caros

Mykonos Santorini
& the Cyclades

Cadogan Guides
27–29 Berwick Street, London W1V 3RF
guides@cadogan.demon.co.uk

The Globe Pequot Press
6 Business Park Road, PO Box 833, Old Saybrook,
Connecticut 06475–0833

Copyright © Dana Facaros 1994, 1998
Illustrations © Suzan Kentli 1993, 1995 and
Horatio Monteverde 1994

Design by Animage
Cover photographs © Ellen Rooney
Maps © Cadogan Guides, drawn by Map Creation Ltd

Editing: Catherine Charles
Proofreading: Linda McQueen
Indexing: Judith Wardman

Series Editor: Rachel Fielding

ISBN 1–86011–079–7

A catalogue record for this book is available from the British Library

Printed in Great Britain by
Redwood Books Ltd.

About the Author

Dana Facaros is a professional travel writer. Over the past fourteen years she has lived in several countries, concentrating on the Mediterranean area. In collaboration with her husband Michael Pauls she has written more than twenty Cadogan Guides on, amongst others, Italy, Spain, France and Turkey. Her roots, however, are in the Greek Islands; her father comes from Ikaria. Dana's guide to all the Greek Islands, now in its seventh edition, was first published in 1979.

Acknowledgements

A big *efcháristo parapolí* to my ever-affable hosts extraordinaire and experts on the Greek condition, Michael and Brian; to my cousin Filia for everything, and Nokos on Folégandros, the new owners of the Ios Club, Petros on Kýthnos, Sophia on Sífnos, Apostoli on Síkinos, Panyioti of Teamwork on Sýros, and all the people on the various island tourist offices who lent a hand. Also a heartfelt round of applause to Catherine for her diligent editing.

Please Help Us Keep This Guide Up to Date

We have done our best to ensure that the information in this guide is correct at the time of going to press. But places and facilities are constantly changing, and standards and prices fluctuate. We would be delighted to receive any comments concerning existing entries or omissions. Significant contributions will be acknowledged in the next edition, and authors of the best letters will receive a copy of a Cadogan Guide of their choice.

Contents

Topics 61–72

Athens and Piraeus 73–108

The Islands 109–244

The Islands (*cont'd*)   109–244

Language   245–53

Glossary of Terms   254

Index   255–62

Maps

Introduction

What weighs the bosom of Abraham and the immaterial
spectres of Christian paradise against this Greek eternity
made of water, rock and cooling winds?

Kazantzakis

There's nothing like the Greek islands, especially a Cycladic island,
to make the rest of the world seem blurred, hesitant and grey.
Their frontiers are clearly defined by a sea that varies from emerald
and turquoise to indigo blue, with none of the sloppiness of a
changing tide; the clear sky and dry air cut their mountainous
contours into sharp outline; the whiteness and simplicity of their
architecture is both abstract and organic. Even the smells, be they
fragrant (lemon blossoms, incense, wild thyme, grilling fish) or
whiffy (donkey flops, caique diesel engines, plastic melted cheese)
are pure and unforgettable. In such an environment, the islanders
have developed strong, open characters; they have bright eyes and
are quick to laugh or cry or scream in fury, or enquire into the
most intimate details of your personal life and offer unsolicited
lectures on politics, how to brush your teeth properly or find a
good husband. 'Greece,' the late president Konstantínos
Karamanlís once said, 'reminds me of an enormous mad house.'

Since the 1970s this clarity and bright madness have been magnets to tourists from the blurred, hesitant, grey world beyond. After shipping, tourism is Greece's most important source of income, to the extent that swallows from the north have become a regular fixture in the seasonal calendar: first comes Lent and Greek Easter, then the tourists, followed by the grape harvest, and, in December, the olives. From June to September, ferries and flights are packed with holiday-makers, both Greek and foreign. Popular sites and beaches are crowded by day, and often by night as well, by visitors unable to find a room—they've been booked for months in advance.

Yet as each island, even in a fairly homogenous archipelago like the Cyclades, has its own character, each has responded to the tourism cash cow in a slightly different way. On some, resort hotels have toadstooled up willy-nilly in search of the fast package-tour buck; some islands have sacrificed many charming old customs, environmental health, and even sanity itself, in their desire to please all comers. And then there are other islands and villages, more self-reliant, clinging stubbornly to their traditions and doing all they can to keep outside interests from exploiting their coasts. Others, including some of the most visited islands, are enjoying a renaissance of traditional arts and customs, often led by the young who are pained to see their centuries-old heritage eroding into Euro-blandness.

Gentle reader, may this book help you find the island of your dreams, whether you want all the mod-cons of home, sports facilities and disco dancing until dawn, or want to visit the ancient sites, study Byzantine frescoes and hone up on your Greek, or perhaps just escape to a secluded shore, where there's the luxury of doing nothing at all. Or perhaps you want a bit of each. For, in spite of all the rush to join the 20th century, the Greek islands have retained the enchantment that inspired Homer and Byron—the wine-dark sea, the scent of jasmine at twilight and nights alive with shooting stars. The ancient Greeks dedicated the islands to the gods, and they have yet to surrender them entirely to us mortals. They have kept something pure and true and alive. Or as the poet Palamas wrote, 'Here reigns nakedness. Here shadow is a dream.'

Choosing Your Island

Within the Cyclades you'll find such constant favourites as Mýkonos, Santoríni and Páros, but also Síkinos, and Anáfi, among the least spoiled islands in Greece. Below are thumbnail sketches of each island, starting with the liveliest, trendiest and most touristy.

Mýkonos is still an attractive holiday destination despite its popularity with the international jet-set. It has great beaches and nightlife (both gay and straight), and is just a short boat ride from the holy **Délos**, now an outdoor archaeological museum. Volcanic **Santoríni** has a lot to live up to as almost everyone's favourite, and is the number one spot for backpackers from both hemispheres, visiting cruise boats, and first-timers to Greece. If you tire of the breathtaking views and chi-chi bars in Firá, the main town, you can escape to smaller villages, although the famous black beaches are now major package resorts. **Íos** is geared towards a younger crowd; ideal if you want to hang around the bar and the beach, although the grown-ups are beginning to discover the quieter coastal villages as new roads improve access. **Páros** has a number of cards up its sleeve: it retains much of its charm, despite being one of the top destinations for backpackers and package tourists, windsurfers, and the jet set, who have carved a niche for themselves at Náoussa. It has very frequent connections to quieter, little **Antíparos**, a slightly alternative, friendly island with its beaches and famous cave. Páros' more family-orientated neighbour, **Náxos** is the biggest, most mountainous and one of the greenest of the Cyclades, with its share of package tourism in the main town and along the main beaches, although the rest of the island is almost untouched, and full of hidden charms; it's the best island for walks in the country. **Ándros** is similar, but on a smaller scale; Greek tourists love its greenery, and a fairly discreet core of package holiday-makers love its beaches, especially at Batsí.

Then there are particular favourites like **Tínos**, the focus each year of two major Greek pilgrimages, which, beyond the main town and church, offers serene, charming landscapes dotted with hundreds of white dovecotes. **Sýros** is another, with the largest city on the islands, the beautiful if atypical neoclassical city of Ermoúpolis, the capital of the Cyclades, plus an attractive array of busy and quiet beaches. **Mílos** is another exception: volcanic like Santoríni and, if not as spectacular, full of geological quirks and exceptional beaches; a newly enlarged airport promises to bring more charter flights but at the time of writing things are still fairly mellow. The attractive islands of **Kéa** (Tzía) and **Kýthnos** are the closest to Athens and especially cater to Greek tourists: Kéa attracts the swells in their yachts, and is by far the hardest Cycladic island on which to find accommodation, without making a reservation long in advance, while Kýthnos is more laid-back.

Arguably the best type of island holiday can be found on islands where there are enough tourists to ensure more than basic facilities—places with a choice of decent tavernas, a bar or two for an evening drink and, most of all, a place to sit out and watch life idle by. **Sífnos, Folégandros,** and **Amorgós** fall happily into this category; all have a mixture of rugged island scenery, typical villages, good restaurants and swimming. Newly trendy **Koufoníssi** has the same, but on a smaller scale; its fellow 'Back Islands' **Schinoússa** and **Heráklia** are beginning to attract their share of visitors in search of peace and quiet and something more 'Greek'. Barren **Sérifos** and **Anáfi** are somewhat similar—not quite your desert island in that they have several places to stay, eat and explore, but beyond that not a lot to do after a couple of days, unless you are resourceful. On **Kímolos** and **Dounoússa** you can treat yourself to some serious introspection and brush up on your modern Greek with the locals.

When to Go

When choosing your island(s), the time of year is important. The main season runs from mid-July to 20 August, when the Greeks are on holiday—the festivals and nightlife are in full swing, so make sure you've arranged somewhere to stay in advance. In June and September you can often just show up and take your pick (many islands now have handy accommodation services next to the port); even further out of season, in the spring (except the week of Greek Easter) and autumn, you can often negotiate prices. Nearly all of the resort hotels close down entirely from October or November to western Easter.

A Note on Pronunciation

There is no general agreement within Greece on a standard method of transliterating the Greek alphabet into Roman letters. This means you will constantly come across many variations in the spellings of place names and words, on maps, in books and on road signs. To help you, this book includes island names and those of major towns in the Greek alphabet. When transcribing, we have used D for the Greek *delta* (Δ), which you may see elsewhere as DH or TH, CH for *chi* (X), which is pronounced like the 'ch' in 'loch' and which you may see written as H, e.g. in Chaniá or Chóra; F for *fi* (Φ), which you may see elsewhere as PH; and G for the Greek *gamma* (Γ), which sounds more like a guttural GH verging on a Y, e.g. with *agios* (saint), pronounced more like 'ayios'. Exceptions to this are made where there is a very common ancient name or modern English spelling such as Phaistos or Rhodes.

Stressing the right syllable is vital to the correct pronunciation of Greek; in this book the stressed letter of each word or name is accented with an acute (´) accent.

See also **Language** pp. 246–254.

Travel

Getting To and Around Greece and the Islands

The bible of travel to and around Greece is the *Greek Travel Pages*, updated monthly. Consult a copy at the National Tourist Organization or a travel agency specializing in Greece, or check out the GTP website: *www.hellas.de/gtp*

By Air

'The air and sky are free,' Daedalus told son Icarus as he planned their ill-fated winged escape from Crete. They aren't free any more, but you can fly for less if you look around. As competition increases in Europe, don't automatically presume charter flights with their restrictions are your best buy; flying the Greek national carrier Olympic opens up very reasonable onward prices to island airports. Students or anyone under 26 will find the most bargains (*see* p.5). The good news is that you can fly 'open jaws' into one Greek airport and out of another. The bad news is that a Greek airport tax (£20 at the time of writing) is added on to some ticket prices.

Charter Flights

Charter flights to Athens are frequent in the summer from Europe, less frequent from North America, and non-existent from Australasia. Europeans also have the luxury of charter flights direct to many islands (notably, from London Gatwick, Luton, Glasgow, Cardiff, Newcastle, Manchester, Belfast and Dublin). Check the travel sections in the major weekend papers, *Time Out*, or the London *Evening Standard* for last-minute discounts on unsold seats, or get advice from your local travel agent or the specialists listed below. Most UK charters run from May to mid-October but some firms feature early specials in March and April depending on when Greek Easter falls, usually from London Gatwick and Manchester.

Charter tickets have fixed outward and return dates with often as not departure and arrival times in the wee hours. They are also governed by several restrictions. Tickets are valid for a minimum of 3 days and a maximum of 6 weeks and must be accompanied by an accommodation voucher stating the name and address of the hotel, villa or campsite; you don't really have to stay there. Although a formality, every so often there is a crackdown aimed at what the Greeks consider undesirables flouting the law. Because they subsidise airline landing fees they want to prevent charter flights being used as a cheap way to get to other countries, especially Turkey. Visitors to Greece using a charter flight may visit Turkey or any neighbouring country for the day, but must not stay overnight, at the very real risk of forfeiting your return ticket home. Travellers with stamps from previous holidays in Turkey will not be barred entry, but if you have Turkish Cypriot stamps check with the Passport Office before you go. Returning from Greece, make sure you confirm your return flight three days prior to departure.

Scheduled Flights from the UK and Ireland

Scheduled flights direct to Athens operate several times daily from London on **Olympic**, **British Airways** and **Virgin Atlantic**. East European companies like **Czech Airlines** also fly to Athens and can work out cheaper in season, but you may have to wait for hours for connections in Prague and supply your own drinks and peanuts. Apex and Superapex flights offer substantially reduced fares, with flights from London to Athens ranging from £190 low season to £280 high season. They must, however, be paid for instantly and are not refundable or flexible. Rates range from £212 return midweek in low season to £298 weekends in high.

Scheduled flights from Ireland to Athens on Olympic and Aer Lingus fly via Heathrow and tend to be considerably pricier than charters.

Olympic Airways	London ✆ (0171) 409 3400
	Dublin ✆ (01) 608 0090
British Airways	London ✆ (0181) 897 4000
	Belfast ✆ (0345) 222 111
	Dublin ✆ (1 800) 626 747
Aer Lingus	Belfast ✆ (01232) 314844
	Dublin ✆ (01) 844 4777
Virgin Atlantic	London ✆ (01293) 747747
Czech Airlines	London ✆ (0171) 409 3400

discounts and special deals

Alecos Tours, ✆ (0171) 267 2092. Olympic Airways consolidator.

Avro, ✆ (0181) 715 0000. Charter and scheduled flights to Athens and major islands from London Gatwick, Luton, Manchester, Glasgow, Cardiff, Newcastle and Birmingham.

Balkan Tours, ✆ (01232) 246 795. Charter flights direct from Belfast.

Delta Travel, ✆ (0161) 272 8455; ✆ (0151) 708 7955; ✆ (0121) 471 2282. Manchester-based agents for scheduled flights from Heathrow to Athens; and from Manchester and Birmingham for Athens; wide range of island charters.

Island Wandering, ✆ (01580) 860733. Reasonable schedules to Athens, island packages and open jaws routes. Use Olympic Airways flights.

Joe Walsh Tours, ✆ (01) 676 3053. Budget fares from Dublin.

Eclipse Direct, ✆ (01293) 554400; ✆ (0161) 742 2277. Flights from Gatwick, Manchester and Birmingham.

Sunset Air Fares, ✆ (01204) 701 111. Bolton-based agent with charters to the islands.

Trailfinders. One of the best for affordable flights. London, ✆ (0171) 937 5400; Bristol, ✆ (0117) 929 9000; Birmingham, ✆ (0121) 236 1234; Manchester ✆ (0161) 839 6969; Glasgow, ✆ (0141) 353 2224.

WT Holidays, ✆ (01) 789555. Charter flights from Dublin.

Scheduled Flights from North America

Olympic, TWA and **Delta** offer daily nonstop flights from New York to Athens in the summer; Olympic also flies direct to Athens from Atlanta, Boston, and Chicago several times a week, depending on the season, and offers connecting flights from Dallas, Detroit, Houston, Los Angeles, Miami, Philadelphia, San Francisco and Washington DC; from Canada Olympic flies direct to Athens from Toronto and Montreal, with connecting flights from Vancouver and Calgary. Usually cheaper **Tower Air** flies direct from New York to Athens two or three times a week. American economy fares (Apex and Superapex/Eurosavers, booked at least three weeks in advance) range from $760 return New York–Athens in low season to $1200 high season; Canadian economy fares to Athens from Toronto or Montreal range from $1020 low season to $1350 high season. When ringing around, take into consideration the large discount Olympic offers its international passengers on flights to the islands; at the time of writing, only $100 US will take you on to any domestic destination in Greece.

From many cities in the US and Canada, European airlines such as **KLM** or **Czech Airlines** offer the best deals to Greece. If you have more time than money, get a cheap or standby flight to London and once there hunt up a cheap ticket to an island (*see* above) although this may be a headache in July or August.

Olympic Airways	US ✆ (800) 838 3600; in Canada: Montreal: ✆ (514) 878 9691; Toronto, ✆ (416) 920 2452
Delta:	US ✆ (800) 241 414
Air Canada	Canada ✆ (800) 555 1212; US ✆ (800) 776 3000
KLM:	US ✆ (800) 374 7747; Canada ✆ (800) 361 5330
Tower Air:	US ✆ (800) 34 TOWER
TWA:	US ✆ (800) 892 4141
Czech Airlines	US ✆ (800) 223 2365
British Airways	US ✆ (800) 247 9297; Canada ✆ (800) 668 1055

discounts and special deals

New Frontiers, US ✆ (800) 366 6387; Canada, in Montréal, ✆ (514) 526 8444.

Travel Avenue, US ✆ (800) 333 3335.

Air Brokers International, US ✆ (800) 883 3273. Discount agency.

Council Charter, US ✆ (800) 223 7402. Charter specialists.

Homeric Tours, US ✆ (800) 223 5570, 🖷 753 0319. Charter flights and custom
tours.

Last Minute Travel Club, US ✆ (800) 527 8646. Annual membership fee gets
you cheap standby deals.

Encore Travel Club, US ✆ (800) 444 9800. Scheduled flight discount club.

Scheduled Flights from Australasia

Olympic flies at least twice a week direct to Athens from Melbourne and Sydney,
and if their fares aren't the cheapest, consider the discounts the Greek carrier offers
international passengers on its domestic flights. Other carriers include Qantas,
Singapore Airlines, Aeroflot, KLM, Thai Airways, British Air, and Gulf Air. Prices in
low season (Nov–Mar) average around $2000 low season, $2350 at other times.
There are no direct flights from New Zealand, but Air New Zealand, Qantas,
Singapore Airways or Alitalia will get you there with only one stop en route. If you
can pick up a bargain flight to London, it may work out cheaper to take that and
find a discount flight from there (*see* above).

Olympic Airlines	Sydney and Brisbane toll free ✆ (008) 221 663; Melbourne, ✆ (008) 9331448; Adelaide, ✆ (008) 331 448; (no office in New Zealand)
Thai Airways	Australia, ✆ (1 800) 422 02 Auckland ✆ (09) 377 3886
British Airways	Sydney ✆ (9258 3300) Auckland ✆ (09) 356 8690
Singapore Airlines	Sydney, ✆ (02) 9236 0144 Auckland ✆ (09) 379 3209
KLM	Australia, ✆ (1 800) 505 474
Aeroflot	Sydney, ✆ (02) 9233 7911
Alitalia	Sydney, ✆ (02) 9247 1308 Auckland, ✆ (09) 366 1855
Qantas	Sydney, ✆ (02) 957 0111 Auckland, ✆ (09) 357 8900
Air New Zealand	Auckland, ✆ (09) 303 5826
Gulf Air	Sydney, ✆ (02) 9321 9199

discounts and special deals

Flight Centres, Sydney ✆ (02) 9241 2422, Melbourne, ✆ (03) 650 2899,
Auckland, ✆ (09) 209 6171; Christchurch, ✆ (03) 379 7145, etc.

Brisbane Discount Travel, in Brisbane ✆ (07) 3229 9211.

UTAG Travel, Sydney, ✆ (02) 956 8399 and branches in other Australian cities.
Budget Travel, Auckland, toll free ✆ (0 800) 808 040.

From Africa

Olympic flies three times a week from Johannesburg by way of Nairobi to Athens; in Johannesburg ✆ (880) 4120, ✉ 880 7075; Cape Town, ✆ (021) 230 260, ✉ 244 166; in Nairobi, ✆ 219 532.

Student and Youth Travel

If you're under 26 or a full-time student under 32 with an **International Student Identity Card** to prove it, you're eligible for **student/youth charters**; these are exempt from the voucher system and are often sold as one-way tickets, enabling you to stay in Greece longer than is possible with a regular charter flight. Students under 26 are sometimes eligible for discounts on scheduled flights as well, especially with Olympic Airways who currently offer 25% discount to ISIC card holders on all connecting flights from Athens to the islands. Young people of Greek origin (age 10–15) may be eligible for Gold Card discounts (contact your country's Greek National Tourist Office). Specialists in youth and student travel include:

Campus Travel, 52 Grosvenor Gardens SW1, London, ✆ (0171) 730 3402; with branches at most UK universities: Leeds, ✆ (0113) 246 1155; Bradford, ✆ (01274) 383261; Bristol, ✆ (0117) 929 2494; Manchester, ✆ (0161) 833 2046; Edinburgh, ✆ (0131) 668 3303; Birmingham, ✆ (0121) 414 1848; Oxford, ✆ (01865) 242067; Cambridge, ✆ (01223) 324283. Runs own youth charters to Athens in summer.

STA Travel, in the **UK**, 86 Old Brompton Road, London SW7 3LH or 117 Euston Road NW1 2SX, ✆ (0171) 361 6161; Bristol, ✆ (0117) 929 4399; Leeds, ✆ (0113) 244 9212; Manchester, ✆ (0161) 834 0668; Oxford, ✆ (01865) 792800; Cambridge, ✆ (01223) 366966 and many other branches; in the **US**, New York City, ✆ (212) 627 3111; outside New York ✆ (800) 777 0112; in **Australia**, Sydney ✆ (02) 9212 1255, elsewhere ✆ (800) 637 444.

USIT, Aston Quay, Dublin 2, ✆ (01) 679 8833; Cork, ✆ (021) 270 900; Belfast, ✆ (01232) 324 073; Galway, ✆ (091) 565 177; Limerick, ✆ (061) 415 064; Waterford, ✆ (051) 72601. **Ireland**'s largest student travel agents.

Council Travel, 205 E. 42nd St, New York, NY 10017, ✆ (800) 743 1823. Major specialist in student and charter flights; branches all over the **US**. Also in the **UK**, 28 Poland St, London W1V 3DB, ✆ (0171) 437 7767.

Travel Cuts, 187 College St, Toronto, Ontario M5T 1P7, ✆ (416) 979 2406. **Canada**'s largest student travel specialists; branches in most provinces.

Children and Pregnancy

Free child places on package holidays and discount air fares for tiny travellers vary from company to company. Get a good travel agent, trawl through the brochures and read all the small print. The big package operators geared to family holidays like Thomson offer a wide range of child discounts and seasonal savers with in-resort amusements, kiddie clubs and baby-sitting as well as deals for children under twelve in hotels and teenagers up to seventeen in self-catering accommodation. On some UK charter flights infants under two travel free on a full fare-paying adult's lap, while on others you may be charged £15–£20 for the baby, or 10% of the adult fare. Children from two to twelve cost between 25%–65%, and over twelve you'll have to fork out full fare. On international Olympic flights you'll pay 67% of the adult fare for children aged two to twelve, 10% for infants under two, while under-12s go for half-fare on all domestic flights. Watch out for birthdays; if your toddler has crossed the magic two-year-old age barrier by the return journey you'll have to pay for another seat. Note that many airlines won't let single mothers travel with two infants, although you may get through the restriction by having one on your lap and one in a car seat; explain your position when you book in case they are adamant on the one child per adult rule or turn you away at the check-in.

If you're pregnant, think before you fly. Although Greek hospitals have improved in recent years, you should make sure your insurance covers repatriation. Most airlines will carry women up to 34 weeks of pregnancy—Olympic even later—but you will have to provide a doctor's certificate after 28 weeks to prove you are well enough to fly. Again check when you book.

Getting to and from Ellinikon Airport, Athens

Athens' Ellinikon Airport is divided into three terminals: East Terminal (used by some charters, all non-Olympic international airlines and Air Greece), West Terminal or Olympiki, used for all Olympic Airlines flights, both international and domestic, and the Charter Terminal; if you're on a charter, double check to make sure you go to the right one. **Express bus 091** connects all three terminals to central Athens, stopping in front of the Post Office in Sýntagma Square and from Stadíou Street by Omónia Square every 20 minutes between 5.21am and midnight and every hour at night from 1.12am–4.12am. Fares are 160dr from 7am to 11.30pm, 200dr otherwise. From Karaiskaki Square in Piraeus, **express bus 19** goes to the airport's three terminals every hour from 6am to midnight, and at 2.30am and 5am. The same buses will take you from terminal to terminal, or catch a taxi (under 1000dr). For more on taxis and getting around Athens, *see* pp.82–3.

There's a **left luggage** facility in the Olympic airport, and another at the international airport, down at the far end beyond the charters' hall.

East Terminal	℗ 969 4111
West Terminal	℗ 926 9111
Charter Terminal	℗ 997 2581

airlines in Athens (℗ 01–)

Aeroflot	14 Xenofóndos, ℗ 322 0986, @ 323 6375
Air Canada	10 Óthonos, ℗ 322 3206, @ 323 1057
Air France	18 Vouliagmenis, Glyfáda, ℗ 960 1100, @ 960 1457; airport ℗ 969 9334
Air Greece	22 Filellínon, ℗ 324 4457, @ 324 4479; airport ℗ 960 0646
Air Zimbabwe	22 Filellínon, ℗ 324 5415, @ 324 5446
Alitalia	577 Vouliagmenis, Argyroupoulis, ℗ 995 9200, @ 995 9214; airport ℗ 961 3621
American Airlines	15 Panepistimiou, ℗ 331 1045
British Airways	10 Óthonos, ℗ 325 0601, @ 325 5171; airport ℗ 961 0402
Continental Airlines	25 Filellínon, ℗ 324 9300
Czech Airlines	15 Panepistímiou, ℗ 323 0174
Cyprus Airways	10 Filellínon, ℗ 324 7801, @ 324 4935; airport ℗ 961 0325
Delta	4 Óthonos, ℗ 331 1668, @ 325 0451; airport ℗ 964 8800
Iberia	8 Xenofóndos, ℗ 323 4523; @ 324 0655; airport ℗ 969 9813
KLM	22 Voúlis, ℗ 988 0177; airport ℗ 969 9733
Lufthansa	East Terminal, ℗ 369 2200, @ 363 6881
Malev	15 Papepistímiou, ℗ 324 1116
Olympic	96 Syngroú, among many branches; reservations ℗ 966 6666, @ 966 6111. Info ℗ 936 3363
Qantas	East Terminal, ℗ 969 9323
Sabena	41c Vouliagmenis, Glyfáda, ℗ 960 0021; @ 960 0219; airport ℗ 961 3903
SAS	E. Terminal, ℗ 960 1003, @ 960 1306; airport ℗ 961 4201
Singapore Airlines	9 Xenofondos, ℗ 323 9111, @ 325 4326, airport ℗ 961 2815

S. African Airways	8 Merlin, ✆ 361 7278, 📠 362 7433
Swissair	4 Óthonos, ✆ 323 5813, 📠 322 5548; airport ✆ 961 0203
Thai Airlines	1 Sekeri St, ✆ 364 7610, 📠 364 7680; airport ✆ 960 0607
TWA	8 Xenofóndos, ✆ 322 6451, 📠 322 8973; airport ✆ 961 0012
United Airlines	5 Syngrou, ✆ 924 2645, 📠 922 9268
Virgin Atlantic	8–10 Tzireon, Makrigianni, ✆ 924 9100, 📠 924 9144; airport ✆ 960 1461

Domestic Flights to the Islands

Flights from Athens to the islands can be booked in advance through **Olympic**; as many planes are small, do this as far in advance as possible. Some only have 18 seats, and are good fun; they seem just to skim over the mountain tops (but note, they can't take off or land in high winds, and you could end up back where you started). Because planes are small, baggage allowances (15kg) tend to be enforced—unless you've bought your ticket abroad, when you're allowed all 23kg. Children under twelve go half-price.

Olympic Airways also offer **island-to-island flights** in season, so you don't need to go to Athens. Although these have a habit of changing from year to year, flights between Santoríni and Mýkonos, and on from either island to Crete or Rhodes, are well-established. It's also possible to get a schedule 'open-jaws' ticket to Athens and on to any permutation of islands, but you have to return home from Athens.

By Train

London–Athens

There are 3 daily trains from London to Athens, the *Athenai Express*, the *Acropolis Express* and the *Hellas Express*, all of which take about 3 days. And a hot, crowded, stuffy 3 days too. Check on trains from Britain to Greece with British Rail International, ✆ (0990) 848 848. The alternative and pleasant (though slightly costlier) route is to go through Italy, either to Ancona or further south to Brindisi, and take the ferry over to Corfu and Pátras.

Hardy souls who deny themselves a couchette or cabin should bring plenty of provisions, including water, and some toilet paper. Wear the oldest and most comfortable clothes you own (and save yourself the trouble of washing them before you go).

London to Athens

Taking a coach from London to Thessaloníki or Athens is always a possible alternative for those who decide that a train trip is too expensive or too easy a route to travel. It isn't usually much cheaper than a standby flight, and takes four days instead of four hours, but it's a chance to see Munich, Belgrade and other fine bus terminals en route. **Eurolines**, 52 Grosvenor Gardens, Victoria, London SW1W 0AU, ✆ (0171) 730 8235, make the journey from London to Athens for around £218 return if you're over 26; there's a £12 saving if you're under 26. Departures from London are on Friday mornings in July, August and September only. **Olympic Bus Ltd**, 70 Brunswick Centre, London WC1 1AE, ✆ (0171) 837 9141 offers 2½-day journeys from London to Athens via Brussels and Italy for a mere £50 one-way, or £100 return, departing London on Friday evenings. In Greece, you'll find agencies selling bus tickets on the most obscure islands, as well as in Athens; **Filellínon Street** near Sýntagma Square is Athens' budget travellers' boulevard, so check there.

Domestic Buses

The domestic bus service in Greece is efficient and regular, and still a bargain. Bus services from Athens relevant to this book are as follows:

Athens to	no. daily	Terminal	✆	Duration
Lávrion (for Kéa)	12	Mavromatéon	821 3203	2 hrs
Pátras (for Italy)	16	Kifissoú	513 6185	3hrs
Rafína	18	Mavromatéon	821 0872	1.30hr

To get to the terminal at **100 Kifissoú Street** (✆ 512 4910) take bus 051 from Omónia Square (Zinonos and Menandroú Sts). Take a tram 5 or 9 towards Areos Park on 28th Octovríou Street for the **Mavromatéon** terminal. In August, reserve seats in advance on the long-distance buses if you can.

There never seem to be enough buses on the islands in the summer, nor is it customary to queue. However, you will not be left behind if it is humanly possible for you to squeeze on. If you can wake up in time, you will find that buses are rarely crowded early in the morning.

The most common sea route to Greece is from Italy, with daily ferry services from Ancona and Brindisi, and frequently from Bari and Venice. Ancona to Pátras takes a day and a half; Brindisi ferries connect with the night train from Rome and arrive in

Pátras the next morning. Passengers are usually allowed a free stopover in Corfu if that island is not their ultimate destination, before continuing to Igoumenítsa or Pátras, but make sure it is noted on your ticket. In the summer, reserve in advance, especially if you bring a car (most travel agents can do this for you). Students and young people can get a discount of up to 20%. Discounts of up to 30% on car prices are also offered when buying a return ticket. As a rule, the costlier the ferry, the faster it sails (Minoan, for instance, takes only 22 hours from Ancona to Pátras). If you're in a big, big hurry, **Catamaran Ferry Lines** (86 Filonos St, 18546 Piraeus, ✆ 429 3903, ✉ 452 3624) link Brindisi with Corfu and Igoumenítsa in under 4 hours. Schedules are posted on the net at *www.greekferries.gr/*

Italy–Greece Ferries

The fares listed below are approximate 1998 prices in drachmas for an airline-type seat, one-way, in low/high season; there are even cheaper deck-class tickets, while cabins are considerably dearer. As a general rule, cars under 4.25m cost a few thousand drachmas more than the low-season seat prices listed overleaf; double that price for taking a car in high season.

Ports	Seat Prices	Company
Ancona–(or Venice)–Corfu–Pátras & Brindisi-Corfu-Igoumenítsa	11,500/23,400dr 8000/14,000dr	Strinzis Lines 26 Aktí Possidónos, Piraeus ✆ 422 5000, ✉ 422 5265
Ancona–Pátras– Trieste–Corfu–Igoumenítsa–Pátras	14,200/25,800 dr 16,500/27,500dr	ANEK Lines 54 Amalías, Athens ✆ 323 3481, ✉ 323 4137
Ancona–Pátras (20 hrs)	18,800/24,800dr	Superfast Ferries 157 Alkyonidon, Voúla, Athens ✆ 969 1100, ✉ 969 1190
Ancona–Igoumenítsa–Corfu–Pátras & Brindisi–Corfu–Igoumenítsa & Venice–Igoumenítsa–Corfu –Kefalonía–Patras	17,000/27,200dr 9000/16,000 dr price on application	Minoan Lines, 2 Vass. Konstantinoú, Athens ✆ 689 8340, ✉ 689 8344
Ancona–Igoumenítsa–Pátras & Bari–Igoumenítsa–Ancona– Piraeus–Heráklion (Crete) July/Aug	14,000/19,500dr 10,000/16,000dr	Marlines, 38 Aktí Possidónos, ✆ 411 0777, ✉ 411 7780

Brindisi–Corfu–Igoumenítsa–Pátras & Brindisi–Kefaloniá–Páxi –Zákynthos–Pátras	6400/17,500dr price on application	Hellenic Mediterranean Lines. PO Box 80057, Piraeus,℡ 422 5341, ✉ 422 5317
Bari–Igoumenítsa–Pátras	11,500/17,400dr	Ventouris Ferries 5 Nikodímou, Athens ℡ 324 0071
Brindisi–Corfu–Igoumenítsa	7000/13,400dr	Fragline, 5a Réthymnou, Athens ℡ 821 1285, ✉ 821 3095
Brindisi–Corfu–Igoumenítsa –Pátras	11,900/15,800dr	Adriatica, 85 Aktí Miaoúli, Piraeus, ℡ 429 0487, ✉ 429 0490

Ferries to the Islands

Comfort on Greek ferries has improved by leaps and bounds in recent years, especially the long-haul ferries: shops, video rooms, air-conditioning, disco bars, slot machines and small swimming pools are added attractions to the old pleasures of lazily watching passing islands, feeling the sea breeze (or tempest, if the wind kicks up), looking out for dolphins during the day or shooting stars at night. Most island ferries have three classes: the first, or 'distinguished' class, with a plush lounge and private cabins (these often cost as much as flying); the second class, often with its own lounge as well, but smaller, porthole-less cabins, segregated by sex, not recommended for claustrophobes; and third or tourist class, which offers access to a typically large room full of airline-type seats, and the deck and the snack bar area. As a rule the Greeks stay inside and the tourists stay out—on warm summer nights in particular this can be the most pleasant alternative, especially if you have a sleeping bag. Drinking water is never very good on the boats, but all sell bottled water, beer, coffee and soft drinks (for about twice as much as on shore). Biscuits and cigarettes complete the fare on the smaller boats, while the larger ones offer sandwiches, self-service dining or full meals (usually adequate and fairly priced) served in a dining room.

Athens' port Piraeus is the busiest in Greece, and gets so busy at peak times that ferries circle about in holding patterns like planes waiting to land. To speed things up, there's a trend to use smaller mainland ports, especially Rafína (for Ándros, Tinos, Sýros, and Ilios hydrofoils to the Cyclades) and Lávrion (for Kéa); both ports are frequently linked by bus to Athens (*see* above, p.10), but most foreign tourists see them as a bother, which means that islands mainly served by these outlying ports tend be quieter and more 'Greek'.

The National Tourist Office publishes a free weekly list of ship departures, both abroad and to the islands; for serious island hoppers, ask for their free booklet, *Greek Travel Routes: Domestic Sea Schedules*. Be aware, however, that any number of factors (weather, health emergencies and unforeseen repairs) can throw timetables out of the window, so if you have to catch a flight home allow for the eccentricities of the system and leave a day early to be safe. For the latest information on departures and arrivals, ring the relevant port authorities (*limenarchíon*). Numbers are listed for each island. For mainland departures numbers are:

Piraeus Port Authority, ✆ (01) 422 6000 (for schedules) or ✆ 451 1311

Rafína Port Authority, ✆ (0294) 22300

Before purchasing a ticket, check timetables in competing agencies—ticket prices will always be the same, but note that some ferries are faster than others, and others can take half a day stopping at tiny island ports. On smaller islands, agents moonlight as bartenders or grocers and may only have a handwritten sign next to the door advertising their ship's departures.

Always keep your ticket with you on a Greek ship, in case of a 'ticket control', a comedy routine necessitated by the fact that the crew doesn't always check tickets when passengers board. Instead, after one or two pleas on the ship's loudspeaker system for passengers without tickets to purchase them forthwith, you suddenly find all the doors on the boat locked or guarded by bored but obdurate sailors, while bands of officers rove about the boat checking tickets. Invariably mix-ups occur: children are separated from their parents, others have gone to the WC, someone has left a ticket with someone on the other side of the immovable sailor, crowds pile up at the doors, and stowaways are marched to the purser's office.

Prices are still reasonable for passengers but rather dear for cars. All ships and hydrofoils are privately owned and, although the Greek government controls prices, some will charge more for the same journey, depending on the facilities offered, speed, etc. In most cases children under the age of 4 travel free, and between 4 and 10 for half-fare. Buying a ticket on board will cost 20% more. In the summer, especially in August, buy tickets well in advance if you have a car or want a cabin. Refunds are given only if the ship never arrives.

Hydrofoils and Catamarans

There are several fleets of hydrofoils, several catamarans, and the occasional 'sea jet' thumping over the Greek seas, and new lines are added every year. Most services run throughout the year but are considerably less frequent between November and May. As a rule hydrofoils travel at least twice as fast as ferries and are twice as expensive. In the peak season they are often fully booked, so buy tickets as early as you can. In a choppy sea a trip may leave you saddle-sore, and beware: if the weather is very bad, they won't leave port. The principal companies departing from the mainland are **Ceres**, with departures from Zéa Marina in Piraeus for the Cyclades, information ℂ (01) 428 0001, reservations can be made up to three months in advance; and **Ilios**, with departures from Rafína to the Cyclades, information ℂ (01) 422 4980 or 322 5253.

Ferry and Hydrofoil Times and Prices from the Mainland

On the following pages is a list of some of the more popular scheduled mainland–island connections. Duration of each boat trip and approximate 1998 prices are given in drachmas but are subject to change without notice. Each port has its own port taxes (the paper bits the agent staples on your ticket) but these are minimal—from 50 to 300drs. You can roughly calculate the car prices on the ferries by multiplying the 3rd class fares by five. Timetables are posted on the web at *http://www.greekferries.gr/*

Piraeus to	1st Class (dr)	2nd Class (dr)	3rd Class (dr)	hours
Amorgós	11,500	5–11,000	4500	11
Anáfi	11–13,000	7050	5800	18
Donoússa	11,070	6000	4560	10
Folégandros	12,500	6640	4080	12
Heráklia	10,500	6500	4200	15
Ios	11–13,000	6–11,000	4000	10
Kímolos	11–13,000	5–6000	4000	8
Koufoníssia	10,500	6500	4200	14
Kýthnos	9–8000	3800	2530	4
Mílos	11–13,500	6000	3700	8
Mýkonos	9000	4160	3520	6
Náxos	9–10,000	5–8000	4000	8
Páros	8–9000	5–8000	4000	6
Santoríni	11–13,000	6–11,000	4500	10
Sérifos	10–11,000	4200	3000	5
Skhínoussa	10,500	6500	4200	14
Sífnos	11–13,000	5200	3550	6
Síkinos	11–13,000	7570	5070	10
Sýros	4470	3640	3220	5
Tínos	8500	4000	3520	5

Cyclades Line

Rafína to

Amorgós	4000	8100	8.00
Ándros	2500	4500	2.30
Mýkonos	3300	7500	5.00
Náxos	3200	7700	6.30
Páros	3100	7700	5.00
Tínos	2900	6500	4.00

Kéa–Kýthnos Line

Lávrion to

Kéa	1700		2.30
Kýthnos	2300		4.00

Tourist Excursion Boats

These are generally slick and clean, and have become quite numerous in recent years. They are usually more expensive than the regular ferries or steamers, but often have schedules that allow visitors to make day trips to nearby islands (though you can also take them one-way), and are very convenient, having largely taken the place of the little caique operators, many of whom now specialize in excursions to remote beaches.

By Car

Driving from London to Athens (and taking the ferry from Italy to Greece) at a normal pace takes around 3½ days. Don't even consider driving down unless you are planning to spend a few weeks on one or two islands, and if that's the case the smaller the better, both for squeezing the car on to the ferry, and for negotiating the sometimes very narrow village roads. Alternatively, there are countless rent-a-car firms on the islands; most are family-run, and fairly reliable (asking around a bit will usually reveal who the stinkers are). If an island has a lot of unpaved roads and not a lot of competition, prices tend to be higher; at the time of writing, hiring a small car varies between 10–15,000dr a day in the summer, and open-air Jeeps at least a third more. Most require that you be at least 21, some 25. Read the small print of your contract with care (look out for mileage limits, etc.), and don't be surprised if you have to leave your driving licence as security. In the off season, negotiate. Arriving at a car hire agent's with a handful of brochures from the competition has been known to strengthen one's bargaining position. Fuel at the time of writing is around 230dr a litre; unleaded (*amólivdi*) a wee bit less.

An **International Driving Licence** is not required of EU citizens. Other nationals can obtain an international licence at home, or at one of the Automobile Club offices in Greece (ELPA), by presenting a national driving licence, passport and photograph. The minimum age is 18 years.

The Motor Insurance Bureau at 10 Xenofóntos Street, Athens, ✆ (01) 323 6733, can tell you which Greek insurance company represents your own, or provide you with additional cover for Greece.

The **Greek Automobile Club** (ELPA) operates a breakdown service within 60km (40 miles) of Athens, Thessaloníki, Laríssa, Pátras and Herákleon: dial ✆ 104. If you belong to an automobile club at home, breakdown service is free anywhere.

Customs formalities for bringing in a car are very easy and usually take very little time. You are allowed a year of free use of the car in Greece, and after that can apply for a 4-month extension. North Americans and Australians are allowed 2 years. If you leave Greece without your car, you must have it withdrawn from circulation by a customs authority. ELPA has a list of lawyers who can offer free legal advice on car problems. They also have a 24-hour number of information useful to foreign motorists; call ✆ 174, and speak English.

While driving in the centre of Athens may be a hair-raising experience, the rest of Greece is fairly easy and pleasant. There are few cars on most roads, even in summer, and most signs, when you're lucky enough to find one, have their Latin equivalents. Traffic regulations and signalling comply with standard practice on the European continent (i.e. driving on the right). Crossroads, tipsy tourists, goats, and poor visibility in the mountains are probably the greatest hazards, along with Greek motorists, arguing and gesticulating while driving (note: if they stick their open palm at you, they are not saying hello, but telling you to go to hell). Where there are no right-of-way signs at a crossroads, give priority to traffic coming from the right, and always beep your horn on blind corners. If you're exploring, you may want to take a spare container of petrol along, as stations can be thin on the ground (especially on the islands) and only open shop hours. There is a speed limit of 50km per hour (30mph) in inhabited areas.

By Motorbike and Moped

Motorbikes and even more popular mopeds are ideal for the islands in the summer. It almost never rains, and what could be more pleasant than a gentle thyme-scented breeze freshening your journey? Scooters (the Greeks call them *papákia*, 'little ducks', supposedly for the noise they make) are both more economical and more practical than cars. They can fit into almost any boat and travel paths where cars fear to tread. Rentals are not expensive, and include third party insurance coverage in most cases. You will have to have a valid driving licence (for Americans, this means an international one). For larger motorbikes (anything over 75cc) you may be asked to show a motorcycle driver's licence. The down-sides: many of the bikes are poorly maintained, many of the roads are poorly maintained, and everyone takes too many risks; hospital beds in Greece fill up each summer with casualties, both foreign and Greek (check your insurance to see if you're covered). Most islands have laws about operating motorbikes after midnight (the 'little ducks', often stripped of their mufflers, tend to howl like a flock of Daffys and Donalds on amphetamines) but they are enforced as often as the helmet requirement. Actually, no: you do see Greeks wearing helmets, but only on their elbows, which, judging by the way they drive their machines must be where they keep their brains. Literally hundreds of people, nearly all young, are killed every year in Greece. Be careful.

By Bicycle

Cycling has not caught on in mountainous Greece, either as a sport or as a means of transport, though you can usually hire an old bike in most major resorts. Trains and planes carry bicycles for a small fee, and Greek boats generally take them along for nothing.

Hitch-hiking

Greek taxi drivers have recently convinced the government to pass a law forbidding other Greeks from picking up hitch-hikers. As with the aforementioned helmet-wearing law, this is regarded as optional, but it is true that you may find hitching slow going; perhaps because of the law, motorized holidaymakers now seem to stop and offer more rides than the locals. The Greek double standard produces the following percentages for hopeful hitch-hikers:

> Single woman: 99% of cars will stop; you hardly have to stick out a thumb.
> Two women: 75% of cars will find room for you.
> Woman and man: 50%; more if the woman is pretty.
> Single man: 25% if you are well dressed with little luggage; less otherwise.
> Two men: start walking.

Entry Formalities

All **European Union** members can stay indefinitely. The only reason you would need special permission to stay would be for working or if complicated banking procedures were involved requiring proof of residence; contact the Aliens Bureau: 173 Leof. Alexandrás, 11522 Athens, ✆ 646 8103. The formalities for **non-EU tourists** entering Greece are very simple. American, Australian and Canadian citizens can stay for up to 3 months in Greece on presentation of a valid passport. South Africans can stay 2 months. If you want to stay longer, take your passport 20 days before your time in Greece expires to the Aliens Bureau or your local police station, and be prepared to prove you can support yourself with bank statements and the like. If you overstay your 3 months, be prepared to pay a fine of 22,200dr.

A complete list is available from the **National Tourist Organization of Greece**
(*see* pp.42–3).

in the UK

British Museum Tours, 46 Bloomsbury Street, London WC1B 3QQ, ✆ (0171)
323 8895. Different archaeological guided tours every year.

Greco-File, ✆ (01422) 375999. Expert advice on where to go, flights and 'couture' holidays to unusual islands for the discerning traveller.

Island Holidays, Drummond Street, Comrie, Perthshire PH6 2DS, ✆ (01764)
670107. Cycladic wind- and water-mills.

Swan Hellenic Ltd, 77 New Oxford Street, London WC1A 1PP, ✆ (0171) 800
2200. Cultural, archaeological and art history tours and cruises.

Travel Companions, 110 High Mount, Station Road, London NW4 3ST,
✆ (0181) 202 8478. Vera Coppard can match you up with a kindred spirit,
for a £40 fee, if you don't want to travel alone.

Waymark Holidays, 44 Windsor Road, Slough SL1 2EJ, ✆ (01753) 516477.
Guided hiking groups on Mílos, spring and autumn breaks.

in the USA/Canada

Aegean Visions, 26 Sixth St, Suite 260, Stamford, CT, 06905, ✆ (203) 667
2524, toll free ✆ (800) GREECE97, ✆ 969 0799. Scuba-diving, hiking,
archaeological, alternative living.

Aegean Workshops, 148 Old Black Point Rd, Niantic, CT, 06357, ✆ (860) 739
0378. Harry J. Danos, a university art teacher, offers watercolour, drawing
and design workshops of 15 to 21 days on Mýkonos or Santoríni.

Avenir Adventures, 1790 Bonanza Drm Suite 207, Park City, UT 84060,
✆ (800) 367 3230. Expeditions by land and sea for small groups.

Central Holiday Tours, Inc., 206 Central Avenue, Jersey City, NJ 07307,
✆ (201) 798 5777, toll free ✆ (800) 935 5000, ✆ 963 0966. Tours in
ancient history and archaeology, mythology and theatre.

Cloud Tours, 645 5th Avenue, New York, NY 10022, ✆ (212) 753 6104, toll
free ✆ (800) 223 7880, ✆ 980 6941. Scuba-diving, biking, honeymoon
tours, women's groups, religious history tours and many others.

IST Cultural Tours, 225 West 34th Street, Suite 913, New York, NY 10122,
✆ (212) 563 1202, toll free ✆ (800) 833 2111, ✆ 594 6953. Customized
tours including yacht cruises and lectures on archaeology.

Metro Tours, 484 Lowell Street, Peabody, MA 01960, ✆ (508) 535 4000, toll free ✆ (800) 221 2810, ✉ 535 8830. Weddings and honeymoons on Santoríni.

Our Family Abroad, 40 W. 57th St, Suite 430, New York, NY 10019, ✆ (212) 459 1800, toll free ✆ (800) 999 5500, ✉ 581 3756. Gay & lesbian tours.

The Greek Island Connection, 418 E. 14th Street, Suite 3, New York, NY 10009, ✆ (212) 674 4072, toll free ✆ (800) 241 2417, ✉ 674 4582. Archaeology, cooking, hiking, biking, gay and lesbian, religion.

Disabled Travellers

Many of the Greek islands, with their ubiquitous steps and absence of suitable transport, would put severe constraints on visitors in chairs, and ferry and hydrofoil access is difficult. Islands that receive lots of visitors (such as Santoríni and Mýkonos) have hotels with facilities—the Greek National Tourist Office has a list.

In the UK, several of the big package holiday companies like **Thomsons** have some suitable tours. Contact **RADAR**, 12 City Forum, 250 City Rd, London, EC1V 8AS, ✆ (0171) 250 4119 or **Tripscope**, ✆ (0181) 994 9294, for advice and referrals.

In the USA similar service is provided by the **Travel Information Service**, Moss Rehabilitation Hospital, 1200 W. Tabor Red, Philadelphia, PA 19141, ✆ (215) 456 9600 and the **Society for the Advancement of Travel for the Handicapped**, 347 Fifth Avenue, Suite 610, New York, NY 10016, ✆ (212) 447-SATH, ✉ 725 8253. **New Directions**, 5276 Hollister Ave, Suite 207, Santa Barbara CA 93111, ✆ (805) 967 2841, ✉ 964 7344. In Canada, the **Jewish Rehabilitation Hospital**, 3205 Place Alton Goldbloom, Montréal PQ H7V 1R2 is a good source of travel info. In Greece, contact **The Panhellenic Association for the Blind**, 31 Veranzérou St, 10432 Athens, ✆ (01) 522 8333, ✉ 522 2112, or **Association Hermes**, Patriárchou 13, Grigouiou E, 16542 Argyroúpolis, ✆ (01) 996 1887.

Yachting, Sailing and Flotilla Holidays

Are we sailing straight, or is the shore crooked?

old Greek proverb

One of the great thrills of sailing the Cyclades is the variety of places to visit in a short time, with the bonus that nowhere in Greece is far from safe shelter or harbours with good facilities for yachtsmen. There is little shallow water, except close to the shoreline, few currents and no tides or fog, and a virtually inexhaustible supply of secluded coves and empty beaches, even at the height of the tourist season. Equally, there are berthing facilities in the most popular of international hotspots—it's all there beneath the blue skies and bright sunshine. The Greek

National Tourist Organization has initiated a programme of rapid expansion in the face of mounting competition from Turkey and Spain; facilities are being improved and new marinas are being constructed throughout the country.

The colour map on the inside back cover shows main yacht supply stations and ports of entry and exit. Greek weather guarantees near-perfect sailing conditions. The only real problem you'll encounter is the strong winds at certain times of the year, notably April to October, when most yachtsmen are at sea. The Aegean Sea is affected by a northwest wind in the south, and a northeasterly in the north, and when the *meltémi* blows in August and September, it can reach force eight, testing all your skills at the helm.

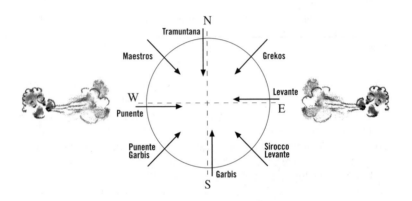

If you wish to skipper a yacht anywhere within the Greek seas, consult the *Compile Index Chart of Greek Seas*, otherwise known as *XEE*, published by the Hellenic Navy Hydrographic Service. Basically it is a map of Greece divided into red squares, each with an index number, from which you can select the appropriate charts and order them accordingly. For non-Greeks, you can buy what is known as *XEE 64*, a booklet of abbreviations explaining the signs on the charts, with texts in English and Greek.

You also need one of the Pilot series books, in this case *Pilot B: Southeastern Greek shores; Crete, Eastern Peloponnese, Saronic Gulf and Cyclades*, which cost 2500dr each and cover the area in great detail, covering geographical data, possible dangers, and the present state of transportation and communication. All ports and marinas are mentioned, including where to obtain fresh water and fuel, and there are descriptions of visible inland features. The Hydrographic Service constantly updates the books and sends additional booklets to authorized sellers and to all port authorities, where you may consult them. The nautical charts are updated using the latest, most sophisticated methods, and follow standardized dimensions. They are on a 1:100,000 scale for bigger areas and 1:750,000 for ports. Heights and depths are given in metres with functional conversion tables for feet and fathoms.

Further information is provided in booklets called *Notes to Mariners*, published monthly and available for consultation at port authorities. These give information on any alterations to naval charts you have purchased for your voyage. Besides all this there is the Navtex service. A special department of the Hydrographic Service keeps you informed about the weather or any special warnings for the day, through telex, or Navtex. The text is in Greek and English, and there are four re-transmission coastal stations covering the Greek seas. Weather forecasts for yachtsmen are broadcast at intervals throughout the day on VHF Channel 16 (in Greek and English); security warnings are also broadcast on this channel, e.g. dangerous wrecks, lights not in operation, etc.

The following is a list of **bunkering ports and supply stations** where fuelling facilities and other provisions may be obtained:

Adámas (Mílos)*, Aegina, Ag. Nikólaos (Kéa), Ag. Nikólaos (Crete)*, Alexandroúpolis*, Álimos Marína, Argostóli (Kefaloniá)*, Chíos*, Corfu Port*, Ermoúpolis (Sýros)*, Flísvos Marína, Goúvia Marína*, Gýthion*, Chalkís*, Chaniá (Crete)*, Hýdra, Itéa*, Kalamáta*, Kálymnos, Kamáres (Sífnos), Kapsáli (Kýthera), Kastellórizo, Kástro (Ándros), Katákolo*, Katápola (Amorgós), Kavála*, Kými (Évia), Korínthos*, Kos*, Lákki (Léros), Lávrion*, Lefkás, Liméni (Máni), Linariá (Skýros), Mýrina (Límnos)*, Mytilíni*, Monemvásia, Mýkonos*, Náfpaktos, Náfplion*, Náxos, Néa Róda, Paléa Epidávros, Paleokastrítsa, Párga, Parikía (Páros), Pigádia (Kárpathos), Pílos*, Póros, Pórto Koufó, Pórto Ráfti, Préveza*, Rhodes (Mandráki)*, Skála (Pátmos)*, Skiáthos*, Skópelos, Spétses, Thessaloníki Marína*, Thessaloníki Port*, Tínos, Váthi (Ithaca)*, Vólos*, Vouliagméni Marína, Zákynthos*, Zéa Marína.

* indicates official ports of entry and exit, where there are port, customs and health authorities, as well as immigration and currency control services. Others are: Égion, Gerakini (Chalkidikí), Glyfáda, Igoumenítsa, Herákleon, Kimássi (Évia), Pátras, Pérama, Pithagórion and Vathí (Samos), Dáfni (Agion Óros), Elefsína, Fíra (Santoríni), Ivira (Agion Óros), Kalí Liménes (Crete), Drépanon (Achaía) and Stilí (Lamia).

Yachts entering Greek waters must fly the code flag 'Q' until cleared by entry port authorities. Upon arrival the port authority (*Limenarchíon*) issues all yachts with a transit log, which entitles the yacht and crew to unlimited travel in Greek waters. It also allows crew members to buy fuel, alcohol and cigarettes duty free. It must be kept on board, produced when required, and returned to the customs authorities on leaving Greece at one of the exit ports. Permission is normally given for a

6-month stay, but this can be extended. Small motor, sail or rowing boats do not require a '*carnet de passage*', and are allowed into Greece duty free for 4 months. They are entered in your passport and deleted on exit. For more information, apply to the Greek National Tourist Organisation, 4 Conduit Street, London W1R 0DJ, ✆ (0171) 734 5997, who produce a useful leaflet *Sailing the Greek Seas*.

Anyone taking a yacht by road is strongly advised to obtain boat registration documentation from the DVLA, Swansea SA99 1BX, ✆ (0792) 783355. The Royal Yachting Association, R.Y.A. House, Romsey Road, Eastleigh, Hampshire SO5 4YA, ✆ (0703) 629962, is a useful source of yachting information.

Yacht Charter

Chartering yachts is very popular these days, and, as the promotional literature says, can be cheaper than staying in a hotel (if you have enough friends or family to share expenses). Between the various firms there are over a thousand vessels currently available in all sizes, with or without a crew (though without a crew—bareboat charter—both the charterer and another member of the party must show proof of seamanship: a sailing certificate or letter of recommendation from a recognized yacht or sailing club). There are various options: motor yachts (without sails), motor sailors (primarily powered by motor, auxiliary sail power) and sailing yachts (with auxiliary motor power). The Greek National Tourist Organisation has a list of Greek charter firms, or contact **The Hellenic Professional Yacht Owners Association**, Zéa Marína A818 536, Piraeus, ✆ 452 6335 and 428 0465, ✉ 452 6335, and **Greek Yacht Brokers and Consultants Association**, 11 Posseidonos Av., Alimos, ✆ (01) 985 0122, 105 57 Athens, ✆ 323 0330. In the UK, the **Yacht Charter Association**, 60 Silverdale, New Milton, Hampshire BH25 7DE, ✆ (01425) 619004, supplies a list of its recognized yacht charter operators and offers advice on chartering overseas.

Flotilla and Sailing Holidays

If you want to float among the islands on the wine-dark sea, but don't own your own yacht, or lack the experience to charter one, a flotilla holiday may be just the answer. A growing number of flotilla companies offer one- or two-week sailing holidays, some of which will take on instructing even the most inexperienced sailors (usually beginning with a week based on land). High season prices for a fortnight's holiday range from £550 per person to £9000 per head, on a four-person yacht. The yachts have 4–8 berths (there are shared boats available for couples and singles) and sail in flotillas, usually from six to a dozen yachts, supervised by a lead boat, with experienced skipper, engineer and social hostess. Plenty of free time built in.

Agemennon Yachts, 213B Karaiskaki St., 26222 Pátras, Greece ✆/@ (00 30) 61 344009, *skp@hi way.gr* . Yacht charters.

BUOYS Cruising Club, 8 Chase Side, Enfield, Middlesex EN2 6NF, England, ✆ (0181) 367 8462. Charters from Athens.

Euroyacht, 22 Akti Themistokleous, 18536 Piraeus, Greece ✆ (00 30) 1 428 1920, ✉ 1 428 1926. Bareboat or crewed sail or motor boats, and flotilla sailing.

Ghiolman Yachts, 7 Filellinon St, Athens, ✆ 323 3696. Besides yachts, can supply mobile phones, helicopters, planes, and even put private islands at your disposal.

Grecian Holidays, 75 The Donway West, Don Mills, Ontario M3C 2E9, Canada, ✆ (800) 268 6786, ✉ (416) 510 1509.

Greek Island Cruise Centre, 4321 Lakemoor Dr., Wilmington, NC, 28405, USA ✆ (800) 341 3030. Yacht charters.

Just Boats, Kontakali 49100 Corfu, Greece, ✆ (00 30) 661 90932, ✉ 90837, *root@ just_boats.ker.forthnet.gr.* Crewed and bareboat yachts, flotilla holidays, caiques.

Interpac Yachts, 1050 Anchorage Lane, San Diego, CA, 92106 USA, toll free ✆ (888) 99 YACHT. Crewed power or sail yacht charters.

The Moorings, 188 Northdown Road, Cliftonville, Kent CT9 2QN, England ✆ (01843) 227140. Offers charters from Athens.

McCulloch Marine, 32 Fairfield Road, London E3 2QB, England ✆ (0181) 983 1487. Offers charters from Athens.

Odysseus Yachting Holidays, 33 Grand Parade, Brighton BN2 2QA, England ✆ (01273) 695094. Flotilla holidays.

Sovereign Sailing, ✆ (01273) 626284, 120 St George's Road, Brighton, E. Sussex, BN2 1EA. England. Flotilla holidays.

Sunsail, The Port House, Port Solent, Portsmouth PO6 4TH, England ✆ (01705) 210345, for dinghies, flotillas, tuitional sailing and watersports.

Valef, 22 Aktí Themistokléous, Piraeus, Greece ✆ (01) 428 1920, ✉ 428 1926 (in the USA: 7254 Fir Rd, PO Box 391, Ambler, Pa 19002, ✆ (800) 223 3845; in Canada, Islands in the Sun Cruises, 10441 124 St, Edmonton, Alberta T5N 1R7, ✆ toll free (800) 661 7958. *VALEF@ix.netcom.com*, *http//ValefYachts.com*). One of the largest and most reputable firms, with more than 300 crewed yachts, accommodating 4–50 people from $300 to $8000 a day.

Windstar Cruises, Standard House, 15–16 Bonhill St, London EC2P 2EA, England, ✆ (0171) 628 7711. Yacht charters.

World Expeditions Ltd, 7 North Road, Maidenhead, Berkshire SL6 1TL, England, ✆ (01628) 74174. Yacht charters.

Women on Watch, West Cottage, Westcliff, Whitstable, Kent CT5 1DJ, England. Sailing holidays for women of all abilities from pedalo to Maiden standards. Skipper Gina Seller based on Póros offers tuitional sailing in the Saronic Islands, Peloponnese and Cyclades from April to October. Experienced sailors interested in becoming skippers welcome.

Womanship, Learn to Sail Cruises For and By Women, USA, ✆ (800) 324 9295. North American company specialising in women-only flotilla holidays in the Greek islands.

yacht repair yards

And in case something goes wrong limp along to:

Glýfada (Athens): ✆ (01) 894 7353. **Piraeus Marina Zéa**: ✆ (01) 428 4100. **Sýros**: ✆ (0281) 86 070 or 88 818.

Practical A–Z

The Aegean enjoys a dry, mild and clear Mediterranean climate, and a blowy one as well, with winds puffing on an average of 120–160 days a year. This is good news in the hot summer, when the Cyclades are cooled by winds, especially the notorious *meltémi* from the northeast, always the most likely to upset Aegean sailing schedules; on the other hand, it's very rare for the mercury to hit the dread 40°C (104°F) mark, as happens so often on the mainland. Winters are mild: there are no mountains and it doesn't snow; in the spring the Cyclades have the earliest wheat harvest in Greece. In general the wet season begins at the end of October or beginning of November, and in December, the rainiest month, it can fall like 'tables and chairs' as the Greeks say. It begins to feel springlike near the end of February, when the first wildflowers reappear.

The Cyclades is one of the driest areas in Greece, with only 65% moisture and rain a real event if it falls between April and September. Until recently the inhabitants depended on the occasional precious spring and their cisterns—the winter rainwater caught off their slightly tilted flat roofs. These days water is imported in big tankers to many islands in the summer, although some people still use their old cisterns to water their flowers and vegetables.

Average Daily Temperatures

	Athens F°	Athens C°	Cyclades F°	Cyclades C°		Athens F°	Athens C°	Cyclades F°	Cyclades C°
Jan	48	11	54	12	July	82	28	76	25
Feb	49	11	54	12	Aug	82	28	76	25
Mar	54	12	56	13	Sept	76	25	74	23
April	60	16	60	17	Oct	66	19	68	20
May	68	20	68	20	Nov	58	15	62	17
June	76	25	74	23	Dec	52	12	58	14

Two uniquely Greek **measurements** you may come across are the *strémma*, a Greek land measurement (1 *strémma* = ¼ acre), and the *oká*, an old-fashioned weight standard, divided into 400 drams (1 *oká* = 3lb; 35 drams = ¼lb, 140 drams = 1lb).

'God gave watches to the Europeans and time to the Greeks,' they say, but if you need more precision, **Greek time** is Eastern European, two hours ahead of Greenwich Mean Time and seven hours ahead of Eastern Standard Time in North America.

Embassies and Consulates

Australia: 37 D. Soútsou, 115 21 Athens, ✆ 644 7303, ✉ 644 3633.
Canada: 4 I. Gennadíou, 115 21 Athens, ✆ 725 4011, ✉ 725 3994.
Ireland: 7 Vass. Konstantínou, 106 74 Athens, ✆ 723 2771, ✉ 724 0217.
New Zealand: 24 Xenia, 115 28 Athens ✆ 771 0112.
Netherlands: 5–7 Vas. Konstantínou, Athens, ✆ 723 9701.
South Africa: 60 Kifissías, 151 25 Maroússi ✆ 680 6459, ✉ 689 5320.
United Kingdom: 1 Ploutárchou Street, 106 75 Athens, ✆ 723 6211, ✉ 724 1872.
USA: 91 Vassilías Sofías, 115 21 Athens, ✆ 721 2951, ✉ 645 6282.

Events and Cultural Attractions

Besides Greek Easter, and religious and national holidays, the Cyclades celebrates a range of other events in the summer. Each island has a section on its own particular feast days, the *panegýria*—direct descendants of the ancient Greek religious festivals, the *panegyries*. The Olympics were the greatest of the ancient *panegyries*; modern ones usually feature a religious service, and a communal meal of some sort, and music and dancing, although not surprisingly the more out-of-the-way villages and islands with fewer tourists hold more authentic celebrations. The main ones are listed in the text, while below is a list of more ambitious annual events. Dates squirm around a lot; ring the National Tourist Organization a month or two before the event to pin them down.

May

Homereia, on Íos. Three days of folklore, art and other culture in honour of the poet.

June–September

Athens Festival. International culture. Modern and ancient theatre, jazz, classical music and dance, often with visiting British companies, in the stunning setting of the Herodus Atticus Odeon beneath the Acropolis. Also a wide range of performances at the Lycabettus Theatre, Likavitós Hill, including the **International Jazz and Blues Festival** in late June.

Epídavros Festival in the Peloponnese. Ancient Greek drama under the stars in the authentic setting, so take a cushion or something to sit on. Special buses from Athens. Festivals Box Office 4 Stadíou Street, Athens, in the arcade, ✆ 322 1459.

June–August

Ermoupouleia, on Sýros, with theatre, music, art and folk music performed in the main square.

July

Simonida Festival, on Kéa, celebrating the work of the island's famous son, lyric poet Simonides, 557–467 BC, with theatre, lectures, exhibitions and dance.

Dáphní Wine Festival, near Athens.

August

Pilgrimage to Tínos, on the 15th: the biggest in Greece.

August–September

International Music Festival, Santoríni, classical music concerts.

Food and Drink

Life's fundamental principle is the satisfaction of the needs and wants of the stomach. All important and trivial matters depend on this principle and cannot be differentiated from it.

Epicurus, 3rd century BC

Epicurus may have given his name to gourmets, but in reality his philosophy was an economical one that advocated maximizing the simple pleasures of life: rather than continually seek novelty and delight in ever greater extremes, Epicurus suggests, make a plate of bread and olives taste sublime by fasting for a couple of days. In that way modern Greeks are all epicureans: centuries of occupation and extreme poverty have taught them to relish food more than cuisine, and they eat with great zest and conviviality.

Meals are not about scaling gastronomic heights, but a daily reminder to the Greeks of who they are and what their country has to offer—fish from the seas, lamb from the valleys, fresh herbs and honey from the mountains, wild young greens from the hills, olives, fruits and nuts from the groves. The method of cooking these things is often quite simple; Turkish and Italian influences remain strong, just as they do in the language. What's more, recent studies show that Greek food not only tastes good, but is remarkably good for you, too.

Nevertheless, Greece has acquired a poor reputation for food. During the 1970s, the relatively few restaurants that existed, especially on the islands, were overrun. Standards fell as they tried to cope with the influx of people; and they fell even lower when making as much money as possible in a few short months became the overriding consideration. Neither did the first generation of taverna-owners in the tourist age see any reason to improve; the masses, mostly travelling on a shoestring, seemed content with cheap village salads, reheated moussaká, kebabs, taramosaláta and more kebabs, often served in a kind of caricature of Greekiness (plastic grapes and Zorba, Zorba, Zorba). Others struggled haplessly to please middle-aged customers from the pale north who swore that they couldn't abide garlic or even olive oil, which in Greece is close to nectar (guide books used to train their readers to say WHORE-is LA-thi, parakaLO —'without oil, please').

While too many tourist tavernas still grind out greasy grub, advertised with plastic idiot-photos of food sun-blasted over the years into greenish plates of flaking scabs (no wonder they have to hire obnoxious touts who drag in clients from the street!), their days seem to be numbered, as diners have come to know and expect better.

The new generation of taverna-owners are making a concerted effort to offer real Greek cooking, reviving recipes handed down from mother to daughter, recipes very much based on what's in season: vegetables like butter beans, green beans and okra in rich tomato and olive oil sauces; *briáms* of aubergines and courgettes; beetroot with hot garlic *skordaliá* dip; stuffed, lightly battered courgette flowers; prawns in filo parcels; octopus *stifádo*; beef stew with baby onions; lamb grazed on mountain herbs baked with fresh dill, yoghurt and lemon; ragout of snails, and whitebait so fresh they're almost wriggling. A simple sun-ripened Greek tomato in August, sprinkled with fresh oregano and anointed with olive oil from the family grove, is enough to jump-start the old taste buds. Just try to reproduce the same sensation back home.

One criticism levelled at Greek food is that it's served cold. It usually is, and that's because Greeks believe tepid food is better for the digestion than hot in the summer (once you get used to it, you realize that many dishes are actually tastier once they're left to cool in their own juices). The pace of life is different as well. There's no rush. Lunches begin late and stretch long into the afternoon and dinners into the small hours. While we tend to shovel down quick dinners in front of the TV, the gregarious Greeks eat to enjoy, to relax, to talk. A night out with friends in a taverna is the best entertainment going.

vegetarians

Of all the people in the European Union, the Greeks now eat the most meat per capita, but they also eat most cheese, more than even the French, and follow only the Italians in eating pasta. Basically they just eat a lot, which means there are plenty of dishes for vegetarians, a wide range of pulses and *ladera* (fresh vegetable main courses cooked with olive oil, invented for the many Orthodox fasts) and salads from artichokes to aubergines as well as okra, beetroot leaves, spinach-style greens with lemon and in some places *cápari*, pickled caper plant which looks like prunings from a rose bush but tastes delicious. There are delicate cheese and spinach pies in flaky filo pastry, and pasta dishes and pizzas up to Italian standards, thanks to the influx of those pickiest of all diners; stuffed peppers and tomatoes; deep-fried courgettes; *dolmádes*, sometimes using cabbage leaves instead of vines.

If you're a vegetarian or used to buying pre-packed, sanitized meat, it's worth pointing out that in many parts of Greece, especially the remoter islands, food comes on the hoof, on the wing or in the net. It's not uncommon to see a kid or sheep despatched near a taverna by day and then turn up on the menu at night. Bunnies hopping round the village also hop into the pot, the family pig turns into sausages, free-range chickens end up being barbecued and after a while the washing line of drying octopus becomes part of the scenery.

Eating Out

So how can you find a good place to eat? As always, follow the locals. Greek families aren't going to throw away hard-earned cash on tourist food. If you're hungry for something a cut above taverna fare, keep an eye open for restaurants that have made an effort to revive traditional Greek décor, austere but colourful with handpainted signs, painted chairs, weaving and so on; their owners usually prove to be just as serious about reviving traditional recipes in the kitchen.

Greek eating places are divided into five categories. **Tavernas** and *estiatória* (restaurants) are found everywhere and the differences between them tend to get a bit blurred. But you'll generally find the *estiatório* has a wider menu and is a bit more upmarket. Tavernas are more like family-run bistros and can range from shacks on the beach to barn-like affairs called *Kéntrikos* that provide music in the evening. There may not be a menu as such. The waiter will reel off what's on or even invite you to have a look for yourself. Mine host may have some special fish, a lobster or 'dish of the day'. Homemade English translations may leave you more baffled than ever (*see* **Topics**); the **menu decoder** on pp.252–4 may help.

A typical Greek meal begins with a basket of bread and a range of starters that everyone shares: *taramosaláta*, *tzatzíki* (cucumbers and yoghurt), prawns, feta cheese, little cheese or spinach pies, *saganáki* (fried cheese sprinkled with lemon), greens in olive oil and lemon sauces, green beans, okra or butter beans in sauce or fried courgettes and aubergines.

These are followed by a shared salad and potatoes, and a main course that you eat on your own—fish, a pasta, an oven dish ('Ready dishes', moussaká, stuffed vegetables, etc.) or else meat: lamb, pork, beef or kid, either stewed, baked in a casserole (*stifádo*, *kokinistó*, veal *youvétsi* with tear-drop pasta are typical) or freshly grilled (*tis óras*, 'the On Times')—chops (*brizóles*), lamb cutlets (*paidhákia*), souvláki (kebabs), meatballs (*keftédes* or *sousoukákia*), sausages (*lukániko*), or chicken (*koutópolou*, usually free-range). Greeks eat very little duck; if you are offered 'Quacker', don't be surprised when you get rolled oats.

Desserts are rare outside tourist places, although you may find some fresh watermelon or yogurt; Greeks make lovely sweets, puddings, cakes, and ice creams (just look at the displays in any **zacharoplasteío** or pastry shop) but tend to eat them in the late afternoon with a coffee after the siesta, or in the early evening, hours before dinner.

At the seaside you'll find the fish tavernas, **psarotavérnes**, specializing in all kinds of seafood from freshly fried calamari, shrimps, giant prawns, to red mullet, swordfish, bream and sardines. Ironically, fish is expensive, because of depletion of stocks in the Med, but you can find cheapies like fresh whitebait (*marídes*), cuttlefish stew (*soupiá*), small shrimps (*garídes*), sometimes cooked in feta cheese; and fish soups like *psarósoupa* or spicy *kakavia*, a meal in themselves with hunks of fresh bread and a bottle of wine. When eating fish soup it's customary to remove the fish, put it on a plate, drink the broth then tuck into the fish. Note that each type of fish has its own price, and portions are priced by weight.

If you're a red-blooded **meat eater** then head for the nearest **hasapotavérna**, which is a grill room attached to a local butcher's shop. Not that common, they offer fresh meat of all kinds, kebabs, home-made sausages and sometimes delicious stews, usually served by the butcher's assistant in a bloodstained apron for added carnivorous effect. The **psistariá** is another version of the theme specializing in chicken, lamb, pork or *kokorétsi*, a kind of lamb's offal doner. You may even find a **mageiria**, simple old-fashioned pots simmering on the stove home-cooking places, often only open for lunch. Other kinds of eateries in Greece need no introduction: the pizzeria (often spelled *pitsaria*) and, in big towns and major resorts, American fast fooderies, along with Goody's, the main Greek clone, and mom-and-pop attempts at the same.

A pitcher or bottle of tap water comes with each meal, and most Greeks order wine or beer. Note that when dining with Greeks it's customary to pour wine for each other—always guests first—and drink constant toasts, glasses chinking—*steen yámass*, good health to us, *steen yássou* or *yássas*, good health to you. By all means clink glasses, but on no account bring your glass down on another person's (unless your intentions for the evening are entirely dishonourable). If a man does it to your glass, it's best to say '*yámass*' and act dumb, unless you want to take him up on it.

Eating out in Greece has always been something of a movable feast. Because of the intense heat in summer, Greek families tend to eat late lunch at home, followed by their siesta or *mesiméri*. Then it's back to work, and around 8 or 9pm, it's time for the evening *vólta* or stroll to see and be seen, catch up on the news, and decide where to go. Greeks eat late, rarely before 10pm, and meals can go on into the small hours. The children are there (they too have a nap in the afternoon) and are more than welcome—babies are rocked, toddlers crawl under the table and the older children get up to goodness knows what. Dinner is often boisterous, punctuated with fiery discussions and maybe bursts of song or dance. The more company round the table the merrier, and the more likely your meal will turn into a spontaneous cabaret that no tour operator's organized 'Greek Night' can match. You may even get your table whipped away from under you in a dancer's jaws. *Kalí órexi!* *Bon appetit!*

prices

A **Greek menu**, *katálogos*, usually has two-tier prices—with and without tax; you pay the highest. **Prices** are fixed according to category, although there can be seasonal fluctuations when they jump, especially at Easter and in August. If you suspect you're being ripped off, the system makes it easier to complain. If you eat with the Greeks, there's no Western nit-picking over who's had what. You share the food, drink, company and the bill, *to logariasmó*, although hosts will seldom let foreign guests part with a drachma. A new law designed to catch tax-evaders insists that you take a receipt (*apóthexi*); the police make periodical checks.

An average taverna meal—if you don't order a major fish—usually runs at around 2500–3000dr a head with generous carafes of house wine (*see* below). Prices at sophisticated restaurants or blatantly touristy places tend to be a bit higher, and places on remote islands can be just as costly because of extra transport prices. Quite a few places now offer set price meals with a glass of wine (often for under 2000dr) some for two people, some better than others. In the 'Eating Out' sections of this book, any price given is per person with house wine.

kafeneíons *and cafés*

Every one-mule village will have at least one **kafeneíon**, a social institution where men (and increasingly women, although they're still outnumbered) gather to discuss the latest news, read the papers, nap in hard wood chairs, play cards or backgammon and incidentally drink coffee. Some men seem to live in them. They are so essential to Greek identity that in at least one instance, on Skópelos, when property

interests threatened the last old *kafeneíon* with extinction, the town hall opened one for its citizens. The bill of fare features Greek coffee (*café hellinikó*), which is the same stuff as Turkish coffee, prepared to order in 40 different ways, although *glykó* (sweet), *métrio* (medium) and *skéto* (no sugar) are the basic orders. It is always served with a glass of water. '*Nes*' aka Nescafé with condensed Dutch milk has by popular tourist demand become available everywhere, though Greeks prefer their instant coffee whipped and iced (*frappé*)—and it's lovely on a hot day. Tea will be a pot of hot water and a bag. Soft drinks, *tsikoúdia* (*rakí*), brandy and ouzo round out the old style *kafeneíon* fare.

Newer cafés (those with the cushy soft plastic chairs under awnings) usually open much earlier and close much later than *kafeneíons*. They are good places to find various kinds of breakfast, from simple to complete English, with rashers, baked beans and eggs, and attempts at cappuccinos. They also serve mineral water (try the sparkling IOΛH), ice cream concoctions, milkshakes, fruit juices, cocktails, pastries, and thick Greek yoghurt (cow, sheep or goat's milk) and honey. They are also a traditional place to stop for a late-night Metaxá; the more stars on the label (from three to seven), the smoother and the higher the price.

bars *(*barákia*)* and ouzeriés

Nearly every island has at least one trendy music bar, usually playing the latest hit records and serving fancy cocktails as well as standard drinks. These establishments come to life at cocktail hour, then again around midnight, when everyone has spent the day on the beach and the earlier part of the evening in a taverna. Bars used to close at dawn, although in 1994 the Greek government decreed a 2am weekday closing, claiming that the nation was nodding off at work after a night on the tiles.

In general bars are not cheap, sometimes outrageously dear by Greek standards, and it can be disconcerting to realize that you have paid the same for your Harvey Wallbanger as you paid for your entire meal half an hour before in the taverna next door. Cocktails have now risen to beyond the 1000dr mark in many bars, but before you complain remember that the measures are triples by British standards. If in doubt stick to beer (Greece has a new brand to try, Mythos) ouzo, *suma* (like ouzo, but often sweeter—each island makes its own) wine and Metaxá (Metaxá and Coke, if you can stomach it, is generally about half the price of a rum and Coke). One unfortunate practice on the islands is the doctoring of bottles: some bar owners buy cheaper versions of spirits and use them to refill brand-name bottles.

Just when it seemed time to write the obituary on a grand old Greek institution, the **ouzerie**, it has come back with a vengeance. The national aperitif, ouzo—the *rakí* drunk by the Byzantines and Venetians, inexplicably renamed ouzo in the 18th century from the Latin *usere*, 'usable'—is clear and anise-flavoured, and served in small glasses or a *karafáki* holding about three or four doses which many drinkers dilute and cloud with water. It is cheap, and famous for making its imbibers optimistic. As the Greeks look askance at drunkenness—as they did in ancient times, when they cut their wine with water and honey—ouzo is traditionally served with a little plate of snacks called *mezédes* which can range from grilled octopus, nuts, olives, chunks of cheese and tomatoes to elaborate seafood platters; for an assortment, ask for a *pikilía* (usually translated as '*seafood various*'). Similar to *ouzeríes* are **mezedopoieíons**, specializing in these Greek tapas, where you can build up an entire meal, sometimes from a hundred choices on the menu, and wash them down with wine or beer.

Wine

Wine in Greek is *krasí*, a word that comes from the *krasis*, the custom of mixing two parts water with one part wine. The Cyclades have a long and honourable wine-growing history: Dionysos, the god of wine, lived on Náxos, and even in Roman times the islands exported a huge variety of wines, mostly strong and used for blending. They tend to be highly regionalized, each island and village offering their own varieties made from indigenous grapes; forget the tyranny of Cabernet Sauvignon and Chardonnay.

These days Santoríni is the leading producer with a national reputation, but ask for the others in the local tavernas; nearly every island makes a bit, especially Páros, Náxos, Síkinos, and Mílos. Ordinary red and white **house wines** are often locally produced bargains—ask for *krasí varelísio* (barrelled wine) or *krasí chíma* (loose wine). These wines are nearly always better than fine, though you may be unlucky and get one that's a stinker; if you're suspicious, order a glass to start with.

The country's best-known wine, **retsína**, has a very distinctive taste of pine resin. In ancient times, when the Greeks stored their wine in clay amphorae sealed airtight with resin, the disintegration of the resin helped prevent oxidation in the wine and lent it its distinctive flavour. It is an acquired taste, and many people can be put off by the pungent odour and sharp taste of some bottled varieties. Modern retsínas show an increasingly restrained use of resin; all retsínas are best appreciated well-chilled.

Draught retsína (*retsína varelísio*) can be found only on some islands (on the Cyclades, only Kýthnos and Kéa make it), but in Athens it is the accepted, delicious accompaniment to the meal. Retsína is admirably suited to Greek food, and after a while you may find non-resinated wines a rather bland alternative. Traditionally it comes to the table in chilled copper-anodized jugs, by the kilo (about a litre), or *mesó kiló* (half) or *tétarto* (250ml) and served in small tumblers. Etiquette requires that they are never filled to the brim or drained empty; you keep topping up your companions' glasses, as best you can.

Greece also produces an ample selection of medium-priced red and white wines in bottles. All the principal wine companies—Boutari, Achaia-Clauss, Carras, Tsantali—have made strides to improve the quality in the past decade, investing heavily in new equipment and foreign expertise, and it shows; even that humblest of bottles (and Greece's best-seller) Deméstika has become very acceptable of late, and bears little resemblance to the rough stuff that earned it some unflattering sound-alike nicknames.

Look out for the nobler labels; Boutari Náoussa is an old-style, slightly astringent red, while Boutari's Grande Réserve is their best red; Lac des Roches is their most popular white on the islands. Peloponnesiakos from Achaia-Clauss is an easy-drinking, light white wine which is faddishly popular at the moment anywhere within exportable distance of the Peloponnese. From Carras, Château Carras is a Bordeaux-style red wine made from the Cabernet Sauvignon and Merlot grapes; if you're lucky you might find Carras Limnio, one of Greece's most distinct red wines. Boutari's Santoríni is their finest island white, while in Rhodes CAIR supplies Greece with its sparkling *méthode traditionelle* white, Caïr. Emery produces some good whites including Villare. The most noble red wines come from Nemea, and are superb with roast lamb.

In recent years small bottle-producers have become very fashionable with the wine-drinking élite. Some of these are superb; others deserve obscurity. But for the most part you are unlikely to come across them in the average taverna. If you're a wine buff, it's worth seeking them out from local recommendations in wine shops (*kávas*) and high-class restaurants.

Health

At the bare minimum there is at least one doctor (*iatrós*) on every island with more than a couple of hundred people. Surgery hours are 9am–1pm and 5–7pm. On bigger islands there are hospitals which are open all day, and outpatient clinics, open in the mornings. EU citizens are entitled to free medical care; British travellers are often urged to carry a Form E111 (apply well in advance on form CM1 from post offices), which will admit them to the most basic IKA (Greek NHS) hospitals for treatment; but this doesn't cover medicines or nursing care. In any case, the E111 seems to be looked on with total disregard outside Athens; expect to pay up front, and get receipts so you can be reimbursed back home. Private doctors and hospital stays can be very expensive, so take out a travel insurance policy and make sure your holiday insurance has adequate repatriation cover; Greek hospitals have improved by leaps and bounds but, as it's still common for families to supply food and help with the nursing, you may feel neglected. Non-Europeans should check their own health policies to see if they're covered when abroad.

Greek general practitioners' fees are usually reasonable. Most doctors pride themselves on their English, as do the pharmacists (found in the *farmakeío*), whose advice on minor ailments is good, although their medicine is not particularly cheap. If you forgot to bring your own condoms and are caught short, they are widely available from *farmakeío* and kiosks, with lusty brand names such as 'Squirrel' or 'Rabbit'. If you can't see them on display, the word *kapótes* (condom) gets results. You can also get the Pill (*chápi antisiliptikó*), morning-after Pill and HRT over the pharmacy counter without a prescription. Be sure to take your old packet to show them the brand you use.

For some reason Greeks buy more medicines than anyone else in Europe (is it hypochondria? the old hoarding instinct?) but you shouldn't have to. The sun is the most likely cause of grief, so be careful, hatted and sunscreened. If you find the olive oil too much, Coca Cola or retsina will help cut it. Fresh parsley is good for stomach upsets. *See* pp.63–4 for possibly unkind wildlife. If anything else goes wrong, do what the islanders have done for centuries: pee on it.

Money

The word for **bank** in Greek is *trápeza*, derived from the word *trapézi*, or table, used back in the days of money-changers. On all the islands with more than goats and a few shepherds there is some sort of banking establishment. If there's no bank, travel agents, tourist offices or post offices will change cash, traveller's cheques and Eurocheques.

If you plan to spend time on a remote island, such as Skhinoússa, it is safest to bring enough drachmae with you. Beware that small but popular islands often have only one bank, where exchanging money can take forever: beat the crowds by going at 8am, when the banks open (normal banking hours are 8–2, 8–1.30 on Fri).

The number of 24-hour **automatic cashpoints** on the islands grows every year: some accept one kind of credit card and not another (VISA is perhaps the most widely accepted). You can also use these to withdraw cash at banks. Major hotels, luxury shops and resort restaurants take cards (look for the little signs) but smaller hotels and tavernas certainly won't.

Traveller's cheques are useful even though commission rates are less for cash. The major brands (Thomas Cook and American Express) are accepted in all banks and post offices; take your passport as ID, and shop around for commission rates.

Running out? Athens and Piraeus, with offices of many British and American banks, are the easiest places to have money sent by cash transfer from someone at home—though it may take a few days. **American Express** may be helpful here; their office in Athens is 2 Ermou St, right by Sýntagma Square, © 324 4975, and there are branches on Mýkonos and Santoríni.

The **Greek drachma** (abbreviated dr, in Greek δρχ) is circulated in the following coins: 100, 50, 20, 10, and 5 drachmae, and in the following notes: 100, 500, 1000, 5000 and 10,000 drachmae.

Museums and Archaeological Sites and Opening Hours

Significant archaeological sites and museums have regular admission hours. Nearly all are closed on Mondays, and open other weekdays from 8 or 9 to around 2, although more important sites now tend to stay open later, until 4 or 5pm. Hours tend to be shorter in the winter. On the other hand, churches are often open only in late afternoon (from 6 to 7pm), when they're being cleaned. Students with valid ID often get a discount on admission fees. These are usually between 400 and 1000dr; more expensive ones are listed as such in the text.

National Holidays

Note that most businesses and shops close down for the afternoon before and the morning after a religious holiday. If a national holiday falls on a Sunday, the following Monday is observed. The Orthodox Easter is generally a week or so after the Roman Easter.

1 January	New Year's Day	*Protochroniá*; also *Ag. Vassílios* (Greek Father Christmas)
6 January	Epiphany	*Ta Fóta/ Theofánia*
February–March	'Clean Monday' (precedes Shrove Tuesday, and follows a three-week carnival)	*Katharí Deftéra*
25 March	Annunciation/ Greek Independence Day	*Evangelismós*
late March–April	Good Friday	*Megáli Paraskeví*
	Easter Sunday	*Páscha*
	Easter Monday	*Theftéra tou Páscha*
1 May	Labour Day	*Protomayá*
40 days after Easter	Pentacost (Whit Monday)	*Pentikostí*
15 August	Assumption of the Virgin	*Koímisis tis Theotókou*
28 October	'*Ochí*' Day (in celebration of Metaxás' 'no' to Mussolini)	
25 December	Christmas	*Christoúyena*
26 December	Gathering of the Virgin	*Sináxi Theotókou*

In Greece, Easter is the equivalent in significance of Christmas and New Year in northern climes, the time when far-flung relatives return to see their families back home; it's a good time of year to visit for the atmosphere, feasts and fireworks. After Easter and May 1, spring (*ánixi*—the opening) has offically come, and the tourist season begins. Festival dates for saints' days listed in the text vary over a period of several given days, or even weeks, owing to the Greek liturgical calendar's calculations for Easter; check these locally. It's also worth remembering that the main partying often happens the night *before* the saint's day.

Packing

Even in the height of summer, evenings can be chilly in Greece, especially when the *meltémi* wind is blowing. Always bring at least one warm sweater and a pair of long trousers, and sturdy and comfortable shoes if you mean to do any walking— trainers (sneakers) are usually good enough. Plastic swimming shoes are handy for rocky beaches, often the haunt of those little black pincushions, sea urchins; you can easily buy them near any beach if you don't want to carry them around with you. Greeks are inveterate night people: bring ear plugs if you don't want to hear them scootering home under your hotel window at 4am.

If you travel in August without any reservations, consider bringing a sleeping bag, just in case your destination is all full up. Serious sleeping-baggers should also bring a Karrimat or similar insulating layer to cushion them from the gravelly Greek ground. Torches come in very handy for moonless nights, caves and rural villages. Note that the **electric current** in Greece is mainly 220 volts, 50Hz; plugs are continental two-pin. Buy an adaptor in the UK before you leave, as they are rare in Greece; North Americans will need adaptors and transformers.

On the pharmaceutical side, bring extras of any prescription drug you need, just in case—other items, such as seasickness remedies, sunscreen, insect repellent, women's sanitary towels and sometimes Tampax, tablets for stomach upsets and aspirin are widely available in pharmacies and even kiosks, but on remote islands you'll need to seek out the *farmakeío*; if there's no pharmacy, you've had it. Soap, washing powder, a clothes line, a knife for picnics and especially a towel are essential budget traveller's gear. A photo of the family and home is always appreciated by new Greek friends.

Let common sense and the maxim 'bring as little as possible and never more than you can carry' dictate your packing; work on the theory that however much money and clothing you think you need, halve the clothes and double the money.

Photography

Greece lends herself freely to photography, but a fee is charged at archaeological sites and museums. For a movie camera of any kind, including camcorders, you are encouraged to buy a ticket for the camera; with a tripod you pay per photograph at sites, but cameras (especially tripod-mounted ones) are not allowed in museums, for no particular reason other than the museum's maintaining a monopoly on its own (usually very dull) picture stock. 35mm film, both print and slide, can be found in many island shops, though it tends to be expensive and the range of film speeds limited. Disposable and underwater cameras are on sale in larger holiday resorts. Busy islands even have one-hour developing services.

The light in the summer is often stronger than it seems and is the most common cause of ruined photographs; opting for slow film or filters will help. Greeks usually love to have their pictures taken, and although it's more polite to ask first, you should just go ahead and take the photo if you don't want them to strike a pose.

You should avoid taking pictures (well, who would want to anyway?) of the aircraft, military installations and barracks, communications systems on mountain tops, and military look-out posts. If you have an expensive camera, it never hurts to insure it. Above all, never leave it alone. Although Greeks themselves very rarely steal anything, other tourists are not so honest.

Post Offices

Signs for post offices (*tachidromío*) as well as postboxes (*grammatokivótio*) are bright yellow and easy to find. Post offices (which are also useful for changing money) are open from Monday to Saturday 7.30am to 8pm; on small islands they may shut for lunch. Stamps (*grammatósima*) can also be bought at kiosks and in some tourist shops, although they may charge a small commission. Be warned that postcards can take up to three weeks to arrive at their destinations, while anything in an envelope will usually get there in a week or so, depending on the route. If you're in a hurry, pay extra for an express service. To send a package, always go to an island's main post office. If you do not have an address, mail can be sent to you poste restante to any post office in Greece, and picked up with proof of identity (you'll find the postal codes for all the islands in the text, which will get your letters there faster). After one month all unretrieved letters are returned to sender. In small villages, particularly on the islands, mail is not delivered to the house but to the village centre, either a *kafeneíon* or bakery.

Shopping

Official shopping hours in Greece are: Mon, Wed, 9–5; Tues, Thurs and Fri 10–7, Sat 8.30–3.30 and Sun closed; in practice, tourist-orientated shops stay open as late as 1am in season. Leather goods, gold and jewellery, traditional handcrafts, embroideries, and weavings, onyx, ceramics, alabaster, herbs and spices and tacky knick-knacks are favourite purchases; also check the text for island specialities.

Non-EU citizens tempted by Greek jewellery, carpets, perfumes and other big ticket items can perhaps justify their indulgences by having the sales tax (VAT) reimbursed—this is 18% of the purchase price (or 13%, on Aegean islands). Make sure the shop has a TAX FREE FOR TOURISTS sticker in the window, spend at least 40,000dr inside, and pick up a tax-free shopping cheque for your purchases.

When you leave Greece, you must show your purchases and get the customs official to stamp your cheques (allow an extra hour for this, especially at the airport), and cash them in at the refund point as you leave. If you are flying out of another EU country, hold on to the cheques, get them stamped again by the other EU country's customs and use their refund point. You can also post your tax free cheques back to Greece for refund (10 Nikis St., 10563 Athens, © (01) 325 4995, @ (01) 322 4701) but they skim off 20% of the amount on commission.

Sports

watersports

Greece was made for watersports and, by law, all the beaches, no matter how private they might look, are public. All but a fraction meet European guidelines for water cleanliness, although a few could stand to have less litter on the sand.

Beaches near built-up areas often have umbrellas and sunbed concessions and snack bars, and if there's a breeze you'll probably find a windsurfer to rent at affordable prices (the favourite windy spot in the Cyclades is Páros—which holds world championships in August).

Bigger beaches have paragliding and jet-skis, and waterskiing is available on most islands and large hotel complexes. The Ministry of Tourism has just allocated huge sums to build up marinas on the islands, which may improve your chances of finding a small sail or motor boat to hire by the day; at the time of writing they are relatively small.

Nudism is forbidden by law in Greece, but tolerated in numerous designated or out-of-the-way areas. On the other hand, topless sunbathing is now legal on the majority of popular beaches as long as they're not smack in the middle of a village; exercise discretion. Even young Greek women are shedding their tops, but nearly always on someone else's island.

Scuba diving, once strictly banned to keep divers from snatching antiquities and to protect Greece's much-harassed marine life, is permitted between dawn and sunset in specially defined coastal areas (so far around Mýkonos only, in the Cyclades; local diving excursions will take you there). For information contact the Hellenic Federation of Underwater Activities, Post Office of the West Air Terminal, 16604 Elliniko, © (01) 981 9961.

Average Sea Temperatures

Jan	Feb	Mar	April	May	June	July	Aug	Sept	Oct	Nov	Dec
59°F	59°F	59°F	61°F	64°F	72°F	75°F	77°F	75°F	72°F	64°F	63°F
15°C	15°C	15°C	16°C	18°C	22°C	24°C	25°C	24°C	22°C	18°C	17°C

land sports

Walking is the favourite activity on every island in the Cyclades; Mílos and Náxos have the most to offer. Increasingly locals are arranging treks, and little, often locally produced maps and guides, are a big help for finding the most interesting country paths. Never set out without a hat and water; island shops have begun to sell handy water-bottle shoulder slings.

Tennis is popular in Athens, with numerous clubs from Glyfáda to Kifissiá, and at all major resort hotels (many are lit up at night so you can beat the heat); often non-residents are allowed to play in the off season. Páros is one of a few islands which offer horse-riding. For more detailed information call the **Riding Club of Greece**, Parádissos, © 682 6128 and Riding Club of Athens, Gerakos, © 661 1088.

Telephones

The new improved Organismós Telefikoinonía Elládos, or OTE, has replaced most of its old phone offices with new card phones, which work a treat, although many on the islands, for some reason, are set up for basketball players only. If you can reach the buttons, you can dial abroad direct (dial 00 before the country code, UK 44, Ireland 353, USA and Canada 1, Australia 61, New Zealand 64, and drop the first number of the area code). Cards for 100 units are 1500dr. For a decent long-distance chat you may need more, although the 500 unit 6500dr and the 1000 unit 11,500dr *telekártas* are hard to find outside of big resort areas. As a last resort, find a telephone *me métriki* (with a meter), which are often more costly and usually located in kiosks (*períptera*), *kafeneíons*, some travel agents, hotels, and shops. As a general rule, calls are cheaper between 3–5pm and after 9pm, but this may change. **Telegrams** can be sent from one of the surviving OTE offices in big cities or from the post office. When **phoning Greece** from overseas, the country code is 30 and you drop the first '0' of the local area code.

Toilets

Greek plumbing has improved dramatically in the past few years, and in the newer hotels you can flush everything away as merrily as you do at home, at least as often as your conscience lets you on arid islands strapped for water. Tavernas, *kafeneíons* and sweet shops almost always have facilities (it's good manners to buy something), and there are often public pay-toilets in strategic areas of the towns. In older pensions and tavernas, the plumbing often makes up in inventiveness for what it lacks in efficiency. Do not tempt fate by disobeying the little notices 'the papers they please to throw in the basket'—or it's bound to lead to trouble (a popular new sticker has Poseidon himself bursting out of the toilet bowl and pricking an offender with his trident). Old *kafeneíons* and bus stations tend to have only a ceramic hole squatter. Always have paper of some sort handy.

If you stay in a private room or pension you may have to have the electric water heater turned on for about 20 minutes before you take a shower. In most smaller pensions, water is heated by a solar panel on the roof, so the best time to take a shower is in the late afternoon, or the early evening (before other residents have used up the finite supply of hot water). In larger hotels there is often hot water in the mornings and evenings, but not in the afternoons. Actually 'cold' showers in the summer aren't all that bad, because the tap water itself is generally lukewarm, especially in the afternoon. A good many showers are of the hand-held variety, which is potentially dangerous (especially if you have kids) because Greeks don't believe in shower curtains and one thoughtless moment means your towel or toilet paper are soaked.

Greek tap water is perfectly safe to drink, but on some islands it tastes less than delicious. On the other hand, inexpensive plastic bottles of spring water are widely available (and responsible for untold pollution, taking up half the available room in landfill sites). On dry islands, remember to ask what time the water is turned off.

Tourist Information

If the National Tourist Organization of Greece (in Greek the initials are **EOT**) can't answer your questions about Greece, they can refer you to someone who can.

Australia and New Zealand

51 Pitt Street, Sydney, NSW 2000, ℡ 9241 1663/4; 📠 9235 2174.

Canada

1300 Bay St, Toronto, Ontario, M5R3K8, ℡ (416) 968 2220, 📠 968 6533.

1233 De La Montagne, Montreal, Quebec, H3G1Z2 ℡ (514) 871 1535, 📠 871 1498.

Great Britain and Ireland

4 Conduit Street, London W1R 0DJ, ℡ (0171) 734 5997 or ℡ 499 4976 📠 287 1369.

Netherlands

Leidsestraat 13, NS 1017 Amsterdam ℻ 625 4212/3/4, ✉ 620 7031.

USA

Head Office: Olympic Tower, 645 Fifth Avenue, 5th Floor, New York, NY 10022, ℻ (212) 421 5777; ✉ 826 6940, *gnto@orama.com*

168 N. Michigan Avenue, Chicago, Illinois. 60601, ℻ (312) 782 1084; ✉ 782 1091.

611 West Sixth Street, Suite 2198, LA, Calif. 90017, ℻ (213) 626 6696; ✉ 489 9744.

in Greece

The most popular islands have EOT offices; the others usually have some form of local tourist office or tourist police (located in an office in the regular police station, although nine times out of ten they're the only people on the island who don't speak any foreign language). If nothing else, they have listings of rooms on the island. **Legal Assistance for Tourists** is available free, but in July and Aug only: in Athens at 43–45 Valtetsiou St, ℻ (01) 330 0673, ✉ (01) 330 1137.

Travelling with Children

Greece is a great country for children, who are not barely tolerated, but generally enjoyed and encouraged. Depending on their age, they go free or receive discounts on ships and buses. However, if they're babies, don't rely on island pharmacies stocking your brand of milk powder or baby foods—they may have some, but it's safest to bring your own supply. Disposable nappies, especially Pampers, are widely available, even on small islands.

Travelling with a tot is like having a special passport. Greeks adore them and spoil them rotten, so don't be surprised if your infant is passed round like a parcel. Greek children usually have an afternoon nap (as do their parents) so it's quite normal for Greeks to be eating *en famille* well into the small hours. You should never have a problem finding a babysitter: indeed some of the larger hotels even offer special supervised kiddies' campgrounds and activity areas so that parents can have some real time off.

Superstitions are still given more credit than you might expect; you'll see babies with amulets pinned to their clothes or wearing blue beads to ward off the evil eye before their baptism. Beware of commenting on a Greek child's intelligence, beauty or whatever, as this may call down the jealous interest of the old gods and some of the nastier saints. The response in the old days was to spit in the admired child's face, but these days, superstitious grannies are usually content with a ritual 'phtew-phtew-phtew' dry spit, to protect the child from harm.

Hotels

All hotels in Greece are classed into six categories: Luxury, A, B, C, D and E. This grading system bears little relationship to the quality of service, charm, views, etc., but has everything to do with how the building is constructed, size of bedrooms, lifts, and so on; i.e. if the hotel has a marble-clad bathroom it gets a higher rating. **Pensions**, most without restaurants, are a confusing subdivision in Greek hotel classifications, especially as many call themselves hotels. They are family-run and more modest (an A class pension is roughly equivalent to a C or D class hotel and is priced accordingly). A few islands still have their government-built hotels from the 1960s, the Xenias, many of which resemble barracks, the fashion in those junta ruled days. On the Internet, *www.greekhotel.com* lists, with musical accompaniment, 8000 hotels and villas in Greece, with forms for more information about prices, availability and booking.

prices

Prices are set and strictly controlled by the tourist police. Off season (i.e. mid-September–mid July) you can generally get a discount, sometimes as much as 40%. Other charges include an 8% government tax, a 4.5% community bed tax, a 12% stamp tax, an optional 10% surcharge for stays of only one or two days, an air-conditioning surcharge, as well as a 20% surcharge for an extra bed. All these prices are listed on the door of every room and authorized and checked at regular intervals. If your hotelier fails to abide by the posted prices, or if you have any other reason to believe all is not on the level, take your complaint to the tourist police.

1998 approximate hotel rates (drachma) for high season (mid-July–mid-Sept)

	L	A	B	C	D
Single with bath	20,000–70,000	15,000–40,000	15,000–23,000	9000–20,000	4000–7000
Double with bath	30,000–200,000	25,000–50,000	20,000–35,000	11,000–28,000	6000–14,000

Prices for E hotels are about 20% less than D rates. Out of season rates are often 30–40% lower.

During the summer, hotels with restaurants may require guests to take their meals in the hotel, either full pension or half pension, and there is no refund for an uneaten dinner. Twelve noon is the official check-out time, although on the islands it is usually geared to the arrival of the next boat. Most Luxury and class A, if not B, hotels situated far from the town or port supply buses or cars to pick up guests. Hotels down to class B all have private en-suite bathrooms. In C most do, as do most Ds; E will have a shower down the hall. In these hotels don't always expect to find a towel or soap, although the bedding is clean.

In the 'Where to Stay' sections of this book, accommodation is listed according to the following price categories:

luxury	29,000 to astronomical
expensive	12,000–30,000
moderate	6000–13,000
inexpensive	4000–7000

Prices quoted in the book are approximate and for **double rooms**.

booking a hotel

The importance of reserving a room in advance, especially during July and August, cannot be over-emphasized. Reservations can be made through the individual hotel, through travel agents, through the Hellenic Chamber of Hotels by writing, at least two months in advance, to 24 Stadíou St, 105 61 Athens, ✆ (01) 322 5449, or in person in Athens, at the Hotels Desk in the National Bank of Greece building, 2 Karageorgi Servias, ✆ 323 7193, open Mon–Thurs 8.30–2, Fri 8.30–1.30, and Sat 9–12.30.

Rooms and Studios

These are for the most part cheaper than hotels and sometimes more pleasant. Although you can still find a few rooms (ΔΟΜΑΤΙΑ, *domátia*) in private houses, on the whole, rooms to rent are found off a family's living quarters, sometimes upstairs or in a separate annexe; an increasing number have en suite baths. One advantage rooms hold over hotels is that nearly all will provide a place to hand-wash your clothes and a line to hang them on. Another is the widespread availability of basic kitchen facilities (sink, table and chairs, at least a couple of gas rings, fridge, utensils and dishes) which immediately turns a room into a **studio**; these obviously cost a bit more, but out of season the difference is often negligible. Depending on facilities, a double room in high season will cost between 4000–8000dr with bath, a studio from 6000–12,000. Until June and after August prices are always negotiable. Owners will nearly always drop the price per day the longer you stay.

Prices also depend a lot on how much competition exists between owners on each island. On some it's good-natured dog eat dog (you can, for instance, get a very good deal on Santoríni, because the locals have overbuilt); when you step off the ferry you will be courted with all kinds of interesting proposals, photos of the rooms and even guidebook reviews of their establishments. On others, room and hotel owners have co-operated to organize accommodation booths by the port to sort out customers; if the room is not within walking distance, they'll collect you in a car or minivan. If you still can't find a room, most travel agencies will be able to dig one up (although these always cost more).

Youth Hostels

Some of these are official and require a membership card from the Association of Youth Hostels, or alternatively an International Membership Card (about 2600dr) from the Greek Association of Youth Hostels, 4 Dragatsaníou Street, Athens, © 323 4107; other hostels are informal, have no irksome regulations, and admit anyone. Most charge extra for a shower, sometimes for sheets. Expect to pay 2000dr a night, depending on the quality of facilities and services offered. The official ones have a curfew, which in Greece means you miss the fun.

Camping Out

The climate of summertime Greece is perfect for sleeping out of doors, especially close to the sea, where breezes keep the worst of the mosquitoes at bay. Unauthorized camping is illegal (the law was enacted to displace gypsy camps, and is still used for this purpose) although each village on each island enforces the ban as it sees fit. Some couldn't care less if you put up a tent at the edge of their beach; in others the police may pull up your tent pegs and fine you. All you can do is ask around to see what other tourists or friendly locals advise. Naturally, the more remote the beach, the less likely you are to be disturbed.

Most islands have at least one privately operated camping ground, though most have only minimal facilities. Islands with no campsites at all usually have a beach where free camping is tolerated. If the police are in some places lackadaisical about enforcing the camping regulations, they come down hard on anyone lighting any kind of fire in a forest, and may very well put you in jail for two months; every year fires damage huge swathes of land.

Camping prices are not fixed by law but these are the approximate guidelines, per day:

Adult	1200dr
Child (4–12)	600dr
Caravan	1800dr
Small tent	700dr
Large tent	1400dr
Car	650dr
Sleeping bag	350dr

On most islands it is possible to rent cottages or villas, generally for a week or more at a time. Villas can often be reserved from abroad: contact a travel agent or the National Tourist Organisation (EOT) for names and addresses of rental agents, or see the list below. In the off season villas may be found on the spot by asking around. Depending on the facilities this can work out quite reasonably per person. On the whole the longer your stay, the more economical it becomes. If you book from abroad, packages usually include flights, and transfers by coach, ferry, hydrofoil or domestic planes.

in the UK

Best of Greece, 23–24 Margaret St, London, W1N 8LE, ✆ (0171) 331 7070. Luxury villas.

Filoxenia Ltd, Sourdock Hill, Barkisland, Halifax, West Yorkshire HX4 0AG, ✆ (01422) 371796, ✉ 310340. Haute couture holidays to Athens and a select range of islands. Suzi Stembridge and family have scoured Greece for unusual holiday places and pass on their favourites to fellow Grecophiles. Houses, villas, tavernas, pensions, fly-drive. Also **Opus 23** for travellers with disabilities.

Greek Islands Club, 66 High Street,Walton-on-Thames KT12 1BU, ✆ (01932) 220477, ✉ 229346; US and Canada ✆ (800) 394 5577; *www.vch.co.uk/villas/*, *info@vch.co.uk.* Well run, established specialists, with helpful yet unobtrusive reps. They also offer an unusually wide choice of personalized activity holidays; their new Private Collection features hide-away hotels and exclusive villas on Santoríni, Mýkonos, Páros and Sýros.

Greek Sun Holidays, 1 Bank Street, Sevenoaks, Kent TN13 1UW, ✆ (01732) 740317. Helpful and family-run company, offering Athens and a range of unusual islands like Síkinos and Mílos. Tailor-made holidays and two-centre breaks.

Ilios Island Holidays, 18 Market Square, Horsham, West Sussex RH12 1EU, ✆ (01403) 259788. Self-catering on Páros and Náxos.

Island Wandering, 51A London Road, Hurst Green, Sussex TN19 7QP, ✆ (01580) 860733, ✉ (01580) 860282. Island-hopping without tears, with hotels or studios on many of the Cyclades, pre-booked before you go or with a wandering voucher system.

Manos Holidays, 168–172 Old Street, London EC1V 9BP, ✆ (0171) 216 8000. Good value holidays to the major resorts and lesser-known islands, island-hopping and two-centres. Ideal for children, low-season specials and deals for singles.

Simply Simon Holidays Ltd, 1/45 Nevern Square, London SW5 9PF, ☎ (0171) 373 1933. Cyclades specialists, covering every island except Tínos and Ándros.

Skiathos Holidays, 4 Holmedale Road, Kew Gardens, Richmond, Surrey GU13 8AA, ☎ (0181) 940 5157. Packages to Páros and Santoríni.

Sunvil, Sunvil House, Upper Square, Isleworth TW7 7BJ ☎ (0181) 568 4499, very friendly, well run company offering good value self-catering and hotel accommodation on most of the Cyclades.

in the USA/Canada

Amphitrion Holidays, 1206 21st St, NWm Suite 100A, Washington DC, 20036, ☎ (800)424 2471, ✆ (202) 872 8210. Houses, villas and apartments.

Apollo Tours, 1051 N. Waukegan Rd, Glenview, IL 60025, ☎ (800) 228 4367, ✆ (847) 724 3277. Upmarket villas and apartments.

CTI Carriers, 65 Overlea Blvd, Suite 201, Toronto, Ontario M4H 1P1, ☎ (800) 363 8181, ✆ (429) 7159. One of the biggest Canadian operators with villas.

Cycladic Environments, PO Box 382622, Cambridge, MA 02238-2622, ☎ (800) 719 5260, ✆ (617) 492 5881. Conservation group with a range of traditional properties to let in Oía on Santoríni. Special rates available for students on fellowships and academic researchers.

European Escapes, LLC, 483 Second Avenue, San Francisco, CA 94118, toll free ☎ (888) EUROLUX, ✆ (415) 386 0477, *http://members.aol.com/euroluxury/*, *EuroEscape@aol.com.* Luxury villas.

Greek Island Connection, 889 Ninth Ave, New York, NY, 10019, ☎ (212) 581 4784, ✆ (212) 581 5890, *grislcon@gte.net.* Customized seaside villas and condos.

Omega Tours, 3220 West Broadway, Vancouver, British Columbia, ☎ (800) 663 2669, ✆ (604) 738 7101. Villas and apartments.

Triaena Tours, 850 Seventh Ave, Suite 605, New York, NY, 10019, ☎ (800) 223 1273, ✆ (212) 582 8815. Long-established operator.

Zeus Tours, 209 W. 40th St, New York, NY 10018, ☎ (800) 447 5667, ✆ (212) 764 7912, *www.zeustours.com.*

in Greece

The Greek National Tourist Organization's programme to restore village houses into guesthouses fitted out in traditional furnishings includes a settlement in Oía on **Santoríni** (houses sleeping two to seven, reservations from: Paradosiakos Ikismos Oias, Oía, Santoríni, ☎ (0286) 71 234).

There's an annexe of the **Athenian School of Fine Arts** at Mýkonos which provides inexpensive accommodation for foreign artists (for up to 20 days in the summer and 30 in the winter) as well as studios, etc. One requirement is a recommendation from the Greek embassy in the artist's home country. Contact the School of Fine Arts, 42 Patission St, ☎ (01) 361 6930 for further information.

Women Travellers

Greece is a choice destination for women travellers, but going it alone is sometimes considered odd. Be prepared for a fusillade of questions. Greeks tend to do everything in groups or pairs and can't understand people who want to go solo.

The good news for women, however, is the dying out of that old pest, the *kamáki* (harpoon). These 'harpoons'—Romeos in tight trousers and gold jewellery who used to roar about on motorbikes or hang out in the bars and cafés, strutting about jangling their keys, hunting in pairs or packs—would try to 'spear' as many women as possible, notching up points for different nationalities. A few professional *kamákia* still haunt piano bars in the big resorts, gathering as many hearts, gold chains and parting gifts as they can; they spend the winter all over the world with different members of their harem.

It is young Greek women who are to thank for the decline in *kamáki* swagger. Following the example set by foreign tourists, as well as the torrid soaps and dross that dominate Greek television, they have decided that they've had quite enough of 'traditional values'. Gone are the days when families used the evening promenade or *vólta* as a bridal market for their carefully sheltered unmarried daughters; now the girls hold jobs, go out drinking with their friends, and move in with their lovers. They laughed at the old *kamákia* so much that ridicule, like bug spray, finally killed them dead.

Working

Casual summer jobs on the islands, legal for EU citizens, on the black for others, tend to be bar or restaurant work in a resort (although with the recent influx of impecunious Albanians low-paying jobs are becoming harder to find). Alternatively jobs might be available as travel reps/greeters/co-ordinators with island travel offices that deal with holiday companies. Expect your wages to pay for expenses but that's about it.

One or other of the seven English/American schools in Athens always seems to be in need of qualified teachers, or if you have a university degree or TEFL (teaching English as a foreign language) qualification you may find a job teaching English in a *frontistírion* or private language school (although this is getting to be harder with new laws that give Greeks or people of Greek origins priority). You can get around this by giving private lessons on your own. All you need to do is advertise: the market for learning English seems wide open, and if you're any good you can make quite a decent living. The *Athens News*, the country's English daily, and *The Hellenic Times*, a rather nationalistic weekly paper, often have classified advertisements for domestic, tutorial, and secretarial jobs. Working legally requires an often unpleasant descent into Greek bureaucracy (the local police will tell you what you must do); if you mean to stay over three months, *see* p.17.

History and Art

Earliest Traces

Geologists believe the Cyclades are all that survive of a prehistoric land bridge, which they call Aigeida, that over the millennia did a slow motion version of Atlantis and slowly sank deeper and deeper into the sea, until only the mountains were left with their heads above water. The exceptions are the volcanic islands of Santoríni, Mílos and Kímolos, part of the great Mediterranean volcanic chain that includes Vesuvius and Etna, and another Greek island, Níssyros, off in the Dodecanese.

People have found these summits convivial enough at least since the Mesolithic era (7500–6000 BC), the date of the oldest settlement, recently discovered just north of Loutrá on Kýthnos. In Neolithic times the settlers belonged to two pre-Hellenic Semitic tribes from Asia Minor, the Karians and Leleges. All their settlements were directly by the sea, and the ancient Greeks referred to them as pirates. Later arrivals were the Aryan, warlike Pelasgians, the sea people. The oldest Neolithic settlements yet found include a fishing hamlet on the tiny islet of Saliagos off Antíparos and another at Kéfala on Kéa, which go back to *c.* 6000 BC. Artistic finds are typical of the Neolithic era around the Mediterranean: dark burnished pottery, decorated with spirals and wavy lines, and fertility goddesses in stone or terracotta.

The fact that neither the Karians nor Pelasgians were known to be artistic suggests that, some time before 3200 BC, the same people (some suspect they may have been the much maligned Philistines) who settled Crete and became the Minoans also settled the Cyclades. But the art left behind for the next thousand years by the inhabitants of Crete and the islands was radically different.

Halcyon Days: The Early Cycladic Civilization (3200–2000 BC)

In the Bronze Age, the islands' contacts and settlers from Anatolia and the Near East brought them to the cutting edge of not only Greek but European civilization for a millennium. The islanders exported obsidian from Mílos for making tools and weapons, the white marble of Páros and Náxos, and deposits of copper, silver and gold. They continued to live in unwalled settlements on the sea and no doubt supplemented their income by piracy. The notion that they also developed a unique civilization began in the 1890s, when Greek archaeologist Christos Tsountas (who had worked with Schliemann at Mycenae) excavated necropoli at Amórgos, Páros, Sýros and Sífnos, and found a culture quite different from that on the mainland, which he called Cycladic. Based on the dismal science of comparative potsherds (especially dismal here because of the often mediocre quality of Cycladic clay and pots) archaeologists have divided the Bronze Age into three periods, marked increasingly by outside influences from the Minoans and the Mycenaeans.

The first thousand years or so of the Early Cycladic period itself went through three distinct phases, beginning with EC I (3200–2800 BC), or the **Pelos-Lakoudes civilization.** Named for the two principal sites on Mílos and Náxos, the awakening culture left behind stout, rather lumpy handmade pots, but also the first marble 'Cycladic idols' that would become the civilization's trademark. These early proto- types are so highly stylized that their discoverers at once nicknamed them 'Fiddle Idols'. Their origins go back straight to the bulbous fertility goddesses of the Neolithic era, although these are flat and smooth, defining only the female essen- tials of breasts and hips and heads. The oldest one known was found in the Neolithic layers of the aforementioned Saliagos.

EC II (2800–2200 BC), or the **Keros-Sýros civilization** marks the height of the period, although life seems to have become more precarious around 2500 BC, when there was a general move inland and the building of walls and towers; the prime example is at Kástri on Sýros, in response to the increased power of the Cretan navy. In some 500 tombs at Chalandrianí, the cemetery of Kástri, Tsountas found some curious ceramics, the so-called Cycladic 'frying pans' covered with engraved spiral decorations; some believe they were once polished mirrors, or per- haps even representations of the womb. Other ceramics are painted all over with a lustreless paint (matt-painted ware), or decorated with black or red candystripes. A few pieces show some Bronze Age humour, such as the pig in the museum in Náxos, or the bear-hedgehog sitting down and holding a bowl, in the National Museum in Athens. Other vessels were made from marble, or from gold or silver, suggesting that the mines, especially on Sífnos, were already being exploited at this early date. The jewellery found in the tombs, especially at Chalandrianí, is fairly simple—pins of silver or bronze used to fasten clothes, decorated with motifs sim- ilar to those found at Troy (double spirals, birds, jugs, pyramids) that passed through the Cyclades on their way to the Greek mainland.

By 2600 BC, the 'Fiddles' had evolved into the famous flat, elegant Cycladic idols, labouriously cut and rubbed into shape using no tools but the abrasive emery found on Náxos. And once the artists got the idols just they way they wanted them, they reproduced hundreds in the same manner, over the next six centuries, in all sizes, ranging from as small as a fly to as big as a human. The archetypal idol is female, with a flat-topped head, ridge nose, long graceful neck, arms folded under small breasts as if protecting their womb, their slender hips and feet together, sometimes with fingers, toes, mouth or pelvic area etched in. Originally touched up with blue and red paint, they are perfect as they are, all white and strikingly modern; the art- loving Minoans were extremely fond of them and imported large quantities to bury with their dead, just as the Cycladic islanders did. Occasionally the idols are preg- nant; others have lines across their bellies, as if they had just given birth.

If the females were fertility figures, the rare male idols are harder to explain. A few stand in the same pose as the female figures and a few are armed. The best display a wonderful *joie de vivre*: the famous harpist and flute player from 2500 BC, found on the island of Keros, the oldest representations of musicians found in the Aegean world (now in the National Archaeology Museum in Athens) and the drinker, seated and raising a toast, in the Goulandris Museum of Cycladic Art in Athens.

The final phase, EC III (2200–2000 BC) or the **Phylakope I civilization** is named after the First City of Phylakope on Mílos, excavated by the British school in the 1860s. Minoan influences grow stronger, and seamlessly merge with Phylakope II in the Middle Cycladic period.

Middle Cycladic and the Minoans (*c.* 2000–1550 BC)

Phylakope on Mílos, Ag. Iríni on Kéa, and especially Akrotíri on Santoríni, 'the Pompeii of the Bronze Age' provides much of what is known about the Middle Cycladic era, a time when the Minoans of Crete, the masters of the sea, ruled the Cyclades and in all likelihood put a halt to their early experiments in piracy. In myth, King Minos of Crete conquered the Aegean Islands in order to rid himself of his overly just brother Rhadamanthys, whom he sent abroad to administer the new colonies. Minos was most likely a hereditary title, like pharaoh, and it lingers in a number of place names throughout the Aegean from Amorgós all the way to Sicily, as well as in the first known name of the Cycladic archipelago—the *Minoides.*

The Cyclades were the Cretans' own backyard and the islanders were probably not too unhappy under their first cultural imperialists—if a culture can be judged at all by its art, the Minoans were precociously talented, sophisticated, nature-loving and full of joy. Their fleet ruled the seas, and back in Crete the Minoans felt sufficiently secure from external or internal threats to build unfortified palaces and cities near the sea. They developed a form of writing known as Linear A and Linear B, which translated proved to be careful accounts of the magazines of oil, honey, wine and grain stored in the huge jars or *pithoi* in their palaces at Knossos and elsewhere. Minoan civilization reached its apogee between 1800 and 1550 BC—now the commonly accepted date for the cataclysmic eruption of Santoríni that put such an abrupt halt to their culture; they limped on afterwards, but it was never the same.

In the Middle Cycladic period, the islanders lived in small fortified settlements near the sea, in two- or three-storey houses decorated with frescoes, on streets equipped with good sewage systems. A charming fresco of a school of flying fish survived at Phylakope, along with the more famous ones from the Minoan colony of Akrotíri, on Santoríni, all now in the National Archaeological Museum of Athens. The fluid style is similar to the frescoes found in the palaces of Crete, perhaps even more lighthearted and cheerful: a flowery landscape, boxing children, exotic animals.

Besides purely Minoan works and Linear A and B tablets found at Middle Cycladic sites, there are local, more naturalistic works, which show a strong Minoan influence. The most characteristic handmade jugs of the period have beak-spouts, and simple black decoration that become increasingly pretty and imaginative near the end of the period; some have little beesting breasts, others have eyes, or pictures of birds. It was only at the end of the period that the Cycladers discovered the potters' wheel—which had been turning on the mainland and Crete since *c.* 2000 BC.

Late Cycladic and the Mycenaeans (1550–1100 BC)

After the devastating blow wreaked by the explosion of Santoríni on the Minoans, the Mycenaeans (who used the same Linear B script) rushed in to fill the vacuum of power and trade in the Aegean, taking over Crete's colonies on the islands; after 1500 BC, Mycenaean influences—more formal, serious, and warrior-orientated—can duly be seen in Cycladic art. A few islands have vestiges of the Achaeans' impressive stone walls, known as cyclopean after their gigantic blocks, so massive that the Greeks in the Classical era thought they could only have been built by the Cyclops; some remain on Mílos at Pláka and at ancient Thíra on Santoríni.

One curious product of the Late Cycladic period was the cache of 19 nearly life-sized terracotta statues of female figures found in a (probably) Bronze Age temple on Kéa and excavated by the University of Cincinnati. The end of the age is marked by the gradual return of the piratical Karians and Leleges; Thucydides, describing the removal of tombs from Delos during the First Purification, notes that half were Karian. The Phoenicians were also on hand, using the islands as trading bases and buying up local stocks of precious metals and purpura, the royal red dye derived from Aegean molluscs. The Cyclades seem to have escaped the disasters that over-whelmed the Mycenaeans on the mainland (1200 BC) and had a century or so left to their own devices, before the next lot of people washed up on their beaches.

Geometric and Archaic (1100–500 BC): the Ionians

The new arrivals were Ionians, from the coast of Asia Minor and the Greek interior, fleeing from the invading Dorians, who destroyed what remained of Aegean unity in the confusing aftermath of the Trojan War and ushered in one of history's Dark Ages. The Dorians settled two islands, Mílos and Santoríni; nearly all the other Cyclades were colonized by the Ionians. At first art in this period took a giant step backwards and is known as Geometric for the simple, abstract pottery designs; traces of Geometric temples, made of brick and wood, are rarer. One of the most complete towns of this period discovered anywhere in Greece is Zagorá on Ándros.

The splintering of the Minoan and Mycenaean world saw less trade but more agri-culture, stay-at-homes, and the evolution of the *pólis*, or city-state; originally each Ionian island was an independent monarchy. The Ionians claimed to be descen-dants of Apollo, and soon after their arrival in the Cyclades they made Delos their religious capital. As times grew less precarious, trade picked up, and the islands were prosperous again; on many the middle classes forced out the kings and oli-garchs and initiated democracies. The 7th and 6th centuries were the Cyclades' golden age. The islands united in an Ionian maritime league, the Amphictyony, and were prosperous enough to found colonies in Sicily and southern Italy.

They also took part in the fertile and imaginative Ionian cultural blossoming known as the Archaic period. Stone, mostly marble on the Cyclades, replaced wood for the building of temples, and there was a return to figurative art. In spite of all the later depredations suffered by the islands, tantalizing clues remain of their glory days: the Lion Terrace on Delos, the mysterious Lion of Kéa, and the stark lintel of the massive, unfinished temple of Apollo on Náxos. The 7th century also saw the development of regional schools of pottery, influenced by the black-figured techniques of Corinth. The Cyclades produced some of the best; there are good collections in the archaeological museums of Mýkonos and Tínos.

If Cycladic idols are the symbol of the early Bronze Age, the Archaic period is perhaps synonymous with the *kouros*, a statue of a nude young man, life-size or even larger, inspired by the Egyptians; poses are stiff, formal, and rigid, one foot carefully placed before the other; the female version is a *kore*, or maiden, dressed in graceful drapery. Unlike Egyptian models, however, the Greek statues are marked by their easy, confident Archaic smiles, as if they were all in on a secret joke. The biggest were produced on Náxos, where flawed ones were abandoned next to their quarries. Páros, with the finest marble in the world, produced a famous school of sculptors; Sífnos, with its fabulous gold mines, paved its streets with marble and built one of the most fabulous treasuries in Delphi, then dared to cheat Apollo of his tithes, provoking a disciplinary invasion of the islands in 550 BC, by the tyrant Polycrates from Sámos, who incidentally grabbed everything that wasn't nailed down. His intrusion sparked another one from Athens, the rising power in Attica, which based on its Ionian roots demanded to become part of the Amphictyony in 540 BC. When Athens insisted on a post-Polycrates expiation of Delos, by purifying the island of its tombs, the other Cyclades were too weak to resist; from now on, their leading roles in their destiny would be taken by other actors.

Classical and Hellenistic Period (500–30 BC): Athens Butts In

With the rise of the Persians in Asia Minor, many Ionians fled westwards to Attica and Athens, leaving the remaining islanders to fall into Persian hands; several (most notably, Páros and Ándros) went as far as to side with the Persians at Marathon and Salamis in 490 and 480 BC. After the Greek victories, the Persian islands revolted to join Athens, which obliged them to enter into the new maritime league at Delos in 478 BC, replacing the older Ionian Amphictyony. Their goals were the eradication of piracy and promotion of commerce; and total Athenian domination of the Aegean was the great city's not-so-hidden agenda. Especially after the naval victory at Salamis it was acknowledged that Athens' fleet was the finest in the Mediterranean, and the only one capable of protecting the islands. Athens thought their island-allies should contribute towards the expense, and soon the once independent islands became *de facto* vassals paying tribute. Their resentment made it hard for the Athenians to collect/extort the islands' annual contribution of money and ships. When Athens was distracted in the Peloponnesian War, resentment flared into open revolt and most of the islands went over to Sparta at least once, although they soon regretted it, as the Spartans proved just as oppressive. Eventually the islands tended to side with the front-runner at any given time.

When Athens recovered from the war in 378 BC, it was only to form a second Delian league, again subjugating the Cyclades. But the centre of power had moved. Thebes took the islands briefly, in 363, and afterwards most of the islands turned to Philip of Macedon as a saviour from the Athenian bullies (338 BC), only to be fought over a generation later by the generals and the descendants of the generals of Alexander the Great, with the Ptolemies in Egypt coming out on top. Their best-preserved monument on the islands is the bright white Tower of Chimárou, standing tall in the wildest and most remote corner of Náxos.

The turmoil and Athenian dominance wasn't good for art on the Cyclades, although it was very good for Athens, especially when it snatched the sacred treasure of Delos and used the money to build the Parthenon. Much of what was built on the Cyclades themselves during the era has been cannibalized and scoured clean over the centuries: there are ruins of the cities and theatres on Mílos and Santoríni (ancient Thira), some good statues in the archaeological museums of Ándros and bits of temples here and there, and memories of the Venus de Milo.

Delos boomed again under the Ptolemies, and then after 146 BC, when the Romans, warring with the Macedonians, took it over and gained its allegiance by declaring it a free port. It became the biggest slave market in the Mediterranean. The money rolled in until another enemy of Rome, Mithridates of Pontus, plundered and wrecked the island in 88 BC. The houses from the wealthy interval have a rather plush air to them, many decorated with beautiful mosaics and frescoes.

Roman and Byzantine (30 BC–AD 1205)

As a rule, the further away its overlords, the less happy the Cyclades. While the Romans helped to rebuild Delos and gave lip service to its ancient rites, they had very little use for the Cyclades except as bases to refurnish their fleet and as places of exile and exploitation, although the chronicles probably exaggerate when they say 150,000 slaves worked in the marble quarries of Páros. The Pax Romana ended the ancient rivalries between the Greek city-states and cut down on one of the traditional Cycladic livelihoods, piracy, beginning the 'desertification' of the islands. Christianity arrived early: Roman Mílos has catacombs, the only ones in Greece.

Rome's slow fall did not improve the situation. The first taste of things to come was an attack by the Goths in 267, followed by the Slavs in 675 and the Saracens based on Crete (823). Although nominally part of the Byzantine Thema of the Aegean, Constantinople did little to protect them from marauders, and the islanders were left to fend for themselves, leaving the shores to build villages in the most inaccessible places. The remains of Byzantine citadels still top many an ancient acropolis.

Byzantine art and architecture began to show its stylistic distinction under Justinian (527–565), while the immediate post-Justinian period saw a golden age in the splendour of the Hagia Sofia in Istanbul and the churches of Ravenna, Italy. On the Cyclades the few surviving Byzantine-era churches are mostly simple three-naved basilicas—with the exception of the 6th-century Ekatontapyliani of Páros. Náxos has the Panagía Drossianí, built in the 5th century, containing excellent frescoes.

After the austere art purge of the Iconoclasm (726–843) the Macedonian style in painting in Constantinople slowly infiltrated the provinces. The old Roman basilica plan was jettisoned in favour of a central Greek cross crowned by a dome, elongated in front by a vestibule (narthex) and outer porch (exonarthex) and at the back by a choir and three apses; Ag. Ioannis Theológos on Amorgós and Ag. Mámas on Náxos are two good 8th-century examples. The Iconoclasm led to the founding of the most striking Byzantine monastery from this period on the Cyclades, the Chozoviótissa on Amorgós, built into the side of a sheer cliff and later rebuilt by Emperor Alexis Comnenus in the 11th century.

1204–1821: Venetians and Turks

From the days of the Greek-Gothic wars in Italy, Byzantium claimed Italy as its heritage from the ancient Roman empire, and for centuries held on to much of the southern and eastern sections of the country, including Venice, 'Byzantium's favourite daughter.' Protected by and often working for Constantinople, the wealthiest and most powerful city of the time, Venice flourished in the Dark Ages and emerged as the greatest and most enduring of medieval Italy's maritime republics. But like all daughters it began to champ at the bit. The Byzantines needed the Venetians as merchants and often as mercenaries, but disliked them for their pride and obsession with money, lack of scruples in dealing with the infidels and, after the Great Schism in 1054, for sticking with the Latin church in Rome. The Venetians in return resented the old despots' feelings of superiority and fickleness; one year they might be granted free trade concessions, the next year their goods could be confiscated, and their merchants imprisoned or slaughtered.

'The favourite daughter' saw her chance to get even and more in the Fourth Crusade. The French knights, whipped up for a Christian *jihad* by Innocent III in the 1190s, commissioned Venice under its blind, 80-year-old Doge Enrico Dandolo to transport 20,000 men to Egypt, one of Venice's most important trading partners. Dandolo, who hated Constantinople, is thought always to have had other plans in store for French chivalry. When they could not raise the massive sums charged by the Venetians for the ships and provisions they had commissioned, Dandolo suggested that in lieu of payment they could do a favour for Venice by supporting the claims of a pretender to the Byzantine throne who promised to bring the Orthodox church into the Roman fold. The French leaders agreed; most of the Crusaders only found out they were sailing to Constantinople when it was too late.

When Constantinople fell, and was ruthlessly plundered, the Crusaders divided up their empire. The Venetians knew exactly what they wanted for their 'Quarter and a Half-Quarter of the Roman Empire'—a quarter of Constantinople itself, and all the major ports and islands in the Aegean to keep their trade routes free and open.

But their resources were limited. There were so many islands to lay hands on, especially in the Cyclades, that Dandolo's successor, Doge Pietro Ziani, decided to appeal to self-interest and free enterprise, and he offered them to any Venetian with money, ships and spunk enough to grab them. The first man to take up the offer was Marco Sanudo, nephew of Enrico Dandolo, then acting as a judge in Constantinople. Sanudo raised eight galleys, gathered a band of fellow 'entrepreneurs', and captured, at least briefly, some 200 islands, which he distributed to the grasping young noblemen. Most took over the existing Byzantine castles and enlarged them, overtaxed the local population, made the Venetian dialect of Italian the official language, and tried to convert the local population to Catholicism, often by persecuting the Orthodox. Most of the Greeks responded by hating their guts, and as time went on betrayed them to the Turks whenever they had the chance.

Piracy was rampant. The Venetians, especially the Gizzi who held Tínos, Ándros, Ámorgos and Mýkonos, were reputedly the worst pirates of all, despite keen competition from the Genoese, Angevins, Catalans and so on, and, soon enough, from the Turks, with whom the Venetians fought an undeclared war for centuries. Unfortunately for the Cyclades, when the pirates couldn't nip out of their coves and capture a fat galley, they preyed on the islanders themselves. In 1320 alone some 15,000 people from the Cyclades are said to have been sold into slavery. Some of the profits filtered back in the form of Catholic monasteries and convents, where some of the most notorious pirates were buried. Some smaller Cyclades, such as Antiparos and Síkinos, impossible to defend, were abandoned all together. Oppressed by their feudal lords, who took all the best land, and terrorized by pirates, life was hard; on Sérifos, one traveller wrote, the people 'lived like beasts'.

When Constantinople fell in 1453 to the Ottomans, Venice stepped in to police the Cyclades. But it was too little, too late, and they fell one by one, many to the fierce admiral Khair-ed-din-Barbarossa who raged across the Aegean in the 1530s. His technique was enough to make defenders fight to the bitter end, and survivors, especially the women, to throw themselves and their children over cliffs rather than fall into his hands: he massacred all the Catholics and men, sent the boys to Constantinople as slaves or janissaries, and made all the women he captured dance before him, to select the most beautiful for himself and his captains, and handing the rest over to his soldiers. By the mid 16th century, with the exception of Tínos, all the Cyclades were under Turkish control, ruled by a puppet Duke of Náxos.

But for the most part Turkish rule in the Archipelago was harsh only in economic terms—the Kapoudan Pasha, or admiral of the fleet, would pass by every year to collect taxes and otherwise leave the islands to govern themselves—often under their same Venetian or Latinized lords. Piracy grew worse, if anything, and when the islanders begged to leave and go elsewhere, the Turks refused, not wanting to lose their tax farms. Through conversion and intermarriage, the Venetians had converted many of the Greeks on the Cyclades, in particular on Sýros, Tínos, Santoríni and Náxos, and under the tolerant Turks both Orthodox and Catholic monasteries thrived: on many islands you can even find churches with Catholic and Orthodox naves built side by side in ecumenical harmony. The Venetians had inspired a good deal of fresco-painting, and under the indifferent Turks many Cycladic chapels were beautifully decorated; some of the finest, in the 17th century, by the Skordílis family of Kýthnos. The French then began to take a passing interest in the Cyclades, not only as defenders of their Catholic populations, but as collectors—in 1673, their ambassador at the Sublime Porte and his pirate Daniel sailed about the archipelago, gathering 'souvenirs' from Páros, Délos, and Náxos.

From 1771 to 74, one of the more outlandish episodes in Greek history brought a brief interlude from the Ottomans: Russia and Turkey were at each other's throats over Poland, so Catherine the Great decided to open a second front in the war by capitalizing on Greek discontent. Her fleet in the Aegean led an insurrection against the Sultan and occupied some of the Cyclades. By the time the Russians gave it up and went home, they had made themselves very unpopular with all concerned, although the Kioutsouk-Kainartzi treaty that ended the conflict included provisions that allowed the islanders to establish their first merchant fleets.

When the Greek War of Independence broke out in 1821, the Cyclades were ready to join; they offered naval support and took on thousands of refugees, especially Tínos, Náxos and Sýros, which, with large Catholic populations, came under the protection of the French and remained officially neutral. The Cyclades were incorporated into the new Greek state from the very beginning, and Sýros, with its new port Ermoúpolis, became the country's most important shipbuilding and mercantile centre in the 19th century; merchants built themselves handsome neoclassical mansions that are one of the unexpected glories of the Cyclades. Up until the Second World War, the shipowners of Ándros controlled a large part of the Greek merchant fleet, and held a near monopoly on shipping to America. But with no one to forbid migration, islanders began to leave for the mainland or beyond, especially after the turn of the century. Those who stayed began to move closer to the ports. Life improved somewhat after the Second World War, when land reform redistributed property until then still held by the descendants of the feudal lords, but even then many of the Cyclades would now be abandoned if it weren't for tourism, which accounts for nearly all the new jobs on the islands in the past 30 years.

Topics

> *I still sigh for the Aegean; shall you not always love its bluest waves and the brightest of all skies?*
>
> Lord Byron

It never shows up on those idyllic holiday pictures of the Cyclades, but the *meltémi* is as much a part of the Cycladic experience as the sugar cube houses, bluest waves and brightest skies. *Meltem* means 'gentle off-shore breeze' in Turkish, but it was stirring up the Aegean long before the Turks, and if it sweeps the islands clean of clouds and moisture, it isn't always gentle.

A curious, somewhat contrived myth explains its origins, starring Aristaeus, a son of Apollo, and the lion-wrestling queen of Libya, Cyrene. Aristaeus was educated in Libya by nymphs who taught him how to build beehives, how to make cheese, and how to cultivate the wild oleaster so it would yield edible olives. As Aristaeus travelled about, passing his know-how on to the Greeks, the Delphic oracle sent him to Kéa, which, along with the rest of the Cyclades, was suffering from a plague caused by the Dog Star Sirius, who blasted them with hot arrows—for unbeknownst to the Kéans, several murderers had taken refuge on their island. These were peasants who had slain Ikarios, the first mortal taught to make wine by Dionysos; the peasants had drunk it, and thought Ikarios had poisoned them. Ikarios' dog (the star, again) had led his daughter to his body, and in despair she hanged herself.

Aristaeus came to the rescue. He built a great altar to Zeus, offered the appropriate sacrifices, and had the murderers put to death, which purified the islands and stopped the shower of flaming arrows. Grateful for the sacrifices, Zeus rewarded Kéa and the Cyclades by sending them a breeze for forty days at the rising of the Dog Star—the Dog Days of August——called the *Etesies* (the 'annuals'). The ancient Kéans, made Aristaeus one of their chief gods, and offered special sacrifices at the beginning of each summer, to make sure the *Etesies* never failed.

There are actually several *meltemia* that freshen up the summer months, from the end of May until October. The 'forerunners' or *prodromoi* blow until July, a wind the Turks call the *kerasmeltem* or cherry wind, as opposed to the later and stronger *etesies*, or watermelon wind *(karpouzmeltem)*. When it blows from the northwest the wind is a *maistros*, from the northeast, the *gregos*. This natural air-conditioning is good for windsurfing—Páros hosts world championships—but can be extremely dangerous for sailors and vexing even for people who just stay on land, when it howls for days on end, and only strategically placed chunks of marble stop doors banging shut with ear-blasting slams. Sometimes the *meltémi* kicks up enough sea spray to make rainbows that dance across the waves. Without it, however, the Cyclades would be unbearable in July and August, and as further proof of its divine origins, the wind nearly always dies down just in time for cocktail hour.

The Environment: Endangered Animals and Plain Old Pests

When Western Europe was busy discovering the beauties of nature in the Romantic era, Greece was fighting for survival; when the rest of the west was gaining its current environmental awareness in the 1960s and 70s, the Greeks were throwing up helter-skelter resorts on their beaches, making Athens the citadel of sprawl it is today, merrily chucking plastic bags of garbage in the sea and killing off the monk seals because they ate too many fish.

Ever so slowly, the average Greek is waking up to the fact that nature can only take so much before she turns on her persecutors. A small but dedicated band of ecologists has been sounding the alarm for decades, but most Greeks only saw their country as something to exploit: if the law forbids building on forested land, the Greek solution was—and sadly, still is—to burn the forest. But now these past excesses are beginning to hurt, not just the environment but where it counts for everyone, in the pocketbook.

Tourism has been responsible for much of the damage, but also for many of the sea-changes in attitude. The great influx of people has contributed to the severe depletion of fishing stocks. Laws limiting industrial fishing and dynamiting are constantly flouted—demand for fish has drained the Aegean's key resource by nearly 60% in recent years, making what used to be the cheapest staple food in Greece the most expensive. There is often talk about a fishing moratorium of a year or two to give the Mediterranean a break, but the economic consequences are simply too overwhelming for the idea to get past the talking stage. On the positive side, tourist concerns about clean beaches (Greece now proudly claims the cleanest in Europe) have resulted in proper sewage systems on most islands and a noticeable decline in litter and junk, although there is still work to do here. The Greeks may return their beer bottles but they recycle absolutely nothing, not glass, not paper, not plastic.

Most of the wildlife on the Cyclades is human. Hedgehogs, rabbits, bats, and several kinds of rodents sum up the native animals, along with the badgers of Tínos. The number of snakes make up for the few animals, among them sand boas, whip snakes, blind snakes, four-lined snakes, leopard snakes, and one species that's poisonous, the viper, a resident of nooks and crannies of stone walls, which only comes out occasionally to sun itself. Vipers will flee if possible, but if they feel cornered they will make a hissing sound like radio static before attacking. The islands of Mílos and Kímolos are the only habitat of one of the most beautiful and rare European snakes, the *vipera lebetina*, although recently collectors illegally exporting them abroad have caused a noticeable decline in their numbers.

Although Greece can claim some 6000 native species of wildflower, the arid Cyclades are not the best place to come looking for them. The best islands for flowers in the spring are Ándros and Náxos. Although the climate hasn't changed much since the islands were inhabited, they were very much greener in the past. Travellers even in the 19th century described extensive forests on Kéa, Náxos and Íos; today, only remnants survive on Náxos after the depredations of fires, woodcutters and especially goats, which effectively keep down any possible saplings. Still, the Cyclades do count 1166 species of native flora that survived from the Tertiary period, when the lost continent of Aegeis that linked the Greek mainland to Asia Minor sank into the sea, leaving only the mountain tops.

As for creatures unfortunately *not* on the endangered list, the wily mosquito tops the list for pure incivility. Most shops stock the usual defences: lotions, sprays and insect coil, or best of all, pick up one of those inexpensive electric mosquito repellents that plug into a wall socket. Greek skeeters don't spread malaria, but bites from their sand-fly cousins can occasionally cause a nasty parasite infection. Wasps have a habit of appearing out of nowhere to nibble that honey-oozing baklava you've just ordered. Pests lurk in the sea as well: harmless pale brown jellyfish (*méduses*) may drift in anywhere depending on winds and currents, but the oval transparent model (*tsoúchtres*) are stinging devils that can leave scars on tender parts of your anatomy if you brush against them; pharmacies sell soothing ungents. Pincushiony sea urchins live by rocky beaches, and if you're too cool to wear rubber swimming shoes and you step on one, it hurts like hell. The spines may break and embed themselves even deeper if you try to force them out; the Greeks recommend olive oil, a big pin and a lot of patience. Less common but more dangerous, the *drákena*, dragon (or weever) fish, with a poisonous spine, hides in the sand waiting for its lunch. If you step on one (rare, but it happens), you'll feel a mixture of pain and numbness and should go to the doctor for an injection.

Greece's shy scorpions hide out in between the rocks in rural areas; unless you're especially sensitive, their sting is no more or less painful than a bee's. Avoid the back legs of mules, unless you've been properly introduced. Since the time of Homer, mountain sheepdogs have been a more immediate danger in outer rural areas; by stooping as if to pick up a stone to throw, you might keep a dog at bay.

On *Kéfi*, Music and Dancing

In the homogenized European Union of the 1990s, the Spaniards and Greeks are among the very few peoples who still dance to their own music with any kind of spontaneity, and it's no coincidence that both have untranslatable words to describe the 'spirit' or 'mood' that separates going through the motions and true dancing. In Spain, the word is *duende*, which, with the hard-driving rhythms of flamenco, has an ecstatic quality; in Greek, the word is *kéfi*, which comes closer to 'soul'. For a Greek to give his all, he must have *kéfi*; to dance without it could be considered dishonest. The smart young men in black trousers and red sashes who dance for you at a 'Greek Night' taverna excursion don't have it; two craggy old fishermen, in a smoky *kafenéion*, who crank up an old gramophone and dance for their own pleasure, do. It has no age limit: teenagers at discos pounding out all the international hits of the moment are really only waiting for 1 or 2am, when the clubs switch over to Greek music and the real dancing and kéfi can start. You can feel the *kéfi* at Easter when an entire village joins hands to dance an elegant *kala-matianó*, an act as simple and natural as it is moving, an enhanced celebration of community that the rest of us are lucky ever to experience.

Greek music has been influenced by Italy, Turkey and the Middle East, and the Balkans, all of whom were once influenced by the Byzantines, who heard it from the ancient Greeks, who heard it from the Phrygians—and so on. Traditional island songs, *nisiótika*, are played on bagpipes (*tsamboúna*), clarinet (*klaríno*), various stringed instruments—the *laoúto* (a large mandolin, used for backing, traditionally picked with an eagle's quill) and the *violí* (violin), the *kítara* (guitar) and occasionally the double-stringed hammer dulcimer (*sandoúri*), once limited to Greek Anatolia and now heard most often on the eastern islands. The best time to hear *nisiótika* is during a summer saint's day feast (*panegýri*) or at a wedding.

Contemporary composers like Mikis Theodorákis often put modern poetry to music, providing splendid renderings of the lyrics of George Seferis, Odysseas Elytis and Yánnis Rítsos; sung by the deep-voiced Maria Farandouri, they are spine-tingling, even if you don't understand a word. Even current Greek pop has surprisingly poetic moments. It owes much of its origins to *rembétika*, the Greek equivalent of the blues, brought over and developed by the more 'sophisticated' Asia Minor Greeks in the 1920s' population exchange, who in their longing and homesickness haunted the hashish dens of Athens and Piraeus. *Rembétika* introduced the *bouzoúki*, the long-necked metallic string instrument that dominates Greek music today, to the extent that nightclubs are called *bouzoúkia*—rougher ones are known as *skilákia*—'dog' shops, where popular singers croon throbbing, lovelorn, often wildly melodramatic music with a Middle Eastern syncopation that offers Greeks some of the catharsis that ancient tragedies gave their ancestors. Although expensive, a night out at one of these nightclubs is an experience not to be missed. Turn up after midnight, buy a bottle of white wine and fruit, and emote. As the evening wears on, members of the audience may take over the microphone, or the singer may be covered with flowers, or even make the enthusiasts forget the law against *spásimo*, or plate-breaking. If enough *kéfi*, or soul, is flowing, you may see middle-aged bank managers dance with wine glasses or bottles on their heads. When the matrons begin to belly-dance on the table, it's time to leave.

Summer festivals and village weddings are the places to see traditional dancing. Every island has its own dances or slight variations, some preserved, some quickly being forgotten. All Greeks dance the *syrtó*, with slow and somewhat shuffling pace, a circle dance dating from remotest antiquity; the *kalamatianó*, a 12-step *syrtó*, is perhaps *the* national dance: everyone joins in, holding hands at shoulder-level, while men and women take turns leading and improvising steps. Nearly as common is the dignified *tsamikó*, where the leader and the next dancer in line hold the ends of a handkerchief; if the leader is especially acrobatic, the handkerchief seems to be all that keeps him from flying away altogether. The jumping that forms an essential part of the dance recalls the ancient belief that it brought good luck and bountiful harvests. Women are the centre of attention in the *tsíphte téli*, a free-spirited, sensuous belly dance from Asia Minor for the loose-limbed, swivel-hipped and well-oiled, but just as often men usually old and fat) steal the show. The traditional couple's dance, the *bállo*, often stars one couple, who often accompany it with an erotic pantomime, egged on with glee by musicians and spectators.

Other dances are usually but not exclusively performed by men. The *zeybékiko* is a serious, deliberate, highly charged solo (or sometimes duo) dance with out-stretched arms, evoking the flight of the eagle; a companion goes down on one knee to encourage the dancer, hiss like a snake and clap out the rhythm. An intro-spective dance from the soul, the performer always keeps his eyes lowered, almost in a hypnotic state; because it's private, you must never applaud. Another intense dance, the *hasápiko*, or butchers' dance, is perhaps better known as the Zorba dance in the West. The *syrtáki* is more exuberant, traditionally performed by two or three men, often to the *rembétika* tune; the leader signals the steps and it requires some practice but is well worth learning—as Alan Bates discovered, when he finally began to fathom *kéfi* from Anthony Quinn at the end of *Zorba the Greek*.

An Orthodox Life

With the exception of a few thousand Catholics in the Cyclades and Protestants in Athens, all Greeks belong to the Orthodox, or Eastern church; indeed, being Orthodox and speaking Greek are what defines a Greek, whether born in Athens, Alexandria or Australia. Orthodoxy is so fundamental that even the sceptics cannot conceive of marrying outside the church, or of not having their children baptized, although Papandréou's government legalized civil marriages in the early 1980s.

One reason for this deep national feeling is that, unlike everything else in Greece, Orthodoxy has scarcely changed since the founding of the church by Emperor Constantine in the 4th century. As Constantinople took the place of Rome as the political and religious capital, the Greeks believe their church to be the only true successor to the original church of Rome. Therefore, a true Greek is called a *Romiós* or Roman, and the Greek language is sometimes called *Roméika*. The Orthodox church is considered perfect and eternal and beyond all worldly change; if it weren't, its adherents could not expect to be saved. One seeming advantage of all this is that the Greeks have been spared the changes that have rocked the West, from Vatican II and discussions over women in the clergy and married priests to political questions of abortion, birth control and so on. Much emphasis is put on ceremony and ritual, the spiritual and aesthetic, and yet at the same time service can be powerfully moving, especially at Easter.

This determination never to change explains the violence of Iconoclasm, the one time someone did try to tinker with the rules. Back in the early 8th century, the Byzantine Emperor Leo III, shamed by what his Muslim neighbours labelled idolatry, deemed the images of divine beings to be sacrilegious. The Iconoclasm opened up a major rift with Rome, which worsened in 800 when the Patriarch of Rome, aka the Pope, crowned Charlemagne as emperor, usurping the title of the Emperor of Constantinople. Further divisions arose over the celibacy of the clergy (Orthodox priests may marry before ordination) and the use of the phrase *filioque*, 'and the son', in the Holy Creed. This point of ideology was the straw that broke the camel's back, causing the fatal schism in 1054 when the Papal legate Cardinal Humbert excommunicated the Patriarch of Constantinople and the Patriarch in return excommunicated the Pope. Ever since the Orthodox hierarchy has kept a patriarchal throne vacant, ready for the day the Pope returns to his senses.

After the fall of the Byzantine Empire (that 'thousand-year-long mass for the dead' as one Greek writer put it), the Turks not only tolerated the Orthodox church, but had the political astuteness to impart considerable powers to the Patriarch. The church helped to preserve Greek tradition, education and identity through the dark age of Ottoman rule; on the other hand it left Greece a deeply conservative country and often abused its power, especially on a local scale. According to an old saying, priests, headmen and Turks were the three curses of Greece and the poor priests (who are usually quite amiable fellows) have not yet exonerated themselves from the list they now share with the king and the cuckold.

But, the fantastic quantity of churches and chapels on even the smallest islands has little to do with the priests. Most were built by families or individuals, especially sailors, seeking the protection of a patron saint or to keep a vow or to give thanks to a saint. All but the tiniest have an *iconóstasis* (altar screen) made of wood or stone to separate the *heirón* (sanctuary), where only the ordained can go, from the rest of the church. Most of the chapels are locked up thanks to light-fingered tourists; if you track down the caretaker, leave a few hundred drachmae for upkeep.

The vast majority of all these chapels have only one service a year, if that, on the name day of the patron saint (name days are celebrated in Greece rather than birthdays: 'Many years!' (*Chrónia pollá!*) is the proper way to greet someone on their name day). This annual celebration is called a *yiortí* or more frequently *panegýri*, and if it happens in the summer it's cause for feasts and dancing the night before or after the church service. If feasible, *panegýria* take place directly in the churchyard; if not, in neighbouring wooded areas, tavernas, town squares or even specially built halls. The food will be basic but plentiful; for a set price you receive more than your share of stewed goat. *Panegýria* (festivals) are also places for traditional music and dancing. Apart from Easter, the Assumption of the Virgin (15 August) is the largest *panegýri* in Greece. The faithful sail to Tínos and to a dozen centres connected with Mary, making mid-August a very uncomfortable time to island-hop, especially in the Cyclades—ships packed to the brim, the *meltémi* huffs and puffs, and Greek matrons, the most ardent pilgrims of all, are also the worst sailors.

Orthodox weddings are a lovely if long-winded ritual. The bride and groom stand solemnly before the chanting priest, while family and friends in attendance seem to do everything but follow the proceedings. White crowns, bound together by a white ribbon, are placed on the heads of bride and groom, and the *koumbáros*, or best man, exchanges them back and forth. The newlyweds are then led around the altar three times, while the guests bombard the happy couple with fertility-bringing rice and flower petals. After congratulating the bride and groom, guests are given a small *boboniéra* of candied almonds. This is followed by the marriage feast and dancing, which in the past could last up to five days.

Baptisms are cause for similar celebration. The priest completely immerses the baby in the Holy Water three times (unlike Achilles, there are no vulnerable spots on modern Greeks) and almost always gives the little one the name of a grandparent. For extra protection from the forces of evil, babies often wear a *filaktó*, or amulet, the omnipresent blue glass eye bead. If you visit a baby at home you may be sprinkled first with Holy Water, and chances are there's a bit of beneficial garlic squeezed somewhere under the cradle. Compliments should be kept to a minimum: the gods do get jealous. In fact many babies are given other pet names until they're christened, to fool supernatural ill-wishers.

Funerals in Greece, for reasons of climate, are usually carried out within 24 hours, and are announced by the tolling of church bells. The dead are buried for three to seven years (longer if the family can pay), then the bones are exhumed and placed in the family box to make room for the next resident. *Aforismós* (Orthodox excommunication) is believed to prevent the body decaying after death—the main source of Greek vampire stories. Memorials for the dead take place three, nine and forty days after death, and on the first anniversary. They are sometimes repeated annually. Sweet buns and sugared wheat and raisin *koúliva* are given out after the ceremony. But for all the Christian trappings, the spirit of Charos, the ferryman of death and personification of inexorable nature, is never far away, as is expressed in perhaps the most famous of myrologies, or dirges, still sung in some places:

> *Why are the mountains dark and why so woe-begone?*
> *Is the wind at war there, or does the rain storm scourge them?*
> *It is not the wind at war there, it is not the rain that scourges,*
> *It is only Charos passing across them with the dead;*
> *He drives the youths before him, the old folk drag behind,*

And he bears the tender little ones in a line at his saddle-bow.
The old men beg a grace, the young kneel to implore him,
'Good Charos, halt in the village, or halt by some cool fountain,
That the old men may drink water, the young men play at the
                                             stone-throwing,
And that the little children may go and gather flowers.'
'In never a village will I halt, nor yet by a cool fountain,
The mothers would come for water, and recognize their children,
The married folk would know each other, and I should never part them.'

The *Períptero* and the Plane Tree

In Greece you'll see it everywhere, the greatest of modern Greek inventions, the *períptero*. It is the best-equipped kiosk in the world: people gather to chat, make phone calls, or grab a few minutes' shade under the little projecting roof. It is a substitute bar, selling everything from water to ice-cream to cold beer; an emergency pharmacy stocked with aspirin, mosquito killers, condoms and Band Aids; a convenient newsagent for publications, from *Ta Néa* to *Die Zeit*; a tourist shop offering maps, guides, postcards and stamps; a toy shop for balloons and plastic swords; a general store for shoelaces, cigarettes, batteries and rolls of film. In Athens they're at most traffic lights. On the islands they are more common than donkeys. You'll wonder how you ever survived before *perípteros* and the treasures they contain.

The other great meeting centre of Greek life is the mighty plane tree, or *plátanos*, for centuries the focal point of village life, where politics and philosophy have been argued since time immemorial. Since Hippocrates the Greeks have believed that plane shade is wholesome and beneficial (unlike the enervating shadow cast by the fig). In Greek the expression *cheréte mou ton plátano* loosely translates as 'go tell it to the marines', presumably because the tree has heard all that nonsense before. The *plátanos* represents the village's identity; the tree is a source of life, for it only grows near abundant fresh water, its deep roots a symbol of stability, continuity and protection—a huge majestic umbrella, as even the rain cannot penetrate its sturdy leaves. Sit under its spreading branches and sip a coffee as the morning unfolds before you; the temptation to linger there for the day is irresistible.

Lamp Chops and Sweat Coffee

For a country cursed with a mindlessly pedantic system of public education, where rote memorization is the only key to academic success, the Greeks speak astonishingly good English. The Greek dislike of, not to mention their thorough incompetence at dubbing the likes of *Baywatch* and *Santa Monica* may have something to do with it, as well as the dogged efforts of thousands of *frontistérion* (private school) teachers, whose task is to get their pupils through their proficiency exams in spite of Greek public education.

This is enough to make the observer of Greek ways suspect that English mistakes on taverna menus are no accident, but part of some crafty plot to keep tourists out of the locals' own secret haunts by making taverna menus such compelling reading that by the time you've spotted the Lamp Chops, Eye Eggs (i.e. sunnyside up), or Sandwitches you're laughing too hard to go anywhere else. Will you have the Rabeet Soupee, Brawn Beans, Stuffed Vine Lives, String Deans, Sours Various, You Court with Gurig and Gogumbers, Eggfish, Chief's Salad or Beet Poots to start? For main course, the Harmbougger sounds distinctly threatening; better stick with dishes you know the Greeks do well: Scabby Shrimps, Staffed Tomatoes, Reformed Schnitzel, Sguids in Spies, See Food Various, Chicken Pain (i.e. breaded), Souvlaki Privates, Grumps Salad, T-Buogne Rum Stake, Veal Gogglets and Shrimp Shave, or vegetable dishes such as Zucchini Bulls, Cheek Pees, Jacked Potatoes, or perhaps Grass Hill (it turned out to be a small mound of boiled greens). You can smack your lips over a Rude Sausage or Rude Meat Pie; on Páros, you can ponder where your parents went wrong over a Freud Juice or Freud Salad; in Mytilíni, either sex can enjoy a delicious (and perfectly correct) Fish in Lesbian Sauce; cannibals can find solace in a place where 'We Serve Hot Tasty Friendly Family!' Then it's off to the Snake Bar for a Sweat Coffee, Kaputsino, or perhaps a Ouisgi before driving off in your Fully Incurable Rent-a-Care from the Vague Travel Agency of Piraeus.

Form and Function: Cycladic Architecture

An intimacy of scale sets the Cyclades archipelago apart from other Greek islands: their relative small size, physical proximity to one another, and distinctive white villages, piled like pristine drifts of snow on the hills against the sapphire sky. Typically hill villages wear a flounced skirt of dry stone terraces running down the rugged slopes, some bare and neglected nowadays, others silvery with olives or green with vines. On their heads, their ancient acropolises, they wear crowns of ruined castle half fused into the rock. In these wild settings, the proto-Cubist villages look as if they were seeded from crystals.

For all their striking good looks, Cycladic towns are practical and ingenious works of architecture. Every detail responds in some unexpected way to the climate, society and needs of the precarious centuries when they were built. Their picturesque, nearly inaccessible settings, hidden from view of the sea, were one of their few defences. Only islands such as Mýkonos and Páros, with enough ships and pirates of their own, could afford to have towns by the sea. In many, such as Antíparos, the backs of the houses were built together to form thick outer walls; the typical narrow, twisting lanes, stairs, and cul-de-sacs visitors find so charming were to designed to confound invaders, and limit the impact of the wind and sun. The lack of a native aristocracy and the innate democractic tendencies of the inhabitants are reflected in the simple, unpretentious and homogenous architecture of the houses. These are often two or three stories tall because of limited building space. Decoration, if any, is discreet—a carved lintel, perhaps an ornate chimney pot or balcony support. The homogeneity continues even into names—the largest village on almost every island is generically, simply called *Chóra*, or 'chief town.'

Houses in the Cyclades are by preference orientated to the southeast, towards the winter sun. Their cellars intercommunicated with one another, forming an escape route in time of emergency. Windows, especially in the oldest houses, tend to be few and small, to keep out the wind and the worst heat of summer. The corners at crossroads are rounded to allow the passage of donkeys or mules laden with baskets, the widest traffic most villages can handle. The flat roofs that so greatly contribute to the sugar cube effect are also utilitarian: tiles never caught on because the *meltémi* sends them flying. Flat roofs also catch a maximum of precious rainwater, linked by stone pipes to the cistern at the bottom of the house; like the cellars, they also provided escape routes in emergencies, and on exceptionally steep terrain, as on Santoríni, someone's roof often serves as another's terrace. Churches are usually domed or barrel-vaulted, adding variety to the roofscape; houses on Santoríni also tend to be vaulted, to stand up better to the frequent earth tremors.

There are subtle differences in style from island to island, but all show a remarkable economy of space. The limited protected area within a Chóra forced people, already unified in an us-versus-them mentality, to live a communal existence. Because of the climate, Greeks have always spent most of their lives out of doors; once outside, privacy is rare. At most, houses have a tiny yard, sometimes enclosed by a low wall, although more often whatever space—an outside stair, wooden balcony, or veranda—meshed into the street, which evolved as a semi-private, semi-public extension of people's living space. People know each other. On the one hand this means plenty of gossip; on the other, even at the end of this millennium, they can claim one of the lowest crime rates in the western world. Alienation is hard to achieve in the intimate world of the village, especially in the Cyclades.

The universal, all-unifying whitewash, renewed two or three times a year, reflects the sun to keep the houses cool; it was also thought to prevent disease (during times of plague, even the frescoes inside churches were whitewashed) and to this day the tidy Greek housekeeper judges his or her neighbour's cleanliness in part by the freshness of their whitewash. Layer upon layer of the stuff renewed over the centuries has rounded off every corner and right angle, most impressively on Mýkonos' famous church, the Paraportianí, which looks as if it were made of melted icing. The whitewash also serves as street lighting; possible hazards—steps in the lanes, protruding stones and the lower parts of tree trunks—are all whitewashed to reflect in the moonlight. In many places, women add happy, fanciful patterns, in between on the little squares and lanes: geometric figures, fish, flowers, hearts and even mermaids. And as Easter is a favourite occasion for renewing the whitewash, you'll often see ΚΑΛΟ ΠΑΣΧΑ! (Happy Easter!)

A Quick Who's Who in Greek Mythology

Like all good polytheists, the ancient Greeks filled their pantheon with a colourful assortment of divinities, divinities perhaps more anthropomorphic than most, full of contradictions, subtleties and regional nuances. Most islands have stories about their doings; some have become part of the familiar baggage of western civilization, others read like strange collective dreams, or nightmares. But as classical Greek society grew more advanced and rational-minded, these gods were rounded up and made to live on the sanitized heights of Mount Olympos as idols of state religion, defined (and already ridiculed) in Homer. The meatier matters of birth, sex, death and hopes for an afterlife—i.e. the real religion—went underground in the mysteries and chthonic cults, surviving in such places as Eleusis (Elefsína) near Athens, and at the Sanctuary of the Great Gods on Samothráki.

The big cheese on Olympos was **Zeus** (Jupiter, to the Romans), a native of Crete, the great Indo-European sky god, lord of the thunderbolt with a libido to match, whose unenviable task was to keep the other gods in line. He was married to his sister **Hera** (Juno), the goddess of marriage, whose special role in myth is that of the wronged, jealous wife, and who periodically returned to her special island of Sámos to renew her virginity. Zeus' two younger brothers were given their own realms: **Poseidon** (Neptune) ruled the sea with his wife Amphitrite (they had special sanctuaries on Tínos, and the famous 'Heliotrope' on Sýros), while **Hades** (Pluto) ruled the underworld and dead and rarely left his dismal realm. Their sister was **Demeter** (Ceres), goddess of corn and growing things, who was worshipped in the mysteries of Eleusis. **Aphrodite** (Venus), the goddess of love, is nearly as old as these gods, born when Zeus overthrew their father Cronus (Saturn) by castrating him and tossed the bloody member in the sea foam.

The second generation of Olympians were the offspring of Zeus: **Athena**, the urbane virgin goddess of wisdom, born full grown straight out of Zeus' brain and always associated with Athens, her special city; **Ares** (Mars), the whining bully god of war, disliked by the Greeks and associated with barbarian Thrace; **Hermes** (Mercury), the messenger, occasional trickster, and god of commerce; **Hephaistos** (Vulcan), the god of fire and the forge and metalworking, married to Aphrodite; **Apollo**, the god of beauty, music, reason, poetry and prophesy, worshipped at Delphi, but also on the Cycladic islands of Delos and Anáfi; his twin sister **Artemis** (Diana), the tomboy virgin moon goddess of the hunt, was also born here but her chief cults were in Asia Minor. Their cross-dressing half-brother **Dionysos** (Bacchus), the god of wine, orgies and theatre, was the favourite on Náxos. In addition to the twelve Olympians, the Greeks had an assorted array of other gods, nymphs, satyrs, and heroes, the greatest of which was **Herakles** (Hercules), the mighty hero who earned himself a place on Olympos, and gods such as **Helios** (Sol), the unassuming sun god, whose special island has always been Rhodes.

Athens and Piraeus

ACROPOLIS, ATHENS

*Love for Athens, a city once famous, wrote these words, a love
that plays with shadows, that gives a little comfort to burning
desire... Though I live in Athens I see Athens nowhere: only sad,
empty, and blessed dust.*

Michael Akominátos, 12th century

Travellers to the Cyclades often find themselves in Athens, and
although it has perked up considerably since the days of Michael
Akominátos it's rarely love at first sight. Look closely, however,
behind the ugly architecture and congestion, and you may be won
over by this urban crazy quilt—small oases of green parks hidden
amidst the hustle and bustle; tiny family-run tavernas tucked away in
the most unexpected places; the feverish pace of its nightlife and
summer festivals of wine and song; and best of all, the Athenians
themselves, whose friendliness belies the reputation of most city
dwellers. Another plus: Athens is the least expensive capital in the
European Union.

Historical Outline: From Cradle to Grave and Back Again

Although inhabited by pre-Hellenic tribes in the Neolithic Age (*c.* 3500 BC), Athens
made its proper debut on history's stage in the second millennium BC, when
Ionians from Asia Minor invaded Attica and established small city-states. Their
main centre was Kekropia, named for the serpent god Kekrops (later identified with
King Erechtheus, the official founding father of Athens and himself a snake from
the waist down). The owl was sacred to Kekropia—as it was to the goddess
Athena, whose worship and name gradually came to preside in the city.

In the 14th century BC Athens, as part of the Mycenaean empire of the Achaeans,
invaded Crete, fought Thebes and conquered Troy, but managed to escape the subsequent Dorian invasion that left the Mycenaean world in shambles. Two hundred
years later, however, it was Attica's turn to meet the uncouth Dorians, who
brought with them Greece's first Dark Age. This endured until the 8th century BC,
far too long for the sophisticated Ionians, who got fed up and went back to their
homelands in Asia Minor and settled many of the Aegean islands.

In the 8th century BC the towns of Attica were peaceably united, a success attrib-
uted to the mythical King Theseus (1300 BC). Athens was ruled by a king (the chief
priest), a polemarch (general), and an archon (civil authority), who were elected
annually. The conflict between the landed aristocracy and the rising commercial
classes gradually brought about the invention of democratic government, beginning
with the reforms of Solon. Yet Solon was still warm in the grave when Pisistratos,
leader of the popular party, made himself boss (545 BC) and began the naval build-
up that for the first time made Athens a threat to the other city-states of Greece.

Pisistratos' son was followed by another democratic reformer, Kleisthenes, who divided the population (the free and male members, at any rate) into ten political tribes. Lots were drawn to choose 50 members of the people's assembly, from which a further lot was drawn to select ten archons, one from each tribe. The head archon gave his name to the Athenian year.

As Persian strength grew in the east, Ionian intellectuals and artists took refuge in Athens, bringing philosophy, science and the roots of Attic tragedy. They prodded Athens to aid Ionia against the Persians, unsuccessfully: the city was landed in the soup when Darius, the Persian King of Kings, decided to subdue Greece, particularly upstart Athens. In 490 BC Darius' army landed at Marathon only to be defeated by a much smaller Athenian force under Miltiades. Powerful Sparta and the other Greek states recognized the eastern threat but continued to leave 'national' defence primarily to Athens and the Athenian fleet, which grew ever mightier under Themistocles. However, it failed to keep the Persians from having another go at Greece. In 480 BC the new King of Kings, Xerxes, showed up with the greatest fleet and army the ancient world had ever seen. Athens was destroyed, but the Persian navy was outmanoeuvred by the Athenian ships at Salamis, while the invaders was repelled by the Athenians and Spartans at the battle of Plateia.

With her superiority at sea, Athens set about creating a maritime empire, not only to increase her power but also to stabilize her combustible internal politics. She ruled the confederacy at Delos, demanding contributions from the islands in return for protection from the Persians. Sea trade became essential as the city's population grew, while new colonies were founded around the Mediterranean not only to release the pressure but also to ensure a continual food supply for Athens. Athenian democracy became truly imperialistic under Pericles, who brought the treasure of Delos to Athens to 'protect it'—and to skim off funds to rebuild and beautify the city and to build the Parthenon. It was the golden age of Athens, of Phidias, Herodotus, Sophocles, Aristophanes, and Socrates.

It couldn't last. The devastating Peloponnesian War (431–404 BC) began over Athenian expansion in the west. Back and forth the struggle went, Sparta and its allies with superiority on land, Athens on the seas, until both city-states were near exhaustion. Finally Lysander captured Athens, razed the walls, and set up the brief rule of the Thirty Tyrants.

Although democracy and imperialism made quick recoveries (by 378 BC the city had set up its second Maritime League), the Peloponnesian War had struck a blow from which ancient Athens would never totally recover. The population grew dissatisfied with public life, and refused to tolerate innovators and critics; Socrates was put to death. Economically, Athens had trouble maintaining the trade she needed. Yet her intellectual tradition held true in the 4th century BC, bringing forth the likes of Demosthenes, Praxiteles, Menander, Plato and Aristotle.

Philip II of Macedon took advantage of the general discontent to bully the city-states into joining the Macedonians (hellenized barbarians, according to the aloof Athenians of the time) for an expedition against Greece's eternal rival, Persia. Athenian patriotism and independence were kept alive by the orator Demosthenes until Philip subdued the city (338 BC). Philip was assassinated shortly before beginning the Persian campaign, leaving his son Alexander, the pupil of Aristotle, to conquer the East. When Alexander died, Athens had to defend herself against his ambitious generals, beginning with Dimitrios Poliorketes (the Besieger) who captured the city in 294 BC. Alexandria, Rhodes and Pergamon became Athens' intellectual rivals, although Athens continued to be honoured by them.

In 168 BC Rome captured Athens, but again granted her many privileges including the island of Delos. Eighty years later, however, when Athens betrayed Roman favour by siding with Mithridates of Pontus, Sulla destroyed Piraeus and the walls of the city. But Rome always remembered her cultural debt; leading Romans attended Athens' academies, and gave the city gifts; and, Romans being Romans, many Greek treasures ended up in Rome. St Paul started the Athenians on the road to Christianity in AD 44. In the 3rd century Goths and barbarians sacked Athens, and when they were driven away the city joined the growing Byzantine Empire.

In 529, Byzantine Emperor Justinian closed the philosophy schools, and converted the temples to churches and the Parthenon into a cathedral. It was a largely symbolic act; by then Athens had lost her place in the world. She next enters history as the plaything of the Franks after they pillaged Constantinople in 1204. St Louis appointed Guy de la Roche as Duke of Athens, a dukedom which passed through many outstretched hands: the Catalans, Neapolitans and Venetians all controlled it at various times. In 1456 it was the turn of the Ottomans, who converted the Parthenon into a mosque and the Erechtheion into a harem. The Venetians made several attempts to wrench it away, and unfortunately they succeeded, briefly. In the siege of 1687 their general Morosini lobbed a cannonball at the Parthenon, until then perfectly intact, with its roof in place, and scored a direct hit on the Turkish gunpowder store. In 1800 Lord Elgin began the large-scale removal of monuments from Athens to the British and other museums.

The revolutionary spirit that swept through Europe at the end of the 18th and beginning of the 19th centuries did not fail to catch hold in Greece, by now more than weary of the lethargic inactivity and sporadic cruelties of the Ottomans. The Greek War of Independence began in the Peloponnese in 1821, and continued for more than six years in a series of bloody atrocities, intrigues and in-fighting.

In the end the Great Powers, namely Britain, Russia and France, came to assist the Greek cause. In the decisive battle of Navarino (20 October 1827), they gave the newly formed Greek government, under President Count John Capodístria of Corfu, the Peloponnese and the mainland peninsula up to a line between the cities of Árta and Vólos. While the Great Powers searched about for a spare member of some inoffensive royal family to make king of the new state, Capodístria (ex-secretary to the Tsar of Russia), affronted the pro-British and pro-French factions in Greece—and also the powerful Mavromikális family who assassinated him in 1831. Before the subsequent anarchy spread too far, the Great Powers produced a king of the Greeks in Otho, a high-handed son of Ludwig I of Bavaria, who immediately offended Greek sensibilities by giving Bavarians all the official posts.

In 1834, Athens—at the time a clutch of war-scarred houses rotting under the Acropolis with a population of 200—was declared the capital of the new Greek state. Otho brought his own architects with him to lay out a new city, based on the lines of Stadíou and El. Venizélou Streets, which still boast most of Otho's neoclassical public buildings. Much of the city's other architecture was built on the quick and cheap by Greeks moving in from the countryside.

The Birth of the Great Idea, and the Great Debacle

The fledgling Greek state was born with the *Megáli Idéa* or 'Great Idea'—to liberate and unite all the Greeks into a kind of Byzantium Revisited, although at first Athens lacked the muscle to do anything about it. Otho's arrogant inadequacies led to revolts and his dethronement in 1862, but the Great Powers replaced him with William George, son of the King of Denmark (a young naval cadet who learned of his new job in a newspaper wrapped around his sardine sandwich). In 1864, the National Assembly made Greece a constitutional monarchy, a system that actually began to work under Prime Minister Trikoúpis in 1875. In the long reign of George I, Greece began to develop, with shipping as its economic base.

In 1910, Elefthérios Venizélos became Prime Minister of Greece for the first time. He used the two Balkan Wars of 1912–13 to further the Great Idea, annexing his native Crete, the Northeastern Aegean islands, Macedonia and southern Epirus. In the meantime King George was assassinated by a madman, and Constantine I ascended the throne. Constantine was married to Kaiser Wilhelm's sister and, when the First World War broke out, he supported the Central Powers while remaining officially neutral, while Venizélos set up his own government with volunteers in support of the Allies in northern Greece. Things turned out Venizélos' way when the Allies forced Constantine to mobilize the Greek army.

The 'War to end all Wars' hardly extinguished the Great Idea. During the signing of the Treaty of Versailles after the war, Venizélos took advantage of the anarchy in Turkey by claiming Smyrna (Izmir), which at the time had a huge Greek population. Believing the claim had the backing of the Great Powers, especially Britain's Lloyd George, Venizélos' successors ordered Greek forces to occupy Smyrna and advance on Ankara. It was, as the Greeks call it, a catastrophe. The Turks, under nationalist leader Mustapha Kemal (later Atatürk) had grown formidable after their defeats in the Balkans, and in August 1922 the invading Greek army was forced back and routed at Smyrna, with enough atrocities committed on both sides to embitter relations for decades. Constantine immediately abdicated in favour of his son George II; the government fell and Colonel Plastiras with his officers took over, ignobly executing the ministers of the previous government. Relations between Greece and Turkey had reached such an impasse that massive population exchanges seemed to be the only solution, leaving Greece, then with a population of 4,800,000, with the difficulties of finding housing and work for over a million Anatolian refugees.

In 1929 a republic was proclaimed which lasted for ten shaky years. Trade unions and the Greek communist party, or KKE, were formed and gained strength. Venizélos was re-elected President and set the present borders of Greece (except for the Dodecanese Islands, which Italy snapped up at Versailles as part of its war prizes). His term also saw the start of another ongoing headache: the first uprising by Greek Cypriots, four-fifths of the population of what was then a British Crown Colony, who desired union with Greece.

Another Catastrophe: the Second World War & the Greek Civil War

The republic, beset with economic difficulties, collapsed in 1935, and King George II returned to Greece, with right wing General Metaxás as his Prime Minister. Metaxás assumed dictatorial control under the regime of 4 August, exiled the opposition, instituted rigorous censorship and crushed the trade unions and all leftist activities. Although a sympathizer with Fascism, Metaxás had sufficient fore-boding to prepare the Greek army in advance against occupation, and on 28 October 1940, as the apocryphal story goes, he responded with a laconic '*Óchi!*' (No!) to Mussolini's demands that his troops massed on the Albanian border be allowed passage through Greece. The first Allied country voluntarily to join Britain against the Axis, Greece's moment of glory came when it not only stopped the Italians, but pushed them back into Albania.

But by May 1941, after the Battle of Crete, all Greece was in the hands of the Nazis, and George II was in exile in Egypt. The miseries and horrors of the Occupation (more civilians died in Greece than any other occupied country; an estimated 500,000 people starved to death) were compounded by political strife and uncertainty over the status of the monarchy in exile. The Communist-organized EAM, the National Liberation Front, and its army, ELAS, led the resistance and had vast popular support, but its politics were hardly palatable to Churchill, who was keen to restore the monarchy and keep Greece out of Communist hands. The proud Greeks saw his manoeuvring as another example of outside interference, and the Greek Civil War—in retrospect the very first campaign of the Cold War—broke out three short months after the liberation of

Greece. It began in Athens, with British troops and a Greek monarchist minority fighting ELAS and their allies Yugoslavia and Bulgaria, followed by long-drawn-out guerrilla campaigns in the mountains, with more of the usual horrific atrocities. At the end of the Second World War, Britain's communist containment policy was taken over by the Truman Doctrine. American money and advisors poured into Greece. The wretched Civil War dragged on until 1949; leftists who were not shot or imprisoned went into exile.

Recovery and Cyprus

Recovery was very slow, even if orchestrated by America, and the Greek diaspora that began in the early 20th century accelerated so fast that entire villages, especially on the islands, became ghost towns. In1951, Greece and Turkey became full members of NATO, an uncomfortable arrangement from the start because of the unresolved issue of Cyprus, still ruled by Britain. General Papagos of the American-backed Greek Rally party won the elections of 1952. Two years later Greek Cypriots, led by Archbishop Makários, clamoured and rioted for union with Greece; the Americans and British turned a deaf ear. Meanwhile Papagos died, and the more liberal Konstantínos Karamanlís replaced him as Prime Minister, inaugurating eight years of stability and prosperity as agriculture and tourism began to make their contributions to the economy, although the opposition criticized his pro-Western policy and inability to resolve the worsening situation in Cyprus. Because one-fifth of the Cypriots were Turkish, Turkey refused to let Cyprus join Greece—the independence or partitioning of the island was as far as Ankara would go. In 1960, a British-brokered compromise was reached, although it had little appeal for the Greeks: Cyprus became an independent republic and elected Makários president. Britain took care to retain sovereignty over its military bases.

To add to the unhappiness over Cyprus, Greece was rocked with record unemployment. The royal family, especially the neo-Fascist Queen Frederíka, were unpopular; there were strikes and powerful anti-American feelings. In 1963 came the assassination of left-wing Deputy Lambrákis (see Costa Gavras' film *Z*) for which police officers were tried and convicted. Karamanlís resigned and lost the next elections in 1965 to George Papandréou of the centre-left opposition. At the same time, King Paul, son of George II, died and was succeeded by his son, the 23-year-old conservative Constantine II. The combination did not bode well; a quarrel with the King over reforming the tradition-bound military led to Papandréou's resignation in 1966. Constantine was meant to call for new elections but, fearing Papandréou's re-election, he tried instead to organize a coalition around Konstantínos Mitsotákis, the future Néa Demokratikí leader. Massive discontent finally forced Constantine to call for elections in May; on 21 April 1967, a coup by an obscure group of colonels established a military dictatorship and imprisoned George Papandréou and his son Andréas (an economics professor at Harvard and

Adlai Stevenson's campaign manager), charging the latter with treason. Colonel George Papadópoulos became dictator of the junta. Constantine II attempted a ridiculous counter-coup and then fled to Rome.

A Vicious 'Moral Cleansing'

The proclaimed aim of the colonels' junta—propped up disgracefully by the CIA—was a 'moral cleansing of Orthodox Christian Greece'. Human rights were suppressed, strict and often absurd censorship undermined the nation's cultural life, and the secret police imprisoned and tortured thousands of dissidents—or their children. The internal situation went from bad to worse, and on 17 November 1973 students of the Polytechnic school in Athens went on strike. Tanks were brought in and many students were killed. After this incident, popular feeling rose to such a pitch that Papadópoulos was arrested, only to be replaced by his arrester, the head of the secret military police, Ioannídes. Greece was in turmoil. Attempting to save the situation by rallying the nation around the Great Idea, Ioannídes tried to launch a coup in Cyprus, to assassinate Makários and replace him with a president who would declare the long-desired union of Cyprus with Greece. It was a fiasco. Makários fled, and the Turkish army invaded Cyprus, occupying 40% of the island. The Greek military rebelled, the dictatorship resigned and Karamanlís hurriedly returned from his exile in Paris to form a new government, release the political prisoners, order a ceasefire in Cyprus and legalize the Communist party.

A New Greek Alphabet: ND, EEC, PASOK

Karamanlís and his conservative Néa Demokratikí (ND) easily won the November 1974 elections; the monarchy did less well in the subsequent plebiscite, and Greece became a republic; the same year Karamanlís realized his fondest dream when the country was anchored to the European Community. Karamanlís brought stability but neglected the economic and social reforms Greece so badly needed; these, along with a desire for national integrity and an independent foreign policy, were to be the ticket to populist Andréas Papandréou's victories, beginning in 1981. His party, PASOK (the Pan-Hellenic Socialist Movement, with a rising green sun symbol) promised much, beginning with withdrawal from NATO and the EEC, and the removal of US air bases; understandably, Papandréou's anti-US and Europe rhetoric was music to Greek ears. PASOK's sun shone over some long-awaited reforms, especially women's rights, and a heady and hedonistic liberalization swept the land. PASOK easily triumphed again in the 1985 elections, in spite of Papandréou's failure to deliver Greece from the snares of NATO, the US or the European Economic Community, or even keep any of his promises on the economic front. Inflation soared, and after the election Greece had to be bailed out by a huge EEC loan accompanied by an unpopular belt-tightening programme. In the end, however, it was scandals and corruption that brought Papandréou down: the old man's open affair and later marriage to a much younger woman—Dímitri (Mimi) Liáni—and the Bank of Crete corruption scandal didn't go down well in an essentially conservative country.

In 1990, Mitsotákis and the Néa Demokratikí (ND) conservatives took a slim majority in the elections, promising to grapple with Greece's severe economic problems. ND immediately launched a wave of austerity measures which proved even more unpopular than Papandréou: a crackdown on tax evasion; a wage freeze for civil servants; privatization of most state-run companies, including Olympic Airways; and steep increases in charges for public services. This sparked off a wave of strikes in 1991 and 1992. By late 1992 Mitsotákis had also had his share of political scandals, and in October 1993 his party fell in the general election, returning rascally old Andréas Papandréou to office, a package that included wife Liáni as chief of staff.

Third time did prove lucky when it came to closing down the US bases in Greece (1994). Otherwise Papandréou kept Greece in his thrall by pushing all the Balkan nationalist buttons: rallying the country around the hallowed name of Macedonia when the new little landlocked country on Greece's border tried to snatch it (as punishment, Greece cut off its links to the sea until November '95) and siding (verbally, mostly) with the Serbs in Bosnia because they too were Orthodox and that was all that mattered. As Papandréou played the gadfly, the once-reviled EU poured funds into the country, resulting in new roads, schools, sewers, and agricultural subsidies. The once low prices that fuelled the Greek tourist boom of the 1970s and 80s inched up to match the rest of Europe, but after 1994 (a record year for tourism with 11.3 million arrivals), the strong drachma brought a steep decline.

In late 1995 Papandréou declined as well, and went into hospital. Seriously ill with kidney failure, he refused to resign as Prime Minister while his wife's faction manoeuvred for power, thwarted in the end by a revolt led by former trade minister Kósta Simítis, a respected but 'bland' technocrat who toughed it out to get the party's nod to finish out the old man's term. Simítis' first weeks at the helm were severely tested when a dispute with Turkey erupted over an uninhabited rock pile in the Dodecanese, nearly bringing the two countries to a shooting war; nationalists blamed Simítis for being soft on agreeing to an American-brokered mutual withdrawal pending mediation, but the feeling after all the rhetoric was that it was not an issue to send young men to die for.

Non-dogmatic, low-key, efficient and untainted by scandal, Simítis has proved to be a hard worker for pragmatic common sense, something all too rare in recent Greek politics. Even before Papandréou's death in June 1996, he broke with the shrill nationalism of his former boss (while keeping old PASOK hands happy by appointing Papandréou's intelligent and sensible son George as deputy Foreign Minister) and has since patched up relations with Greece's neighbours. Under Simítis Greece has become a regional leader and prime investor in the Balkans; he has encouraged talks led by Richard Holbrook to come to an agreement over Cyprus; the paranoia index has plummeted, and a truce of sorts has kept Greek-Turkish relations from flying off the handle, in spite of political instability in Turkey. Although economically still sharing the European Union cellar along with Portugal, Simítis' Greece is doggedly trying to better itself: improving the country's infrastructure, providing a climate for capital investments, building new ties with Eastern Europe and Russia, and, in 1997, letting the drachma slide to make Greece more attractive to tourism, which today represents 15 per cent of the annual income, by far the biggest foreign currency earner.

Today the Hellenic vortex, greater Athens, squeezes in over three million lively, opinionated inhabitants—a full third of the population of Greece—who, thanks to native ingenuity and EU membership, are now more prosperous than they have been since the age of Pericles. Unfortunately this translates into a million cars, creating the worst smog problem east of Mexico City and one that threatens to choke this unique city. The word for smog is *néfos*, and if you happen to arrive on a brown day you'll soon know too much about it. To relieve the congestion, the first lines of the new metro are under construction but making things worse before they get better.

Modern Athens may never win any beauty prizes, but it's as alive as it is ugly—the opposite of its old master Venice, which is stunningly beautiful, and stunningly dead. And of late Athens is undergoing a quiet renaissance under Mayor Dimitris Avramópoulos: neoclassical buildings are being restored, trees planted, car-less oases created in the central shopping districts and Pláka; construction of a new airport has begun at Spata, 20km away, and new immigrants from Eastern Europe and the Balkans are giving the city a new cosmopolitan buzz (even the Albanian crime wave that traumatized Athens a few years back seems to have stabilized). Losing the 1996 Olympics to Atlanta may have been a kick in the *fustanella*, but it also concentrated Athens' attention on its problems like nothing before. The hard work was rewarded by its selection, at long last, for the 2004 Olympics—94% of the population were in favour of 'bringing the games home'.

Getting Around

by bus

The free map of Athens distributed by EOT (*see* below) marks the main city bus (the blue ones) and trolley routes. Purchase tickets (75dr) before boarding, and punch in the machine; if you're caught without a ticket the fine is 2000dr. Note that all trolleys except 1, 10 and 12 pass in front of the

National Archaeology Museum; for the Acropolis and Thesion, catch bus 230 from Sýntagma Square's post office. For info, call ✆ 185 between 7am and 9pm.

by metro

The metro is an important means of getting across Athens, especially from Piraeus. It runs as far as Kifissiá, stopping at Thissío (Theseum) Monastiráki (flea market, near Pláka) Omónia (Athens' Times Square) and Plateía Viktorías (near Areos Park). The network is being extended 20km with major excavations throughout the city; work is supposed to be finished in 2000, and might be, if the quibbling stops.

by taxi

Compared to other Western cities, Athenian taxis are cheap, but a pain in the butt. Because fares are so low, the only way cabbies can make a decent living is by sharing, which makes hailing a cab a sport not for the faint-hearted; the usual procedure is to stand by the street, flag down any passing cab and, if they slow down and cock an ear, shout out your general destination. If the taxi is going that way, the driver will stop, if not, not. If there's more than two of you, flagging a cab is hopeless, and you might as well walk to the nearest taxi stand or call a radio taxi. Check the meter when you board (although some taxis now have two meters) and pay from there, with a small surcharge, but more often than not the cabbie will try to nail you to the full fare on the meter. The only thing to do is start writing down the taxi's licence number and threatening to go to the police, which usually settles the issue on the spot.

The meter starts at 200dr, and the 60dr per kilometre doubles if you leave central Athens. There's a 300dr airport surcharge, a 150dr bus station/port surcharge, 50dr per bag luggage surcharge, and all prices double from midnight to 5am and on major holidays such as Easter. A taxi between Athens and the airport should cost about 1500dr. Piraeus is particularly prone to cowboys preying on unsuspecting tourists heading from and to the ferries; take proper yellow taxis with meters and official licence numbers or be prepared to be ripped off. **Radio taxis** charge a 300dr callout fee. Some numbers to try: ✆ 513 0640; ✆ 922 1755; ✆ 411 5200; ✆ 582 1292.

driving

Just don't. If evil chance finds you behind a wheel, note that parking in the central Athens Green Zone is forbidden outside designated areas. Green Zone borders are the following streets: Sékeri, Botássi, Stoúrnara, Marni, Menándrou, Pireás, Likourgoú, Athinás, Mitropóleos, Filellínon, Amalías and Vassilís Sofías.

National Archaeological Museum

TOSSITSA

Exarchia Square

28 OKTOVRIOU (PATISSION)

ZAIMI

SP TRIKOUP

STOURNARI

SOLOMOU

AHARNON

MARNI

TRITIS SEPTEMVRIOU

AKADIMIAS

THEMISTOKLEOUS

EM BENAKI

ZOODHIOU PIGIS

HARILAOU TRIKOUPI

MAVROMIHALI

IPPOKRATOUS

ASKLIPIOU

ERESSOU

NEAPOLI

KAROLOU

MARNI

National Theatre

AGIOU KONSTANTINOU

Omonia Square

M

P. TSALDARI

MENANDROU

SOKRATOUS

STADIOU

EL VENIZELOU

SKOUFA

ANEMONISTOPOULOU

OMIROU

SINA

AKADIMIAS

SOLONOS

LIKAVITOU

University

PINDAROU

AMERIKIS

PIREOS

SOFOKLEOUS

Theatrou Square

EVRIPIDOU

Eleftherias Square

ATHINIAS

EOLOU

PRAXITELOUS

EVRIPIDOU

Klafthimonos Square

Ag. Theodori

Athens City Museum

M

KOLOKOTRONI

National Historical Museum

LEKA

i

Benaki Museum

Keramikos

Keramikos Museum

ERMOU

AG ATHANASSIOS

M

SARI

AGION ANARGIRON

AG DIMITRIOU

APOSTOLOU TAKI

KARA SKAKI

MONASTIRAKI

Kapnikaria

Monastiraki Square

AREOS

ERMOU

Syntagma Square

MITROPOLEOS

Parliament Building

National Gardens

POULOPOULOU

AKIEOU

IRAKLIDON

APOSTOLOU PAVLOU

AKAMANDOS

Theseum

Stoa of Attalus

Ancient Agora

Agii Apostoli

DIOSKOURON

Mitropoli Square

Cathedral

Popular Musical Instruments Museum

Roman Forum

Kanelopoulos Museum

THEORIAS

APOLONOS

ADRIANOU

PLAKA

Great Folk Art Museum

Jewish Museum

AMALIAS

Zappeion

OTRINEON

PNIKA

SMITH

Areios Pagos

Acropolis

Lysikratos Monument

LISSIKRATOUS

VASILISSIS OLGAS

Hadrian's Arch

The Pnyx

Dionysus Theatre

Temple of the Olympian Zeus

Lofos Nymfon

DIONISSIOU AREOPAGITOU

ROBERTOU GALLI

MAKRIGIANI

HATZIHRISTOU

ATH.DIAKOU

ARDITOU

Socrates' Prison Cell

Filopappos Monument

Filopappos Theatre

MAKRIGIANI

ANDREA SYNGROU

VEIKOU

DIMITRAKOPOULOU

KALLIROIS

84

Lycavitos
Theatre

*Lycavitos
Hill*

NEAPOLI

KOKALI

Ag.Georgios

Funicular
Railway

VASILISSIS SOFIAS

ARISTIPOU

PAPADIAMANDOPOULOU

PINDAROU   Dexameni

CHARITOS

PATRIARHI IOAKIM

National
Gallery

PLOUTARHOU

KOLONAKI

Goulandris Museum
of Cycladic Art

MIHALAKOPOULOU

SOFIAS

Benaki
Museum

VASSILIS

War Museum

Byzantine
Museum

IRODOU ATIKOU

VASSILEOS KONSTANDINOU

PANGRATI

National
Gardens

Zappeion

Athens Stadium

N

500 metres
500 yards

Athens

85

Sýntagma (ΣΨΝΤΑΓΜΑ) (**Constitution**) **Square** is the centre of the city, site of the **Parliament Building** which backs on to the **National Gardens** and **Záppeion Park**, a cool haven of green and shade to escape the summer heat, with ducks to feed and benches to snatch forty winks. Traffic is slowly being syphoned away, so you can hear yourself think at the outdoor tables of the overpriced cafés and the great big McDonald's. The McPresence may be a golden arch-blasphemy for old Athens hands, but it's packed just the same, mostly with Greeks who don't give a hang about culture pollution. At the time of writing Sýntagma Square is further convulsed with the construction of the new $2.8 billion metro; a 3rd-century AD Roman bath and villa with lovely murals, an 11th-century BC grave and the tomb of a little dog were found under all the traffic; archaeological finds from the digs will be displayed in a smart underground concourse.

From Sýntagma Square it's a short walk down to the **Pláka** (ΠΛΑΚΑ), the medieval centre under the Acropolis, where many of the older houses have been converted into intimate tavernas or bars, each tinkling away with its own bouzouki. This is also a good place to look for mid-priced accommodation, now that cars have been banished. On the very top of Pláka, at the foot of the Acropolis, **Anafiótika** (ΑΝΑΦΙΟΤΙΚΑ) is a charming uncommercialized enclave left by the builders of Otho's palaces, who came from the island of Anáfi and, homesick, tried to re-create their village here.

During the day meander through Athens' nearby flea market district, to the west of **Monastiráki** (ΜΟΝΑΣΤΙΡΑΚΙ) **Square** (and the metro station), where bulging shops sell everything from good quality woollen goods and fake Caterpillar boots to furniture and second-hand fridges. Several streets en route all claim to be the flea market, but are nothing more than tourist trap alley; aim for Avysinias Square. Just north of Monastiráki, across Ermoú, **Psirri** is an inner-city workers' neighbourhood of winding little streets that in the past couple of years has become one of the trendiest spots to eat and play in Athens, where retro is definitely in. A ten-minute walk east from Sýntagma will take you to **Kolonáki Square**, Athens' Knightsbridge in miniature, complete with fancypants shops, upmarket restaurants and plenty of well-heeled 'Kolonáki Greeks'—Athenian Sloane Rangers—to patronize them. Above the square rises **Lykavitós** (ΛΥΚΑ-ΒΕΤΟΣ) hill, illuminated like a fairytale tower at night (a long walk, but there's a funicular every 10 minutes from the corner of Aristippoú and Ploutarchoúis). The summit offers the best panoramic views of Athens and Piraeus, *néfos* permitting, and the chapel of **St George**, a restaurant/bar, a lovely outdoor theatre and a cannon fired on national holidays.

For something different, a 15-minute walk north of Sýntagma past the University (Panepistímou) will bring you to funky **Omónia** (OMONIA) **Square**, the Athenian Times Square, open 24 hours a day and embracing a useful metro stop, as well as fast food, huge news-stands, porn-mongers and screwballs. The **National Archaeology Museum** is further north, and behind it lies **Exárchia**, Athens' Latin Quarter, home of trendies, students and literati. Terra incognita for tourists, Plateía Exárchia is one of the city's liveliest centres after dark, with traditional *ouzeries* and *boîtes* where you're likely to find rave alongside bluesy, smoke-filled *rembétika* clubs. For establishment Athens, Exárchia is synonymous with Anarchia, and home to druggies, disaffected youth and graffiti-sprayers. But it's tame by London or New York standards.

Two other areas off the tourist trail and pleasant places to stay are residential **Veikoú** and **Koukáki**, reached from the southern slopes of the Acropolis or Filopáppou Hill, both on the nos.1, 5 and 9 trolley-bus routes. Proper Greek neighbourhoods, the local shops, tavernas and *ouzeries* have few concessions to tourism and excellent, authentic food. Good places to go for a leisurely lunch or to round off an evening.

A 20-minute walk from Sýntagma, along Vass. Sofías, brings you to the Hilton Hotel, a useful landmark. Behind it are the essential Athenian neighbourhoods of **Ilíssia** and **Pangráti**, the best place to get a feel for everyday life in the city. Lose yourself in their back streets and you may find your own little taverna (of which there are plenty), rather than restrict yourself to the tourist haunts in the centre. Across Konstantínos Avenue from Záppeion Park, the landmark is the big white horseshoe of the **Olympic Stadium**, site of the 3rd-century BC original used during the Panathenaea festival, and rebuilt for the first modern Olympics, in 1896. Behind this you'll find **Mets**, an old-fashioned neighbourhood popular with artists and media folk with some fine old houses and small pensions. If you don't mind the walk into the centre of Athens, it's a good place to stay with authentic tavernas and *kafenéions*.

From Záppeion Park buses run frequently down to the coast and suburbs of **Glyfáda**, **Voúla** and **Vouliagménis**. Glyfáda, close to the airport, is a green and pleasant suburb that has grown into a busy resort and rival of fashionable Kolonáki. Smart city dwellers shop at the ritzy boutiques, and berth their gin palaces in the swish marina, ready for weekend jaunts over to Kéa and other nearby islands. At the other end of the scale it's the hub of British package holidays to the so-called Apollo Coast. Here and further down the coast at Voúla are pay beaches run by EOT, usually jammed with well-heeled Athenians. There are all kinds of facilities and the sea is cleaner at some than others—watch out for that sewage outfall—but nothing like the crystal waters of the more remote islands. There's also good swimming beyond Voúla in the rocky coves at Vouliagménis, a smart place for a fish lunch and haven for Greek yachties. En route, **Kavoúri** has excellent fish restaurants, ideal for a romantic dinner overlooking the sea. Beyond Vouliagménis, the road continues along the coast to **Várkiza**, another beach playground, and winds to stunning **Cape Soúnion** and its **Temple of Poseidon** (440 BC), famous for its magnificent position and sunsets and where there's always at least one tourist searching for the column where Byron carved his name.

Major Museums and Sites in Athens

The Acropolis

© 321 0219; open summer Mon–Fri 8–6.30, Sat and Sun 8–2.30; winter Mon–Fri 8–4.30, Sat and Sun 8.30–2.30; adm exp.

Acropolis in Greek means 'top of the town', and many Greek cities have similar naturally fortified citadels crowned with temples, but Athens has *the* Acropolis, the ultimate, standing proud above the city from a hundred different view points. First inhabited at the end of the Neolithic Age, it had a Cyclopean wall and the palace of Athens' Mycenaean king, although this was later replaced by a temple of Poseidon and Athena, after the two divinities took part in a contest to decide who would be the patron of the city. With his trident Poseidon struck the spring Klepsydra out of the rock of the Acropolis, while Athena invented the olive tree, which the Athenians judged the better trick. In later years the tyrant Pisistratos ordered a great gate to be constructed in the Mycenaean wall, but Delphi cursed it and the Athenians dismantled it. In 480 BC the temple's cult statue of Athena was hurriedly bundled off to Salamis, just before the Persians burnt and smashed the Acropolis. Themistocles built a new rampart out of stones of the old Parthenon, and under Pericles the Acropolis as we see it today took shape.

The path to the Acropolis follows the Panathenaic Way, laid out at the consecration of the Panathenaic Festival in 566 BC. The Acropolis entrance is defended by the **Beulé Gate** (named after Ernest Beulé, the archaeologist who found it); the monumental stairways were built by the Romans and the two lions are from Venice. Themistocles' reconstructed Panathenaic ramp leads to the equally reconstructed **Propylaia**, the massive gateway built by Pericles' architect Mnesikles to replace Pisistratos' cursed gate. The ancient Greeks considered the Propylaia the architectural equal of the Parthenon itself, although it was never actually completed because of the Peloponnesian War. On either side of the Propylaia's entrance are two wings; the north held a picture gallery (Pinakothéke) while the smaller one to the south consisted of only one room of an unusual shape, because the priests of the neighbouring Nike temple didn't want the wing in their precinct. The original entrance had five doors, the central one pierced by the Panathenaic Way.

Temple of Athena Nike

The Ionic Temple of Athena Nike, or *Wingless Victory*, was built by the architect Kallikrates in 478 BC of Pentelic marble. It housed the cult statue of Athena, a copy of a much older wooden statue; its lack of wings, unlike later victory statues, gave the temple its second name. In 1687 the Turks destroyed the temple to build a tower. It was rebuilt in 1835 and again in 1936, when the bastion beneath it threatened to crumble away. Cement casts replace the north and western friezes which were taken to England by Lord Elgin. From the temple of Athena Nike the whole Saronic Gulf could be seen in pre-*néfos* days, and it was here that King Aegeus watched for the return of his son Theseus from his Cretan adventure with the Minotaur. Theseus was to have signalled his victory with a white sail but forgot; at the sight of the black sail of death, Aegeus threw himself off the precipice in despair and, although he was miles from the water at the time, gave his name to the Aegean Sea.

The Parthenon

The Parthenon, the glory of the Acropolis and probably the most famous building in the world, is a Doric temple constructed between 447 and 432 BC under the direction of Phidias, the greatest artist and sculptor of the Periclean age. Originally called the Great Temple, brightly painted and shimmering with gold, it took the name Parthenon (Chamber of Virgins) a hundred years after its completion. Constructed entirely of Pentelic marble, it held Phidias' famous chryselephantine (ivory and gold) statue of Athena, who stood over 36ft high. The builders of the Parthenon wrote the book on mathematical perfection, subtlety, grace and *entasis*, the art of curving a form to create the visual illusion of perfection. Look closely, and you'll see that there's not a straight line to be seen: the foundation is curved slightly to prevent an illusion of drooping caused by straight horizontals. The columns bend a few centimetres inward, and those on the corners are wider to complete the illusion of perfect form.

The outer colonnade consists of 46 columns and above them are the remnants of the Doric frieze left behind by the beaverish Lord Elgin: the east side portrayed the battle of giants and gods, the south the Lapiths and Centaurs (mostly in the British Museum today), on the west are the Greeks and the Amazons, and on the north the battle of Troy. Little remains of the pediment sculptures of the gods. Above the interior colonnade, the masterful Ionic frieze designed by Phidias himself shows the quadrennial Panathenaic Procession in which the cult statue of Athena in the Erechtheion was brought a golden crown and a new sacred garment, or *peplos*.

The Parthenon, used as a church and then a mosque, was intact until 1687, when a Venetian bomb hit the Turks' powder stores and blew the roof off; an earthquake in 1894 was another serious blow. Entrance within the Parthenon has been forbidden, to save on wear and tear. Preserving the building, as well as undoing the damage of previous restorations, has been the subject of intense study over the past 15 years, when the alarming effects of the *néfos* on the marble could no longer be ignored: while discovering how to use hot, pressurized carbon dioxide to re-harden stone surfaces, Greek scientists have learned about ancient building techniques, and after all these years are picking up the pieces to reconstruct as much of the temple as possible, stringing column drums on new non-rusting titanium rods.

The Erechtheion

The last great monument on the Acropolis is the Erechtheion, a peculiar Ionic temple that owes its idiosyncrasies to the various cult items and the much older sanctuary it was built to encompass. Beneath the temple stood the Mycenaean House of Erechtheus, mentioned by Homer, and the primitive cult sanctuary of Athena; on one side of this grew the Sacred Olive Tree created on the spot by Athena, while under the north porch was the mark left by Poseidon's trident when he brought forth his spring. The tomb of the snake man Kekrops, the legendary founder of Athens, is in the Porch of the Caryatids, where Erechtheus died at the hand of either Zeus or Poseidon.

Within the temple stood the ancient primitive cult statue of Athena Polias, endowed with the biggest juju of them all, solemnly dressed in the sacred *peplos* and crown. After the Persian fires, the sanctuary was quickly restored, but the marble temple planned by Pericles was not begun until 421 BC. Converted into a church in the 7th century, the Turks made it a harem and used the sacred place of the trident marks as a toilet.

Basically the Erechtheion is a rectangular temple with three porches. Inside were two cellas, or chambers: the East Cella dedicated to Athena Polias, the smaller to Poseidon-Erechtheus. Six tall Ionic columns mark the north porch where the floor and roof were cut away to reveal Poseidon's trident marks, as it was sacrilegious to hide such divine work from the view of the gods. The famous maidens or caryatids gracefully supporting the roof on their heads are another Ionian motif. Lord Elgin nicked parts of this temple as well, including one of the six caryatids (now in the British Museum); the other girls, said to weep every night for their missing sister, have also come in from the *néfos* and have been replaced by casts.

The Acropolis Museum

This was built to house sculptures and reliefs from the temples, in particular the Erechtheion's caryatids, the statues of Kores, or Maidens offered to Athena, and the 6th-century BC Calf Bearer (*Moschoforos*). Anti-*néfos* filters have been installed to show the British parliament that Greece is ready to care for the Elgin marbles properly, if they should ever vote to give them back. Below the Acropolis to the west is the bald **Areópagos**, or hill of the war god Ares, with a marble portal to mark the seat of the High Council, who figured so predominantly in Aeschylus' play *The Eumenides* where mercy defeated vengeance for the first time in history during the trial of the matricide Orestes. Although Pericles removed much of the original power of the High Council, under the control of the ex-archons it continued to advise on the Athenian constitution for hundreds of years.

Beyond it, tucked in the side of Philopápou hill, is the **Pnyx**, where the General Assembly of Athens met and heard the speeches of Pericles and Demosthenes. On assembly days citizens were literally rounded up to fill the minimum attendance quota of 5000, but they were paid for their services to the state. Later the assembly was transferred to the theatre of Dionysos. On the summit of the big hill is the **Philopáppos Monument** (AD 114) built in honour of Caius Julius Antiochos Philopáppos, a Syrian Prince and friend of Athens. Come up here for the romantic sunsets and views of the Acropolis; just below is the Dora Stratou Theatre, where Athens' folk dance troupe performs nightly.

The Theatres

Two theatres are tucked into the south flank of the Acropolis. The older, in fact, the oldest in the world if you don't count the 'theatre' at Knóssos, is the **Theatre of Dionysos** (*open daily 8.30–2.30, adm*). Built in the 6th century BC when Thespis created the first true drama, it was continually modified up to the time of Nero. Here 17,000 could watch the annual Greater Dionysia, held in honour of Dionysos, the god of wine and patron divinity of the theatre; the dramatic competitions were awarded prizes, many of which went to the works of Aeschylus, Sophocles, Aristophanes and Euripides. The stage that remains is from the 4th century BC, while the area before the stage, or *proskenion*, is decorated with 1st-century AD scenes based on the life of Dionysos. A couple of streets east in Pláka, the **Monument of Lysikrates** was built by an 'angel' who funded the play that won top prize in 334 BC. It later passed into the hands of Capuchin friars, who hosted Lord Byron; another Lord, Elgin, wanted to take the monument to London but was thwarted this time by the friars.

The second theatre, the **Odeon of Herodes Atticus** (AD 161) was originally covered with a roof when it was built by the Rockefeller of his day, Herodes Atticus (whose life reads like something out of the *Arabian Nights*: he inherited his extraordinary wealth from his father, who found a vast golden treasure outside Rome). The Odeon hosts the annual mid-May and September **Festival of Athens**, where modern European and ancient Greek cultures meet in theatre, ballet, and classical music concerts performed by companies from all over the world.

The Heart of Ancient Athens: the Agora, Theseum & Stoa of Attalus

© 321 0185; open 8.30–2.45, closed Mon; adm.

The Agora was not only the market but the centre of Athenian civic and social life. Here citizens spent as much time as possible, where they discussed the issues of the day and were buttonholed by Socrates. After the Persians destroyed all the buildings of the Agora in 480 BC, it was rebuilt on a much grander style; since then many landmarks have suffered, mostly from angry Romans, firebug barbarians or Athenians in need of cheap building stone. Only the foundations remain of the council house or **Bouleuterion** and the neighbouring Temple of the Mother of the Gods, the **Metroön**, built by the Athenians as reparation for the slaying of a priest from her cult. The round **Tholos** or administration centre is where the *prytanes* worked, and as some had to be on call day and night like modern police, kitchens and sleeping quarters were included. To the right of the Tholos is the **horos**, or boundary stone; a path from here leads to the foundations of the prison where Socrates spent his last days and drank the fatal hemlock. Opposite the Metroön, only a wall remains of the **Sanctuary of the Eponymous Heroes of Athens**, the ten who gave their names to Kleisthenes' ten tribes. The **altar of Zeus Agoraios** received the oaths of the new archons, a practice initiated by Solon.

The 4th-century **Temple of Apollo** was dedicated to the mythical grandfather of the Ionians, who believed themselves descended from Apollo's son Ion; the huge cult statue of Apollo it once held is now in the Agora museum. Almost nothing remains of the **Stoa Basileios** (or of Zeus Eleutherios), the court of the annual archon, where trials concerning the security of the state were held. By the Stoa of Zeus stood the **Altar of the Twelve Gods**, from which all distances in Attica were measured. Alongside it ran the sacred **Panathenaic Way**, the ceremonial path that ascended to the Acropolis, where devotees celebrated the union of Attica; some signs of its Roman rebuilding may be seen by the Church of the Holy Apostles. South of the Altar of Twelve Gods stood a Doric **Temple to Ares** (5th century BC). The **Three Giants** nearby were originally part of the **Odeon of Agrippa** (15 BC); parts of the orchestra remain intact after the roof collapsed in 190 AD. Both the site and giants were reused in the façade of a 5th-century AD gymnasium, that a century later became the University of Athens, at least until Justinian closed it down. Near the **Middle Stoa** (2nd century BC) are ruins of a **Roman temple** and the ancient shops and booths. On the other side of the Middle Stoa was the people's court, or **Heliaia**, organized by Solon in the 6th century BC to hear political questions; it remained active well into Roman times.

Between the **South and East Stoas** (2nd century BC) is the 11th-century **Church of the Holy Apostles** (Ag. Apóstoli), built on the site where St Paul addressed the Athenians; it was restored, along with its fine paintings, in 1952. Across the

Panathenaic Way run the remains of **Valerian's Wall** thrown up in AD 257 against the barbarians, its stone cannibalized from Agora buildings wrecked by the Romans. Between Valerian's Wall and the Stoa of Attalos are higgledy-piggledy ruins of the **Library of Pantainos**, built by Flavius Pantainos in AD 100 and destroyed 167 years later. Artefacts found in the Agora are housed in the **museum** in the **Stoa of Attalos**, the 2nd-century BC portico built by one of Athen's benefactors, King Attalos II of Pergamon, and reconstructed by a later benefactor, John D. Rockefeller of Cleveland, Ohio.

Adjacent to the agora, the mid 5th-century BC **Theseum** is nothing less than the best-preserved Greek temple in existence. Doric in order and dedicated to Hephaistos, the god of metals and smiths, it may well have been designed by the architect of the temple at Sounion. It is constructed almost entirely of Pentelic marble and decorated with *metopes* depicting the lives of Heracles and Theseus (for whom the temple was misnamed in later centuries). Converted into a church in the 5th century, it was the burial place for English Protestants until 1834, when the government declared it a national monument.

National Archaeology Museum

> *Patissíon and Tossítsa Streets, © 821 7717, open Mon 12.30–6.45; Tues–Fri 8–6.45, Sat and Sun 8.30–2.45; adm exp.*

This is the big one, and deserves much more space than permitted here. It contains some of the most spectacular and beautiful works of the ancient Greek world—the Minoan frescoes from Santoríni, gold from Mycenae (including the famous 'mask of Agamemnon'), statues, reliefs, tomb stelae, and ceramics and vases from every period. The Cycladic collection includes one of the first known musicians, the 2500 BC sculpture of a harpist that has become the virtual symbol of the Cyclades. The star of the sculpture rooms is a virile bronze of Poseidon (5th century BC) about to launch his trident, found off the coast of Evia in 1928; around him are some outstanding archaic Kouros statues and the Stele of Hegeso, an Athenian beauty, enveloped by the delicate folds of her robe, seated on a throne. The museum has a shop on the lower level, with reproductions of exhibits by expert craftsmen, so accurate that each piece is issued with a certificate declaring it an authentic fake so you can take it out of the country.

Other Museums and Sites in Athens

Athens City Museum: 7 Paparigopoulou St, © 324 6164, *open Mon, Wed, Fri and Sat, 9–1.30; adm*. Located in a former residence of King Otho, this new museum contains photos, memorabilia and a model of Athens as it was soon after it became the capital of modern Greece.

Benáki Museum: On the corner of Vassilís Sofías and Koumbári Street, ✆ 361 1617 (*Closed indefinitely for renovation; shop open*). António Benáki spent 35 years amassing Byzantine and Islamic treasures in Europe and Asia, dating from 6th to 17th centuries. There are two icons painted by El Greco before he left his native Crete for Venice and Spain—the *Adoration of the Magi* (1560–65) and the *Evangelist Luke* (1560). There is a section on folk art, dating from the Ottoman occupation, which contains a superb collection of costumes and artefacts from the Ionian islands to Cyprus.

Byzantine Museum: 22 Vassilís Sofías, ✆ 723 1570, *open 8.30–3, closed Mon; adm.* A monumental collection of religious treasures ranging from the Early Byzantine period to the 19th century—not only icons but marble sculptures, mosaics, woodcarvings, frescoes, manuscripts and ecclesiastical robes. There are three rooms on the ground floor arranged as chapels, one Early Christian, another Middle Byzantine, and the third post-Byzantine.

Goulandris Museum of Cycladic and Ancient Greek Art: 4 Neofýotou Doúka (just of Vass. Sofías), ✆ 722 8321, *open 10–4, Sat 10–3, closed Tues and Sun.* Stop here before going out to the islands. The Goulandris' collection of Cycladic figurines and other art going back to 3000 BC, as well as ancient art from other parts of Greece, may be second to the collection in the National Museum, but it's better documented and intelligently displayed. Don't miss the Cycladic figure raising his cup in a toast, or the 5th-century BC cat carrying a kitten in her mouth. As of 1992 the museum includes the elegant Stathatos Mansion.

Greek Folk Art Museum: 17 Kydathinaíon St, Pláka, ✆ 322 9031, *open 10–2, closed Mon; adm.* Exquisite Greek folk art, embroideries, wood carvings, jewellery, paintings by naïve artists, and nearby, in a renovated mosque, a superb collection of ceramics.

Ilias Lalaounis Jewellery Museum: 41 Karyatidon St, Acropolis, ✆ 922 1044, *open Mon and Wed 9–9, Thurs–Sat 9–3, Sun 10–3, closed Tues, adm.* Showroom and workshop.

Jewish Museum: 36 Amálias, ✆ 323 1577, *open Mon–Fri 9–2.30 and Sun 10–2.30, closed Sat.* Most of Greece's Jewish population arrived in the 16th century, escaping the Spanish Inquisition, and most of their descendants were killed in the Second World War; documents and artefacts chronicle the time in between.

Kanellópoulos Museum: Theorias and Panos, Anafiótika, ✆ 321 2313, *open 8–2.30, closed Mon.* In a neoclassical mansion, a highly eclectic private collection.

Keramikós and Museum: 148 Ermoú Street, ✆ 346 3552, *open 8.30–3, closed Mon; adm.* The ancient cemetery or Keramikós was used for burials from the 12th century BC into Roman times, but the most impressive and beautiful finds came from the rich private tombs built by the Athenians in the 4th century BC. Large stone vases mark the graves of the unmarried dead, while others are in the form of miniature temples and stelae; the best are in the National Museum. Excavations for the metro have revealed over a thousand more graves.

National Gallery: 50 Vass. Konstantínou, across from the Athens Hilton, ✆ 723 5937, *open 9–3, Sun and holidays 10–2, closed Tues; adm*. The National Gallery concentrates on painting and sculpture by modern Greek artists. Works by the leading contemporary painter, Níkos Hadzikyriákos-Ghíkas, are permanently displayed on the ground floor, while the lower level is used for rotating exhibitions.

National Historical Museum: 13 Stadiou Street, ✆ 323 7617, *open 9–1.30, closed Mon; adm*. In the imposing neoclassical Old Parliament of Greece, guarded by a bronze equestrian Theodóros Kolokotrónis, hero of the War of Independence, are exhibits on Greek history, concentrating on the War of Independence. Highlights are the 25 paintings narrating Greek history, from the fall of Constantinople to the War of Independence, commissioned by General Makriyiánnis, who described the events to the painter Zographos (another set of the paintings are in Windsor Castle's library); also see Byron's sword and helmet and his famous portrait dressed as a *klepht.*

Popular Musical Instruments Museum: 1–3 Diogenous St, Pláka. ✆ 325 0198, *open daily 10–2, Wed 12–6, closed Mon.* Fascinating collection of old and new Greek instruments.

Roman Forum: Located between the Agora and the Acropolis, at Pelopia and Eolou Sts, ✆ 324 5220, *open 8.30–3, closed Mon; adm*. At the end of the Hellenistic age, the Romans built their own marketplace, or Forum, feeling uncomfortable in the Greek Agora, especially after they wasted it. The Forum contains the celebrated 1st century BC **Tower of the Winds**, or Clock of Andronikos, which was operated by a hydraulic mechanism, so the Athenians could know the time, day or night. Note the frieze of the eight winds that decorates its eight sides, although it has lost its ancient bronze Triton weathervane. The Forum also contains the **Gate of Athena Archegetis**, built by money sent over by Julius and Augustus Caesar; there is also a court and ruined stoae, and the Fehiye Camii, the Victory or Corn Market Mosque.

Temple of Olympian Zeus: Vass. Ólgas and Amalías, ✆ 922 6330, *open 8.30–3, closed Mon; adm*. Fifteen columns recall what Livy called 'the only temple on earth of a size adequate to the greatness of the god'. The foundations were laid by the tyrant Pisistratos, but work ground to a halt with the fall of his dynasty, only to be continued in 175 BC by a Roman architect, Cossutius. It was half finished when Cossutius' patron, Antiochos IV of Syria, kicked the bucket, leaving the Emperor Hadrian to complete it in AD 131. Nearby are the ruins of ancient houses and a bath and at the far end stands **Hadrian's Arch**, in Pentelic marble, erected by the Athenians to thank the emperor for his help; the complimentary inscription reads on the Acropolis side: 'This is Athens, the ancient city of Theseus', while the other side reads: 'This is the city of Hadrian, not of Theseus'. The Athenians traditionally come here to celebrate the Easter Resurrection.

War Museum of Greece, Vass. Sofías and Rizari Sts, ✆ 729 0543, *open Tues-Fri 9–2, Sat and Sun 9.30–2, closed Mon.* Weapons and battle relics past and present.

Byzantine Churches and Monasteries

Agii Theódori: This 11th-century church in Klafthmónos Square at the end of Dragatsaníou St is notable for its beautiful door; the bell tower and some decorations inside are more recent.

Kapnikaréa: A few blocks from Agii Theódori, on Ermoú Street, is the tiny Kapnikaréa (the chapel of the University of Athens), built in the late 11th century in the shape of a Greek cross, its central cupola supported by four columns with Roman capitals.

Panagía Gorgoepikoos: 'Our Lady who Grants Requests Quickly', the loveliest church in Athens is in Mitropóleos Square. Known as the little cathedral, it was built in the 12th century almost entirely of ancient marbles: note the ancient calendar of state festivals and the signs of the zodiac. The adjacent 'big' **Cathedral** or Metropolitan was built in 1840–55 with the same collage technique, using bits and pieces from 72 destroyed churches. The Glucksberg Kings of Greece were crowned here between 1863 and 1964, and it contains the tomb of the unofficial saint of the Greek revolution, Gregory V, the Patriarch of Constantinople, hanged in 1821.

Moní Pendéli: Buses from Mouseío to Paliá Pendéli. Founded in 1578, in a lovely wooded setting on the mountain of Pentelic marble, this is one of the biggest monasteries in Greece, a popular weekend refuge from the *néfos*. Greek families come out for lunch under the gargantuan plane tree at the excellent **O Telis**, ✆ 804 0484.

Dafní and its Wine Festival: 10km from Athens; take bus 860 or 880 from Panepistímiou St by E. Benáki, ✆ 581 1558, *open 8.30–3; adm.* The name Dafní derives from the temple of Apollo Dafneíos (of the laurel), built on the Sacred Way from Athens to Eleusis. A walled monastery by the 6th century, its new church was built in 1080 and decorated with the best Byzantine mosaics in southern Greece. These are dominated by the figure of Christ Pantokrátor in the dome, his eyes spellbinding and tragic, 'as though He were in flight from an appalling doom' according to Patrick Leigh Fermor. From mid-August until September, every evening from 7.45pm–12.30am, the monastery park holds a festival with over 60 Greek wines (free once you've paid the admission) accompanied by poor overpriced food, singing and dancing, an event well-attended by Athenians and visitors alike.

Athens is a big noisy city, especially so at night when you want to sleep—unless you do as the Greeks do and take a long afternoon siesta. Piraeus (*see* below) may be a better bet, no less noisy but much more convenient for catching those up-at-the-crack-of-dawn ferries. If you can't find a room, try the Hotel Association's booking desk in Sýntagma Square, in the National Bank building (*open Mon–Thurs 8.30–2, Fri 8.30–1 and Sat 9–1, ☎ 323 7193*).

luxury

The beautiful **Grande Bretagne**, Sýntagma Square, ☎ 333 0000, ✆ 322 8034 (*lux*) was built in 1862 for members of the Greek royal family who couldn't squeeze into the palace (the current Parliament building) up the square. Now run by Sheraton, it is the only 'grand' hotel in Greece worthy of the description, with a vast marble lobby, elegant rooms (now air-conditioned and appointed with such modern conveniences as direct dial phones and colour TV), a formal dining room, and a grandeur, style and level of service that the newer hotels, with all their plushness, may never achieve. It was used by the Nazis as their headquarters during the war. Winston Churchill spent Christmas 1944 here and was lucky to escape a bomb meant for him, planted in the hotel's complex sewer system.

Down from the Grande Bretagne on Sýntagma Square the **Meridian Athens**, 2 Vass Geórgiou, ☎ 325 5301, ✆ 323 5856 (*lux*) is a modern favourite. All rooms are soundproofed; it has a very respectable restaurant.

On a less exalted level, but with a far more fetching view, is the **Royal Olympic Hotel** at 28 Diákou, ☎ 922 6411, ✆ 923 3317 (*lux*), facing the Temple of Olympian Zeus and Mount Lykavitós. Rooms here are American in spirit, with a number of family-sized suites, and if you have the misfortune to get a room without a view, there's a wonderful panorama from the rooftop bar.

In Kolonáki, **St George Lycabettus**, 2 Kleoménous (Plateía Dexaménis) ☎ 729 0711, ✆ 729 0439 (*lux*) has an intimate, family-run atmosphere and wonderful views of the Parthenon or out to the sea, and a pool, too. The Grand Balcon dining room has views that take in most of Athens.

New luxury chain hotels are mushrooming up everywhere just outside the city centre—among them, the **Ledra Marriott** at 113–115 Syngroú, ☎ 934 7711, ✆ 935 8603 (*lux*), featuring a Chinese-Japanese restaurant, and a hydrotherapy pool you can soak in with a view of the Parthenon. If you want to stay out of the centre, you can't beat the gorgeous old

Pentelikon, 66 Diligiánni St, Kefalári, in the northern suburb of Kifissiá, © 808 0311, ✆ 801 0314 (*lux*) with a lovely garden and pool.

expensive

Close to Pláka, the **Electra Palace** at 18 Nikodímou, © 324 1401, ✆ 324 1875 (*A*) has views of the Acropolis and a wonderful rooftop swimming pool in a garden setting—something you don't find every day in Athens. Rooms are air-conditioned and there's a garage adjacent to the hotel. More reasonable, just off Sýntagma Square, the **Astor**, 16 Karagiórgi Servías, © 325 5555, ✆ 325 5115 (*A*) also has fully air-conditioned rooms and a rooftop garden restaurant. The **Parthenon**, 6 Makrí St, © 923 4594, ✆ 923 5797 (*A*) is not far from the Acropolis, and has a pretty outdoor breakfast area. **Titania**, 52 Panepistímou, © 330 0111, ✆ 330 0700 (*B*) has pleasant rooms and a very fashionable rooftop terrace planted with old olive trees, and gorgeous views over the Acropolis and Lykavittós. The **Athenian Inn**, 22 Cháritos in swanky Kolonáki, © 723 8097, ✆ 724 2268 (*C*) was the favourite of Lawrence Durrell.

moderate

Adam's, 6 Herefóntos, © 322 5381 (*C*) is in a quiet but central location on the edge of the Pláka, 3 minutes from Hadrian's Arch; rooms are traditional, comfortable, and good value. Also in Pláka, the 19th-century **Akropolis House**, 6–8 Kodroú, © 322 3244, ✆ 324 4143, has modernized rooms but in a traditional style, with antique furnishings, frescoes and a family welcome. **Pension Adonis**, 3 Kódrou, © 324 9737, a gem, clean and well run by the Greek who managed the Annapolis Hilton. All rooms have balconies, and there's a lovely breakfast roof garden and bar with views (rates include breakfast). **Museum**, 16 Bouboulínas, © 360 5611, ✆ 380 0507 (*C*), right at the back of the Archaeology Museum, has similar rooms, but the prices are a bit higher. **Tembi**, 29 Eólou, © 321 3175, ✆ 325 4179 (*D*), near Monastiráki, is nothing special, but is cheaper, with kind owners, and washing facilities. **Hermes**, 19 Apollónos, © 323 5514, ✆ 323 2073, near Sýntagma (*C*) is comfortable and friendly, with a small bar and roof garden with Acropolis views. **Hera**, 9 Falírou at Veikoú, © 923 6683, ✆ 924 7334 (*C*) is modern but tasteful with a garden on the ground and roof.

Out in posh Kifissiá, **Katerina**, 3 Mykónou, © 801 9826 (*C*) is one of the least expensive and friendliest places. In Chalándri, a bit closer to Athens, the **Akropol**, 71 Pentélis Ave, © 682 6650, ✆ 684 5057 (*C*) is very nice with a garden, popular with business people, American tourists and anyone who wants to stay above the *néfos* line. **Art Gallery** at Eréchthiou 5,

Veíkoú, ✆ 923 8376, 📠 923 3025 (*E*) is a pleasant place at the lower end of this category, though Pláka is a 20-minute walk.

inexpensive

The first six on this list are in Pláka: **Phaedra**, 16 Cherefóndos St, ✆ 323 8461 *(D)* just off Filellínon St, has free hot showers, an unreconstructed pre-war interior, and pleasant staff. **John's Place**, 5 Patróou St, ✆ 322 9719 (near Metropóleos St) (*E*) is simple and cheap, with bathrooms down the hall. **Kouros**, 11 Kódrou St (just off Kidathinéou St), ✆ 322 7431 (*E*), an old house in a quietish backwater near the Greek Folk Art Museum, opposite the small park area on Kidathinaíon. The **Student Inn**, 16 Kidathinéon, ✆ 324 4808, is ideal for the rowdy younger crowd (1.30am curfew). Very near Monastiráki, the **Pella Inn**, Ermou 104, ✆ 321 2229, is simple but welcoming. **Aphrodite**, Apollonos 21, ✆ 322 3357, 📠 322 6047, has little character, but good rooms on a quiet street. In Exárchia, book early for **Dryades**, E. Benáki 105 and Anaxartísias, ✆ 382 7191, 📠 380 5193 (*D*); the top three rooms have lovely views (the same owner also runs the even cheaper **Orion**, (*D*) adjacent). **Marble House**, 35 A. Zínni, in Koukáki, ✆ 923 4058 (*E*) is a comfortable Greek-French-run pension. The **Student's Hostel** at 75 Damaréos St, Pangráti, ✆ 751 9530, 📠 751 0616, is central and not a member of YHA. Athens' nearest **campsites** are at Dafní Monastery, and down on the coast at Voúla.

hotels near the airport

If you have an early or delayed flight, or just a day in Athens, there are a few hotels by the airport. They do tend to be desperately noisy—some are practically on the runway. **Emmantina**, 33 Vass. Georgíou, Glyfáda, ✆ 898 0683, 📠 894 8110 (*A; exp*) is one of the better ones, with a pool on the roof and an airport shuttle bus. Convenient, moderate choices in Glyfáda include: the **Blue Sky**, 26 Eleftherías, ✆ 894 7722, 📠 894 3445; **Avra**, 5 Gr. Lambraki, ✆ 894 7185 📠 898 1161; and **Beau Rivage**, 87 Vass. Geórgiou, ✆ 894 9292. **Kreoli**, 17 Vass. Georgíou, ✆ 894 4301, 📠 894 8986 (*B*) is basic, but friendly and family-run, with a pool and breakfast room. Front room and ear plugs essential, air-conditioning extra.

Eating Out in Athens

Athenians rarely dine out before 10 or 11pm, and they want to be entertained afterwards. If it's warm they'll drive to the suburbs or the sea. Glyfáda, near the airport, and outer Piraeus (Kalípoli) are popular on a summer evening: the cool sea breeze is a life-saver after the oppressive heat of Athens. The following places are all Greek, but ethnic food, especially Asian, is just as easy to find.

Pláka

Pláka is the place to head for pleasant restaurants and al fresco dining in the evening—the tinkling glasses, music, chatter and laughter ricochet off the medieval walls. Although scores of places cater for the passing tourist trade (very easy to spot) it remains a perennial favourite with both Greeks and visitors. **Platanos**, 4 Diogénis, ✆ 322 0666, the oldest taverna in Pláka, is near the Tower of the Four Winds and serves good wholesome food in the shade of an enormous plane tree (*around 3000dr*). *Closed Sun*. In the heart of Pláka, in Filomousón Square, where you will land up sooner or later, you can eat well at **Byzantino**, 18 Kidathinéon, ✆ 322 7368, which serves big portions (the fish soup and lamb fricassee are excellent) at its tables under the trees (*3000dr*). It's also one of the few decent places open for Sunday lunch. **Bacchus**, 10–12 Thrasyllou, ✆ 322 0385 has a lovely cloistered outdoor dining area under the Parthenon; try one of the savoury pies (*around 4000dr*). For a cut above taverna fare, dine at **Daphne's**, 4 Lysikrátous (by the Lysikratos monument) ✆ 322 7971, a neoclassical mansion with an elegant dining room with Pompeiian frescoes and beautiful courtyard—a rarity in Athens—serving refined, traditional Greek and international dishes (*around 9000dr a head*). Athens' oldest vegetarian restaurant, **Eden**, 12 Lissíou and Mnissikléous, ✆ 324 8858, with vegetarian quiches and soya moussakas (*around 2500dr*). *Closed Tues*.

Under Pláka: Psirri/Monastiráki/Thísio

Among the many new restaurants and *ouzéries* in Psirri, the first remains outstanding for fun: **Taki 13**, at 13 Táki, ✆ 325 4707 has a superb atmosphere: simple food but a great party bar, often featuring live music (jazz/blues Tuesday and Wednesday, Greek on weekends) and sing songs till 1.30 am. Weekend afternoons bring similar outbursts of drinking and singing at the more bohemian **Café Abysinnia**, in Place Abysinnias, in the centre of Monastiráki, ✆ 321 7047; so-so food but excellent atmosphere, *closed Mon*. If you have a hankering for an excellent *souvláki* and *gýros*, get yourself to **Thanassis**, 69 Mitropoléos, in Monastiráki, ✆ 324 4705, open till 2am. **Vrachakia**, Ortynon 7, nearer the Thesion, overlooks the Acropolis and offers a bizarre 1950s ambiance to go with its taverna classics (*5000dr*). In the same area, **Phanari**, Irakleidon 19A, has some of the best and most economical fish dinners in Athens (*from 4000dr*) and tables in the middle of a street that comes alive after dark.

Kolonáki and Around

The legendary **Gerofinikas**, 10 Pindárou, ✆ 362 2719, still has the ancient palm tree that gave it its name, growing right out of the middle of the restaurant; the food is famous, expensive (*around 7000dr a head*) and the whole meal an experience. *Closed holidays*. Behind the Hilton, the Cypriot restaurant **Othello's,** 45 Mikalakopoúlou, © 729 1481, serves delicious, authentic cuisine (*around 4500dr for a meal*). Out towards the US embassy, **Vlassis**, 8 Pasteur St, © 642 5337 is a superb family-run taverna, *the* place to find true Greek cuisine and one of the rare ones with excellent wines and desserts, too (*around 5000dr*). *Book. Closed Sun.* **Salamandra**, Matzarou 3, © 361 7927, has some of the least expensive but tastiest food in Kolonáki, served in a pretty old house (*under 3000dr*). *Closed Sun.*

Around Omónia Square

Sleazy Omónia Square is a great place to try Greek street food. If you're anywhere near the Central Market, don't miss one of the best *mageiria* in Athens: **Diporto**, Theatrou and Sofokléous, an Athens institution, serving simple but delicious dishes and salads with barrelled retsina (*lunch only, around 3000dr*). **Athinaiko**, 2 Themistokléous, east of Omónia, © 383 8485 is a great place to fill up on tasty *mezédes* and swordfish kebabs while watching the passing crowds. On the same street, at No.18, **Andreas**, © 362 1522 offers tasty seafood at reasonable prices, and tables outside. The traditional Greek hangover cure, tripe soup (*patsas*) and meaty Hellenic soul food is dished up in the early hours to trendy drunkards at **Monastiri**, the butchers' restaurant in the central meat market.

Exárchia

In Exárchia, **Kostayiannis**, 37 Zaími, © 821 2496, behind the National Archaeology Museum, has a succulent display of food in the glass cabinets near the entrance preparing you for a memorable culinary evening. Apart from the superb seafood, the 'ready food' is unbeatable—roast pork in wine and herb sauce or the rabbit *stifádo*, accompanied by barrelled retsina. Prices here are very reasonable (*3500dr for a full evening meal*). To enjoy the after-theatre ambience, don't get there too early. *Closed lunchtimes, Sun, and Aug*. **Galatia**, 50 Valtetsiou, © 380 1930, offers authentic Cypriot fare in relaxed surroundings. For a night out, book a table at **Strephis**, Athineas 5 and Poulcherias 8, © 882 0780, in a historic house at the foot of Stefi hill, where Xanthis, owner and disciple of Theodorakis leads the public in old Greek songs; good, plentiful food (*evenings only; around 4500dr*). Among several tavernas along Methonis street, try **Ama Lachi**, at No.66, © 384 5978, cheap, good and pleasant; there's another clutch of inexpensive places around Plateía Exárchia.

Entertainment and Nightlife

The summer is filled with festivals attracting international stars from around the world; at other times, classical music fans should try to take in a performance at the **Mégaron**, on Vass. Sofías and Kokkáli, ✆ 728 2333, Athens' brand new acoustically wonderful concert hall. Maria Callas got her start at the **Greek National Opera House**, 59-61 Academías St, ✆ 361 2461, which is shared with the national ballet. From May to September there are nightly folk dance performances at the **Dora Stratou Theatre** on Philapapou Hill (✆ 921 4650. *Rembétika*, the Greek blues, is in full revival in Athens; the real thing may be heard live at **Stoa Athanaton**, Sophokleous 19, ✆ 321 4362 (*closed Sun*) or **Rota**, Ermou 118, ✆ 325 2517 (*closed Mon and Tues*), and often at **Diogenis Palace**, 259 Syngroú (also a useful street for big bouzouki clubs, or if you're looking for a transvestite), ✆ 942 4267. Irakleidon street in Thissio has popular rock bars, such as **Stavlos** and **Berlin**. For jazz, try **French Quarter**, 78 Mavromicháli in Exárchia, ✆ 645 0758 or **Half Note**, Trivonianou 17 in Mets, ✆ 923 3460, which alternates between Greek and foreign artists. In summer, young fashion slaves and beautiful Athenians head out to the bars and clubs in Glyfáda or by the airport: here you'll find **Vareladiko**, 4 Alkondidon St, ✆ 895 2403, the first 'hyper-club' in Greece, with the latest Greek hits; **Romeo**, 1 Ellinkikou, ✆ 894 5345, a *skyladiko* club for a wild Greek night out, and **Amfitheatro**, Vass. Georgiou , ✆ 894 4538, Athens' biggest rave venue. Gay Athens gathers in Makrigiánni, the neighbourhood just south of the Acropolis: **Splash**, **Lamda** and **Granazi**, are popular dancing bars with cover charges, all along Lembessi St, off Syngroú. In the summer, outdoor cinemas are a treat and all the films are in their original language: two of the nicest are in Kolonáki: **Dexameni**, in Dexameni Square halfway up Lykavittós, ✆ 360 2363 and **Athinaia**, 50 Charitos St, ✆ 721 5717.

Piraeus

The port of Athens, Piraeus (ΠΕΙΡΑΙΑΣ)—pronounced pi-ray-A or the old way, Pirevs—was the greatest port of the ancient world and remains today one of the busiest in the Mediterranean. In Greece, a country that derives most of its livelihood from the sea in one way or another, Piraeus is the true capital, while Athens is merely a sprawling suburb where the bureaucrats live. Still, it takes a special visitor to find much charm in the tall grey buildings and dusty hurly-burly in the streets, although Marína Zéa and Mikrolimáni with their yachts, brightly lit tavernas and bars are a handsome sight, as are the neon signs flashing kinetically as you sail from Piraeus in the evening.

Historical Outline

Themistocles founded the port of Piraeus in the 5th century BC when Pháliron, Athens' ancient port, could no longer meet the growing needs of the city. From the beginning Piraeus was cosmopolitan and up-to-date: the Miletian geometrician Hippodamos laid it out in a straight grid of streets that have changed little today. The centre of action was always the huge agora in the middle of the city. In the shelter of its *stoae* the world's first commercial fairs and trade exhibitions were held, including some on an international scale. All religions were tolerated, and women were allowed for the first time to work outside the home.

As Piraeus was so crucial to Athens' power, the conquering Spartan Lysander destroyed the famous Long Walls that linked city and port in 404 BC, at the end of the Peloponnesian War. Piraeus made a brief come-back under Konon and Lykurgos, who rebuilt its arsenals. After the 100-year Macedonian occupation and a period of peace, Sulla decimated the city to prevent any anti-Roman resistance, and for 1900 years Piraeus dwindled away into an insignificant village with a population as low as 20, even losing its name to become Porto Leone (after an ancient lion statue, carved in 1040 with runes by future king of Norway Harald Hadraada and his Vikings, then later carted off by Morosini to embellish Venice's Arsenal). With Athens the capital of independent Greece, Piraeus has regained its former glory as the reigning port of a seagoing nation, although nearly everything dates from after 1944, when the departing Germans blew the port sky-high.

Getting Around

In Piraeus this usually means getting out of town as quickly as possible. **Ships** are grouped according to their destination (*see* map) and almost anyone you ask will be able to tell you the precise location of any vessel. The cluster of ticket agents around the port is very competitive, but prices to the islands are fixed, so the only reason to shop around is to see if there is an earlier or faster ship to the island of your choice. For complete non-biased ferry schedules call the **Piraeus Port Authority** © 422 6000.

The **metro** is the quickest way into central Athens, while **buses** on the main 'Green' line (no.040) will take you directly to Sýntagma Square/Filellinon St. The express line no.19 bus service to East and West Airport leaves from Karaiskáki Square.

The Sights

Piraeus has its own fine **Archaeology Museum** at 31 Char. Trikoúpi Street, © 452 1598 (*open 8.30–3, closed Mon*) with an above average collection of antiquities, many discovered off the Attica coast; pride of place goes to the five bronzes found in the port in 1959: an archaic Kouros, two Artemises, the Piraeus Athena

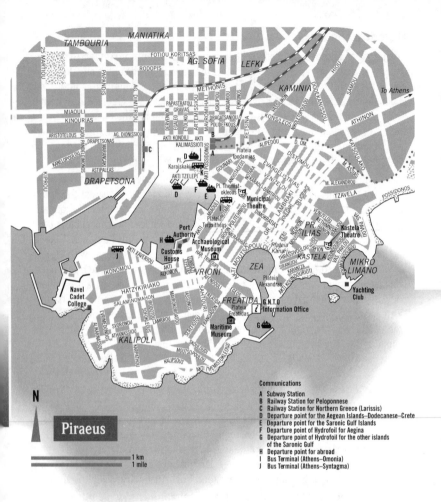

Communications

A Subway Station
B Railway Station for Peloponnese
C Railway Station for Northern Greece (Larissis)
D Departure point for the Aegean Islands–Dodecanese–Crete
E Departure point for the Saronic Gulf Islands
F Departure point of Hydrofoil for Aegina
G Departure point of Hydrofoil for the other islands
  of the Saronic Gulf
H Departure point for abroad
I Bus Terminal (Athens–Omonia)
J Bus Terminal (Athens–Syntagma)

Piraeus

1 km
1 mile

and a tragic mask, as well as the fine 7th-century BC Protoattico amphora. The **Maritime Museum** on Akti Themistoklés by Freatídos Street, ℭ 451 6822 (*open 8.30–2, Sun 9–1, closed Mon*), has intriguing plans of Greece's greatest naval battles, ship models and mementoes from the War of Independence. If you find yourself in Piraeus with time to kill on a Sunday morning, prowl through the flea market in and around Hippodamias Square, where you may well happen across some oddity brought back by a Greek Sinbad.

Beaches are not far away, although the sea isn't exactly sparkling. Kastélla is the closest, followed by Néo Fáliron. Buses go to Ag. Kósmos by the airport, where you can play tennis or volleyball; at Glyfáda and Vouliagméni, further east, there's more wholesome swimming and a golf course. Zéa, Glyfáda and Vouliagméni are the three **marinas** organized by the National Tourist Organization. Piraeus is also the place to charter yachts or sail boats, from 12ft dinghies to deluxe twin-screw yachts, if you've missed your island connection (*see* pp.19–24).

Where to Stay in Piraeus

Hotel accommodation in Piraeus is geared towards businessmen, and less so towards people who have arrived on a late-night ship or plan to depart on an early-morning one. There are plenty of sleazy hotels within a 10-minute walk of the metro station.

expensive

Kastella, 75 Vass. Pávlou, © 411 4735, @ 417 5716 (*B*) is a nice place on the waterfront beyond Mikrolimáni, with a roof garden. Even more swish is the **Cavo d'Oro**, 19 Vass. Pávlou, © 411 3744 (*B*), with a restaurant and disco, and the most expensive of all, **Mistral**, Vass. Pávlou 105, © 412 1425, @ 412 2096 (*B*) comes with a pool, restaurant and air-conditioning.

moderate

If you want to be within walking distance of the docks, the **Triton**, 8 Tsamadou, © 417 3457, @ 417 7888 (*B*) is one of the best of the many in the area. **Lilia**, 131 Zéas, Passalimáni, © 417 9108, @ 411 4311 (*C*) is pleasant and offers free transport to the port. The **Ideal**, 142 Notará, © 429 4050, @ 429 3890 (*C*), 50m from the customs house, offers air-conditioning, but should be renamed the So-So.

inexpensive

Known to seasoned travellers as the One Onion, the **Ionian**, 10 Kapodistríou, © 417 0992 (*C*) is getting smellier by the year but is very convenient for an early ferry or if you've just fallen off one. Others are **Achillion**, 63 Notará Street, © 412 4029 (*D*), **Aenos**, near the main harbour, © 417 4879 (*C*), **Santorini**, © 452 2147 (*C*), and **Acropole**, © 417 3313 (*C*), all used to backpackers.

Eating Out in Piraeus

Around the port the fare is generally fast food or tavernas so greasy it's a wonder they don't slide off the street. The bijou little harbour of Mikrolimáni, once the traditional place to go, is now an overpriced tourist trap. On the other hand, Piraeus has one of Greece's top seafood restaurants in the elegant

tourist information

The National Tourist Organization (EOT) has thankfully opened a proper tourist information office in the heart of Athens, after 20 years of waiting. It's right near Sýntagma Square at 2 Amerikis Street, ℗ (01) 331 0561 (*open Mon–Fri 9–6.30, Sat 9–2, closed Sun*). EOT also have a branch at the **East Airport**: ℗ (01) 969 9500. On Internet try Welcome to Athens with maps, hotels, and practical info at *http://agn.hol.gr/hellas/attica/athens.htm*.

emergencies

Ambulance ℗ 178. Doctors on duty: ℗ 105. Fire: ℗ 199. Police: ℗ 100. Pharmacies: ℗ 107.

The Athens tourist police are out at Dimitrakopoúlou 77, Koukáki, ℗ 925 3396, ℗ 924 3406 but they have a magic telephone number—**171**; Agent 171 not only speaks good English, but can tell you everything from ship departures to where to spend the night, 24 hours a day. Piraeus tourist police are in the cruise ship New Passengers Terminal on Aktí Miaoúli, ℗ 429 0665.

left luggage

Pacific LTD, 26 Níkis (just down from Sýntagma Square), ℗ 324 1007, offers left luggage service, open regular business hours and useful if you have time to kill before taking a plane/boat out and want to visit Acropolis/Pláka etc. In Piraeus, the left luggage store next to the HML ticket agency opens at 7am and stays open until midnight, 300dr an hour, or 500dr for the whole day.

Varoulko, 14 Deligiorgi, near Zéa Marina, ℗ 411 2043 (*book*), where the denizens of the deep are exquisitely prepared and brought to you without a menu; huge wine cellar and prices over 10,000dr to match. *Closed Sun.*

Its chief rival, **Thalassinos**, is just behind the Onassis hospital in Kallithéa, at Liskratous 32, ℗ 930 4518, serving more utterly fresh seafood, beautifully prepared, in the same price range. *Closed Sun eve and Mon.*

On Piraeus' highest hill (it's worth taking a taxi), **Rigas** is an excellent family taverna. It's a favourite destination for Sunday lunch, with a huge choice of starters, and some unusual main courses to go along with the old favourites (*around 3500dr*). Nip across the road and top it off with a coffee on the terrace of the **Bowling Club** opposite, to enjoy the superb view over Piraeus.

If you leave something on a bus, taxi or metro, try ✆ 642 1616.

shopping

To find bargains, visit the Monastiráki flea market in the morning (don't miss the arcade off Andrianou, selling traditional crafts); to spend lots of money, the latest in Greek designer fashion (Carouzos, Prince Oliver, Parthenis, etc) is on display in the boutiques along Kolonáki's Tsakalof and Milioni streets.

For food, Athens' **Central Market** is on Athinás Street, between Evripidou and Sophokleous; food shops continue all the way to Omónia Square.

On a number of islands you can visit workshops where women make carpets, but there's only one place to buy them: **EOMMEX**, 9 Mitropoleos St, ✆ 323 0408. Other fine handicrafts are on sale at the shops run by the **National Welfare Organization**, at 6 Ipatiás and Apóllonos Sts, ✆ 325 0524 and at 135 Vass. Sofiás, ✆ 646 0603.

If you need a good book in English try **Eleftheroudakis**, 4 Níkis, ✆ 322 9388 or **Compendium**, 28 Níkis ✆ 322 1248, both near Sýntagma; also **Pantelides**, 11 Amerikí, ✆ 362 3673, with a wide selection of more academic titles. For used books, try **Koultoura**, 4 Mantazarou, ✆ 380 1348 or **Bibliopolion**, 22 Ifestou St, in Monastiráki. **Metropolis**, 64 Panepistímiou, ✆ 383 0404, has the biggest selection of old, rare and new Greek recordings.

But if it's fish you must have, head over to Fratídas, around from the Zéa Marína yacht harbour, where several moderately priced places offer fresh fish and sea views or, better still, continue along the coast to Kalípoli (bus 904 or 905 from the Metro) where *ouzeries* and fish tavernas line the road, and you can watch the ferries pass and the sun set over Salamína.

Diasimos, 306 Aktí Themiksoleous, ✆ 451 4887, is one of the best in this area; Athenians drive down on Sundays to enjoy the sea views and seafood. For something less pricey but equally memorable, try to locate the Naval School near here: the favourite for excellent fish, salad and wine is **Margaro**, at the gate on Hatzikyriakoú St, ✆ 451 4226. Although there's absolutely no view at all, the variety, freshness and reasonable price of the seafood is its own reward.

An alternative if it's packed: walk up the road away from the Naval School, pass the traffic lights and look out for the *psarotaverna* **Anna**.

Towards the airport at Kalamáki, the **Apaggio**, 8 Megístis Street, ✆ 983 9093, specializes in Greek regional dishes. The menu changes daily, but often includes rarely seen delicacies such as lamb with prunes and almonds and onion pie. It's one of the in-places for Greek foodies and will set you back around 6000dr. *Bookings essential; closed Mon.*

The Islands

Here lies harmony, here lies human scale.

Le Corbusier, on the islands, in 1936

Say 'Greek island', and many people picture one of the Cyclades: a cluster of nearly barren mountain tops rising from a crystal blue sea, where the hills spill over with little villages of asymmetrical white houses and narrow labyrinthine streets, a pocket-sized church squeezed in at every corner, stone terraces striping every slope. Few places are so irresistibly stark and clear, so visually pure and honest, so sharply defined in light and shadow; none of the islands is very large, and you can always see several floating dreamily on the horizon, beckoning, framing a sunset or a rosy-fingered dawn.

The name 'Cyclades' was first used by Herodotus in the 5th century BC, and comes from *kyklos*, 'circling', because the islands encompass sacred Delos. Scattered across the Aegean, they look like (and have often served as) the Stepping Stones between East and West, or, more vividly, the 'stigmata on the skin of a sea panther'.

They come in a wide range of moods. Islands that missed the first onslaught of international tourism have developed as quiet, more relaxed, 'Greeker' alternatives. But even Mýkonos, the busiest, manages to retain an air of class in spite of the hordes it attracts. This is as jet-setty as you can get, with great beaches and the best nightlife. On Íos you'll feel old at 25; the emphasis here is definitely on pubbing and beachlife. The main centres of lovely Páros and Náxos get swamped by mass package tourism, although Náoussa on Páros is now as trendy as Mýkonos. Spectacular, volcanic Santoríni gets the most cruise ships and honeymooners.

Less familiar islands such as Sífnos, Folégandros, Mílos, Amorgós and Sýros offer a seductive mixture of rugged scenery, typical villages, good restaurants and swimming. Then there are special gems like Tínos, a mecca for pilgrims and popular with Greeks. The islands closest to Athens, Kéa and Kýthnos, are favourites for passing yachtsmen and are mostly visited by Greek tourists; Ándros is similar, but with a sprinkling of international resorts. If you're seeking peace and quiet, there's Síkinos, Kímolos, Sérifos, or Anáfi. The tiny islands east and south of Náxos, Koufoníssi, Schinoússa and Heráklia, used to be very quiet but now get quite busy in summer, especially trendy Koufoníssi.

The arid climate of the Cyclades, more than anywhere else in Greece, is influenced by the winds. Winter is plagued by the *voreas,* the north wind that turns ship schedules into a fictional romance. After March the *sirocco* blows from the south, warming islands still green from the winter rains. By July many of the Cyclades look brown and parched, except where there are sources of underground water. From July to September the notorious *meltémi* from the Russian steppes huffs and puffs like the big bad wolf, quadrupling sales of Dramamine in the ports. If you're really a landlubber you can fly: Páros, Mýkonos, Mílos, Santoríni, Náxos and Sýros have airports. Another high summer consideration is the sheer number of visitors; without a reservation you can expect only frustration on the more popular islands, or the smaller ones with a limited number of beds. Don't assume that the more isolated the island the cheaper the accommodation, as supply and demand dictate the prices. You could well pay more for a room in Folégandros, for example, than on Páros, where rooms are far more plentiful. Out of season you can pick and choose, and places with a high percentage of Greek tourists (Kýthnos, Kéa), who tend to go for a six-week burst in the height of summer, are a bargain. October is calmer, and a bit cooler, but usually still warm enough for the beach.

Because islands are so popular with visitors, efforts have been made to ensure they and their new hotels have ample water supplies, even in August. Before the advent of tourism, the population of the Cyclades dropped to an all-time low; it was simply too hard to make a living from the dry, rocky soil. Even now, the winter months can be lonely as many islanders retreat to flats in Athens.

Amorgós (ΑΜΟΡΓΟΣ)

> How very much I loved you only I know
> I who once touched you with the eyes of the Pleiades,
> Embraced you with the moon's mane, and we danced on the
> meadows of summer...

Nikos Gatsos, *Amorgos VI*
(trans. by Edmund Keeley and Philip Sherrard)

Easternmost of the Cyclades, Amorgós is also one of the most dramatically rugged islands in the archipelago. On the south coast cliffs plunge vertically into the sea, and until 1995 crossing the island from north to south by road was so bone-rattling that most people preferred to get about by caique. Long, narrow, and mountainous, it's virtually two islands, with the main port of Katápola in the southwest almost a stranger to Aegiáli in the northeast. For years an island of political exile, Amorgós gradually became a destination for the adventurous, then whoosh!—suddenly travellers arrived en masse seeking the quiet Cycladic life of their dreams, swooping off the ferries until there were people camping out in the streets. There still aren't enough rooms to accommodate everyone in high season, so if you come in August without a reservation be prepared to sleep under the stars.

History

Both Amorgós and its neighbouring islet Kéros were inhabited as far back as 3300 BC. In 1885 the German archaeologist Dummler uncovered 11 ancient cemeteries, producing many fine ceramics and marbles now to be seen in the museums of Oxford and Copenhagen; the artefacts pointed to Bronze Age trade with Mílos and Egypt. Under the Ionians, a commonwealth of three ancient independent cities shared Amorgós, each minting its own coins and worshipping Dionysos and Athena: Kástri (modern Arkesíni) was settled by Naxians, Minoa by Samians, and Aegiáli by Milians. The island was perhaps best known for its lingerie, the kind sold nowadays by Ann Summers: chitons of transparent silk, dyed red from a lichen that still grows on the island, and very much in demand among the ancient Athenian and Corinthian courtesan set.

After Alexander the Great, Amorgós like most of the Cyclades came under the rule of his general, Ptolemy of Egypt, who made it a centre of worship of the Alexandrian gods Serapis and Isis. The Romans were the first to use the island as a place of exile, beginning a downhill trend which continued as Goths, Vandals and Slavs savaged and ravaged it during the Byzantine period. One bright moment in this dark history came during the War of the Iconoclasts, when a miraculous icon sailed to Amorgós, set adrift, according to tradition, by a pious lady from Constantinople. As the icon showed a distinct preference for staying by the cliffs on Amorgós' south coast, Emperor Alexis Comnenus founded the Chozoviótissa monastery there in 1088.

In 1209 the Duke of Náxos, Marco Sanudo gave the island to the Gizzi brothers of noble Venetian stock, who built the town castle and went on to acquire a reputation as the worst pirates in the Cyclades. Mostly ignored under the Turkish occupation, Amorgós prospered in the 17th century from the export of exquisite embroideries made by the women, some of which are now in the Victoria and Albert Museum in London. So many of these extraordinary pieces were sold that War of Independence hero General Makriyiánnis threatened to declare war on Amorgós should the island send any more abroad. Rather than fight Makriyiánnis,

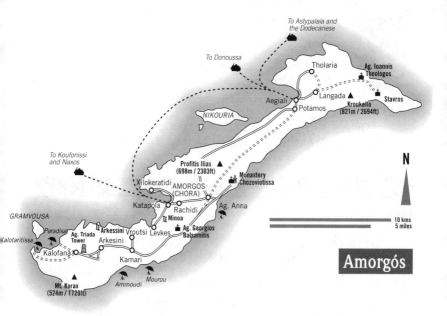

the island's women just stopped making them, although occasionally you can spot older women wearing fine, translucent scarves that suggest the art was never totally forgotten.

The island resumed its sad role as a place of exile for political prisoners during the sixties under the colonels' junta. The filming here of Luc Besson's cult 1988 movie *Le Grand Bleu* attracts trendy tourists, especially the French, keen to see the wreck of the *Olympia* to the west of the island which figured largely in the film.

Amorgós ☎ (0285–)   **Getting There and Around**

By sea: most **ferries and hydrofoils** call at both Katápola and Aegiáli, but check. Daily links in summer with Náxos, Koufoníssi, Schinoússa and Heráklia; 5 times a week to Donoússa, Piraeus, Náxos, Páros, Sýros, Tínos, Mýkonos; twice a week with Astypálaia, Santoríni, and Rafína via Ándros. **Port authority**: Katápola, ☎ 71 259. Aegiáli, ☎ 73 032.

By road: frequent **bus service** from Katápola to the Chóra (Amorgós town) and Aegiáli; others via Chóra to the Chozioviótissa Monastery, Ag. Ánna and Paradísi beaches, and to Langáda and Thólaria from Aegiáli. A summer bus runs from Katápola to Kalotaritissa beach. There is also an ancient **taxi** in Katápola; call ☎ 71 255.

Information office on the quay in Katápola, ℭ (0285) 71 278; also regular police, ℭ 71 210. Naomi at the Aegialis Tourist Information bureau, ℭ 73 394, is also very helpful.

Festivals

1 July, Thólaria; **26 July**, Ag. Paraskeví at Arkesíni; **15 August** at Langáda; **29 August**, Vroutsí; and **21 November** at the Chozoviótissa Monastery.

Middle Amorgós: Katápola and Chóra

Katápola (ΚΑΤΑΠΟΛΑ) sits on a pretty, sheltered horseshoe bay looking out towards the island of Kéros. It has everything you need, including a beach, which is a bit grotty but beloved of the local ducks. The harbour actually links two other villages—**Rachídi** on the hillside in the middle and **Xýlokeratídi**, the fishing port at the northern end. The whole is a bustling, workaday and very Greek port with smallholders selling produce from their trucks and villagers sending parcels via the bus to families in the Chóra. From Katápola you can walk up the hill Mudulias to the ancient city of **Minoa**, where walls, bits of the acropolis, a gymnasium and a few remains of a temple to Apollo can still be seen; the name suggests it may have begun as a colony of Crete. Amorgós has yielded up many treasures: the largest Cycladic figurine in the National Archaeological Museum in Athens was unearthed near Katápola. Beyond Minoa is the little village of Léfkes, from where you can visit **Ag. Geórgios Balsamítis** (St George of the balsam), with good frescoes, built on the site of an ancient 'aquatic' oracle where people came to have their fortunes told by signs on the surface of a sacred spring. There's an old Venetian towerhouse and watermill nearby.

The island capital, **Amorgós Town**, or **Chóra**, is a typical white Cycladic town, perched more than 400m above sea level, with a neat spinal ridge of decapitated windmills—each family had its own—which once laboured with the winds that rose up the dizzying precipices from the sea. It has a perfect, plane-shaded *plateía*, lanes all painted with big flowers and hearts and abstract patterns, and more churches than houses; especially note the way ancient and Byzantine inscriptions and reliefs are incorporated over the doors. One, with three vaulted aisles, melts like a meringue into the wall behind it; another, **Ag. Iríni**, only slightly larger than a phone box, is the smallest church in Greece. There's also a tiny **archaeological museum**, but it's rarely open. Steps lead up a huge rocky thumb rising out of the centre of town to **Apáno Kástro,** the well-preserved Venetian fortress built by Geremia Gizzi in 1290 (get the key before you go). From Chóra, it's an easy hour's walk down to Katápola, partly following the path; the views as you descend are especially dramatic around sunset.

The Monastery of Chozoviótissa

Open 8–2 and 5–8; donation; strict dress code, although long gowns are available if you fail to meet it.

A road has been built to the island's most astonishing sight, the spectacular **Monastery of Chozoviótissa**, one of the most astonishing buildings in the whole of Greece; a rubbly *kalderími* path goes there from the helipad in Chóra, zig-zagging down the magnificent natural amphitheatre. Even if you take the bus, be prepared for a 20-minute walk up. Built high above the sea into sheer 600ft orange cliffs, the monastery resembles a stark white fort embedded in the living rock, supported by two enormous buttresses. Within are some 50 rooms, two churches, and a library containing 98 precious manuscripts, although these are only visible by special request. The monastery was founded *c.* 800 by monks from Hozova in Asia Minor, fleeing the Iconoclasm with their miraculous icon painted by St Luke. They were guided to the site by a mysterious spear stuck in the cliff that finally fell off a few years back, not unlike Roland's sword, still embedded in the cliff in Rocamadour, France. Rebuilt in 1088, the monastery had 100 monks by the 17th century. It now gets by with three. Below the bus continues down to the pebble beaches at **Ag. Ánna**. The series of coves lead to a larger bay, popular with nudists, a trifle sacrilegious given the neighbours.

The South: Káto Meriá

The paved road and occasional buses continue south into the least visited and most traditional part of Amorgós: the fief of ancient Arkesini, better known these days as Káto Meriá. The landscape is dotted with curious old churches, sometimes three or four linked together. Extensive tombs, walls, a subterranean aqueduct, and houses of ancient **Arkesini** are near the mountain village of **Vroútsi**. The easiest way to get there is to get off the bus at **Kamári**—there's a taverna—and head north. A well-preserved 4th-century BC Hellenistic tower, the **Pírgos Ag. Triáda**, is near modern Arkesíni, another mountain village. **Kalofana** is the most remote of all, but near several quiet beaches: **Paradísa** and **Kalotaritissa** on the west coast are especially delightful; **Moúros** and **Ammoúdi** on the south coast is also popular.

Aegiáli

Small, charming **Aegiáli** (ΑΙΓΙΑΛΗ), also known as **Ormós Aegiáli**, is Amorgós' northern port and main resort, thanks to the island's one genuine sandy beach and its striking views over the great granite lump, the islet **Nikouriá**, once a leper colony. You can follow the path over the headlands to a series of isolated sand or shingle coves, bathing costumes optional, or take one of several boat excursions to quieter beaches; the Amorgos Diving Centre offers lessons for those in search of Le Grand Bleu.

From Aegiáli you can take in the scant remains of ancient Aegiáli or take the bus to the pretty hill villages of **Tholária**, named for its vaulted tholos tombs from the Roman period, and **Langáda**, one of the island's prettiest villages, under a rocky thumb similar to Chóra. Both have rooms and tavernas. A circular walk along the herb-scented hill ridge links them and the port; the section from Langáda's church of the Panagía to Tholária poignantly passes through 'the valley of the old, useless, doomed donkeys' and takes about an hour and a half. From Langáda another path leads up to the decapitated windmills, by way of a frescoed cave church, **Yero Stavros**; another path leads out east in about an hour to frescoed **Ag. Ioannis Theológos**, an 8th-century monastery, recently restored; one window is said to be a replica of a window in Hagia Sophia in Istanbul. The path continues to another church, **Stávros**, and down to an abandoned bauxite mine.

Amorgós ✉ *84008,* ✆ *(0285–)*   ***Where to Stay and Eating Out***

Katápola

The new **Ag. Georgios**, ✆ 71 228, ✆ 71 147 (*C; mod*) is the most comfortable hotel, while the **Minoa**, set back from the square, ✆ 71 480, ✆ 71 003 (*C; mod*), is more traditional, but might be noisy. Set around a garden full of geraniums, **Voula Beach Rooms**, ✆ 71 221 (*inexp*), near the port police, all have en suite baths. The basic but friendly **Amorgos**, ✆ 71 214 (*mod–inexp*) is handy for the ferry; **Anna**, ✆ 71 218, ✆ 71 084 (*inexp*), with its rose-covered trellis, offers rooms, studios, and breakfasts set back a bit from the waterfront. Quiet **Villa Catapoliana**, ✆ 71 064 (*mod–inexp*) has nice rooms with fridges set in a courtyard, around a small archaeological dig, and a roof garden with views. Towards Xylokeratídi, **Maroúsa Studios**, ✆ 71 038, ✆ 71 883 (*mod*) are quiet and set back in a garden 50 yards from the sea. **Katapola Camping**, ✆ 71 257, is by the beach and has a pleasant café.

Vitzentos, ✆ 71 518, is a deservedly popular seafront taverna in Xylokeratídi, where arriving late could mean missing the day's speciality. Try the kid and potato casserole (*patatáto*, the island's speciality), or stuffed aubergines with tomatoes, mushrooms, parsley and onion. **Taverna Minos**, at the quieter south end of the waterfront, is an old-fashioned place with good home-cooking; try the tuna *souvláki* or rabbit *stifado*.

Psaropoula is an amiable *psarotavérna* where you choose your fish from wooden trays before it's hurled on to the barbecue. Tourists flock to **Mourayio** but the locals hang out at **Kamari**, further along the quay. Along the front at Xýlokeratídi the cocktail bar **Le Grand Bleu** is stylish and popular for aperitifs and nightcaps with screenings of the Luc Besson film. The **Moon Bar** gets packed after dinner but it's a pleasant place to linger over a pricey beer or cocktail and listen to anything from REM to The Doors.

Chóra

Just outside the village, **Pension Chora**, ✆ 71 110 (*mod*) is comfortable with a minibus pick-up service; **Panorama** at the beginning of the village is small and OK, but no phone and grumpy owners, while the **Loudaros** family's rooms, ✆ 71 216/541 (*mod*) are in a pretty house with a walled courtyard. Tiny **Kastanis** is a good, inexpensive and very Greek taverna; **Liotrivi**, ✆ 71 700 on the edge of town with a roof gardens has more elaborate dishes such as *kalogíros* (aubergine with veal, feta and tomatoes), *exichiko* (lamb and vegetables in a pastry) and baked vegetarian *briams*. The **Vegera Café** serves the likes of carrot cake and milkshakes to go with its views. **Café Loza** is an authentic *ouzerie*. **To Plateoki** in the upper square is always popular with the café crowd in the late afternoon. Night owls hang out until 4am at **Lithos**, a little music bar in the centre.

Aegiáli/Langáda/Tholária

Lakki, ✆ 73 253, ✉ 73 244 (*B; mod*), is set back from the beach in lovely gardens with a tree house for kids. Cycladic-style, immaculate self-contained rooms, excellent food served outdoors from their taverna. Isolated, across the harbour, the **Aegialis**, ✆ 73 393, ✉ 73 395 (*B; mod*) is a smart hotel complex with pool and taverna, the trendy nightclub Corte, a great sea view from the veranda and a minibus service. **Mike**, ✆ 73 208, ✉ 73 633 (*C; mod*), the port's first hotel, has recently had a facelift. **Akrogiali**, ✆ 72 208 has rooms with en suite baths (*mod–inexp*) or there's **Camping Amorgos**, ✆ 73 500, in a field off the Tholária road, with decent facilities and a café. The favourite grazing ground is **To Limani**, known to all as **Katerina's**, packed out for its great food, wine from the barrel and mellow sounds. The **Korali** has tasty fish and the best sunset views. **Passepartout** and the **Selini Bar** are popular after-dinner hangouts, and there are two discos by the beach, **Disco the Que** and **Delear**.

Up in Langáda, **Nikos**, ✆ 73 310 (*inexp*) has clean, comfortable rooms and bougainvillea cascading over the terrace; it specializes in roast kid and baked aubergines; **Pension Artemis**, ✆/✉ 73 315 (*inexp*) and the

Taverna Loza, run by the kind Dimitri Dendrinos, are both simple and pleasant; **Yianni Sinonies** is also good. In Tholária, the **Vigla**, ✆ 73 288, @ 73 332 (*B; mod*) has views, bar and restaurant. There are also rooms over the friendly and excellent fish taverna **Adelfi Vekri**, ✆ 73 345/254 (*mod–inexp*). The **Panorama** has wonderful views; **Tholaria** fills up fast thanks to its good food and an exuberant atmosphere.

Between Amorgós and Náxos: the Back Islands

Between Amorgós and Náxos lie a bevy of tiny islands in a sparkling sea known as the Back Islands because they're in the back of beyond—Schinoússa, Koufoníssi, Donoússa and Heráklia (or Iráklia) are the four inhabited ones. Once a hide-out for pirates, and for partisans in the last war, all are now firmly on the holiday map. All now have post offices to change money, and most have tourist agencies as well. The islands are quiet in low season, with sandy beaches and wonderful walking country. Although Koufoníssi and Heráklia have geared up for an increase in guests, Donoússa can't cope with the seasonal invasion; fresh produce can be scarce.

Getting There

By sea: the islands are served daily in summer by the old rust bucket *Skopelitis*, which rolls its way between Náxos and Amorgós, and the occasional **ferry** from Piraeus. There are two ferries a week via Sýros, Páros and Náxos, Tínos and Mýkonos. The **hydrofoil** from Amorgós also calls in at the islands apart from Donoússa.

Koufoníssi (ΚΟΥΦΟΝΗΣΙ)

Koufoníssi is tiny and flat—you can walk around it in about three hours—and it has a thriving fishing fleet and exerts such a compelling charm on its visitors that many become addicts and can't stay away. Once the hideaway of intrepid independent travellers, it now gets jammed in July and August with trendy Athenians and Italians into spear-fishing and perfecting their tans. The *meltémi* rages at exactly the same time, and has been known to launch tents into space from the free but unsheltered campsite by Fínikas Beach. The village, on a low hill above the quay, has its back to the sea. Life centres on the cobbled main street; in summer it turns into a big party and fashion parade with batik-clad island-hoppers carousing at the tables outside every taverna and *ouzerie*. Koufoníssi has gorgeous beaches, some with shade, tucked under golden rocks eroded into bulging *mille feuille* pastries. The first, **Fínikas**, east of the village, is lined with sleeping bags in high season. Over a rocky spit there are two more lovely beaches, **Charakópou** and **Porí**. There are daily excursions in season on the caique *Prásinos* to **Káto Koufoníssi**, the island just opposite, for skinny-dipping, and the occasional excursion to the beaches on the abandoned island of **Kéros**. This has the ruins of a Neolithic-Bronze Age settlement at **Daskálio** on the west coast, where the 'Treasure of Keros' was unearthed in the 1950s and 60s, including a magnificent selection of fine Cycladic figurines (including the famous 'Harpist' in the Archaeology Museum in Athens). There's also an abandoned medieval settlement in the north.

Koufonísssi ℭ *(0285–)* **Tourist Information**

The **Prassinos agency** next door to the post office, ℭ 71 438, changes money; the owner sells ferry tickets on the quay and runs excursions. **Port authority**: ℭ 71 735.

Koufoníssi ✉ *84300,* ℭ *(0285–)* **Where to Stay**

New pensions and studios are sprouting up like crazy, and most offer generous off-season discounts. The neo-Cycladic **Keros Studios**, ℭ 71 600 (*exp in season*), with a garden and bar by the sea, is open all year; rooms have telephones. **Christina's House**, ℭ 71 735, is similar but on a more modest scale (*mod*). **Villa Ostria**, at Ag. Geórgiou, ℭ/℗ 71 671 (*exp*) has a pretty veranda over the sea and 10 comfortable rooms, with phones, fridges and music.

Petros Club, ℭ 71 728 (*mod*), is near the sea, and has a large garden and restaurant, mini bars in each room. *Open July–Sept only.* **Hondros Kavos**, ℭ 71 707 and **E. N. Simos**, ℭ 71 445, are both brand new (*mod*). **Finikas**, ℭ 71 368 (*C; mod*) has self-contained double rooms in a cluster of white buildings near Fínikas beach; the owner meets ferries. **Katerina**, ℭ 71 455 (*mod*), with ebullient landlady, is just up the hill from the port. There's a free campsite to the east of the port behind Fínikas beach, with two areas each fronted by tavernas.

Koufoníssi ℭ *(0285–)* **Eating Out**

Taverna Melissa on the main street is great value, with Greek favourites served on the terrace; **Afroessa** is also popular, as is **Lefteris** on the front. In the village the **Ouzerie** serves octopus, *kalamári* and shrimps from an outside brazier. *Evenings only.* **The Mill**, an old windmill atop the village converted into a bar, is a great place to watch the sun set and, in the summer, nights in the bars are rarely dull.

Schinoússa (ΣΧΟΙΝΟΥΣΣΑ)

Schinoússa is scenically less attractive than the other small islands, but it's still very Greek and charming, if not entirely undiscovered. There are only 85 inhabitants in winter, increasing in summer to around 200, most of them farmers trying to make ends meet. The tiny port of **Myrsíni**, where the ferries dock, has a good taverna and rooms, but the main settlement is the **Chóra**, also known as **Panagía**, less than a mile up the hill. You can take the old cobbled mule track for a short-cut.

Chóra has rooms to rent and village life goes on regardless of tourists. From there a steep track runs down to the grey sand beach at **Tsigoúra**, fringed by tamarisk trees, with a rather expensive taverna and disco. There are about seventeen beaches on the island, many bleak and littered by the wind, but **Psilí Ámmos** is worth the 45-minute walk from Chóra across the island via the ghost hamlet of **Messariá**. A rough cobbled track leads to the duny sands with crystalline turquoise waters; in summer it's a favourite unofficial camping spot. Schinoússa is blessed with fresh springs, and a species of mastic bush grows on its relatively flat terrain.

Tourist Information

The **Gripsos Tourist Center** agency in Chóra, ✆ (0285) 71 175, 🖷 71 176, at the top of the path from Myrsíni, run from a mini-market, arranges accommodation, ferry tickets and round-island trips. **Port authority:** ✆ 22 300.

Schinoússa ✆ (0285–)   ### Where to Stay and Eating Out

Room owners often meet the ferries. In the Chóra, **Anesi** ✆ 71 180 (*mod*) is on the main street with wonderful views. **Provaloma**, ✆ 71 936, just outside Chóra, offers more fine views, minibus service, rooms with bath, and a good taverna, with food cooked in an old-fashioned stone oven.

Other rooms to let are over the **Panorama Taverna**, which also supplies basic home cooking, great views to Tsigoúra, and locals playing backgammon.

To Kentro general store cum *kafeneíon* serves beer, snacks and pungent home-made cheese; **Schinoussa** does the usual Greek fare and pizzas. In Myrsíni the **Taverna Myrsini**, ✆ 71 154, is deceptive. Its spartan kitchen conjures up delicious seafood in the evenings and it doubles as a left-luggage store by day. There are simple rooms above **Snack Bar**, ✆ 71 159, which serves everything from breakfast to burgers, octopus and ouzo under its vine-clad trellis.

Donoússa (ΔΟΝΟΥΣΑ)

Donoússa, due east of Náxos, and northernmost of the chain, is more remote than the others and has only half as many ferry links, although there are two private caiques, Elias Skolitis, © (0285) 51 571 and Kostas Markoulis, © 51 569, which provide services to Náxos, Amorgós and Koufoníssi as well as excursions. Larger and more mountainous than Schinoússa and Koufoníssi, it's a good place for walkers and hermits; most of the tourists so far are German.

Donoússa (or Stávros), the port and village, has rooms to let, tavernas and a shop; the sandy beach **Kédros** is a 15-minute walk away. Resources are stretched with the influx of tourists in high season. There's a summer-only bakery, but food and water can get scarce. A Geometric-era settlement (900–700 BC) was excavated by Vathí Limenarí, but most of its visitors come for its fine sandy beaches, at **Livádi** and **Fýkio**, reached in two hours by foot via the fertile hamlets of **Charavgí** and **Mersíni** (or 20 minutes by caique); another beach, **Kalotarítissa**, is an hour's walk to the north.

Heráklia (ΗΡΑΚΛΕΙΑ)

Heráklia, or Iráklia, the most westernly and the largest of the Back Islands, is only an hour's ferry hop from Náxos, but even in mid-August it remains quiet and friendly. Unusually for the Cyclades, it's a good time to visit and join in the celebrations for the Festival of the Panagía on August 15, with three days of non-stop eating, drinking and dancing. There are rooms to let in the attractive port, **Ag. Geórgios**, set in a crook in the hills, with a small tamarisk-lined beach and a little fishing fleet. From here it's a 20-minute walk to the large sandy beach at **Livádi**, popular with Greek families and campers.

The old Chóra, **Panagía**, named after its main church, is about an hour's walk into the hills, but you might hitch a lift with the baker. It's sleepy and primitive but pretty, and it's unlikely you'll find anywhere to stay. There is, however, an excellent **bakery**—the baker picks wild sesame seeds for his bread on his journey from the port. From Panagía a path leads to sandy **Alimniás Beach.** Another excursion is the three-hour walk along the mule path southwest from Ag. Geórgios to the large stalactite cave of **Ag. Ioánnis**, overlooking Vourkaria Bay, with two chambers over 240ft long (bring a flashlight and non-slip shoes); the chapel at the entrance sees a huge *panegýri* on 28 August.

Gavalos Tours, ℭ/✆ 71561 may help you find a room. In
Ag. Geórgios there are basic, inexpensive rooms above
Melissa, ℭ 71 539/561, a taverna, *kafeneíon* and general
store with a good budget menu; there are also rooms
above the nameless waterside taverna, ℭ 71 488.
Dimitris Gavalas is the best eating place with Greek

dishes, sometimes pizza, served beneath the pine tree. Most of the island's
tourist infrastructure is at Livádi: **Zografos**, 700m back, ℭ 71 578 (*mod*)
has rooms with verandas, baths, fridges and a communal barbecue to grill
your own fish. **Mary**, ℭ 71 485 has rooms and apartments and meets ferries. **Livadi,** on the beach, serves good food and plays old *rembétika* songs
and has rooms to let (*inexp*); the owner Geórgios organizes boat trips to
Alimniás Beach and meets the ferries with his truck.

Anáfi (ΑΝΑΦΗ)

Anáfi, the most southerly of the Cyclades, looks like a tadpole with a tail swollen
like the Rock of Gibraltar. But it's friendly and unpretentious, the ideal place for
peace and solitude. If the crowds and noise seem too thick elsewhere, Anáfi may be
the antidote: the islanders go about their lives as they always have, with few concessions to tourism. But be warned: if the weather breaks, ferries may not dock and
you could get marooned, so allow plenty of time to get back. Little contact with the
outside world means that old customs have been preserved; some scholars have
found in the Anáfiots' songs and festivals traces of the ancient worship of Apollo.

The Island of Over-sexed Partridges

Apollo always had a particularly strong cult on Anáfi. Myth has it that
Jason and the Argonauts were sailing from Crete after killing the
bronze giant Talus with the help of Medea when a violent storm
kicked up. At Apollo's command, an island—Anáfi—rose from the
waves to shelter them. Anáfi was the island the most closely associated with partridges (one of Talus' other names was Perdix,
'partridge'), a bird much noted even back then for its lascivious
behaviour; Aristotle and Pliny wrote that a hen partridge merely had
to hear or smell a cock partridge to become impregnated, and further noted
that if the females were out of commission on their nests, the males practised
sodomy to relieve their sexual feelings. Partridges become so obsessed during
their ritual mating dances that they don't notice if someone comes up and

kills a few of the dancers next to them. The ancient Greeks used this knowledge to catch them, luring them into traps with a decoy—a lusty male partridge they had captured and hobbled so it couldn't fly away. The ideas of a ritual dance and death lure, of a hobbled male (Medea killed Talus by pulling the plug from his heel) and 'virgin' births are all potent images in the mythopoeic mind, and it has been suggested that the Minoan bull cult on Crete supplanted a partridge cult, that the spiral dancing at Knossós began as a ritual partridge dance, and that the Minotaur was the original decoy to lure in sacrificial victims. On Anáfi, according to the descriptions that have come down to us, the rites of Apollo (who after all began his career c. 1200 BC as a mouse demon) were those of Radiant Apollo, the Sun God, but infused with a good deal of old-fashioned partridge eroticism.

History

Anáfi's history isn't as exciting as its mythology, although in the 15th century BC it gained a certain stature in the form of volcanic rock, 5m thick in some places, carried to the island by wind and tidal wave after the explosion of Santoríni. The twelfth Duke of Náxos, Giacomo Crispi, gave Anáfi to his brother who built a castle, but his fortification had little effect when Barbarossa turned up in 1537 and enslaved the entire population. Anáfi remained deserted for a long time after that. When King Otho arrived in Athens, he asked for the best builders in Greece to

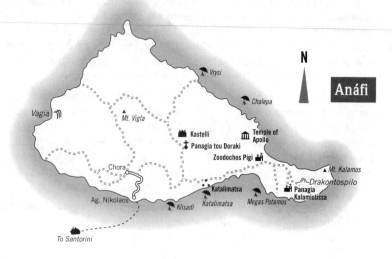

make him a place, and he was sent a contingent of Anafiots, who built themselves the delightful neighbourhood Anafiótika at the foot of the Acropolis, taking advantage of the law that stated that if you could erect four walls and a roof by sunrise, the place was yours.

Anáfi © (0286–)

Getting There

By sea: ferries twice a week connecting with Piraeus, Santoríni, Íos, Náxos and Páros, once a week with Amorgós and Sýros; occasional catamaran from other Cyclades islands and Piraeus. **Port authority**: © 61 216.

Tourist Information

None, but the tourist agency **Protoapa** may help, © (0286) 61 290.

Festivals

8 September, Panagía at the monastery, known for its authentic folk-dances.

Around the Island

The island's one village, quiet, laid-back **Chóra** (pop. 260), an amphitheatre of white domed houses and windmills with views all around, is a short but steep walk up from the landing, **Ag. Nikólaos**, although the new road and a bus makes life considerably easier. Guglielmo Crispi's **Kástro** is to the north of the village and half-ruined; a path leads up to its rocky height. There are attractive **beaches** along the coast around Ag. Nikólaos, from **Klisídi** east of the port, with a popular snack bar, to a range of bays signposted from the Chóra road, dotted here and there with the tents of freelance campers. The only spring is at **Vagia**, on the west coast.

The favourite path on Anáfi runs east of Chóra to **Kastélli** (about two hours), site of the ancient town and the country chapel **Panagía tou Doráki**, decorated with a pair of Roman sarcophagi and the trunk of a statue. Another hour's walking from Kastélli, past the ruined hamlet of **Katalimátsa**, will bring you to the summit of the tremendous tadpole-tail, **Mount Kálamos.** Along the way, huge square blocks mark the temple of Apollo Aiglitos, dedicated by the grateful Jason. Other blocks went into the construction of the nearby **Monastery of Zoodóchos Pigí**.

On top of Kálamos, the pretty 16th-century **Monastery of Panagía Kalamiótissa** (450m over the sea) is Anáfi's most important, built where an icon of the Virgin was found hanging on a cane; it enjoys tremendous views, especially sunrises (bring

supplies and a sleeping bag). Nearby you can also poke around in an old dragon's lair, the **Drakontóspilo**, with stalactites and stalagmites.

Anáfi ✉ *84009,* ☎ *(0286–)*   **Where to Stay**

Room-owners travel down from Chóra by bus to meet ferries. Otherwise, your classiest bet is **Villa Apollon**, above Klisídi beach, ☎ 61 348, ▦ 61 287 (*mod; open May–Oct, out of season ring Athens (01) 993 6150*) with a garden, and fridges in each room. **Ta Plagia**, ☎ 61308, Athens (01) 412 7113 up by Chóra (*inexp*) has similar, and a restaurant (*open May–Sept*), or try **Anatoli** rooms in Chóra, ☎ 61 279.

Anáfi ☎ *(0286–)*   **Eating Out**

Because everything has to be imported, prices are a bit high. In the Chóra **To Steki** is cheap and cheerful, **Alexandra's** more upmarket. **Kyriakos** is another option for dinner. In Ag. Nikólaos try **Roussos**.

Ándros (ΑΝΔΡΟΣ)

> *The sea is my mother,*
> *My sister is the wave*
> *and my lovers are the little fishes by the shore*
>
>   an old song from Ándros

Lush and green on one side, scorched and barren on the other, split-personality Ándros is the northernmost and second-largest of the Cyclades. It's long been a haunt for wealthy Athenian shipping magnates who descend for long stays in high summer and breed horses on their spectacular country estates in the wooded hills. Package holidaymakers, mainly from the UK, Germany and Scandinavia, are more recent arrivals on the scene. And as it's easy to reach from Rafína, Ándros is also a popular weekend playground for trendy young Athenians who patronize the island's chic cocktail bars, discos and the odd toga party.

In the south only the narrowest of straits separates Ándros from Tínos, while in the barren north the blustery Cavo d'Oro Channel, long dreaded by sailors, divides the island from Évia. However, the same irksome wind also makes Ándros, and especially its capital, one of the coolest spots in the Aegean in July and August. Crossed by four parallel mountain ridges, it has green valleys; water gushes from the marble fountains and mossy springs of the villages; flowers, orchards and forests cover the south, and fields are divided by dry stone walls, *xerolithiés*, split from the local schist, with flat upright pieces of slate at intervals. Ándros is a prosperous island, neat, well-ordered, adorned with white dovecotes first built by the Venetians and famed for its captains and shipowners; many from elsewhere come here to retire.

History

Originally known as Hydroussa ('watery'), the island is thought to derive its name from the Phoenician Arados, or from Andrea, the general sent by Rhadamanthys of Crete to govern the island. In 1000 BC Ionians colonized Ándros, leading to its early cultural bloom in the Archaic period. Dionysos was the most popular god worshipped at the pantheon of Palaiopolis, the leading city at the time, and a certain temple of his had the remarkable talent of turning the water running out of a spring into wine during the five-day festival of the Dionysia in January.

For most of the rest of its history, Ándros has been the square peg in a round archipelago. After the Athenian victory at Salamis, Themistocles fined Ándros for supporting Xerxes. The Andrians refused to pay up, and Themistocles besieged the island, but was unsuccessful and had to return home empty-handed. Although the islanders later assisted the Greeks at Plateía, Athens continued to hold a grudge against Ándros, and in 448 BC Pericles divided the island between Athenian colonists, who taxed the inhabitants heavily. In response, the Andrians abetted Athens' enemies whenever they could: when the Peloponnesian War broke out, they withdrew from the Delian league and sided with Sparta, supporting those neurotic reactionaries throughout the war, in spite of another Athenian siege led by Alcibiades and Konon. Spartan oppression, however, proved just as awful as Athenian oppression, and things were no better during the succession of Hellenistic rulers. For resisting their conquest, the Romans banished the entire population to Boetia, and gave Ándros to Attalos I, King of Pergamon. When permitted to return, the inhabitants found their homes sacked and pillaged. Byzantium proved a blessing compared with the past: in the 5th century Ándros maintained a Neoplatonic philosophy academy, where Proclos and Michael Psellos taught, and in the 11th it became an important exporter of silk fabrics embroidered with gold, an industry that lasted into the 18th century.

In the Venetian land-grab after the Fourth Crusade, Marino Dandolo, a nephew of Doge Enrico Dandolo, took Ándros. If he was a benign absentee landlord, later Venetian rulers, the Somaripas, were nasty and incompetent and Barbarossa took the island without a fight in the 1530s. Apart from collecting taxes, the Turks left it to its own devices, and 10,000 Albanian refugees, many from nearby Kárystos (Évia) settled on Ándros. In 1821 Ándros' famous son, the philosopher Theóphilos Kaíris, declared the revolution at the cathedral of Ándros, and the island contributed large sums of money, ships, and weapons to the struggle. Thanks to the astuteness of its seamen and captains, Ándros' merchant fleet was one of the few in the Cyclades to grow in the 19th century; in the 1880s they purchased steamships that ranged across the Mediterranean and up the Danube, and not long after to North America;

N

Ándros

5km
3 miles

by 1914 one out of every ten Greek merchant vessels was from Ándros, and between the two world wars, the number rose to one out of five. In 1943 the Germans bombed the island for two days when the Italians refused to surrender.

Ándros © (0282–)   ***Getting There and Around***

By sea: daily **ferry, catamaran,** and **hydrofoil** connections with Rafína, Tínos and Mýkonos, less often with Sýros, Páros, Náxos, Amorgós, Íos, and Karystos (Évia). **Port authority:** © 71 213.

By road: buses (© 22 316) run from Chóra to Batsí, Gávrion, Apoíkia, Strapouriés, Steniés, and Kórthi; buses for Batsí,

Chóra and Kórthi leave from near the dock at Gávrion, linking with the ferries. **Cars** and **bikes** are widely available for rent. **Taxis**: in Gávrion, ✆ 71 561, in Batsí: ✆ 41 081.

Ándros ✆ *(0282–)*   **Tourist Information**

There is a sporadically open **tourist office** in a converted dovecote in Gávrion, ✆ 71 785. The Dolphin Hellas travel office in Batsí is very helpful, ✆ 41 185; so is Batis Travel in Gávrion, ✆ 71 040, 🖷 71 165.

Festivals

Theoskepastí, **15 days before Easter**, and Análipsis, **19 June** (approx.) both at Ándros Town; **15 August**, at Kórthinon; **23 August**, at Ménites.

Gávrion and the West Coast

All ferries dock at the main port, **Gávrion** (ΓΑΒΡΙΟ) on the northwest coast of Ándros. Long one of the dustiest dumps on the islands, it is in the throes of a total makeover, with fancy street lights, tiled pavements, flower beds and the works to go with its beach, bars and tavernas. From Gávrion, it's a 40-minute or so walk east up the **Pyrgós Ag. Pétros**, the best-preserved ancient monument on Ándros. Dating from the Hellenistic era, this mysterious tower stands some 70ft high—the upper storeys were reached by ladder—and its inner hall is still crowned by a corbelled dome. The landscape around here seems to squirm with stone walls, or *xerolithiés*, resembling huge, arched caterpillars. There are good beaches north of Gávrion: **Ormos Felós** is the best but Athenians are developing the coastline with villas. **Amólochos**, on the road crossing the island to the remote beach at Vitáli Bay, is an isolated mountain village famous locally for its beauty.

Kybí, south of Gávrion, is another fine sandy beach, near the junction for the 14th-century convent of **Zoodóchos Pigí**, 'Spring of Life', which has icons from that century onwards. A handful of nuns run a weaving factory (*open until noon*). Further down the coast, **Batsí** (ΜΠΑΤΣΙ), built around a sweeping sandy bay, is Ándros' biggest resort, with a little fishing harbour and a cute, rather artificial charm oozing from its maze of narrow lanes up the white steps. The BBC TV series *Greek Language and People* put it on the map, and it's been very popular with UK package companies ever since. The tree-fringed town beach gets busy with families, so head along the coastal track to **Delavóyas Beach** for an all-over tan. From Batsí a road ascends to shady well-watered **Arnás**, a garden village on the northern slopes of Ándros' highest peak, Mount Pétalo (994m).

Palaiópolis, 9km down the coast, was the original capital of Ándros, founded by the Minoans and inhabited until around 1000 AD when the people moved up to

Messariá. An earthquake in the 4th century AD destroyed part of it, and over the years pirates mopped up the rest. The current edition of Palaiópolis is on top of a steep hill, from where 1039 steps lead down to the ancient site, partly underwater; there are walls and part of the acropolis, and ruins of buildings and temples. The road to Chóra continues through rolling countryside dotted with dovecotes and the ruined stone tower-houses of the Byzantine and Venetian ruling classes.

Ándros Town/Chóra

The capital, **Ándros** (ΑΝΔΡΟΣ) or **Chóra** (ΧΩΡΑ), sits on a long, narrow tongue of land, decorated with the grand neoclassical mansions of the island's wealthy ship-owning families. One of their legacies in Chóra is a rare sense of public spiritedness and tidiness. At the edge of the town, a stone arch is all that survives of the bridge to the Venetian castle, **Mésa Kástro**, built by Marino Dandolo and damaged in the 1943 bombardment by the Germans; the ruins are guarded by the beckoning statue of the **Unknown Sailor** by Michael Tómbros in **Plateía Ríva**. There's a small **museum** dedicated to Ándros' seafaring history, but you may have to ask around for the key. **Káto Kástro**, the maze of streets that forms the medieval city and the mansions of the Ríva district, is wedged between **Parapórti** and **Embórios** bays, with steps down from the central square, **Plateía Kaíri**. These beaches are sandy but often windswept, and holiday bungalows and rooms to let are springing up at Embórios, where the ferries used to dock.

The pedestrianized main street, paved with marble slabs and scented with cheese and custard pies made at the local bakery, is lined with old mansions converted into public offices; post and telephone offices and banks are in the centre of town, and the bus station just a few steps away. A small white church, **Ag. Thalassíni**, guards one end of Embórios harbour from a throne of rock. The cathedral, **Ag. Geórgios**, is built on the ruins of a 17th-century church. A legend is told about a third church, **Theoskepastí**, built in 1555. When the wood for the church's roof arrived in Ándros from Piraeus, the priest found that he couldn't afford the price demanded by the captain of the ship. Angrily, the captain set sail again, only to run into a fierce, boiling tempest. The sailors prayed to the Virgin Mary, promising to bring the wood back to Ándros should she save their lives. Instantly the sea grew calm again, and Theoskepastí, or 'Sheltered by God', was completed without further difficulty. It was dedicated to the Virgin Mary, who apparently is on a hotline to the miracle-working icon inside the church.

Just north of Plateía Kaíris are the museums endowed by Basil and Elise Goulandrís of the ship-owning dynasty. The **Archaeology Museum** (*open Tues–Sun 8.30–3; adm*) houses the outstanding *Hermes Psychopompos*, Conductor of the Dead, a 2nd-century BC copy of a Praxiteles original, discovered by farmers in Palaiópolis. Other exhibits include the *Matron of Herculaneum*, finds from the ancient cities of

Zagora and Palaiópolis, architectural illustrations and pottery collections. The island's other gem, the **Museum of Modern Art**, in Plateía Kaíris (© 22 490, *open Wed–Mon, 10–2 and 6–9*) occupies two buildings, with exhibitions of international modern artists, contemporary Greek artists, and sculptures by Michael Tómbros.

Villages Outside Chóra

Lovely villages surround Chóra: **Steniés**, 6km north, is the most beautiful village on the island, its lanes closed to traffic and heavy with the scent of flowers and blossoms in spring. A few mulberries remain; in the old silk-making days the precious cocoons would be brought into the houses in the winter to keep them warm. The sandy beach, **Gialyá**, is close by, with a good and affordable fish taverna. The famous Sáriza mineral water flows in the hill village of **Apíkia**, above Steniés, where a luxury hotel overlooks the spring; a certain problem with contaminated bottle tops closed down the bottling plant. The village owns the 16th-century monastery **Ag. Nikólaos** to the north.

The main west coast road passes through the fertile **Messariá Valley** with its numerous farming villages. One old custom may still be heard: in the evening after a hard day's work, the patriarch will pipe the family home from the fields. **Messariá** itself has a Byzantine church, **Taxiárchis** built in 1158 by the Emperor Emmanuel Comnenus. Another church, **Ag. Nikólaos**, has an icon made by an 18th-century faith-healing nun from her own hair. Further west, lush, green **Ménites** has springs gushing from marble lion-head fountains, and the church of **Panagías tis Kóumoulous**, the 'Virgin of the Plentiful', which may have been the site of Dionysos' miraculous water-to-wine temple. The village is known for its nightingales and cool, spreading trees, and there's a peaceful taverna overlooking the stream. From there an hour's steep walk takes you to the most important monastery on Ándros, **Panachrándou**. Now home to just three monks, it was founded shortly after Niképhoros Phokás' liberation of Crete in AD 961, and supposedly visited by the emperor himself. Southwest of Messariá, at **Aladinó**, you can visit a stalactite cave called Cháos—bring a light.

The **Bay of Kórthion** (ΟΡΜΟΣ ΚΟΡΘΙ) is 30km southeast of Chóra, at the bottom of a lush valley with a beach and some modest tourist development. To the north of the bay, the ruined Venetian fort is known as the **Castle of the Old Woman**, after a gritty old lady who abhorred the Venetians. She tricked them into letting her inside the fort, and later secretly opened the door to the Turks. Appalled at the subsequent slaughter of the Venetians, the old woman leapt from the castle and landed on a rock now known as '**Tis Grias to Pidema**' or 'Old Lady's Leap'. The inland villages of **Kapariá** and **Aidónia** have the prettiest dovecotes on the island.

On the west coast, **Zagorá** (ΖΑΓΟΡΑ) was inhabited until the 8th century BC, when it boasted a population of 4000; it was solidly defended, for sheer cliffs surrounded it on three sides, while on the fourth the Zagorans built a mighty wall. Within, inhabitants lived in small, flat-roofed houses (some remains still exist) and cultivated the fields outside the wall. Excavated by Australians in the 1960s, finds from Zagorá are now in the island's museum.

Ándros ✆ (0282–)   *Where to Stay and Eating Out*

Like Kéa, Ándros is an island where the tourism infrastructure is geared to long-term stays, and it may well be difficult, especially in the capital, to find a place that will let you stay for only a few nights. If there's a room, owners often meet the ferries.

Gávrion ✉ 84501

Gávrion might be the only place you'll find rooms in high season. The smartest place is **Andros Holiday**, ✆ 71 443, ✉ 71 097 (*B; exp*), on the beach with half-board, swimming pool, tennis, sauna and gym. **Ostria Studios**, ✆ 71 551, ✉ 71 554 (*C; mod*) are upmarket self-catering apartments just out of town; **Galaxias**, on the waterfront ✆ 71 228 (*D; mod–inexp*) also has a good taverna, with house specialities; **Aphrodite**, ✆ 71 209, is nice, too (*mod–inexp*).

Camping Andros, ✆ 71 444, is an attractive site along the Batsí road with a mini-market, swiming pool, outstanding taverna and a van to meet the ferries. Halfway to the camp site, look out for **Karlos**, an excellent restaurant a bit hidden away, where the locals come for traditional dishes and low prices. The **Sunset**, en route to the Andros Holiday Hotel, also has a reputed kitchen where you can try the Ándros speciality, *froutália*, an omelette made with potatoes and local sausage. If you have a car, drive 5 minutes along the Batsí road to **Yiannoulis**, set on a sandy beach, with superb food and low prices.

Batsí ✉ 84503

The refined **Aneroussa**, shaded by banana groves, ✆ 41 044, ✉ 41 444 (*exp–mod, inc. breakfast*) tops the cliff at Apróvato like an iced cake and has private sands next to Delavóyas Beach, popular with nudists. **Chryssi Akti**, ✆ 41 236 (*C; mod*) is OK, on the beach; the smaller **Skouna**, ✆ 41 240 (*C; mod*) is also a good seafront bet; the **Avra**, ✆ 41 216 (*D; inexp*) is the cheapest pension with shared facilities; others are up the steps or out towards the Apróvato neighbourhood. The wide range of eateries do justice to Ándros' old reputation as an island of chefs. **Stamatis** has good food and rooftop views over the harbour. **Takis** is good for fish: take the first steep concrete road on the right as you leave (by the mirror) and at the end of the road is a friendly, inexpensive family-run taverna. The place opposite the Dolphin Hellas agency is excellent, famous for its lamb parcels.

Chóra ✉ 84500

The elegant, long-established **Paradise**, ✆ 22 187, ✉ 22 340 (*B; exp*) is a graceful, neoclassical confection, with a pool and tennis and colour TVs and other luxuries in the air-conditioned rooms; the restaurant serves international and Greek cuisine. The traditional **Aegli**, ✆ 22 303, ✉ 22 159 (*C; mod*), between the two squares, is also air-conditioned. *Open all year.*

Irene's Villas, by the sea, ✆ 23 344 (*exp–mod*) are charming, set in lush flower gardens, and sleep 4–6. *Open all year.* In a garden, **Saint Louis**, ✆/✉ 23 965, has pretty studios with verandas at low prices outside of July and August. Just north in pretty Steniés, **Soula Tzoumeni** rents rooms, ✆ 23 130.

Chóra has two fine restaurants, **Platanos** and **Delfinia**. Also try **Parea** on the main square, with an excellent Greek menu, or follow the locals out to **Achipelagos**, on the edge of town towards Giálya beach, for great traditional food, service and prices.

Apíkia ✉ 84500

The swish **Pigi Sarisa** ✆ 23 799/999, ✉ 22 476 (*B; mod*), almost on top of the famous mineral spring, has lovely views over the Aegean. An all-inclusive holiday complex, it has a pool and games facilities, restaurant and minibus for transfers. *Open all year.* There are also rooms to let in the village.

At Ménites the **Kardyies Restaurant** has tables overlooking the stream and specialities like *froutália* and tomatoes stuffed with chicken.

Kórthion ✉ 84502

Family-run **Korthion**, ✆ 61 218, ✉ 61 118 (*C; mod*) is spotless, right on the sea, and has a restaurant; blue and white **Villa Korthi**, ✆ 61 122, ✉ 62 022 (*mod*) is a pleasant choice, in spitting distance of the sea.

Entertainment and Nightlife

Ándros, especially Batsí, is full of slick cocktail bars, dancing bars and discos which change names from season to season, or there are organized **Greek nights** at three tavernas in Katákilos above Batsí. Batsí also has an open-air **cinema**. In Chóra, nightlife is more Greek-orientated, centring round the bars and clubs.

Folégandros (ΦΟΛΕΓΑΝΔΡΟΣ)

Bleak, arid and mountainous, long an island of exile (Socialist Prime Minister George Papandréou, father of Andreas, was once an unwilling guest), Folégandros is now a popular place to get away from it all by choice. With sheer cliffs and the breathtaking Chóra built to defy pirates, it's one of the most alluring in the Cyclades and the perfect base since 1984 for the Cycladic Centre of Art.

With 600 inhabitants (down from 4000 in the 1940s) Folégandros is one of the smallest islands in Greece with a permanent population, swollen several times over in the summer with Danes, Italians and others seeking genuine island life or partied out by the fleshpots of Íos. In myth, Folegandros was a son of King Minos of Crete, and his legacy on the island can be seen in the labyrinthine paths across the island, laid out to confound invaders. Linguists, however, say the name Folégandros comes from the Phoenician *Phelekguduri*, 'rock-built'; one ancient nickname was Aratos, 'the Iron-bound'. In fact, many of the landscapes look as if they had been whipped to a froth by a furious god, then suddenly petrified, an effect curiously softened by a smattering of churches with breast-shaped domes.

Folégandros ✆ (0286–)   **Getting There and Around**

By sea: 4–5 times a week to Piraeus, Íos, Santoríni and Síkinos; less frequently with Kímolos, Mílos, Sífnos, Sérifos and Kýthnos, Náxos, and Páros. Excursions to Ag. Nikólaos and other beaches and Sikínos. **Port authority**: ✆ 41 249.

By road: the island **buses** link the port Karavostássi to Chóra and meet all the ferries, no matter how late they arrive; another bus goes from Chóra to Angáli and Áno Meriá.

Folégandros ✆ (0286–)   **Tourist Information**

Sottovento Agency, in Chóra, near the Áno Meriá bus, ✆/✉ 41 430, is very helpful and speaks English.

Festivals

At **Easter** an icon is paraded and trips are made in boats around the island; Ag. Panteleímon, **27 July** in Áno Meriá; **15 August** at Panagía.

Around Folégandros

Boats land at **Karavostássi**, the tiny harbour on the east coast, with a tree-fringed pebbly beach, restaurants and rooms to rent. Shady **Livádi** beach is a 15-minute walk or short drive from the port, while **Katergo** beach, one of the prettiest, facing a big sea rock, is another 45 minutes. A rough path from the inland hamlet of Livádi takes an hour to remote **Evangelístra monastery**, dominating the rocky southern shores of the island.

A newly improved road leads up to the **Chóra**, the capital, a stunning sight perched on the pirate-proof cliffs some 1000ft above the sea; the tall houses turn their backs on the sea, fused along the ridge of the cliff with a sheer drop below. Part of the charm is the lack of cars, which are confined strictly to the periphery. Life revolves around four interlinking squares. The first, shaded by rowan trees, has a taverna and is the hub of nocturnal action; the second is quieter; the third has *kafeneía* frequented by locals, and **Ag. Antonis** with a charming portal; the fourth is home to the post office. All get packed out in summer. Newer parts of town look distinctly Andalucian. An arcade leads into the fortified **Kástro** quarter, built in the 13th century by Marco Sanudo, a maze of dazzling paved alleys filled with geraniums and bougainvillea and white houses sporting distinctive wooden balconies reached by steps. There's a pretty 17th-century church, **Pantánassa**, and if you are interested in drawing classes (*May–Oct*) you can usually find the teacher, Fotis Papadopoulos, up here somewhere.

From Chóra, a zig-zag path climbs the hill of Paleokastro to the landmark church of the **Panagía,** set on a 1000ft sheer cliff over the sea, illuminated at night (get the key from the town hall). According to legend, raiding pirates once stole a silver icon of the Virgin and kidnapped an islander. As they made their getaway they capsized and drowned, all except the local who clung to the icon and floated unscathed to the foot of the cliff and built the church at the top in gratitude, just coincidentally on the site of an ancient temple to Artemis. Every year the icon goes on an island tour, to bless the houses and bring the fishermen luck. The castle that stood here is long gone, but beyond it, a large grotto, **Chríssospiliá** ('Golden Cave') has huge stalactites and legends that Barbarossa's treasure is buried in its depths. A thorough exploration in 1988 produced no treasure but some ancient tombs and Classical-era inscriptions. Access is difficult; ask in Chóra for someone to guide you.

A bus, departing from the far side of town, serves the island's other settlement, **Áno Meriá** (ΑΝΩ ΜΕΡΙΑ) 5km west, really a string of farming hamlets straddling the road surrounded by terraced fields. There are three tavernas, a limited number of rooms (ask at the Papadópoulos Kafeneíon), and wonderful sunsets; on a clear day you can see Crete. Áno Meriá also has an excellent **Folk Museum** (℡ 41 387, *open daily 5–8*) with exhibits reconstructing traditional peasant life. With decent shoes and water, you can walk down to remote beaches at **Ampeli, Livadáki** and **Ag. Geórgios Bay**; the bus will drop you off at the appropriate track. Between Áno Mería and Chóra a road descends to the main sandy beach **Angáli**, with a steep scramble down to the sands; there's a donkey-hire service at the top of the road. There are two tavernas, pine trees, some rooms to let and freelance camping is

Íos (ΙΟΣ)

Although desperately trying to change its image from the Benidorm or Fort Lauderdale of the Aegean, Íos remains the mecca for throngs of young people who spend their days lounging on the best beach in the Cyclades and their evenings staggering from one watering hole to another. To discourage raucous parties and late-night revellers sleeping out on the beach, four lovely campgrounds have been provided, but rows of sleeping bags by night and naked bodies by day are still the norm. The seasonal Irish invasion is so great that the island's name has been re-interpreted as the acronym for 'Ireland Over Seas'. If you're a raver or party animal then it's the place for you. Otherwise, despite the loveliness of the island, its glorious sands and pretty Chóra with blue-domed churches, you may well feel disenchanted, unless you take refuge in one of the upmarket resort hotels on the coast, far from the thumping discos. In early spring, when the locals reclaim it, you might find Íos as Lawrence Durrell did, full of 'silences, fractured only by some distant church bell or the braying of a mule'.

Íos ✆ (0286–) | Getting There and Around

By sea: Íos is well connected. There are daily ferries and in summer hydrofoils to all the major Cyclades and Piraeus, and frequently to minor ones and Rafína; also 2–3 times a week to Crete, Kárpathos, Kássos, Chálki, and Rhodes; **excursion boats** to nearby islands. **Port authority**: ✆ 91 264.

The **bus** service is the best on any island, calling at Koumbára, Gialós, Íos town to Milapótas beach every 10 minutes throughout the day and night; 3-day unlimited travel cards are available. Less frequent buses go to Ag. Theodotis beach.

Íos ✆ (0286–) | Tourist Information

Information office in the port of Gialós, ✆ 91 028 (open for bookings when ferries arrive). Also in Íos town next to the town hall, ✆ 91 505, ✉ 91 228. Íos also has its own web site: *www.iosgreece.com*

Festivals

Mid May, three day Homer festival; **26 July**, Ag. Barbára, at Perivóli; **29 August**, Ag. Ioánnis Kálamos, the island's biggest *panegýri*; **8 September**, Ag. Theodótis, with food and dancing.

Gialós and Íos Town

The island's name, also rendered Níos (the locals say Nío), comes from the Ionians who built cities on the sites of Gialós and Íos town, when the island was famous for its oak forests. Over the centuries, the oaks became ships and Íos became an arid rockpile; after the earthquake of 1951, when all the water was sucked out of Íos Bay and rushed back to flood and damage Gialós, the island might have been abandoned had not the first tourists begun to trickle in.

Gialós (ΓΙΑΛΟΣ), the port, also known as Ormós (ΟΡΜΟΣ), has grown up to be a bustling resort in its own right. Under the Turks, its nickname was 'Little Malta' because it was a favourite loafing place for young pirates (some things never change). To the left of the port, note the pretty 17th-century chapel of **Ag. Iríni**, with separate Catholic and Orthodox altars. Gialós has a beach but it tends to be windy and you're better off walking 15 minutes or catching the bus to **Koumbára**, where a long stretch of sand ends at a big rock that's fun for snorkelling; rooms and tavernas and bars can handle most other desires. There are other quieter beaches sprinkled all along the coast to the north.

Íos Town, 'the Village', one of the finest in the Cyclades, a dream vision of white houses and domed churches with tall palms rising up like masts, is increasingly hard to find at street level through the mist of overcharged hormones behind the discos, bars, gýros/burger stands and shops selling rude T-shirts. Of the 18 original windmills behind the town, 12 remain in various states of repair. Traces of the ancient walls are preserved, and only a bit more survives of the fortress built in 1400 by the Albanians. Piracy was so bad on 14th-century Íos that the island had been completely abandoned, until Marco Crispi, whose family had succeeded the Sanudos as Dukes of Náxos, brought in Albanians to repopulate the island; a traveller wrote that every morning when they opened the town gates they'd send out their oldest women; if the women returned, they presumed the coast was clear.

Here **Panagía Gremiotissa**, 'Our Lady of the Cliffs', at the very top houses a miraculous icon that floated to Íos from Crete then stubbornly refused to be put anywhere else, because it is the only spot on Íos from where Crete is (sometimes) visible. Íos Mayor Poussaios, a Homer enthusiast, has just built a new **town theatre** to host quality concerts to lure culture vultures back to town.

Amidst all the hubbub it's worth recalling a story from more innocent days. When Otho of Bavaria, the first King of Greece, paid a visit to Íos, he greeted the villagers in the *kafeneíon*, treated them to a round of drinks and promised he would pay to have the village cleaned up for them. The grateful Niots, scarcely knowing what majesty Otho pretended to, toasted him warmly: 'To the health of the King, Íos' new dustman!'

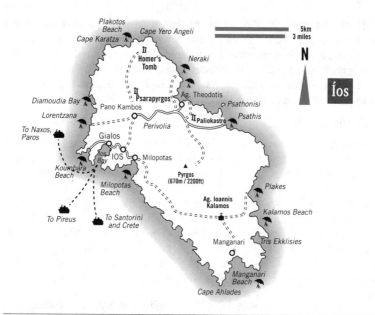

Beaches around Íos

Íos has 35 beaches, but only a handful have been developed. Leading the list is **Milopótas** (ΜΥΛΟΠΟΤΑΣ), with its superb sandy beach filmed in Luc Besson's *Le Grand Bleu*, hosting every conceivable water sport, posh hotels, and campsites. Don't count on getting much shut-eye near the sands: Íos' all-night beach parties are infamous, and have unfortunately ended in several deaths caused by various kinds of overdoses. For something less Babylonian, you can hire a motorbike or catch an excursion; boats leave Gialós every day for the chic golden crescent coves of **Manganári Bay**, where nudism rules and new hotels have been planted; long sandy/pebbly quiet **Kalamós Beach** is a 30-minute walk north on a track (do-able on a motorbike) beginning at the pretty church of **Ag. Ioánnis Kálamos**. For even more isolation, walk over to **Plakes**, a beach where there's often no one at all.

Once remote but now accessible by bus, **Ag. Theodótis** (ΑΓ. ΘΕΟΔΟΤΗΣ) has a fine beach looking out towards Heráklia island. The beach is overlooked by the ruined windswept 15th-century Venetian fortress of **Paliokástro**, with a well-preserved Byzantine church inside. Marauding pirates once bored a hole in the fortress gate, big enough to allow one man in at a time, only to be scalded to death in burning oil poured on them by the besieged villagers; the door is on display in the church of Ag. Theodótis. A soon-to-be-paved road continues to the coarse golden sands of **Psáthi**, where a church dedicated to the Virgin fell into the sea—rather a prophetic statement on raunchy Íos. Psáthi is a favourite for windsurfing and loggerhead turtle nests. It's now the haunt of wealthy Athenians, and has a pair of tavernas (one, Alonistra, has some unusual specialities) and rooms. **Perivóla**, in the middle of the island, has Íos' fresh-water springs and trees. **Páno Kámbos**, once inhabited by a hundred families, now just three or four, is another pretty place. Nearby, at a place called **Helliniká**, are monoliths of mysterious origin.

Plakotós and Homer

Tradition has it that Homer's mother came from Íos, and it was here that the great poet came at the end of his life. Some say it was a riddle told by the fishermen of Íos that killed Homer in a fit of perplexity: to wit, 'What we catch we throw away; what we don't catch, we keep' (not wanting any readers to succumb to a similar fate, the answer's below). Homer's tomb is on the mountain at **Plakotós**, and although earthquakes have left only the rock on which it was built, the epitaph was copied out by ancient travellers: 'Here the earth covers the sacred head of the dean of heroes, the divine Homer.' Plakotós once had a temple to Apollo, but like the church at Psáthi it slid down the cliff. You can look down and see the ruined houses; only one tower, **Psarápyrgos**, remains intact to mark the town.

Íos ✉ *84001,* ☎ *(0286–)*   **Where to Stay and Eating Out**

Íos, paradise of the footloose and fancy-free, can be reasonable, though you can pay 8000dr for a cramped room in peak season; if you can't find a place try the **Rooms Association**, ☎ 91 205. The rule of thumb seems to be that the young and wild head up for 'the Village', oldies and less riotous types stay down in Gialós. Before Guinness, Íos' speciality was *meyífra*, a hard white cheese, mixed with perfume and fermented in a goatskin—hard to find these days (all the better, some might add). Don't confuse it with *mezíthra*, the soft ricotta-like sheep's-milk cheese. But *meyífra* cheese is not the answer to Homer's riddle: what the fishermen caught was lice.

Gialós (Ormos)

Petra Apartments, ☎/🖷 91 049 (*C; mod*) is a lovely luxurious Cycladic village complex at the far end of the beach with stylish open-plan apartments. **Poseidon**, ☎ 91 091, 🖷 91 969 (*C; mod–inexp*) has immaculate rooms just off the waterfront and a panoramic pool; the **Mare-Monte**, ☎/🖷 91 585 (*C; mod*) is another harbour option. **Ios Camping**, ☎ 91 329, again is just off the front, but beware mosquitoes. **Psarades** is a good place for fish and the excellent **Polydoros** at Koumbára is popular for the best traditional Greek dishes, fish soup, seafood and vegetarian meals.

Íos Town

Homer's Inn (there had to be one!) ✆ 91 365, 🖷 91 888 (*C; mod*), with a pool, is a good bet; **Sunrise**, ✆ 91 074, 🖷 91 064, on the next hill has stunning views over town, a pool and bar. Halfway to Milopótas, try **Petradi**, ✆/🖷 91 510 (*C; mod*), with balconies, private baths and a terrace restaurant with great views over Sikínos; in the same area, **Hermes**, ✆ 91 471, 🖷 91 608 (*mod*) has pretty sea views and a snack bar. **Violetta**, ✆ 91 044 (*E; inexp*) is cheapest of all with basic rooms; **Afroditi**, on the Gialós road, ✆/🖷 91 546 (*D; mod–inexp*) is one of the best for value.

The **Ios Club**, on the footpath up from the harbour, has long been renowned for views of the sunset over Sikínos, good drinks and classical music and jazz. In the centre of the village, the **Lord Byron** is an oasis of Greek tradition and sanity, specializing in an array of Anatolian *mezédes*, with *rembétiko* music. **Pithari**, near the church, is one of the best places on the island, serving excellent Greek food and barrelled wine. **Vesuvius** serves decent Italian fare and pizzas.

Milopótas Beach

The **Dionyssos Hotel**, ✆ 91 215, 🖷 91 633 (*B; exp*) is built in traditional style and has a swimming pool, tennis, air-conditioning and transfer service. **Ios Palace**, ✆ 91 224, 🖷 91082 (*B; exp*), on the beach, designed and decorated in the old island style, has two pools, tennis, billiards, jazz bar and good views of the bay. A few minutes from the beach the **Far Out Hotel**, ✆ 91 446, 🖷 91 701 (*C; exp*), named because of guests' reactions to the view, has comfortable rooms in Cubist style clustered on the hillside with a pool.

Markos Beach, ✆ 91 571, 🖷 91 671 (*C; mod*) has standard rooms with showers on the beach. The beach has three campsites: **Camping Stars**, ✆ 91 302, **Milopotas**, ✆ 91 554 and posh **Far Out Camping**, ✆ 91 468, 🖷 91 560, apparently just that, with a restaurant, minibus, pool, and sports facilities (including the **Ios Diving Centre**, with traditional instruction, but also night diving and life-saving courses).

Manganári Bay

The German-owned **Manganari Bungalows**, ✆ 91 200, 🖷 (01) 363 1904 (*B; exp*) offers luxury rooms and suites, with a restaurant and nightclub for those who like their entertainment sane and close to home. *Open June–Sept only*.

The village is one long rave-up, all the bars offering different amusements from videos to rock bands, and happy hours that stretch into morning. Serious drinkers pack the main square bars after midnight and go on until dawn. Each music bar and disco posts its nightly programme so you can pick and choose: among the classics are **Slammer**, in the main square, **The Dubliner** with its DJs and **Sweet Irish Dream** until the wee hours; down in Milopótas, **Scorpion** is the biggest disco in the Cyclades. In more staid Giálos, bars show videos outdoors at night instead, usually in English.

Kéa/Tzía (KEA/TZIA)

Closest of all the Cyclades to Athens, Kéa with its fine beaches has for many years been a favourite place for Athenians to build their summer villas—the island can be reached from the metropolis in less than 4 hours, and it's guaranteed to have no room on holiday weekends, when jeeps, dogs, boats and windsurfers pile off the ferries and the jet-set sails over to Vourkári from Glyfáda in a flotilla of gin palaces; if you want to make a short stay, time it for mid-week.

Kéa feels very different from the other Cyclades, with lush valleys and terraces of fruit trees, fields grazed by dairy cattle and grubbing pigs; since antiquity it has been famed for its fertility, its red wines, lemons, honey and almonds. Its traditional architecture may lack the pristine white Cubism of its sister isles but there's almost a touch of Tuscany about its capital town of Ioulís, with its red-pantiled houses and higgledy-piggledy lanes.

History

Traces of a Neolithic fishing settlement dating back to 3000 BC were discovered at Kefala on Kéa's north coast. These first settlers were no pushovers; when the mighty Minoan thalassocrats founded a colony *c.* 1650 BC on the peninsula of Ag. Iríni, they were forced to build defences against attacks, not from the sea but by land. The colony, discovered in 1960 by John L. Caskey of the University of Cincinnati, coincides nicely with the myth that Minos himself visited Kéa and begat the Kéan race on a native named Dexithea; it also reveals a fascinating chronicle of trade and diplomacy with the Minoans and, later, with the Mycenaeans.

In the Classical era, Kéa was divided into four towns: Ioulís, Karthaea, Poiessa and Korissía. One of these produced the great poet Simonides (557–467 BC), and they're still proud of him today. He is best known for his epitaph that rallied the Greeks after the Battle of Thermopylae (480 BC) when King Leonidas and his 300 Spartans were all killed, defending the narrow pass against the Persians:

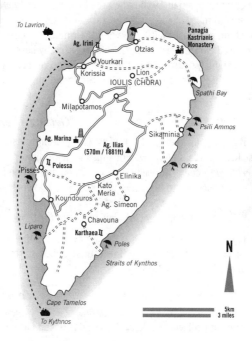

Kéa/Tzia

Of those who died at Thermopylae
Glorious is their fate, beautiful their death.
Their tomb is an altar; for lamentation they have
                                    remembrance; for sorrow, praise
Mould will never darken such a shroud
Nor time which conquers all.
This shrine of brave men has drawn to itself
All the glory of Greece. Leonidas, king of Sparta, too,
Is witness to it, leaving the grand glory of his courage
And undying fame.

Other famous sons of Kéa include Simonides' lyrical nephew Bacchylides, the philosopher Ariston, and the physician Erasistratos. Rather less to their credit, Kéa was also famous for its retirement scheme called the *geroktonia*: citizens were required to take a glass of conium (like hemlock) when they reached 70, although the Kéans claim it was only enforced when the island was besieged by the Athenians and food was low.

Kéa's name crops up again in 1916, when the hospital ship *Britannic*, sister-ship to the *Titanic*, sank 3 miles offshore after an explosion. Of the more than a thousand people aboard, only 21 lost their lives when their lifeboat capsized. Speculation at the time produced two theories: that the ship had secretly been carrying munitions, which had accidentally exploded in the hold, or that the British had scuttled the ship themselves, hoping to pressure Athens into forbidding enemy craft from navigating freely in Greek waters.

Kéa ℂ (0288–)   ***Getting There and Around***

By sea: daily **ferry** and **Flying Cat** (75 minutes) connections with Lávrion (passing by way of sinister Makrónissos, a prison island and torture chamber used in the Civil War and by the Junta; poet Yánnis Rítsos spent years there); 3 to 4 times a week with Kýthnos and once a week to Sýros. Daily **hydrofoil** service in summer with Kýthnos and Piraeus (Zéa). Port authority: ℂ 21 344.

By road: the **bus** runs 3–4 times a day from Ioulís to Vourkári, and is seldom seen anywhere else; the tourist police have the ever-changing schedule. Taxis: ℂ 22 444.

Kéa ℂ (0288–)   ***Tourist Information***

The **tourist police** are in Korissía, ℂ 21 100, and have lists of rooms to let.

Festivals

10 February, Ag. Charálambos, patron of Kéa, at Chóra; **17 July**, Ag. Marína; **15 August**, Panagía, at Chóra; **7 September**, Ag. Sózonta, at Otziás.

Korissía and Ag. Iríni

Kéa's port **Korissía** (ΚΟΡΗΣΣΙΑ) has a few pretty neoclassical buildings and a lovely church but otherwise it's an ordinary, functional little place with a bust of Simonides in the centre. Anxious to become a resort like Kéa's other coastal villages, it boasts a few boutiques and an art gallery among the waterfront tavernas and cafés. Korissía, of course, recalls the ancient town that once stood on the site; most locals, however, still call it Livádi, as they continue to call their island Tzía instead of the official Kéa. The bay sweeps round to the sandy if not especially tidy town beach; a footpath over the headland leads past the old castle-like country house of the Maroúli family, then north to small, sandy **Gialiskári** beach and a popular taverna shaded by a pine wood. A playground for rich Athenians, the area bristles with holiday villas, high gates and guard dogs.

A kilometre further north, on attractive Ag. Nikólaou Bay, **Vourkári** the pretty fishing village has metamorphosed into a smart little resort, where the pleasure-cruiser brigade loaf on their sundecks. There are few fishing boats now, and even fewer under sail. Around the bay, on the church-topped peninsula of **Ag. Iríni**, are the excavations of the **Minoan–Mycenaean settlement**. It's not difficult to make out the Bronze Age temple, the oldest in the Aegean, near a late Minoan megaron, walls and a street. Inscriptions in the Minoan Linear A were among among the finds, most of which can be seen in the Archaeological Museum in Ioulís.

From here the coastal road continues to the delightful, very popular beach resort at **Otziás** (OTZIAΣ), its bay ringed with lacy almond blossom in early spring. From here you can walk up to wind-whipped **Panagía Kastriáni**, with panoramic views down the coast. The 18th-century monastery is noted for its miracle-working icon of the Panagía. There are two churches, the first built in 1708 after shepherds saw a strange glow on the mountain pinpointing the presence of the icon.

Ioulís (Chóra) and the Happy Lion

High above Korissía, the island's capital **Ioulís** or Ioulída (IOΥΛÍΔΑ) is hidden inland, like so many Cycladic towns, from sea-going predators. As the bus climbs, the views down the terraced hillside to the sea are stunning. En route note the school on the hill, built in the neoclassical style, one of the finest in Greece. Ioulís also boasts the largest collection of **windmills** in the Cyclades: 26 stand sentinel on the Mountain of the Mills.

The town is a pretty place to wander around with its flower-filled balconies and covered galleries known as *stegadia*, a maze of alleys and archways, the white houses topped with red-tiled roofs. The fine neoclassical Town Hall, topped with statues of Apollo and Athena, has a sculpture of a woman and child found at Karthaiea and ancient reliefs set into niches.The **Kástro** quarter, reached through a dazzling white archway (note the coat of arms of the Pangalos family, with its loaf of bread and two cockerels) occupies the site of the ancient acropolis and Temple of Apollo. In 1210, the Venetian Domenico Michelli cannibalized its marbles to build himself a castle; in the 1860s the Greek government dismantled the castle in turn to put the Classical bits in a museum. Bits and blocks remain, as well as a few Venetian mansions and Byzantine churches. The **Archaeological Museum** (✆ 22 079; *open Tues–Sun, 8.30–3; adm free*) contains Minoan finds from Ag. Iríni, and the nearly life-sized Bronze Age terracotta female figures from the 14th-century BC temple–the oldest one yet found in the Aegean. Made after the fall of Minoan Crete, the figures are very much in the style of the bare-breasted Cretan goddess, and yet unlike anything every found on Crete, handmade over wooden skeletons, no two quite alike and brightly painted yellow, white and red. If not goddesses, they could have represented permanent worshippers at the sanctuary. There are also artefacts from ancient Kéa's four cities, as well as a copy of the wonderful Kouros of Kéa, discovered in Korissía and now in the National Archaeological Museum in Athens.

A 10-minute walk east of Chóra leads to the island's watchdog—the 6th-century BC **Lion of Kéa**, the *'Leonda'*, an ancient guardian 10ft high and 19ft long, gently smiling down over Ioulís. Tales about the lion abound: one says he symbolizes the Kéans' bravery, another recounts how evil nymphs were killing the wives of Ioulís and the men, fed up, were ready to abandon the city. The priest prayed to Zeus to send the nymphs away, and he delivered an enormous lion, which chased them across the water to Kárystos in Evía. The Kéans then carved the lion in stone, to keep the nymphs permanently at bay; others say this is the lion himself, as still as stone, ready to spring at the mere whiff of a bad fairy.

The countryside north of Ioulís, the **Paraméria**, still has its oakwoods and simple, traditional country houses. Above Peraméria the lush valley of Spathí ends at sandy **Spathí Bay**. Another road east from Ioulís branches for three fine beaches: **Sykamiá**, **Psíli Ammos** and **Orkós**.

Southern Kéa

The main road south of Ioulís leads 5km through rolling green countryside to the ruined monastery of **Ag. Marína**, built around a square, three-storey Hellenistic tower; one of the finest in Greece, its masonry has withstood time better than the monastery. From here the road cuts across to the west-coast resort community **Písses** (which perhaps should consider reviving its ancient name, Poiessa, of which a few traces remain). Backed by a lush valley full of orchards and olive groves, Písses has a huge sweeping sandy beach, one of the finest on the island. The next bay along, sandy **Koúndouros**, is just as lovely, and has several smaller coves, as well as a crop of bungalows for Athenian weekenders. Another gorgeous beach is further along the coast at **Liparó**.

On the southeast shore at Póles Bay (with another beach) stood **Karthaea**, once Kéa's most important city, set high on the headland. Simonides had his school of poetry here; now you'll only find remains of massive walls, the theatre, temples of Apollo, Demeter and Athena and other buildings. It's possible to walk the Hellenistic road from **Káto Meriá** or **Ellinciká**.

Kéa ✉ *84002,* ✆ *(0288–)*   **Where to Stay and Eating Out**

Most of Kéa's accommodation is in the form of furnished seaside apartments aimed at Greek families. Simple rooms to rent are like gold dust at weekends or in high season, with prices to match. The **Kastrianí Monastery**, ✆ 21

348, on the north coast, has guest rooms if you get desperate. Although foreign visitors have begun trickling in, Kéa is still very Greek and the tavernas serve up unadulterated Greek fare at fairly reasonable prices. Look for *pastéli*, a delicious sticky bar made from local thyme honey and sesame seeds. Other specialities include smelly *kopanistí* cheese and *paspallá*, preserved fat pork, usually eaten at Christmas.

Korissía

I **Tzia Mas**, ✆ 21 305, 🖥 21 140 (*C; mod*) fronts the town beach but it's right on the main road, so isn't very peaceful. Off the harbour the **Karthea**, ✆ 21 204 (*C; mod*) is a bit gloomy; better to head for **Korissia**, ✆ 21 484, 🖥 21 355 (*E; mod*), in a quiet backwater with a nice terrace, bar and large rooms or studios. Nearby, the **United Europe Furnished Flats**, ✆ 21 362, 🖥 21 122 (*A; exp–mod*) are a smart self-catering option close to the beach. Other furnished apartments worth trying are **To Korali**, ✆ 21 268, and **To Oneiro**, ✆ 21 118 (*exp–mod*). **I Apolavsi** ('The Enjoyment'), ✆ 21 068 (*inexp*), above Kostas Taverna has comfortable, basic studios and a huge sun-terrace overlooking the harbour. In the alley behind, **Kyria Pantazi**, ✆ 21 452, has very basic but quaint village rooms, but no view.

As you get off the ferry, there are eating places offering anything from pizza to *mezédes*. **Apotheki**, in a whitewashed ruin, has a large choice of menu, or you can spend a pleasant evening over a grilled fish or moussaka at **Faros** or **Kostas Taverna**, a basic, hectic and popular haunt with local workmen. Further along the harbour the smart **Ouzerie Lagoudera**, in a refurbished neoclassical house, has an excellent menu and tasty prawn *saganáki*; next door **To Mouragio** does pizzas as well as Greek fare.

Vourkári/Otziás

At Vourkári there are furnished apartments to let (*all exp–mod*), including **Nikitas,** ✆ 22 303, on the waterfront, **Lefkes**, ✆ 21 443, and **Petrakos**, ✆ 21 197.

Vourkári is the place for seafood at a price where the yachties and cruisers can moor up a few feet away from their tables. **Aristos** is among the best for good Greek cooking and, if the wind has been blowing the right way and there's been a good haul of fish, a delicious *kakavia* (Greek *bouill-abaisse*) will be on the menu. **Nikos**, ✆ 21 486, next to the art gallery, and **To Oraío Bourkari** are also popular for lunch and dinner. In Otziás the **Coaldi Club**, ✆ 21 093, 🖥 21 109, has furnished apartments overlooking the sands and there are also several *domátia* places. **Iannis** is the favourite fish taverna.

Ioúlis

There are two pensions full of character, **Ioulis**, ✆ 22 177 (*C; mod*) and **Filoxenia**, ✆ 22 057 (*E; inexp*) which has shared bathrooms. The café and pastry shop near the bus stop is a nice place to have a drink and a snack as you soak up the view; through the main archway the **Piatsa Restaurant** is in a lovely setting while the **Ioulis**, on the town hall square is a good place to have a grilled lunch, again with sensational views. **To Steki** and **Taverna Argiris** also have a good range of Greek fare.

Písses/Koúndouros

Among the furnished apartments in Písses, try the **Galini**, ✆ 31 316, or any run by the Polítis family, ✆ 31 343/318. There's also **Kea Camping**, ✆ 31 332, run by Ioánnis Polítis. Two respected fish tavernas are **Simitis** and **Akroyiali**. In increasingly popular Koúndouros, **Kea Beach**, ✆ 31 230, 🖂 31 234 (*B; exp*) is a swish complex in traditional village style complete with a restaurant, pool, and watersports. **Nikolas Demenegas,** ✆ 31 416 has tidy studios in a garden (*mod*). Or sleep (4–6 people) in a **stone windmill**, complete with a kitchen; contact Nikolas Tsirikos, ✆ (01) 897 4534. **Politis** is a favourite taverna.

Entertainment and Nightlife

Ioulís is now the in place to spend the evening: **Kamini, Quiz, Apano** and **Leon** are popular, and **Milos** has live *rembetiko*. In Vourkári at night, **Kouros** and **Prothikos** are popular music bars and **Vinilio** is good for a dance. In Korissía, **Clue** is a popular after-dinner haunt or go out towards Písses for a bouzouki night at **Sklavanikolas**. The island's *panegýria* are known for their spectacular dances to music played on traditional instruments like the *tsamboúna*, *doubi* and lute.

Kímolos (ΚΙΜΩΛΟΣ)

Kímolos is Mílos' little sister, and until fairly recently they were Siamese twins, connected by an isthmus with a town on it, dating back to the Mycenaeans. But the isthmus sank into the sea, leaving a channel only a kilometre wide. Once known as Echinousa, or sea urchin, which it proudly depicted on its coins, the island gave its modern name to *kimolía* ('chalk' in Greek), and to cimolite in English, a mineral similar to soft, chalk-like Fuller's Earth, an essential ingredient in the dying of cloth. Kímolos remains one of the world's top producers of cimolite; you can see the workings as the boat pulls in. If it hasn't rained lately, the island may be coated with fine white cimolite dust—the despair of local housewives.

Kímolos with its 720 souls is a quiet, untainted Greek island with plenty of beaches and freelance camping: a perfect place to relax and do nothing, with no cars and few tourists, even in August. Although rocky and barren ever since the Venetians set the olive groves ablaze in 1638, there are patches of green, and 140 species of rare plants, mostly on the southeast coast where you may also sight the island's rare blue lizards. The largest building on the island is a retirement home built by local philanthropist Geórgios Afendákis, where the elderly live free of charge.

Kímolos ✆ (0287–) **Getting There**

By sea: connections five times a week with Piraeus, Mílos, Kýthnos, Sérifos and Sífnos, three or so a week with Folégandros, Síkinos, Íos and Santoríni; **water taxi** 3 times a day to Apollónia on Mílos; caiques to the beaches. **Port authority**: ✆ 51 332.

Kímolos ✆ (0287–) **Tourist Information**

Just the police, ✆ 51 205.

Festivals

20 July, Profítis Ilías; **27 July**, Ag. Panteleímon; **15 August**, Panagía; **27 August**, Ag. Fanoúris; **21 November**, traditional music and dancing.

Chóra and Around

From the pretty little port, **Psáthi** (ΨΑΘΗΣ), which has a good taverna, a beach café and the 'doctor's mill' on the hill above, it's a 2km, 15-minute walk up to **Kímolos** or **Chóra**. On the way up you'll pass the Afendákis Foundation building, with a statue of the benefactor; a small museum in the basement takes in whatever potsherds and ancient bric-à-brac the locals happen to dig up. Blizzard-white, Chóra is a tangle of paved lanes with flowers at every turn. It's divided into two settlements: **Mésa Kástro** (or **Palío Choró**, the bit in the castle walls) and **Éxo Kástro**, or **Kainoúrio Choró**, on the outside. The houses of Mésa Kástro form the inside of the fortress with loophole windows and four gates. The outer village has a few small cafés and tavernas, and a beautiful domed cathedral church, **Panagía Evangélistra**, built in 1614. Other impressive churches are the **Panagía Odygítria**, 1873; **Taxiárchis**, 1670; and **Chrisóstomos**, 1680, and the ruins of the Catholic church, the **Madonna of the Rosary**. One of the six windmills still grinds wheat—the last truly functioning one in the Cyclades.

From Chóra you can walk up to the ruined Venetian castle built by Marco Sanudo at Kímolos' highest point (355m). Within its forbidding walls is the island's oldest church, **Christós**, dating from 1592, according to the wall inscription. Another walk by way of **Alíki** (with a beach, rooms and a taverna) ends at **Ag. Andréas** and the **Ellinikó necropolis**—all that survives of the city that sunk with the isthmus—and its graves from the Mycenaean period (1500 BC) to the early centuries AD. You can end with a swim at the beach at **Ellinikó** (where loggerhead turtles make their nests, so take care) or **Kambána**.

There are other beaches along the east coast. A path from Chóra descends to Goúpa, a small hamlet with the most abundant fish in the Aegean these days, and here, supposedly, people used to scoop them out by the basketful. It's a very pretty little place, with a good beach untouched by tavernas or snack bars. Beyond Goúpa there's another lovely beach at Klíma, and 7km north at Prássa, where the cimolite is extracted, are radioactive thermal springs especially good for rheumatism. Goats are the only inhabitants of Políegos, the large islet facing Psáthi, although the rare monk seal has been sighted as well.

Where to Stay and Eating Out

If you want to stay you'll have to ask around in the bars and tavernas to see who has a vacant room. Camping is usually 'no problem' as the Greeks say—try Klíma and Alíki beaches. Up in Chóra three tavernas all serve standard Greek fare at low prices: **Ramfos**, **Panorama** and **Boxoris**, which also has rooms.

Kýthnos (ΚΥΘΝΟΣ)

Time your visit right and you can have this island to yourself, avoiding the Athenian invasion of July and August. Like its neighbour, Kéa, Kýthnos attracts relatively few foreigners, and even the majority of Greek arrivals are not tourists, but folks full of aches and pains who come to soak in the thermal spa at Loutrá; the locals often call their island Thermia after the springs. Since the closure of Kýthnos' iron mines in 1940, the 1500 islanders who closed their ears to the siren song of emigration have got by as best they could by fishing, farming (mostly figs and vines), basket-weaving and making ceramics; the one thing that has stopped the population from dropping any further is the construction of a harbour mole in 1974, allowing ships to dock.

Perhaps to make up for its slow start, Kýthnos became the first Greek island (1982) to get all of its electricity from renewable resources—wind in the winter and sun in the summer—inspiring similar projects on Mýkonos, Kárpathos, Samothráki and Crete. Perhaps because of their frugal, hard lives Kythniots tend to celebrate *panegýria* with great gusto, donning their traditional costumes; carnival is a big event here. There are quiet sandy beaches, a dramatic, rugged interior great for walkers, and the people are welcoming. Best of all, it's the kind of island where the old men still offer to take you fishing.

History

In Classical times the tale was told that Kýthnos was uninhabited because of its wild beasts and snakes, and Ofiohousa ('snaky') was one of the island's ancient names. Recently, however, archaeologists have uncovered a Mesolithic settlement (7500–6000 BC) just north of the port of Loutrá that not only spits in the eye of tradition, but currently holds the honour of being the oldest settlement yet discovered in the Cyclades. Much later the Minoans held the island, followed by the Driopes, a semi-mythical tribe who were chased out of their home on the slopes of Mount Parnassos by Heracles and scattered to Évia, Cyprus and Kýthnos; their king Kýthnos gave his name to the island and their old capital is still called Drýopis. During the Hellenistic period Kýthnos was dominated by Rhodes.

Two great painters came from the island, Kydian and Timatheus (416–376 BC), the latter famous in antiquity for his portrait of Iphigenia. In 198 BC all Kýthnos was pillaged, except for Vyrókastro, which proved impregnable. Marco Sanudo took the island for Venice, and for 200 years it was under the rule of the Cozzadini family, who maintained control by diplomatically paying taxes both to the Venetians and to the Turks. To this day the Cozzadini live happily in Bologna. Is there a lesson there?

By sea: daily with Piraeus, Sérifos, Sífnos and Mílos, 2–3 times a week with Lávrion, Kéa, Kímolos, Folégandros, Síkinos, Íos and Santoríni. Kýthnos has two ports; all ships these days put in at Mérichas on the west coast, though when the winds are strong they'll come in to Loútra in the northeast. **Hydrofoil**: daily *Flying Dolphin* to Kéa, Piraeus. **Port authority**: ☎ 32 290.

By road: there are two **buses** which run regularly to Chóra and Loutrá and to Drýopida and Panagía Kanála. **Taxis**: Kýthnos, ☎ 31 272, Drýopida ☎ 31 290.

Tourist police: Chóra, ☎ 31 201. There are several ticket agencies in Mérichas, including GATS Travel, ☎/⊚ 32 055, which also arrange accommodation and excursions. The Cava Kythnos off-licence is also the Bank of Greece branch and hydrofoil agency.

Festivals

On **Sundays** you can often hear the island's music at Drýopida. **15 August** and **8 September** there are Panagías at Kanála; **2 November**, Ag. Akíndinos, at Mérichas.

Beaches, Chóra and Loutrá

Mérichas (ΜΕΡΙΧΑΣ) is a typical Greek fishing harbour, the ferry dock and yacht berths giving way to a tree-fringed bay backed by lively tavernas. It's a laid-back, cheerful place, kept tidy by the village oldies who also tend the ducks that live on the sandy beach. Nailed to a tree near the litter-bins, a sign proclaims, 'The sea is the spring of life and joy.' In the morning fishermen sell the day's catch; forklifts buzz about delivering sacks of potatoes and cases of beer. Up the steps from the harbour and a short walk off the Chóra road is the much nicer little beach of **Martinákia**, popular with families, which has an excellent taverna and rooms to let. Just to the north are the unexcavated Hellenistic ruins of the once impregnable **Vyrókastro**, set on the headland above the lovely beaches at **Episkópi,** and **Apókrousi**, although the prettiest sandy beach on the island, **Kolona** is just beyond; caiques make the trip.

The 7½km bus trip north from Mérichas to the capital **Chóra**, also known as Messária, winds through barren hillsides rippled with stone-wall terraces, deep wrinkles filled with oleanders, wider ones planted with fruit trees and vines, and the occasional dovecote. Although as Cycladic towns go it's not that spectacular,

Kýthnos

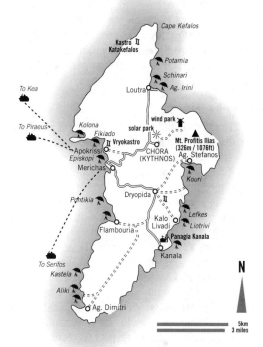

Cape Kefalos

Kastro II
Katakefalos

Potamia

Schinari

To Kea

Loutra · Ag. Irini

wind park

Kolona · solar park

To Piraeus · Fikiado

Vryokastro

Mt. Profítis Ilias
(326m / 1076ft)

Apokrissi · CHORA
(KYTHNOS) · Ag. Stefanos

Episkopi

Merichas

Kouri

Pontikia

Dryopida

Lefkes

Kalo · Liotrivi
Livadi

Flambouria · Panagía Kanala

Kanala

To Serifos

Kastela

Aliki

Ag. Dimitri

N

5km
3 miles

it's an authentic, workaday town with a certain charm. The pavements are especially beautiful, every square inch carefully painted with mermaids, fish, flowers and patterns. It has several pretty churches including **Ag. Sávvas**, founded in 1613 by the Cozzadini, who decorated it with their coat-of-arms. The oldest church is **Ag. Triáda**, a domed, single-aisle basilica. Other churches in Chóra claim to have icons by the Cretan-Venetian master Skordílis, while the **Prodrómos** ('the Scout' or St John the Baptist) has a valuable 17th-century screen. Just outside Chóra are the solar park and modern windmills which provide the island's power.

The buses continue to **Loutrá** (ΛΟΥΤΡΑ), the most important thermal spa in the Cyclades. Iron impregnates the water, leaving a characteristic reddish deposit. Since ancient times Loutra's two springs, **Kakávos** and **Ag. Anárgyri**, have been used for bathing and as a cure for gout, rheumatism, eczema and 'women's problems'. The **hydrotherapy centre**, ✆ 31 277, is *open from 8–noon*. Carved marble baths dating from ancient times are now inside the Xenia Hotel, from which steaming water bubbles down a gulley and out to sea. A straggling, windswept resort with castle-like villas and holiday homes, Loutrá has several tavernas and places to stay. There's a sandy beach and over the headland two more bays, pebbly **Ag. Iríni** and **Schinári**, exposed to the north winds. The aforementioned Mesolithic settlement was found on the promontory just to the north. A hard hour's walk from Loutrá towards the northernmost tip of Kýthnos will bring you to the medieval citadel **Kástro Katakéfalos**; you can poke around its derelict towers, houses and churches (one, **Our Lady of Compassion**, still has some frescoes), all abandoned around the middle of the 17th century.

Drýopida and Kanála

The other road and bus out of Mérichas heads up to **Drýopida** (ΔΡΥΟΠΙΔΑΣ) or Drýopis, the only other inland village and the island's former capital, in part because of nearby **Katafíki cave**, where the people hid during pirate raids. Huddled on the sides of a small canyon, Drýopida could be in Tuscany or Spain with its red-pantiled houses—it's one of the few villages in the Cyclades suffi-ciently sheltered to permit such a luxury. There are two districts, **Péra Rouga**, by the river valley, where they grow crops, and **Galatás**, the upper village, a labyrinth of crazy-paved lanes, neatly white-washed, still crossed by the odd mule train. There are a few cafés and tavernas and even fewer tourists. Once a great ceramics centre, only one pottery remains, in the Milás family for five gen-erations. Kýthnos was also a centre of icon-painting in the 17th century, led by the famous Skordílis family; much of their work can be still be seen, including the iconostasis in **Ag. Mínas**, which also has an Easter bier with folk-art decora-tions. It takes a good hour to walk to Chóra along the ancient, scenic cobbled way, or you can go down to the beaches at **Ag. Stéfanos**, a chapel-topped islet linked by a causeway, or **Léfkes** where there are rooms to let.

The bus terminates at **Kanála**, a popular summer resort where Greeks have hol-iday homes. A village has sprung up around the church of **Panagía Kanála**, the island's patroness, housing a venerated icon, painted by St Luke himself (or more likely, by a member of the Skordílis clan). Chalets dot the peaceful grounds, pine trees shade picnic areas and, below, families laze and splash in a string of sandy coves. There are wonderful views over to Sýros and Sérifos and the water is so shallow that you feel you can almost walk across. A rough track leads to **Flamboúria** beach on the west coast with rooms to let, but you need transport to get to **Ag. Dimitríou** way down at the southern tip.

Kýthnos ✉ *84006,* © *(0281–)*   ***Where to Stay and Eating Out***

Mérichas

Mérichas is the most convenient place to stay. The friendly but basic **Kythnos**, © 32 092 (*mod–inexp*), with smart blue and white striped canopies, is slap on the waterfront over a *zacharoplasteío* that does breakfast as well as home-made rice-puddings and jellies. On the hillside behind, the new **Panorama** rooms, ✆ 32 184/182 (*mod–inexp*), and **Paradissos**, ✆ 32 206/165 (*mod–inexp*), with vine-shaded terraces, are both comfortable with stunning views over the bay.

Among the many village rooms, **Kaliopi**, ✆ 32 203/323, has a nice garden and **Chryssoula Laranzaki**, ✆ 32 051, has quiet rooms with views. The **Martinakia** on the beach of the same name has a friendly parrot in the garden and rooms to let (*mod*) and serves good *kalamária* and grills.

Back in Mérichas, **Yialos** (or **Sailors**), ✆ 32 102, has tables on the beach and do a fine *pikilía* of Greek starters and good specialities such as *kalogíros*, a casserole of meat, aubergines, tomatoes and feta; ask to try Kýthnos' wine. At the far end of the beach (towards the derelict hotel), **To Kantouni**, ✆ 32 220, with tables at the water's edge, specializes in grills and *sfougáta*, feather-light rissoles made from the local cheese, *thermiotikó*; also barrelled retsina and romantic view across the bay. Family-run **Kissos**, ✆ 32 370, is also good for Greek favourites and fish at reasonable prices. After midnight head for the ultra-violet lights at the **Byzantino,** or to the **Akrotiri,** an open-air night club on the far side of the port.

Chóra/Drýopida

Chóra has no rooms but a couple of tavernas, **To Steki** and **To Kentro**. Night owls from around the island flock to **Kousaros** and **Apocalypse** music bars. In Dryopída, there's basic **Taverna Pelegra** behind the butcher's shop (at least the meat's fresh) and look out for local sausages drying on the balcony next door; opposite the **Psistaria O Giorgilos** is your other option for grills.

Loutrá

Loutrá is geared to long stays by spa customers. The most luxurious places are the **Kythnos Bay**, ✆ 31 218, 🖷 31 444 (*C; exp*), and **Porto Klaras** apartments, ✆ 31 276, 🖷 31 355 (*A; exp–mod*), beautifully appointed family suites or doubles. All have sea-view terraces. **Meltemi**, ✆ 31 271, 🖷 31 302 (*C; mod*) are more modest flats; EOT-run **Xenia Anagenissis** overlooks the beach, ✆ 31 217 (*C; mod–inexp*), popular with old ladies taking the waters. **Aneza**, ✆ 31 432, with sea views, are among the nicest rooms to let.

Taverna Despina has good fresh fish and fish soup, and meat from Kýthnos. **Taverna Katerina** at Schinári beach has stunning views.

Kanála

Oneiro, ✆ 32 515, and **Nikos Bouritis**, ✆ 32 350, both have pleasant inexpensive rooms. There are good fish tavernas, and **To Louloudi Taverna** in the church grounds, serving authentic home-cooking from local vegetables to liver and goat stew. At Ag. Dimitríou, **Yiannis Kallilas**, ✆ 32 208, has rooms and a restaurant by the sea.

Mílos (ΜΗΛΟΣ)

Like Santoríni, Mílos, the most westerly of the Cyclades, is a volcanic island. But where the former is a glamorous beauty associated with misty tales of Atlantis, Mílos is a sturdy fellow who has made his fiery origins work for a living. Few places can boast such a catalogue of geological eccentricities: hot springs bubble in its low rolling hills, rocks startle with their Fauvist colours and fantastic shapes, and the landscape is gashed with obsidian, sulphur, kaolin, barium, alum, bensonite and perlite quarries begun in the Neolithic era. In a beach beauty contest Mílos would score over Santoríni hands down with miles of pale golden sands, among the finest in Greece; long strands and weird fjord-like inlets all lapped by deep turquoise waters, some bubbling with the geothermal springs. It seems an odd trick of Mother Nature to so endow such an out-of-the-way island with this mineral cornucopia. Yet in spite of all its strange and wonderful rocks, Mílos still mourns for the one it lost—the renowned Venus, now in the Louvre.

Walks through the gently undulating countryside will bring you down to tiny whitewashed chapels at the water's edge, or unique little settlements that sit on the water, with brightly painted boat garages beneath their balconies. Not surprisingly, Mílos gets more tourists every year (especially Italians and Germans), numbers that will only increase once the new jet runways are complete and the yacht marina is in place in the island's magnificent harbour.

History

But Mílos has long been a popular place. In the early Neolithic era, people braved the Aegean in papyrus boats to mine Mílos' abundant veins of obsidian, the petroleum of its day, a hard black volcanic glass prized for the manufacture of tools. Until the recent discovery of the Mesolithic settlement in Kýthnos, Mílos laid claim to the oldest town in the Cyclades, at Phylakope, settled by either Karians or Cypriots; under Minoan and later Mycenaean rule the island became rich from trading obsidian all over the Mediterranean.

As the inhabitants of Mílos in later years were predominately Dorians, related to the Spartans, they declared themselves neutral in the Peloponnesian War. In the 17th year of the war (415 BC), Athens sent envoys to change their minds. Their

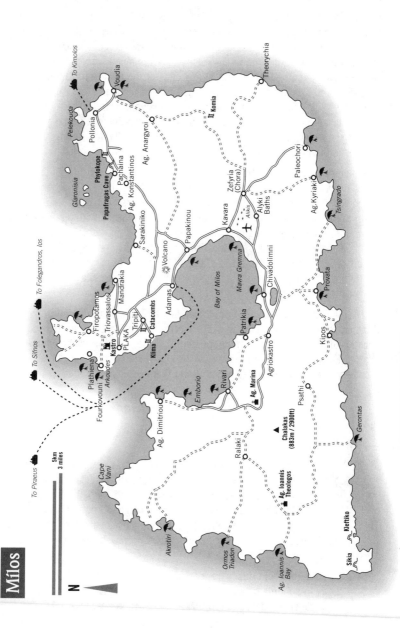

Mílos

N

5km
3 miles

To Kimolos
Pelekouda
Voudia
Theorychia
Pollonia
Phylokope
Papafragas Cave
Pachaina
Komia
Ag. Anargyroi
Glaronisia
Ag. Konstantinos
Paleochori
Zefyria
(Chora)
Sarakiniko
Kavara
Alyki
Baths
Ag. Kyriaki
Tsingrado
Papakinou
Aliki
Volcano
Firopotamos
Triovassalos
Mandrakia
Bay of Mílos
Mavra Gremna
Chivadolimni
To Folegandros, Ios
Tripiti
Catacombs
Adamas
Provata
To Sifnos
PLAKA
Kastro
Klima
Patrikia
Kipos
Plathiena
Arkoudes
Agriokastro
Psathi
Fourkovouni
Emborio
Rivari
Ag. Marina
To Piraeus
Ag. Dimitriou
Chalakas
(883m / 2900ft)
Gerontas
Cape
Vani
Ralaki
Ag. Ioannis
Theologos
Kleftiko
Akrotiri
Ormos
Triadon
Sikia
Ag. Ioannis
Bay

famous 'might makes right' discussion, known as 'the Milian Dialogue', in the fifth chapter of Thucydides, is one of the most moving passages in Classical history. Athens, by that point, had lost most of its fine progressive democratic feelings and was fighting a war of conquest. When Mílos remained unconvinced by the *realpolitik* arguments of the envoys, asking only for the right to remain friendly to both sides and foes to none, the Athenians besieged the island for two years, and when the Milians unconditionally surrendered they massacred all men of fighting age, enslaved all the women and children, and resettled the island with 500 colonists from Athens. These were famous in antiquity for raising the best, toughest roosters—for cock fights.

Christianity came early to Mílos in the 1st century, and the faithful built a great series of catacombs—the only ones in Greece. Marco and his brother Angelo Sanudo captured Mílos, and later placed it under the Crispi dynasty. The Turks laid claim to the island in 1580, even though Mílos was infested with pirates. One of them, John Kapsís, declared himself King of Mílos, a claim which Venice recognized for three years, until the Turks flattered Kapsís into coming to Istanbul, and ended his pretensions with an axe. In 1680 a party from Mílos emigrated to London, where James, Duke of York, granted them land to build a Greek church—the origin of Greek Street in Soho.

In 1836 Cretan war refugees from Sfakiá fled to Mílos and founded the village Adámas, the present port. During the Crimean War the French navy docked at the harbour of Mílos and left many monuments, as they did during the First World War; at Korfos you can see the bases of the anti-aircraft batteries installed during the German occupation in the Second World War.

Mílos ☎ (0287–)   **Getting There and Around**

By air: three flights daily from Athens in summer, two in winter. Airport: ☎ 22 381.

By sea: **ferry** 6 times a week from Piraeus, Sífnos, Sérifos and Kýthnos, 2 or 3 times a week with Crete, Folégandros, Santoríni, Íos and Sikínos; once a week with Kárpathos and Kássos. **Taxi boat** 3 times a day from Pollónia to Kímolos; round-island **excursion boats**, with stops for lunch and swims, or hire the *Apollonia* for your own excursion from Manolis Galanos, ☎ 51 385. **Port authority**: ☎ 22 100.

By road: frequent **buses** from Adámas square to Pláka, via Tripití; 3 times a day to Pollónia by way of Filikopi and Pachera; also to Paleóchora and Zephyria once a day, and Provatás and Paleóchori Beaches.

Mílos ✆ *(0287–)*

Municipal tourist information, on the Adámas quay, ✆ 22 445, has accommodation lists. **Vichos Tours** ✆ 22 286, 🖃 22 396 on the front are very helpful for tickets, accommodation all over the island, and car hire.

Festivals

Easter, Triovassálos; **fifty days after Greek Easter**, Ag Triáda in Adámas; **19 July**, Profítis Ilías on the mountain, Chalákas and Tripití; **26 July**, Ag. Panteleímonos at Plakotá; **5 August**, Sotíris at Paraskópou; **15 August**, Assumption of the Virgin, Ag. Charálambos, Adámas; **7 September**, Panagía Eleoúsa at Psathádika; **16 September**, Ag. Sofía, Chalákas; **25 September**, Ag. Ioánnis Theológos at Chalákas.

Adámas and the Beaches around the Bay

If you arrive by sea, you can see a sample of Mílos' eccentric rocks before you disembark: a formation called the **Arkoúdes**, or bears, rises up from the sea on the left as you turn into the largest natural harbour in the Mediterranean—so large it feels like a vast lake. The port, bustling **Adámas** (ΑΔΑΜΑΣ), is also the main tourist centre, bustling and friendly. The Cretans who founded the town brought their holy icons along, now displayed in the churches of Ag. Tríada and **Ag. Charálambos**, at the highest point in town; in the latter, one ex-voto, dating from 1576, portrays a boat attacked by a raging fish; the captain prayed to the Virgin, who resolved the struggle by snipping off the fish's nose.

West of town you can ease your aches and pains wallowing in the warm sulphurous mineral waters of the municipal **spa baths**, in an old cave divided into three bathrooms (*open daily 8–1, take a towel; adm*). Beyond is small **Lagáda Beach**, popular with families; a monument at Bombarda commemorates the French who died there during the Crimean War. Further along the track, reed-beds with gurgling hot mud pools mark the route to the '**Volcano**', really a glorified steaming fissure in the rock.

The vast, sandy **Bay of Mílos** is fringed with a succession of beaches like **Papikinoú**, backed by hotels and apartments. There's a quieter beach at **Alýkes,** the salt marshes before the Mávra Gremná, or the black cliffs, with fantastical rock formations; at several places out in the bay the sea bubbles from the hot springs released below. The generous spring near the airport is supposedly a sure cure for sterility in women. Past the salt-beds, industrial area and the airport clutter stretches the spectacular sandy beach at **Chivadólimni**, the island's longest, with a deep turquoise sea in front and a saltwater lake behind, named after the clams who live there; it's also the freelance campers' favourite. Other golden beaches along the coast are **Patrikia** and **Rivári**, the latter backed with a lagoon once used as a vivarium by the monks up at **Ag. Marína Monastery**, and **Emboriós** with rooms to let and a quaint taverna. Further north **Ag. Dimitríou** is often battered by winds.

Pláka: Ancient Melos and its Catacombs

Buses leaves frequently for **Pláka** (ΠΛΑΚΑ), the labyrinthine, sugar-cube capital, 4km uphill, blending into the windmill-topped suburb of **Tripití** (ΤΡΥΠΗΤΗ). Next to the bus stop is the **Archaeology Museum** (*©* 21 629, *open 8.30–3, closed Mon; adm*). Just inside is a plaster copy of Venus, a thoughtful consolation prize from Paris, but the real treasures are from the Neolithic era and Bronze Age: terracotta objects and lily-painted ceramics from Phylakope, including the famous *Lady of Phylakope*, a decorated Minoan-style goddess. There are Hellenistic arte- facts from Kímolos and several statues, but, like Venus, the famous marble *Poseidon* and the *Kouros of Mílos* are not at home but in the National Archaeological Museum in Athens. Signs point the way to the **Museum of Popular Arts** (*©* 21 292, *open Tues–Sat 10–1 and 6–8*), housed in a 19th-cen- tury mansion; it's especially fun if you can find someone to tell you the stories behind the exhibits, which include everything down to the kitchen sink.

Steps lead up to the Venetian **Kástro** set high on a volcanic plug. Houses formed the outer walls of the fortress. Perched on top was an old church, Mésa Panagía, blown up by the Germans during the Second World War. After liberation, a new church was built lower down, but the old icon of the Virgin reappeared in a bush on top of the Kástro. Every time they moved the icon it returned to the bushes so they gave in and built another church, **Panagía Skiniótissa**, 'Our Lady of the Bushes'. There are stunning views from here, and on the way up from **Panagía Thalassítras**, 'Our Lady of the Sea', 1228, where the lintel bears the arms of the Crispi family, who overthrew the Sanudi as dukes of Náxos. The church houses fine icons by Emmanuel Skordílis. **Panagía Rosaria** is the Roman Catholic church built by the French consul Louis Brest, and **Panagía Korfiátissa**, on the edge of a sheer cliff to the west of the village, has Byzantine and Cretan icons rescued from the ruined city of Zefýria.

Pláka itself is built over the acropolis of ancient **Melos**, the town destroyed by the Athenians after the dialogue and resettled by the Romans. In the 1890s the British school excavated the site at **Klíma**, a short walk below Pláka (if you take the bus, ask to be let off at Tripití), where you can visit a termitiary of **Catacombs** (*©* 21 625, *open daily except Mon, 8.45–2*), dating from the 1st century AD. One of the best-preserved Early Christian monuments in Greece, it has long corridors of arched niches carved in the rock. When first discovered, they were still full of bones, but contact with the fresh air quickly turned them to dust. Some held five or six bodies; others were buried in the floor. On some, inscriptions in red remain, as well as later black graffiti. The habit of building underground necropoli (besides the many at Rome, there are catacombs in Naples, Sicily and Malta) coincides with the presence of soft volcanic tufa more than with romantic notions of persecution and secret underground rites; interring the dead underground saved valuable land. (Curiously, the modern cemetery near Pláka resembles a row of catacombs above ground, the more posh ones even done out with carpets). A path from the catacombs leads to the spot where Venus was discovered—there's a marker by the fig tree.

The Venus de Milo, or Unclear Disarmament

On April 8, 1820, farmer Geórgios Kentrotás was ploughing a field when he discovered a cave containing half of a statue of the goddess Aphrodite. A French officer, Olivier Voutier, who just happened to be visiting Mílos at the time, urged the farmer to look for the other half. He soon found it, along with a 6th-century BC statue of young Hermes and Hercules as an old man—an ancient art lover's secret cache, hidden from the Christians. Voutier sketched the Aphrodite for Louis Brest, the French vice consul for Mílos. Brest sent this on to the French consul in Constantinople, who decided to obtain Aphrodite for France, and immediately sent an envoy over to complete the deal. But meanwhile Kentrotás, persuaded by the island's elders, had sold the statue to another man on behalf of the translator of the Turkish fleet, the Prince of Moldavia, Nichólas Mouroúzis. The statue was in a caique, ready to be placed aboard a ship for Romania just when the French ship sailed into Adámas. Eventually, after some brisk bargaining, the envoy and Brest managed to buy the Aphrodite as a gift for Louis XVIII (although some say the French sailors attacked the caique and grabbed her by force). On 1 March 1821 she made her début in the Louvre. Somewhere along the line—in the caique battle?—she lost her arms and pedestal with the inscription *Aphrodites Nikiforos* 'Victory-bringing Aphrodite'. The French cadet's sketch showed the arms, one hand holding an apple.

The path continues past the ancient Cyclopean city walls to the well-preserved **Roman Theatre**, where spectators looked out over the sea, excavated and reconstructed to something approaching its former glory; a company from Athens sometimes performs in the theatre in August. Remains of a **temple** are on the path back to the main road. From there you can take the road or an old *kalderími* pathway down to the picturesque fishing hamlet of **Klíma**, with its brightly painted boat garages, *syrmata*, carved into the soft volcanic tufa, with rickety balconies above and ducks waddling on the beach below. A museum-style reconstruction shows how the fishing families once lived around their caiques.

Around Pláka

Near Pláka, the market village **Triovassálos** merges into **Péra Triovassálos**. The churches in Triovassálos contain icons from the island's original capital Zefýria. The great rivalry between the two villages expresses itself on Easter Sunday, when, after burning an effigy of Judas, the young bloods of Triovassálos and Péra Triovassálos hold a dynamite-throwing contest on the land dividing the villages; the most ear-splitting performance wins. Tracks lead down to a wide selection of beaches, some adorned with wonderfully coloured rocks. One of the best beaches is **Pláthíena** near the Arkoúdes, with dazzling orange and white rock formations; it's also the best place on Mílos to watch the sun set. The old path from Pláka leads past **Fourkovoúni** with picturesque *syrmata* hewn into the cliffs. **Mandrákia**, under Triovassálos, is one of the island's most outstanding beauty spots, a stunning little cove studded with boat garages and topped by a white chapel. Further north, **Firopótamos** is another pretty fishing hamlet.

The North Coast: Phylakope and Pollónia

The road from Adámas or Pláka to Pollónia offers a pair of tempting stops along the north coast. A side road descends into the bleached moonscape of **Sarakíniko**, of huge rounded rocks and pointed peaks whipped by the winds into giant white petrified drifts, with a tiny beach and inlet carved in its bosom. To the east the fishing hamlets of **Pachaina** and **Ag. Konstantínos** have more *syrmata*; from the latter it's a short walk to **Papafrángas Cave**, three sea caves, where the brilliant turquoise water is enclosed by the white cliffs of a mini fjord, once used by trading boats as a hiding place from pirates. Bring an air mattress to paddle about on.

On the other side of Papafrángas, **Phylakope** (ΦΥΛΑΚΩΠΗ) is easy to miss but was one of the great centres of Cycladic civilization, and one of the first major sites excavated in Greece by the British, in 1869. The dig yielded three successive levels of habitation: Neolithic/Early Cycladic (from 3500 BC), Middle Cycladic (to around 1500 BC) and Late Cycladic/Mycenaean. Even in Early Cycladic days Mílos traded obsidian far and wide, especially to Crete—pottery found in the lowest levels showed an Early Minoan influence. Grand urban improvements characterize the Middle Cycladic period: a wall was built around the more spacious and elegant houses, some with frescoes—a charming blue and yellow one, now in the National Archaeology Museum in Athens, depicts a school of flying fish, that in the absence of Venus has become the artistic symbol of Mílos. A Minoan-style palace contained fine ceramics imported from Knossós, and there was trade with the coasts of Asia Minor. In this period Mílos, like the rest of the Cyclades, may have come under the direct rule of the Minoans; a tablet found on the site is written in a script similar to Linear A. During the Late Cycladic age, the Mycenaeans built their own shrine, added a wall around the palace, and left behind figurines and ceramics. Phylakope declined when metals replaced the need for obsidian. Yet for all its history the actual remains at the site are overgrown and inexplicable.

The bus ends up at Apollo's old town, **Pollónia** (ΠΟΛΛΩΝΙΑ) on the east coast, a popular resort with a tree-fringed beach, fishing boats, and tavernas. There's quite a bit of new holiday development with apartments and bars on the **Pelekóuda** cape. Water taxis leave Pollónia harbour for Kímolos, five times a day, weather permitting. **Voúdia** beach to the south has a unique view of the island's mining activities.

In the Centre: Zefýria, Paleochóri, and Around

Buses cross the island to **Zefýria** or Chóra, the capital of Mílos from 800 to 1793. **Panagía Portianí** was the principal church of the village; its priest was accused of fornication by the inhabitants, and although he steadfastly denied it, the villagers refused to believe him. With that the priest angrily cursed the people, a plague fell on the town, and everyone moved down to Pláka. Today Zefýria is a very quiet village of old crumbling houses, surrounded by olive trees. A new paved road and the bus continues to popular sandy **Paleochóri Beach**; quieter **Ag. Kyriakí**, to the west, has rooms and tavernas, too. **Kómia**, east of Zefýria, has ruined Byzantine churches, and nearby at **Demenayáki** are some of Mílos' obsidian mines.

South and West Mílos

If eastern Mílos is fairly low and green, the south and west are mountainous and dry. Just south of Chivadólimni, **Provatás** has another sandy beach and hot springs, **Loutrá Provatá,** where you can examine remains of Roman mosaics, followed by a natural sauna to ease your rheumatism, recommended by no less than Hippocrates himself. **Kípos**, further along the coast, has two churches: one, the 5th-century **Panagía tou Kipou**, is the oldest in Mílos. To the west, in the wild **Chalákas** region, where the last remnants of the cedar forests that once covered the island still survive in little canyons, the old monastery at **Ag. Marína** is worth a trip; from here you can climb to the top of **Profítis Ilías**, with a god's-eye view over Mílos and neighbouring islands.

Down in the southwest, at the famous monastery of **Ag. Ioánnis Theológos Siderianós**, St John is nicknamed the Iron Saint—once during his festival, revellers were attacked by pirates and took refuge in the church. In response to their prayers, the saint saved them by turning the church door to iron (you can still see a scrap of a dress caught in the door as the last woman entered). The pirates could not break in, and when one of them tried to shoot through a hole in the church dome, Ag. Ioánnis made his hand wither and fall off, still holding the pistol. Another miraculous story from April 1945 tells of a shell from an English warship zapping through the church door and embedding itself in the wall without exploding. Ask if you can camp on the beach below; the warden usually says yes.

A Geological Mystery Tour

From Adámas excursion boats tour the island's fascinating rock formations from the sea. Highlights include the **Glaroníssia**, four cave-pocked basalt islets, shaped like organ pipes off the north coast; **Paleoréma** on the east coast with a disused sulphur mine which turns the water emerald-green; and on the southwest corner, the sea caves of **Sikía** where the sun's rays slant through the roof to create dramatic colours in the water; and **Kléftiko**, the pirates' hideaway with another set of fantastic cream and white rocks rising from the sea. You can also sail near **Andímilos** to the northwest, a reserve for the rare Cretan chamois goat, or *kri-kri.*

Mílos ✉ *84800,* ✆ *(0287–)*　　　***Where to Stay and Eating Out***

Mílos fills up to the brim from 15 July–15 September, so be sure to book. If you get stuck call the **Rooms to Let Association**, ✆ 23 429.

Adámas

Kapetan Georgadas ✆ 23 215, ✆ 23 219 (*C; exp*) are re-vamped traditional-style apartments, small but exclusive, with satellite TV, mini bars, air-conditioning. *Open all year.* **Delfini**, ✆ 22 001 (*D; mod*) is a friendly family-run hotel with a nice breakfast terrace; the same family also runs the smart new **Seagull Apartments**, ✆ 23 183/193 (*lux–exp*). **Adamas**, ✆ 22 322/581, ✆ 22 580 (*C; mod*) has well-equipped air-conditioned rooms perched above the harbour. On the other side of town, **Popi's**, ✆ 22 286, ✆ 22 396 (*C; exp*) is comfortable with very helpful management. *Open all year.* **Semiramis**, ✆ 22 118, ✆ 22 117 (*D; mod*) is excellent with a pretty vine-clad terrace—help yourself to grapes—bar, transfer minibus and rent-a-bike service. **Chronis,** ✆ 22 226, ✆ 22 900 (*C; exp–mod*) features fully equipped stone cottages in a pretty pistachio and banana orchard but is under miserable management. White and quiet **Mílos**, ✆ 22 087, ✆ 22 306 (*C; mod*), on the seafront, doesn't look much but has an excellent restaurant popular with Greeks.

Adámas has most of the island's restaurants; if you come in the right season, look for clams from Chivadólimni. On the waterfront the best bet for fair-priced Greek home-cooking is **Barko**, with good barrel wine. Friendly **Flisvos** has the usual fish and oven-ready dishes; next door **Kynigos** serves similar fare in unpretentious but pleasant surroundings. **Vendema**, above the ferry port, serves tasty Greek and Middle Eastern dishes. Fish come up to feed beneath the terrace at **Trapatseli's**, which has an excellent menu, especially for fish dishes. The *spetsofái* fish stew and *soupiés*, cuttlefish *stifádo*, are good as well as the local *dópio* hard cheese; next door **Navayio** also has fresh fish and local *mezédes*. **Ta Pitsounakia** spitroasts all kinds of meats and *kokorétsi*, while **Aktaio** by the water is popular for breakfasts, pizza and ice-cream.

Pláka/Tripití/Klíma

In Pláka, the **Plakiotiki Gonia** is a sweet little taverna with local dishes like cheese pies and country bread with tomatoes; **Kastro**, in Pláka's square, is also popular, with views up to the castle.

At Tripití, **Popi's Windmill**, ✆ 22 287, 🖅 22 396 (*lux–exp*) has rooms that sleep 4–5 in two beautifully converted mills. There are lots of new tavernas here; **Mayeriko** is the best. The *ouzerie* **Methismeni Politia**, the 'Drunken State', specializes in *mezédes*, wines and ouzo in a romantic garden setting with views across the gulf.

In Klíma the **Hotel/Restaurant Panorama**, ✆ 21 623 (*C; exp–mod*), has rooms with private bath, and a dining terrace with great views; a good bet for lunch.

Pollónia

Kapetan Tassos, 100m from the beach, ✆ 41 287, 🖅 41 322 (*A; exp*) has rather smart Cycladic-style apartments. **Apollon** apartments and studios, ✆ 41 347 (*exp*) have views over Kímolos, and home-cooking at the family taverna. Other favourites are **Petrakis** and **Kapetan Nikolas.**

Paleochóri /Ag. Kyriakí

At Paleochóri, the **Artemis Restaurant** has bungalows, ✆ 31 222, and the **Pelagos** taverna has great food. **Thirios Restaurant** at Ag. Kyriakí has rooms, ✆ 22 779/058.

Entertainment and Nightlife

Mílos has quite a sophisticated nightlife with scores of dancing bars and discos; there's even a roller-skating rink in Adámas. Locals hang out at **Yanko's**, near the bus stop, **To Ouzerie** on the front or **To Kafeneion** for cocktails and Greek music in a flower-filled courtyard. Otherwise in Adámas hot spots are **Notos Club** on the north end of town, **Milo Milo** disco at Langáda beach, and the **Dancing Club** at Triovassálos, or **Vipera Libertina Bar**, and **Puerto** for Greek music. In Pollónia head to **8 Bofor**, 8 ΜΠΩΦΟΡ, at Pelekoúda for jazz, blues and rock.

Mýkonos (ΜΥΚΟΝΟΣ)

This dry, barren island, frequently plagued by high winds but graced with excellent beaches and a beautiful, colourful, cosmopolitan town, has the most exciting and sophisticated nightlife in Greece. This, plus its proximity to ancient Delos, has made it the most popular island in the Cyclades. If the surge in tourism in recent years caught the other islands unawares, Mýkonos didn't bat a mascaraed eyelid, having made the transformation long ago from a traditional economy to one dedicated to the whims of the international set.

If you seek the simple, the unadorned, the distinctly Greek—avoid Mýkonos like the plague. But the party will go on without you; Mýkonos' streets are jammed with some of the zaniest, wildest, raunchiest and Most Beautiful People in Greece. It also has the distinction of being one of the most expensive islands, and the first officially to sanction nudism on some of its beaches; it is also the Mediterranean's leading gay resort, though it's also very popular with a mixed crowd with money to spend.

History

The Ionians built three cities on Mýkonos: one on the isthmus south of Chóra, the second at Dimastos, over an older site dating back to 2000 BC, and the third at Pánormos near Paliókastro. In 88 BC, during the war between the Romans and Mithridates of Pontus, all three were destroyed.

Chóra was rebuilt during the Byzantine period, and the Venetians surrounded it with a wall that no longer exists; however, at Paliókastro a fort built by the Gizzi still remains. Chóra is one of the few old Cyclades capitals at shore level, perhaps because the islanders were among the most notorious pirates in the Aegean, and in 1537 it fell without resistance to Barbarossa, and then simply carried on as it had been, settled with pirate families, who ran a very profitable plunder market, fencing goods to European merchants.

Centuries of training at sea primed the islanders for the front lines in the war for independence; the island fleet of 22 ships was led by Mantó Mavroyénous, the local heroine, who donated all of her considerable fortune to the cause.

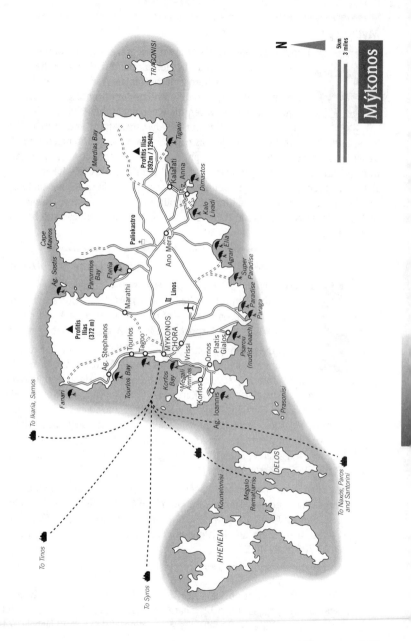

N

5km
3 miles

Mýkonos

TRAGONISI

Merdias Bay

Profitis Ilias
(392m / 1294ft)

Tigani

Kalafati

Ag. Anna

Dimastos

Cape
Mavros

Paliokastro

Kalo
Livadi

Ag. Sostis

Panormos
Bay

Ftelia

Marathi

Ano Mera

Elia

Agrari

Profitis
Ilias
(372 m)

Stephanos

Tourlos

Linos

Super
Paradise

Paradise

Fanari

Tourlos Bay

Tagoo

MYKONOS
HORA

Vrissi

Paraga

Psarou
(nudist beach)

Ag.

Megali
Ammos

Ornos

Platis
Gialos

Korfos Bay

Korfos

Ag. Ioannis

Prasonisi

To Ikaria, Samos

To Tinos

Kounelonisi

Megalo
Rematiarisi

DELOS

To Syros

RHENEIA

To Naxos, Paros
and Santorini

Mythology

In myth Mýkonos is best known as a graveyard, site of the rock tombs of the giants slain by Hercules and that of Ajax the Lokrian, one of the heroes of the Trojan War. This Ajax was known as Little Ajax to differentiate him from Big Ajax, who committed suicide when the weapons of the dead Achilles were not given to him but to Odysseus. After the capture of Troy, Little Ajax proved himself just as pathetic a hero when he raped Priam's daughter Cassandra, who had sought protection in a temple of Athena. Athena avenged this blasphemy by wrecking Ajax's ship off the coast of Mýkonos. Poseidon saved him in a sea storm but, defiant as ever, Ajax declared that he would have been able to save himself without the god's assistance. Poseidon's trident finished Ajax then and there, and his Mycenaean tomb can still be seen at Pórtes.

Mýkonos ☎ *(0289–)*   *Getting There and Around*

By air: several daily with Athens, several times a week with Thessaloníki, Santoríni, Rhodes, and Herákleon (Crete). Olympic Airways office is on the edge of town, at the end of Ag. Efthimiou street, ☎ 22 490. **Airport**: ☎ 22 327. Buses stop by the airport.

By sea: daily connections with Piraeus, Rafína (for catamarans and hydrofoils), Ándros, Tínos, Sýros, Páros, Náxos, Íos and Santoríni; several times a week with Herákleon (Crete), Amorgós, Astypálaia, Kos, Karystos, (Évia), Rhodes, Koufoníssia, Schinoússa and Heráklia. Twice a week with Síkinos, Folégandros, Ikaría, Sámos, Skiáthos, Skýros, and Thessaloníki, once a week with Sífnos, Sérifos, Pátmos and Lípsi. **Excursion boats** to Délos daily between 8 and 10; also to Paradise, Super Paradise, Agrari and Eliá from both Chóra and Platís Gialós, **Port authority**: ☎ 23 922.

By road: there are two **bus** stations. The one by the Archaeology Museum serves Ag. Stefanos, Tourlos, Áno Merá, Eliá, Kalafátis, and Kaló Livádi. The one by Olympic Airways is for Ornós, Ag. Ioánnis, Platís Gialós, Psaroú, the airport, and Kalamopodi. For information, ☎ 23 360. **Taxis**: ☎ 23 700 or 22 400.

Tourist Information

On the quay, **tourist police** ☎ 22 482 (run by the one man on Mýkonos who doesn't speak English!) share the same complex as the Hotel Reservations Office, ☎ 24 540, the Association of Rooms and Flats, ☎ 24

860, open 10–6; and the camping information office. On the Net, try *http://mykonos.forthnet.gr/skaphp1.htm*.

Festivals

15 August, Panagía Tourliani. But then every day's a party on Mýkonos.

Chóra

Prosperity has kept the homes of **Chóra** (XΩPA), the island's picture-postcard capital and port, well-maintained, gleaming and whitewashed, with brightly painted wooden trims. During the day it is a quiet place as everyone hits the beach; at night it vibrates. In the main square a bust of war heroine Mantó Mavroyénous once served as the island's guardian of left luggage; now dire little notices keep the backpacks away. Further up the waterfront is the departure quay for the boats to Délos. The pelican mascot of Mýkonos, the successor of the original Pétros, may often be found preening himself in the shadow of the small church.

On the hill overlooking the harbour are several thatched **windmills**; one from the 16th century has been restored to working order (*open June–Sept 4–6*). They are a favourite subject for the students at the School of Fine Arts, as is **Little Venice**, the houses of Alefkándra, tall and picturesque and built directly on the sea just below the windmills, each house now accommodates a cocktail bar from where there are pretty sunset views.

Mýkonos claims to have 400 churches, some no bigger than bathrooms, and the most famous of these, just beyond Little Venice, is the oft-photographed snow-white **Panagía Paraportianí**, an asymmetrical masterpiece, four churches melted into one. Just opposite, the **Folklore Museum** (*open Mon–Sat 5.30–8.30pm, Sun 6.30–8.30*), houses old curiosities, a traditional bedroom and kitchen, and a gallery of 19th-century prints of sensuous Greek odalisques gazing dreamily into space; downstairs is an exhibition, 'Mýkonos and the Sea'.

The **Nautical Museum**, in the centre at Tria Pigádia, (*open summer 10.30–1; 6.30–9.30pm*) has rooms containing ships' models from ancient times and a collection of paintings, prints and coins. Old anchors, ships' wheels, cannons, and copies of ancient tombstones of shipwrecked sailors fill the garden. Nearby, **Lena's House** (*open April–Oct, 7–9pm*) is a branch of the Folklore Museum: a 19th-century middle class home of Léna Sakrivanoú, preserved as she left it, with everything from her needlework to chamber pot.

Towards the ferry quay, beyond the ducks and geese on Ag. Anna beach, the **Archaeology Museum** (*open 8.30–3, closed Mon; adm*) was built in 1905 in the jailhouse style to imprison ceramics, many boldly decorated with sphinxes, lions, birds and horses, from the necropolis islet of Rhéneia (*see* Délos, p.173). But the finest single item was found on Tínos: a red 7th-century BC funeral pithos with relief scenes from the Fall of Troy, like comic book strips, of the death of Hector's son, and a delightful warrior-stuffed Trojan horse, fitted with airplane windows.

Around Mýkonos: Inside and Around the Edges

In ancient times Mýkonos was the butt of many jokes and had the dubious distinction of being famous for the baldness of its men, and even today the old fishermen of the island never take off their distinctive caps. Despite all the changes, they have kept their sense of humour, and if you speak a little Greek they'll regale you with stories of the good old days—before all the tourist girls (and boys) began chasing them around. You may find a few old fellows to chat up at **Áno Merá** (ANΩ MEPA), Mýkonos' other town, where the 16th-century **Panagía Tourlianí Monastery** with its sculpted marble steeple protects Mýkonos from harm; it has a carved Florentine altarpiece, fine Cretan icons, an ecclesiastical museum and farm tool museum (*to visit, ring ahead,* © *71 249*). Below, sandy windswept **Pánormos Bay** was the site of one of Mýkonos' three ancient cities; here **Fteliá** and **Ag. Sostis** are favourite wild beaches for windsurfers. At **Lino** by the airport are the remains of a Hellenistic tower and walls.

North of Chóra, the beaches at **Tagoú, Toúrlos** and **Ag. Stephanós** have a lot of accommodation and a lot of people to fill them up: **Fanári** to the north is considerably quieter. The nearest beaches south of Chóra are **Megáli Ámmos, Kórfos** and **Ornós**, all of which are built up, especially Ornós, with its cute little port. The biggest resort is **Platís Gialós**, to the east, with its own system of boat excursions to the other beaches and Délos, while jet-setters like to jet-ski at **Psaroú**, just before Platís Gialós. **Paradise** with its campsite, diving school, and Cavo Paradiso (a pool-bar-restaurant Hard Rock Café clone) and **Super Paradise** are the once notorious nudist beaches on the island, both much less notorious; little **Agári**, just east of Super Paradise, has missed out on being exploited. **Eliá**, a once quiet beach accessible by bus, is divided into straight and gay precincts; just inland sports the new **Watermania water park**, © 71 685. **Ag. Ánna** is a quieter beach, and there's the fishing hamlet and the family beach at **Kalafátis**, also worth a trip. At **Pórtes** you can spit on the 'tomb' of Ajax the troublemaker. **Dragonísi**, the islet off the east coast of Mýkonos, has numerous caves, and if you're very lucky you may see a rare monk seal in one of them.

Mýkonos ✉ *84600,* © *(0289–)*   ***Where to Stay and Eating Out***

There's certainly no lack of places to stay on Mýkonos, although prices tend to be higher than almost anywhere else in Greece and you should book from June on. Sleek new hotels, many incorporating elements of the local architecture, occupy every feasible spot on the coast, especially along the road to Platís Gialós. When you step off the ferry you'll be inundated with people offering rooms, but beware that many of these are up the hill above Chóra, in a barren, isolated and ugly area of holiday apartments. You'll probably do better using the accommodation desks just beyond.

Chóra (Mýkonos Town)

Leto, ℰ 22 207, ℰ 23 985 (*A; exp*) has a wonderful view over the harbour and town, and was for many years the classiest place to stay on the island. **Adonis** ℰ 22 433, ℰ 23 449 (*C; mod*) is comfortable and central; **Zorzis** ℰ 22 167 (*C; exp–mod*) is a small American-run hotel in an old house on Kalogéra Street. Overlooking town, **Elysium**, ℰ 23 952, ℰ 23 747 (*C; exp*) adds a fitness centre, jacuzzi and pretty pool to the views from its bungalows. The cheerful little **Delos**, ℰ 22 517 (*C; exp–mod*) is a nice choice near the post office; **Manto**, 1 Evangelístrias, ℰ 22 330 (*C; mod*) is convenient for connoisseurs of the night scene. The delightful **Philippi**, ℰ 22 294 (*D; mod*) in the heart of Chóra at 32 Kalogéra Street has rooms scented by the hotel's lovely garden. **Angela's Rooms**, ℰ 22 967 on Plateía Mavrogénous are some of the cheapest (*mod–inexp*). **Bellou**, ℰ 22 589, ℰ 27 093 (*C; mod*), at Mégali Ámmos beach just south of Chóra, is quiet with no frills. Just inland at Vríssi, the **Kipos Sourmeli**, ℰ 22 905 (*E; mod*) has a pleasant garden, and pleasant rates.

Chóra has food for every pocket and every appetite. **Philippi** *(see* above; ℰ 22 295 to book) has the best reputation in town for international and Greek cuisine, served in the garden (*count on 7000dr*). **Edem**, ℰ 22 855, offers a varied international menu around a courtyard pool next to Panachrandou church. Centrally placed **Katrin's**, again fairly expensive, has many French specialities.

If you need to be reminded that you're in Greece, head for **Niko's Taverna**, behind the town hall, or **Maky's**, just around the corner, with good dinners in the *2500dr* range. A notable exception to the rule that the back streets hide the best, secret tavernas is **Antonini's**, slap in the middle of the activity on taxi square; genuine Greek food at fair prices: varied and excellent *mezé*, shrimp salad and very tasty veal or lamb casserole (*2000dr*). For fish, dine out at **Kounelas**, at the end of the waterfront, where the owner, a colourful character, promises consistently fresh seafood (*4000dr*). English-run **Sesame Kitchen**, ℰ 24 710 is a vegetarian's haven. If you take the complimentary bus out of Chóra, there's even a (real) **Hard Rock Café** where you can eat expensive fast food and lounge by a pool.

North of Chóra

On the beach, within walking distance of town at Tagoú, is the award-winning Cubist beauty **Cavo Tagoo**, ℗ 23 692, ✆ 24 923 (*A; lux*), 'pour les lucky few', with seawater pool, beautiful view of Mýkonos, and the chance to rub shoulders with the stars. **Aegean**, in Tagoú, ℗ 22 869 (*B; exp*) is well-appointed but still family-run and friendly; just out of town **Manoula's Beach**, ℗ 22 900, ✆ 24 314 (*C; exp–mod*) is the pretty bungalow complex where they filmed *Shirley Valentine*. Toúrlos Beach has the **Rhenia**, ℗ 22 300, ✆ 23 152 (*B; exp*) with tranquil bungalows overlooking Chóra and Délos, and the small but stylish **Iliovassilema**, ℗ 23 010, ✆ 23 931 (*D; mod–inexp*). **Matthew Taverna** is slick and well patronized. Favourite of Jane Fonda is the **Princess of Mýkonos** ℗ 23 806, ✆ 23 031 (*B; lux–mod*) at Ag. Stephanós, with pool, sauna, jacuzzi and the works. It isn't in the heart of the action, but only a taxi-ride away; still in that area, the **Artemis Apartments**, ℗ 22 345 (*C; mod*), or the smaller D-class **Mina**, ℗ 23 024, both have perfectly acceptable rooms with bath. Further north, just before Fanári at Choulakia beach, little **Vaggeli**, ℗ 22 458, ✆ 25 558 (*mod*) is quiet, small and very Greek, with a good restaurant.

South Coast Beaches

At Ornós, **Kivotos**, ℗ 24 094, ✆ 22 844 (*C; exp*) is one of the 'Small Luxury Hotels of the World' with Olympic squash courts, antique shops and a wet bar in the seawater pool; another choice, **Yannaki**, ℗ 23 393, ✆ 24 628 (*C; exp–mod*) is traditional style, but with mod cons like air-conditioning, pool, TV, fridges, bars and a pool. At Platís Gialós the ritzy **Petinos Beach** ℗ 24 310, ✆ 23 680 (*A; lux–exp*) has every facility, pool, and water sports. Psaroú's **Grecotel Mykonos Blu**, ℗ 27 800, ✆ 27 783, built in 1996, has the works and a gourmet restaurant. Between Parága and Paradise, the spanking new **San Giorgio**, ℗ 27 474, ✆ 27 481 (*A; exp*) has a seawater pool and all comforts, including minibars. At Kalafítis, the new **Anemoessa** ℗/✆ 71 420 is built in the Cycladic style, air-conditioned, and serves a big American buffet breakfast. The Italian seafood restaurant **Marcos** is an old standby. In nearby Ag. Ánna, at the end of the road that crosses the island, **Nikola's** is authentic and a local favourite. The **Ano Mera** at Áno Merá, ℗ 23 310, ✆ 24 814 (*A; lux–exp*) is one of the island's best hotels with pool, restaurant and disco. The Stavrokopóulos family's **Taverna Vangelis**, on the square, is the place for local food including Mýkonos cheese, *kopanistí*. All campers are referred to the barracks-like **Paradise Beach**, ℗ 22 582, ✆ 24 350 and next-door **Mykonos Camping**, Parága Beach, ℗ 24 578. Both have good facilities, minibuses and continuous boat service from Platís Gialós.

The international and gay set still bop the night away in venues ranging from the cosy to the crazy. Mýkonos has its own little **Internet Café** on Kouzi Georgoul 23, ☎ 22 992 (*netcafe@skagias.myk.forthnet.gr*). Lower tech types have **Veranda Bar** in a converted mansion, a place to relax with a pleasant view of the windmills; **Bolero**, in the centre of town, has good music and cocktails; **Kastro's** in Little Venice will be forever famous for its sunset views, classical sounds and strawberry daiquiris; if you prefer piña coladas, try **Katerina's** next door. Live music and snazzy cocktails can be had at the **Piano Bar** above taxi square, but get there early for a seat; **Monna Lisa**, also here, plays lots of salsa and other latin sounds. High-tech **Astra Bar** is the cool yuppie hang-out. The **City Club** has a nightly transvestite show. **Thalami**, below the city hall, has Greek music and dancing, as does the perennial favourite, the **Mykonos Dancing Bar**; the Greeks themselves get down to the Hellenic top ten at **Nine Muses. Pierro's** just back from the main waterfront remains the most frenzied of the lot, where hordes dance to the loud, lively music and spill out into the square.

Délos (ΔΗΛΟΣ)

Many are your temples and shaded groves
Every peak, cliff and mountain high
Are loved by you, and the rivers that flow to the sea
But Phoebus, Delos is your heart's delight
Where the Ionians in their long robes gather
With their children and honoured wives
To give you pleasure on your holy days
With boxing, dance and song
In all their competitions.
To happen upon the Ionians gathered there
A man would call them deathless and unageing
For he would see how all are graceful
And his heart would take delight in watching them
The men and fine-girdled women
Their fast ships and their many belongings...

Homeric Hymn to Apollo (8th century BC)

Délos, holy island of Apollo, one of the most beloved gods of the ancient Greeks, centre of the great maritime alliance of Archaic and Classical times and commercial hub, is now a vast open-air museum. A free port in Hellenistic times that controlled much of the east–west trade in the Mediterranean, today the island is deserted except for the lonely guardian of the ruins—and the boatloads of day-trippers. Even though the ancients allowed no burials on Délos, the islet is haunted by memories of the 'splendour that was Greece'; the Delians themselves have been reincarnated as little lizards, darting among the poppies and broken marble.

Mythology

Zeus, they say, once fancied a very ancient moon goddess named Asteria. Asteria fled him in the form of a quail, and Zeus turned himself into an eagle the better to pursue her. The pursuit proved so hot that Asteria the quail turned into a rock and fell into the sea. But Asteria, in an older version of the story, was actually the sacred ship of the sky, crewed by the first Hyperboreans, who after thousands of years of wandering the heavens alighted in Egypt and sailed up the Nile to this spot. The ship-rock was called Adelos, 'the invisible', as it floated all over Greece like a submarine just below the sea's surface.

Zeus subsequently fell in love with Asteria's sister Leto, and, despite the previous failure of the bird motif, succeeded in making love to her by turning them both into quails. But Zeus' jealous, Thurberesque wife Hera soon got wind of the affair and begged Mother Earth not to allow Leto to give birth anywhere under the sun, and sent the serpent Python to pursue her. All over the world wandered poor, suffering, overripe Leto, unable to find a rock to stand on, until in pity Zeus turned to the South Wind and his brother Poseidon and asked them to lend a hand. The South Wind blew Leto to Ortygia ('quail' island), later known as Rheneia, where she gave birth to Artemis, the goddess of the hunt and virginity; meanwhile Poseidon ordered Adelos to halt, and anchored the islet with four columns of diamond; thus the Invisible, not under the sun but under the sea, became Delos, or 'Visible'. The newborn Artemis helped her mother over the narrow strait between the islands on to Delos, although the little island was still reluctant to host Leto, fearing her divine offspring would give the island a resounding kick back into the sea. But Leto promised the islet that no such thing would happen; indeed, her son would make Delos the richest sanctuary in Greece. The island conceded, and after nine days' labour on Mt Kýthnos, standing between a date palm and olive tree, she gave birth to Apollo, the god of reason and light. He was hardly born when he picked up his bow and arrows, shot some goats, and erected the first altar to himself from their horns. Zeus intended him to go straight to Delphi from there to give the Hellenes their laws and sent a swan-drawn chariot for that purpose; but Apollo instead used it to fly to the blessed land of the Hyperboreans, 'the beyond-the-north-wind people' where he remained for a year, only returning to Delphi at midsummer.

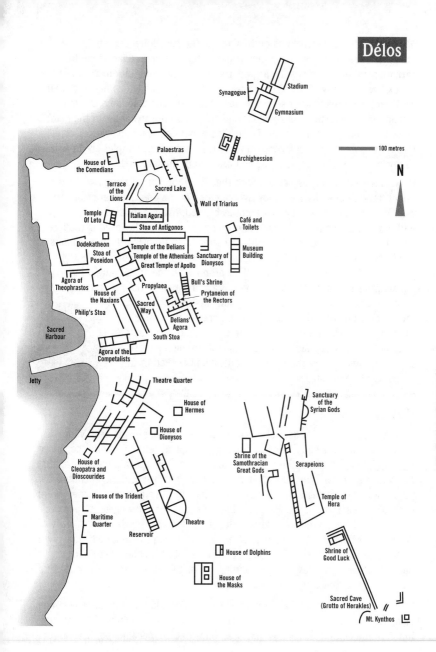

Délos

Stadium
Synagogue
Gymnasium

Palaestras
House of
the Comedians
Terrace
of the
Lions
Sacred Lake
Archighession

100 metres

N

Temple
Of Leto
Italian Agora
Wall of Triarius
Café and
Toilets
Stoa of Antigonos
Dodekatheon
Stoa of
Poseidon
Temple of the Delians
Temple of the Athenians
Great Temple of Apollo
Sanctuary of
Dionysos
Museum
Building
Agora of
Theophrastos
House of
the Naxians
Propylaea
Bull's Shrine
Philip's Stoa
Sacred
Way
Delians'
Agora
Prytaneion of
the Rectors
Sacred
Harbour
South Stoa
Agora of the
Competalists
Jetty

Theatre Quarter
House of
Hermes
Sanctuary
of the
Syrian Gods
House of
Dionysos
House of
Cleopatra and
Dioscourides
Shrine of the
Samothracian
Great Gods
Serapeions
House of the Trident
Temple of
Hera
Maritime
Quarter
Reservoir
Theatre
House of Dolphins
Shrine of
Good Luck
House of
the Masks
Sacred Cave
(Grotto of Herakles)
Mt. Kynthos

Délos   175

Apollo was the archetypal god of the Greeks, the pan-Hellenic deity representative of all the things they believed that set them apart from the barbarians: the love of beauty, art, poetry, music and moderation. Yet even the Greeks, as the story of his birth attests, considered him a latecomer into their pantheon. Leto his mother seems to have been an Asiatic goddess Lat, and Apollo, or rather aspects of Apollo, originated there (for instance, in the *Iliad*, he and Artemis are both on the Trojans' side, both had female priestesses— rare for the western Greek gods—and their most ancient temples are in Asia Minor) while other aspects of the god came from the far north.

He was always closely associated with the Hyperboreans, although who they might have been and where they lived are one of the great mysteries of antiquity: Pindar and others describe them as blessed, living a thousand years without war or the need to work, and spending day after day playing the lyre and flute, feasting and dancing with bay wreaths in their hair (some scholars think they may have been Siberian shamans, who taught Apollo the gift of going into a trance or ecstasy to deliver prophesies, the art he taught his female priests). Throughout his career as a god, Apollo would spend three winter months with them, which explains his traditional if incorrect association with the sun, which also spends its winter in the north. It is also interesting to note that Apollo's cult, rather unusually back then, had proselytizers, and among his most devout followers were the Pythagoreans, who believed in the transmigration of souls.

History

By the 3rd millennium BC Delos was settled by Karians from Asia Minor. By 1000 BC the Ionians had made it their religious capital, centred around the cult of Apollo, the father of Ion, the founder of their race. The worship on Delos is first mentioned in the aforementioned Homeric hymn, which specifically mentions the participation of women in the games—unlike in Olympia, where they were excluded on pain of death. People came from all over the Aegean to pay their respects, and bring precious offerings; for the first few centuries, the sanctity of Delos was such that the treasure lay about, openly and unguarded, in a town without walls. In 550 BC Polycrates, the Tyrant of Samos, conquered the Cyclades but respected the sanctity of Delos, putting the islet Rheneia under its control, and symbolically binding it to Delos with a chain.

With the rise of Athens, notably under Pisistratos, Delos knew its greatest glory and its biggest headaches. Athens, as an Ionian city, demanded to join the Ionians' maritime Amphictyonic league. What was once sacred became political as the

Athenians invented stories to connect themselves to the islet—didn't Leto, before giving birth, take off her belt on an isthmus in Attica? Didn't Erechtheus, the King of Athens, lead the first delegation to Delos? After slaying the Minotaur on Crete and abandoning Ariadne on Náxos, didn't Theseus stop at Delos and dance around the altar of Apollo with his companions (five women, and two men dressed in drag), the origins of the ancient *geranos* or crane dance, imitating the twists and turns of the Labyrinth? In 543 BC, Pisistratos somehow managed to get the oracle at Delphi to order the purification of the island after its 'corruption' by the Samian invaders, which meant removing the old tombs within sight of the temple of Apollo to the island of Rheneia, a manoeuvre designed to alienate the Delians from their past and diminish the island's importance in comparison to Athens. Even dogs were banned because they might kill the island's cats and rabbits.

In 490 BC the population of Delos fled to Tinos before the Persian king of kings, Darius, who, according to Herodotus, not only respected the sacred site and sacrificed 300 talents' worth of incense to Apollo, but allowed the Delians to return home in safety; an unusual measure, as the Persians had their own gods and usually wrecked all the Greeks' temples. After the Persian defeat at the Battle of Salamis, the Athenians, to counter further invasions, organized a new Amphictyonic league, again centred at Delos. Only their fleet, they claimed, could guarantee protection to the islands, who in return were required to contribute a yearly sum and ships to support the navy. Athenian archons administered the funds. No one was fooled in 454 BC when Pericles, in order better to 'protect' the league's treasury, removed it to Athens' acropolis; the money went not only to repair damage incurred during the previous Persian invasion, but to beautify Athens in general.

Shortly afterwards, divine retribution hit Athens and Pericles himself in the form of a terrible plague, and as it was determined to have been caused by the wrath of Apollo, a second purification of Delos (not Athens, mind!) was called for in 426 BC. This time, not only did the Athenians remove all the tombs, but they forbade both birth and death on Delos, forcing the pregnant and the dying to go to Rheneia, completing the alienation of the Delians. When the people turned to Sparta for aid during the Peloponnesian War, the Spartans remained unmoved: since the inhabitants couldn't be born or die on the island, they reasoned that Delos wasn't really their homeland, and why should they help a group of foreigners? In 422 BC Athens punished Delos for courting Sparta by exiling the entire population (for being 'impure') to Asia Minor, where all the leaders were slain by cunning. Athenian settlers moved in to take the Delians' place, but Athens was punished by the gods and suffered many setbacks against Sparta. After a year, hoping to regain divine favour, Athens allowed the Delians to return, but obviously Apollo was not impressed, and, in 403 BC, Sparta defeated Athens. Delos had a breath of freedom for ten years before Athens formed its second Delian alliance. It was far less forceful, and 50 years later the Delians had plucked up the courage to ask the league to give the Athenians the boot altogether. But the head of the league at the time, Philip II of Macedon, refused, wishing to stay in the good graces of the city that hated him most.

In the confusion following the death of Philip's son, Alexander the Great, Delos became free and prosperous, supported by the pious Macedonian general-kings. New buildings and shrines were constructed and by 250 BC Delos was a flourishing cosmopolitan commercial port, inhabited by merchants from all over the Mediterranean. When the Romans defeated the Macedonians in 166 BC they returned the island to Athens, which once again exiled the Delians. But by 146 BC and the fall of Corinth, Delos was the centre of the east-west trade, and declared a free port by the Romans in order to undermine the competition at Rhodes. People came from all over the world—Phoenicians, Egyptians, Jews, Syrians, Palestinians, Romans—to settle in this ancient Greek Hong Kong, and set up their own cults in complete tolerance. Roman trade guilds centred on the Italian Agora. New quays and piers were constructed to deal with the heavy flow of vessels. Slave markets thrived; on some days 10,000 human beings exchanged hands

In the battle of the Romans against Mithridates of Pontus in 87 BC, Delos was attacked by Mithridates' general Menophanes, who slew 20,000 people and enslaved the rest, threw the statues in the sea and wrecked the temples. The island never recovered. Sulla soon reconquered it, but 19 years later Delos was again pillaged by pirates allied to Mithridates, who once more sold the entire population into slavery. General Triarius retook the island and fortified it with walls, and Hadrian attempted to revive the waning cult of Apollo with new festivities, but by this time wretched Delos had fallen into such a decline that when Athens tried to sell it in the second century AD no one offered to buy it, and it eventually passed on to Mykonos. In AD 363, Emperor Julian the Apostate tried to jumpstart paganism on Delos, holding one last festival in the face of oracles that warned: 'Delos shall become Adelos'. To prevent it from ever happening again, Theodosius the Great banned pagan ceremonies altogether in 380. A small Christian community survived until the 6th century, but with few defences; the island was abandoned afterwards, and remained abandoned. House-builders on Tínos and Mýkonos used Delos for a quarry, taking the square blocks and throwing the statues and reliefs into the lime kiln; the Turks removed the bronze clasps that held the buildings together, while the rest was slowly covered with a thick layer of dust, as Delos indeed became Adelos; its once busy temple and markets became a pasture for the flocks of Mýkonos.

After the War of Independence, Delos and Rheneia were placed in the municipality of Mýkonos. Archaeological excavations were begun in 1872 by the French School, and were rather at random at first; surface evidence of the topography by then was almost nonexistent, and all the ancient sources, including an eight-volume guidebook to Delos written by a certain Semes, and Artistotle's *Treatise on the Republic of the Delians*, were lost. Digging began at Mount Kýthnos and spread to the plain, and continues to this day.

Getting There and Around

By sea: tourist boats from Mýkonos leave between 8 and 10am daily (except Mon), returning between 12 noon and 2pm, for around 1400dr return. Guided tours (4500dr), are available from agencies, or hire a **private boat** at the main harbour.

The Excavations

*A trip to **Délos** (© (0289) 22 259, open Tues–Sun 8.30–3), begins as you clamber out of the caique and pay the 1200dr entrance fee. Sensible shoes, sunhat, and water are essential. The quality of 'official' guides varies, and you have to fit in with their timetables. Major sites are labelled, badly translated guidebooks are on sale, and in the summer the crowds can make it hard to get much of a feeling for the place. To get your bearings, head up the hill, **Mount Kýthnos**, which has a great view over the site and the neighbouring islands of Mýkonos, Tínos and Sýros.*

As you disembark, to your left from the landing stage is the **Agora of the Competalists**. *Compita* were Roman citizens or freed slaves who worshipped the Lares Competales, or crossroads gods. These were the patrons of Roman trade guilds, while others came under the protection of Hermes, Apollo or Zeus; many of the ruins in the Agora were offerings built to them. Trade and commerce were part of Délos from the start. The temple acted as a bank, taking in taxes and rents from the properties donated by the faithful, and loaned the sacred money to earn interest; archaeologists found extensive records of the debts, paid and delinquent, which were posted in a public place for all to see.

A still discernible Sacred Way, once lined with statues, leads from here to the sanctuary of Apollo. To the left of the road stood a tall and splendid Doric colonnade called **Philip's Stoa**, built by Philip V of Macedon in 210 BC, and now marked only by its foundations; it once held a votive statue dedicated by Sulla for his victory over Mithridates. The kings of Pergamon built the **Southern Stoa** in the 3rd century BC, and you can also make out the remains of the **Delians' Agora**, the local marketplace in the area.

The **Sanctuary of Apollo** is announced by the **Propylaea**, a gateway built of white marble by the Athenians in the 2nd century BC. Just inside was an open area, where the temple's books and records were displayed, along with gifts. The cult was so important that a good deal of attention was given to public witnessing of every rite and ritual and donation; fragments of the annual lists engraved in stone, compiled by the sanctuary officials, carefully noting the donor and weight of each golden wreath, necklace, coin, and cups. Within the Propylaea stood a number of buildings, of which the most venerable was the long, narrow **House of the Naxians** (7th century BC), with granite walls. Of a huge and famous *kouros*, four times life size, representing Apollo as a young man, only the pedestal remains, bearing the inscription: 'I am of the same marble, both statue and base.' According to Plutarch, the *kouros* fell over when a nearby bronze palm tree donated by the pious Athenian general Nicias toppled over in the wind. The palm not only recalled the tree clutched by Leto in giving birth, but the custom initiated by the Athenian hero Theseus, who made a palm frond the prize of the Delian games. Nicias, later to be known for his leading role in Athens' climactic defeat at Syracuse, which caused it to lose the Peloponnesian War, also brought over one of the wonders of the day: an elegant disassembled pontoon bridge made of wood, covered all over with a thin coating of gold and ornament. Assembled and erected between Délos and Rheneia during the night before the opening of the Delian games, it caused a sensation when the Athenian dignitaries made their procession over to the sacred island, dressed in fine robes and garlands of wild flowers.

Next come three temples in a row. The first and largest, the **Great Temple of Apollo**, was begun by the Delians in 476 BC, and was crammed with offerings on its shelves and in coffers, including treasures such as the tiller from Agamemnon's trireme and the helmet that Leonidas wore at Thermopylae. The second is a small, exquisite **Athenian Temple** of Pentelic marble, built during the Second Purification, designed as a kind of private retreat for Apollo, where only the priests and a handful of magistrates had access, although worshippers could make sacrifices on the altar outside. The third, the smallest, of porous stone, the **Temple of the Delians**, was made by the 6th-century Athenian tyrant Pisistratos to house the sacred *Asteria*, the 'ship of the sky', represented by a moon setting in the sea. The Hellenistic warlord, Dimitrios the Besieger contributed the nearby **Bull's Shrine**, which held a model of another ship, a trireme in honour of the sacred delegation ship of Athens—the one Theseus sailed in on his return to Athens after slaying the Minotaur, and whose departure put off executions (most famously that of Socrates) until its return to Athens. Other buildings in the precinct were of an official nature—the **Prytaneion of the Rectors** and the **Councillor's house**. Towards the museum is the **Sanctuary of Dionysos** (4th century BC), flanked by lucky marble phalli; like Apollo, Dionysos was an outsider (from Thrace) and latecomer to the Greek pantheon. Even before Nietzsche's famous essay, the two complimented each other in curious ways—when Apollo was with the Hyperboreans, Dionysos usually took his place, as at the Oracle in Delphi. The **Stoa of Antigonos** was built by a Macedonian dynasty of that name in the 3rd century BC. Outside is the **Tomb**

of the Hyperborean Virgins, which was too sacred to move and the only one to stay put during the purifications. The story goes that once they sent two virgins with an escort of five youths to Delos as ambassadors to deliver gifts, but the two girls died, and the Hyperboreans, after waiting years for their return, became even more remote, and henceforth only sent gifts to Delos wrapped in straw, passed in a mysterious relay hand to hand.

On the opposite side of the Stoa of Antigonos the **Minoan fountain** dates from the 6th century BC. Through the **Italian Agora** you can reach the **Temple of Leto** (6th century) and the **Dodekatheon,** dedicated to the twelve gods of Olympos in the 3rd century BC. Beyond is the famous **Terrace of the Lions**, ex-votos made from Naxian marble in the 7th century BC; of the curiously lean and elongated half lions crouching on their haunches five remain of the original nine (or perhaps sixteen); one now guards the Arsenal in Venice and three have gone missing. They look east, towards the site of the **Sacred Lake**, which once hosted a flock of swans, marked by a small wall and a palm tree, but the water all evaporated in 1925, when Délos' torrent Inopos stopped flowing. Along the shore are two **Palaestras** (for exercises and lessons) along with the foundation of the **Archighession**, or temple to the first mythical settler on Délos, worshipped only here. Besides the **Gymnasium** and **Stadium** are remains of a few houses and a **synagogue** built by the Phoenician Jews in the 2nd century BC.

A dirt path leads from the tourist pavilion up to holy Mount Kýthnos. Along the way stand the ruins of the **Sanctuary of the Syrian Gods** of 100 BC with a small religious theatre within. Next is the first of three 2nd-century BC **Serapeions**, all temples dedicated to Serapis, the first and only successful god purposely invented by man—Ptolemy I of Egypt—who combined Osiris with Dionysos to create a synthetic deity to please both Hellenistic Greeks and Egyptians; syncretic Délos was one of the chief centres of his worship. Between the first and second Serapeions is the **Shrine of the Samothracian Great Gods**, the Cabiri or underworld deities. The third Serapeion (still housing half a statue) was perhaps the main sanctuary, with temples to both Serapis and Isis. In the region are houses with mosaic floors, and a **temple to Hera** from 500 BC. The **Sacred Cave**, where Apollo ran one of his many oracles, is en route to the top of Mount Kýthnos. Later it was dedicated to Heracles. On the mountain itself is the **Shrine of Good Luck**, built by Arsinoë Philadelphos, wife of her brother, the King of Egypt. On the summit of 113m Mount Kýthnos, signs of a settlement dating back to 3000 BC have been discovered, but better yet is the view, encompassing nearly all the Cyclades.

The exclusive **Theatre Quarter** surrounded the 2nd-century BC **Theatre of Délos**, with a 5500 capacity; beside it is a lovely eight-arched **reservoir**. The surviving records of property transactions on the holy island show a high rate of inflation; speculators would buy up blocks and demolish them to make ever grander houses. The houses that survive here date from the Hellenistic times and are among the best preserved in Greece, thanks to their long abandonment. As there was an excess of marble chips on the island, nearly all had mosaic floors: some 300 have survived, including some of the most lavish to survive from the period in Greece, such as in the **House of the Dolphins** and the **House of the Masks**. All have a cistern beneath the floor, spaces for oil lamps and sewage systems. Some are built in the peristyle 'style of Rhodes', with a high-ceilinged guest room; colonnades surround the central courts left open to the sun. The House of the Masks, with 19 rooms, may have been a fancy hotel for actors, and had its own slave quarter and sunken baths. Also seek out the **House of the Trident** and the **House of Dionysos**, both with mosaics, and the **House of Cleopatra and Dioscourides**, where the statues stand a headless guard over the once bustling town.

Surrounding Délos are the islets **Ag. Geórgios** (named after its monastery), **Karavoníssi**, **Mikró** and **Megálo Rematiáris**, the last consecrated to Hecate, the Queen of the Night. **Rhéneia**, also known as Greater Délos, lies just west of Délos and is just as uninhabited. Here came the pregnant or dying Delians—a large number of little rooms were excavated in the rock to receive them—before they moved into the realm of tombs and sepulchral altars. A 'purification pit' near the shore was the repository of the bones and grave goods exhumed by the Athenians in the second purification, where most of the vases in the museum in Mýkonos were discovered. On the other side of Rhéneia are the ruins of a lazaretto, once used by Sýros-bound ships sent into quarantine.

Where to Stay and Eating Out

You can't. Near the museum there's an overpriced café for the tourists. Don't be caught out; bring snacks and water with you.

Náxos (ΝΑΞΟΣ)

Náxos, 448sq km in area, is the largest of the Cyclades and the most mountainous, its highest point, Mount Zas, crowning the archipelago at 1004m. The second most populated, with 17,000 year-round residents, it can also claim to be the most fertile, the only one that could get by without importing food, its valleys a refreshing green even in the height of the sun-browned Cycladic summer. Sacred to Dionysos, Náxos makes excellent wine, and Kítron, a fragrant liqueur distilled from citron leaves, although seed potatoes are the main export. The entire west coast is almost one uninterrupted beach of silvery sands.

Náxos was Byron's favourite island, perhaps because it comes in romantic proportions: rugged mountains and lush valleys, sprinkled with the ruins of the ancient

Greeks, the gilded Byzantines, and his beloved Venetians. There are plenty of tourists, including heavy German and Scandinavian contingents, but they stay by the beaches, leaving the rest of the big island for wanderers and poets.

History

Náxos was one of the major centres of the Neolithic Cycladic civilization. Around 3000 BC, as now, the main settlements were near Chóra, on the hill of the Kástro, and at Grótta, where the sea-eroded remains of the Bronze Age town can still be seen in the clear water. Tradition has it that the island was later colonized by a party from Karia, led by a son of Apollo named Naxos. Although later Naxians were Ionians, their most troublesome enemy was Miletus in Ionia proper, where some Naxian refugees, eager to take back the island for themselves, helped stir up trouble. According to Plutarch, many battles were fought between the two rivals at the fort called Delion, of which a few vestiges remain near Náxos town.

One story has come down: once, when Miletus attacked Náxos, the beautiful island heroine Polykrite arrived at Delion too late and found the fortress gate closed against her. One of the Miletan leaders found her, fell in love with her and proved it by telling her of all the movements of his armies. His information enabled the Naxians to make a sudden attack on the Miletians, but in the confusion of the battle Polykrite's lover was also killed, and the girl died of sorrow the next day.

Náxos was one of the first islands to work in marble. In the Archaic period Naxian sculptors produced the lions of Délos and *kouros* statues of colossal size. Big was beautiful on Náxos; in 523 BC the tyrant Lugdamis declared he would make Náxos' buildings the highest and most glorious in Greece, although only the massive lintel from the Temple of Apollo survives to tell the tale of his ambition.

Náxos next makes the history books when the fertile, centrally located island, with a fine Byzantine castle, T'Apaliróu already in place, was chosen by Marco Sanudo to be the seat of his Aegean duchy. By the time Sanudo's buccaneers arrived in 1207, however, the Genoese, Venice's arch rivals, had got there first and put up a fierce resistance. To encourage his men, Sanudo burnt all of his ships, and that old trick worked; they ousted the Genoese, and Sanudo declared himself Duke Marco I of the Archipelago ('Archipelago' was a corruption of 'Aegean' as it appeared on Byzantine sea charts, *Aigaíon Pélagos*—under Sanudo and his successors, it took on its current meaning as a group of islands). Although officially the Duchy was under the Latin Emperor at Constantinople, it remained Venetian to the core, but was not exceptionally popular; by the end of the 14th century so many of the island's men had been forced into service that there was no one for the women to marry, and by the end of the 16th century the island was in open revolt. Even after the Turks took Náxos in 1564, the Dukes remained in nominal control of the Cyclades, although paying a tribute and answerable to the Sultan.

Mythology

After slaying the Minotaur, Theseus, the young hero from Athens, and Ariadne, the Cretan princess who loved him and saved his life with her ball of thread, stopped to rest at Náxos on their way to Athens. Yet the next morning, while Ariadne slept, Theseus set sail and abandoned her. This, even in the eyes of the Athenians, was dishonourable, especially as Theseus had promised to marry Ariadne in return for the assistance she had rendered him in negotiating the Labyrinth. Various explanations for Theseus' ungallant behaviour have sprung up over the centuries. Was she shot with arrows by Artemis in the temple of Dionysos, and left for dead, as the *Odyssey* says? Did Theseus simply forget her, did he find a new mistress, or did the god Dionysos, who later found and married Ariadne, somehow warn Theseus off?

Everyone agrees that it was the jilted bride's curse on Theseus that made him forget to change his black sails to white to signal his safe homecoming, causing his father to commit suicide in despair. Ariadne lived happily ever after with Dionysos, who set Ariadne's crown, the Corona Borealis, amongst the stars; the Celts called it Ariansrod, where their heroes went after death. The story inspired later artists as well, including Richard Strauss' opera *Ariadne auf Naxos*.

Náxos ☎ (0285–)

Getting There and Around

By air: two or three flights a day from Athens; charters from London and Manchester. **Airport**: ☎ 23 292.

By sea: daily to Páros, Sýros, Íos, Santoríni, Mýkonos, and Piraeus; almost daily boat or ferry to Amorgós via Koufoníssia, Heráklia and Schinoússa; 3–4 times a week with Donoússa, Herákleon (Crete), Tínos, Ándros, Sífnos, Sérifos, Anáfi, Astypálaea, Sámos, Ikaría, Rafína, Síkinos and Folégandros, to Rhodes and most of the Dodecanese, and Thessaloníki. **Hydrofoil**: frequently with Rafína, Mýkonos, Tínos, Ándros, the Back Islands, Íos, Santoríni, and Amorgós. Excursion boats to Délos, Mýkonos, Heráklia, Koufouníssi, and Santoríni, **Port authority**: ☎ 22 300.

By road: frequent **bus** service down to Ag. Ánna Beach; 5 times to Apiranthos, Filoti and Chalki; 2–3 times to Apollonía, Komiaki, Melanes and Kouros, ☎ 22 291. **Taxi** rank near bus station: ☎ 22 444.

Náxos

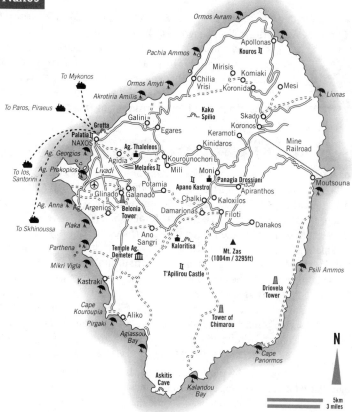

Ormos Avram

Apollonas
Kouros II

Pachia Ammos

Mirisis
Komiaki

To Mykonos

Ormos Amyti
Chilia Vrisi
Koronida
Mesi

Akrotiria Amilis
Lionas

To Paros, Piraeus

Galini
Kako Spilio
Skado

Grotta
Egares
Koronos

Palatia
NAXOS
Keramoti

Ag. Thaleleos
Kinidaros
Mine Railroad

Ag. Georgios
Agidia
Kourounochori
Moni

Ag. Prokopios
Melanes II
Mili

To Ios, Santorini
Livadi
Panagia Drossiani

Ag. Anna
Glinado
Galanado
Potamia
Apano Kastro
Apiranthos
Moutsouna

To Skhinoussa
Ag. Argenios
Belonia Tower
Damarionas
Chalki
Kaloxilos
Filoti

Plaka
Ano Sangri
Danakos

Parthena
Temple Ag. Demeter
Kaloritisa
Mt. Zas
(1004m / 3295ft)

Mikri Vigla
T'Apilirou Castle
Psili Ammos

Kastraki
Driovela Tower

Cape Kouroupia
Aliko
Tower of Chimarou

Pirgaki
Agiassou Bay
Cape Panormos

N

Askitis Cave
Kalandou Bay

5km
3 miles

Tourist Information

Orbit Travel, ℮ 22 454, are very helpful for accommodation and excursions and also represent Olympic Airways; the privately run **Náxos Tourist Information Centre**, ℮ 24 358, right on the quay, manages the Chateau Zévgoli Hotel and sells Christian Veke's helpful *Walking Tours in Náxos*. Also look for the Harms Verlag map of Náxos, available in shops, with all the paths, the best ones marked in red. The island has a better web site than most: *http://naxosnet.com/index.html*

Some of the many celebrations are: **23 April**, Ag. Geórgios at Kinídaros; **1 July**, Ag. Anargýroi at Sangrí; **14 July**, the biggest of all for Ag. Nikódimos, patron saint of Náxos, with a procession of the icon and folk festival; **17 July**, at Kóronos; the **first week of August** usually sees the Dionýsia festival in Náxos town, with folk dancing in local costume; free food and wine in the central square; **15 August**, Panagía at Filotí; **23 August**, at Trípodes; **29 August**, Ag. Ioánnis at Apóllon and Apíranthos.

Náxos Town

Náxos, the island's port and capital, is a hustling bustling place that has sprawled along the waterfront, leaving the old districts on the hill above intact. As you pull into port, the island's Π-shaped trademark, the massive doorway to nowhere, the **Portára** of Lugdamis' unfinished **Temple of Apollo** (522 BC), stands out like an ancient version of the enigmatic monolith in *2001: A Space Odyssey*. Set on the islet of **Palátia**, linked by an ancient causeway to the port, it comes in handy as a dramatic frame for sunset photos. The ancient **harbour mole** was rebuilt by Duke Marco Sanudo; in front of the port, a little chapel sits on its own islet. Statues of two famous sons of Náxos greet you: Michaeli Damiralis (d. 1917), who translated Shakespeare into Greek, and the slightly disappointed-looking Pétros Protopapadákis, who planned the Corinth canal but had the misfortune of serving as Minister of Economics during the 1920–22 catastrophe in Asia Minor; he was executed with five other members as scapegoats by the subsequent regime.

Near the main waterfront, by the Agrarian Bank, is the 11th-century church of **Panagía Pantanássa**, once part of a Byzantine monastery and famous for its very early icon of the Virgin. Lanes here lead up into old Náxos, a fine Cycladic town, although some people find its twisting streets under the archways almost claustrophobic and bewildering, which is just as the natives intended them to be, to confuse invading marauders. The town was divided into three neighbourhoods: Boúrgos where the Greeks lived, Evraiki, the Jewish quarter, and up above, Kástro, where the Venetian Catholic nobility lived. In **Boúrgos**, the Orthodox cathedral, the **Metropolis of Zoodóchos Pigí**, was built in the 1780s out of an old temple and older churches, with impressive blocks of granite; the elaborate interior has an iconostasis by Dimítrios Valvis of the Cretan school, and guards a precious Old Testament, donated by Catherine the Great. Archaeologists would gladly knock it down for a slam-bang dig if only the bishop would let them; as it is they've had to be content with the adjacent square, future site of the new archaeology museum, due to be finished by 1999.

The **Evraíki** district, or Jewish ghetto, is just above, but any traces of its former inhabitants have been obliterated, in spite of a long history. Náxos had a strong Jewish population in 1153, when it was visited by Arab geographer Edrizi; it had its own synagogue, and later in the 16th century the Duchy of the Archipelago was actually ruled by a Jewish financial agent named Joseph Nasi, who kept it for Sultan Selim the Sot. Above, at the highest point of Chóra, the introspective, high-walled **Kástro** was the neighbourhood of the Venetian overlords. The walls were built by Marco Sanudo out of a temple of Apollo; one of its seven original towers survives, guarding one of only three entrances into the district. Not surprisingly, the Kástro with its airs was always resented by the Greeks, at least until the 1950s, after the land reform eliminated many of their privileges. Some 19 Venetian houses still bear their coats-of-arms—something you'll almost never see in Venice proper, where displays of pride were severely frowned upon; another decoration you might see are the holders for the flagpoles that once held their proud Venetian standards. Many of the Kástro's current residents still claim Venetian descent, and many of their ancestors' tombstones in the 13th-century **Catholic Cathedral** boast grand titles. The cathedral, clad from head to toe in pale grey marble with a marble floor, was founded by Marco Sanudo for the Catholic archbishop that Venice sent out in 1208; inside the icons show a strong western influence. Near here, the church of **Panagía Theoskepásti** has fine icons by the Cretan school. Sanudo's own palace, or what remains of it, can be seen directly across the square.

During the Turkish occupation Kástro had a reputation for its School of Commerce, run by Catholic friars, attended for two years by Níkos Kazantzákis. This 17th-century building now houses the **Archaeology Museum**, at least until the new one is built (*open Tues–Sun, 8.30–3; adm*) with artefacts from the 5th millennium BC to 5th century AD, including a superb collection of Cycladic figurines in all sizes, including a funny ceramic pig about to be sick in a sack from 2800 BC, Minoan finds from the Grótta and the tombs at Kanini and Apolomata, Mycenaean pottery (note the *hydria* painted with fishermen) and a 4th-century BC mosaic of Europa on the bull, discovered at Aplomata. Náxos was once the centre of Cycladic culture and, by all accounts, the collection should be much larger, but in the 1960s, antique dealers stripped the island's great Bronze Age cemeteries, in what has been called one of the biggest archaeological disasters of the century.

On the north coast, Chóra looks down over **Grótta**, named for its numerous caves (naturally re-dubbed Grotty by Brits); if it's not windy you can see remains of the Cycladic town and a road under the water; one hollow in the rock is the 'Bath of Ariadne'. Further east along the road stands ancient **Fort Delion** (ΔHΛION), scene of starcrossed love. A road from Delion winds up the hill to the 18th-century **Moní Chrystostómou**.

South of Náxos Town

Further south, numerous hotels and a whole new suburb, Néa Chóra, have sprung up around popular **Ag. Geórgios** beach. Much of the rest of holiday Náxos is built up along the sandstrewn coast further south. The road then skirts the fertile **Livádi** plain, where Náxos grows its famous spuds; here, rather incongruously near the potatoes and airport at Iria, a **Temple of Dionysos** was discovered in 1986.

The Gift of Dionysos

Old gods never really die, but are often retired underground, as superstitions or spooks. In Greece, where Christianity triumphed very early on, several divinities of the old religion were syncretized into saints, especially in rural areas or on the islands, often with only a slight change of spelling—think of all the hill-topped chapels named after the prophet Elijah—Elias, or Ilias in Greek, which is only a breath away from Helios, the sun god. Long centuries without proper schools, living hand to mouth, eliminated any more precise memory of the pagan gods of old; in the 19th century, visiting philhellenes, clutching their Homer and Sophocles, were astonished by the Greeks' complete ignorance of their Classical heritage.

Occasionally, however, enough local memory survived for a god to enter the realm of folk tale. Naxians tell the story that when Dionysos was young, he was travelling back to his beloved isle and had stopped to rest when he saw a beautiful plant growing nearby. He decided then and there to transplant it to Naxos and dug it up by the roots, but it was very hot and the plant began to wilt. The young god then came upon the bone of a small bird and carefully slid the plant into the hollow of the bone to protect it. As he was a god, the plant kept growing as he went, and soon the bird bone was too small to hold the plant. He then found a lion bone, and it was large enough to contain both the bird bone and plant.

Still the plant continued to grow and sprout, and Dionysos realized that only a larger bone would do. He found the shinbone of an ass, into which all fitted perfectly well. By the time he arrived in Naxos, it was impossible to remove the plant from its triple sheath of bones, so he planted it in the ground as it was, and it became the first vine. When the grapes were ripe, he made wine and offered it to the Naxians. They declared it was a miracle. After the first couple of glasses they sang like birds; after a few more glasses they were as mighty as lions, as they drank even more they made asses of themselves.

The road continues to **Ag. Prokópios**, with nice coarse non-sticky sand, and then **Ag. Ánna**, the most popular beach, well sheltered from the notorious *meltémi*, and **Pláka** just south, considered by many the best in Náxos—white sand, dunes, and a variety of watersports on offer, and a popular alternative camp site. From Ag. Ánna, boats continue south to the beaches; by road you have to divert inland, by way of **Ag. Arsénios** (if you get off the bus here, you can take a lovely path down to the beaches, past windmills and a 30ft-high Hellenistic watch tower, the **Paleó Pírgos**). The vast white sandy beaches to the south begin at **Parthéna**, excellent for surfing and swimming; followed by **Mikrí Vígla**, where the sea is brilliantly clear; **Sahára** is well equipped for sea sports, and merges into **Kastráki**, again with sparkling sea and white sands, ideal for letting the kids run wild. Above the road stands **Pírgos Oskéllou**, a ruined Mycenaean fortress, built over the remains of a Cycladic acropolis. If the above beaches are too busy for your taste, there's a more remote strip of sand beyond Kastráki on either side of **Cape Kouroúpia**.

Inland Villages, South: Venetian Towers and Olive Groves

A few km east of Náxos town the main inland road forks, the southerly right-hand branch heading first to **Galanádo**, site of the restored Venetian **Belonia Tower**, bearing the lion of St Mark and the Venetian church of **St John**, with a Catholic chapel on the left and an Orthodox on the right: a typical arrangement on Náxos. There are a number of typical Cycladic windmills a mile or so south of the tower at **Bíblos**, while the main road continues toward Sangrí, passing by way of the island's first cathedral, the recently restored 8th-century **Ag. Mámas**, dedicated to the patron saint of thieves, located a short walk from the road. **Sangrí** (ΣΑΝΥΚΡΙ), actually three small villages picturesquely spread out over the plateau, got its name in circular manner, from the Greek pronunciation of Sainte Croix, which in turn is French for the 16th-century tower monastery Tímiou Stavroú or True Cross. There are many Byzantine frescoed chapels (usually locked) and medieval towers in the vicinity and, a pretty mile's walk south of Áno Sangrí, a 6th-century BC **Temple of Demeter**. A church on the site used much of the stone, but archaeologists have taken revenge on the Christians and dismantled the church and scoured surrounding farms for other bits to fit the temple back together like a giant jigsaw. A much more strenuous walk southeast of Áno Sangrí will take you up to the ruins of **T'Apalaróu**, the Byzantine castle high on its rock, where the Genoese defied Marco Sanudo and his mercenaries for two months.

Inland Villages: the Tragéa and Slopes of Mount Zas

From Sangrí the road rises up to the beautiful Tragéa plateau, planted with fruit trees and lilacs, flanked on either side by Náxos' highest mountains. Olives are the main product of the numerous small villages in the valley, including **Chálki** and the Byzantine **Frankópoulo**. In both, you can see Venetian tower houses, most in various stages of disrepair. Surrounded by walls which enclose a large courtyard, the main building of these fortified country villas was used for living quarters, while auxiliary buildings served as store-rooms for food, produce, as stables, wine-presses, etc. Built out of local stone, they are forbidding (most are crowned with swallowtail battlements, and some even had wooden drawbridges) and yet, without the all-pervading whitewash, they blend in nicely with the surrounding countryside. The few doors and windows, especially in the front were topped by sculpted marble lintels, similar to those of the mansion-houses in the Kástro.

From Chálki, a steep, difficult path will take you to one of the oldest tower houses, the 13th-century **Apáno Kástro**, used by Marco Sanudo as a summer hideaway. He was not, however, the first to enjoy the splendid panorama from the summit; the fortress sits on Cyclopean foundations, and Geometric era and Mycenaean tombs have been discovered just to the southeast and, rare for Greece, there's even a menhir. In Chálki itself there are two fine churches with frescoes: 12th-century **Panagía Protóthronis** (*usually open*) and 9th-century **Ag. Diasorítis**. A paved road leads up to a shady glade sheltering the most striking church on Náxos, **Panagía Drossianí**, built in the 5th century and crowned with ancient corbelled domes of field stones. Open most mornings (offering expected), it contains excellent frescoes of the Pantokrator, Virgin, and two saints.

The main road continues on to **Filóti** (ΦΙΛΟΤΙ) on the slopes of Mount Zas, the largest village in the Tragéa, with splendid views and the chance to eavesdrop on everyday village life, where contented ewes and nannies produce the island's best cheese. Monuments include the Venetian towerhouse of the De Lasti family, the churches **Koímisis tis Theotókou** with a fine carved marble iconostasis and **Panagía Filótissa**, with a marble steeple. There are many scenic paths, one leading up the slopes of **Mount Zas**, passing by way of an ancient inscription ΟΡΟΣ ΔΙΟΣ ΜΗΛΩΣΙΟΥ ('Mount Zeus, Herd-Protector'). There's a sacred cave near the summit, where one story says baby Zeus, born in the Diktean Cave on Crete, was briefly deposited for a spell—a typical story to knit a local cult into the national Greek story. Be careful and bring a light if you want to explore; the only inhabitants now are bats. A 3-hour path from Filóti (or dirt road) follows the west flanks of the mountain south to the isolated and hence excellently preserved Hellenistic **Tower of Chimárou**, built by Ptolemy of Egypt of white marble blocks, lost in the wildest part of Náxos.

From Filóti the road skirts the slopes of Mt Zas on its way to **Apíranthos** (ΑΠΕΙΡΑΝΘΟΣ), where the Venetian families Crispi and Sommaripa built towers. Many contemporary families, however, are Cretan, descended from migrants who came during the Turkish occupation to work in Greece's only emery mines, worked since the Bronze Age, to carve and polish Cycladic statues. It's the most picturesque village on Náxos, nicknamed *Marmarino* ('made of marble'), its narrow winding paths paved with the stuff, covered with archways and overhung by flowering balconies; the houses are topped with unique 'twin' chimney pots that are said to draw twice as well. Don't miss the ancient barber shop, and you'll also find a few women still weaving on looms, and farmers selling their produce. Byron loved Apíranthos so much that he declared that he wanted to die here (there are a few rooms to rent if you feel the same way). In August, though, the atmosphere changes with cocktail bars and revelry. Apíranthos' churches, to saints Georgios, Sofia, and Ilias, are built on ancient temples belonging to the gods they replaced, Ares, Athena and Helios respectively. There's a small **Cycladic Museum**, mostly devoted to Neolithic finds (*open 8.30–3; adm free*) and a **Geological and Folklore Museum** in the school, founded by Manolis Glezos, famous in Greece for his exploit as a 19-year-old in May 1941, when with fellow 19-year-old Lakis Sandas he sneaked through the secret Mycenaean passage in the Acropolis in Athens and pulled down the Nazi swastika exactly a month after it was first raised in Greece, keeping a bit as a souvenir and throwing the rest down a well. The bold exploit was broadcast on the BBC within hours, and was the beginning of Greek resistance in the War, although in the madness and confusion of Greece Glezos was to be sentenced to death three times, and live in prison and exile for 16 years after Greece was liberated.

A road from here descends to the port of **Moutsoúna**, where the emery is brought down from the mountains near Kóronos by a rope funicular (more successful than the disastrous one used in *Zorba the Greek*) and loaded on to ships. Moutsoúna has a fine beach; from here a dirt road follows the east coast south to the remote beach of **Psilí Ámmos**.

The North: Mélanes to Apollónas and Down the West Coast

The left branch of the main road from Náxos Town leads to **Mélanes** and the ancient marble quarries in the heart of Náxos; at Flerio, 700m off the road (it's signposted), lies a 7th-century BC 20ft-high *kouros* in a cypress grove. In the Archaic period such statues—highly stylized, stiff figures, arms hugging their sides, one foot stepping forward—were inspired by Egyptian art; the young men they portray are believed to have been Zeus' ancient guardians (the Cretan Curetes) or perhaps the Ionian god Apollo. This one was abandoned because of a broken leg; a second one, 300m south, is in poorer shape. At **Kourounochóri** near Mélanes stand ruins of a Venetian castle; **Ag. Thaléleos** in the same area has a monastery with a fine 13th-century church. Náxos' marble is almost as fine as Páros', and is still quarried to the east at **Kinídaros.** One of the most beautiful walks on Náxos begins here; the path descends past the chapel of the woodland goddess Ag. Artemis, and follows the Xerotakari river valley down to Egarés. The Xerotakari is the only river in the Cyclades to flow in August; it has little waterfalls and provides a pleasant home for turtles and eels, as well as drinking water for Náxos town.

A paved road links **Kóronos** to **Liónas** beach, while the main road north turns into a winding, hairpin serpent leading to pretty **Komiakí**, highest of the island's villages, with stunning views over terraced vineyards. The road leads back down to **Apóllonas** (ΑΠΟΛΛΩΝΑΣ), a dreary little town with a (very) public sandy beach, several tavernas patronized by tour buses, and some mid-range pensions. Ancient marble quarries are carved out of the slopes of the mountain, and steps lead up to a colossal, 33ft long *kouros*, abandoned in the 7th century BC because of flaws in the marble. As Apóllonas was sacred to Apollo (an inscription is still visible on the marble wall) the statue is believed to represent the god; even more intriguingly, the long-vanished temple that stood here is part of a perfect equilateral triangle formed by the temples of Apollo on Délos and Páros.

Apóllonas is as far as the bus goes; by car you can chance the road along the north coast back to Náxos Town, passing the isolated beaches of idyllic **Ormós Ábram**, with a taverna and rooms, and a curious giant marble head abandoned on a rock, and **Pachiá Ámmos** near the **Monastery of Faneroméni** (from 1606). There are lovely beaches along this coast, although when the *meltémi* roars you'll want to give them a miss.

Náxos ✉ *84300*, ☎ *(0285–)*   **Where to Stay and Eating Out**

If you don't have any accommodation, the booking desk by the quay will find you a room. Many rooms are in Néa Chóra, unlovely but handy for the beach; if you stay there, make sure you can find your way 'home' through its anonymous streets.

Náxos Town

Staying up in car-free Chóra is delightful. The plush **Château Zevgoli**, ☎ 22 993, ☏ 25 200 (*C; exp–mod*), in an old mansion, is small and exclusive with roof garden, antique décor and a four-poster for honeymooners. Nearby, the friendly **Anixis**, ☎/☏ 22 112 (*D; mod*), overlooking the sea, has tidy rooms all with balconies, above a fragrant garden terrace. **Despina Panteou's Rooms**, ☎ 22 356 (*inexp*) are nice doubles in an old house near the Kástro with a terrace. Of the small hotels in Boúrgos, just outside Kástro's walls, **Panorama**, ☎/☏ 24 404 (*C; mod*), on Amphitris Street, is the loveliest, with a marvellous sea view; **Pantheon**, nearby, ☎ 24 335, is a restored town house. **Nisaki**, ☎ 25 710, ☏ 23 876 (*C; mod-exp*) offers a bar, pool and restuarant. In a lush setting by the beach, **Naxos Beach**, ☎ 22 928, ☏ 24 805 (*C; mod*) has a pool and bungalows, as well as hotel rooms. The **Grotta**, ☎ 22 215 (*C; mod*) is very pleasant with wonderful sea views; the owner will collect you from the quay. Five minutes from the centre, **Anatoli**, ☎ 24 426, ☏ 23 999 (*C; mod*), has a pool and sea views.

Just south at Ag. Geórgios there's a wide selection, including the family-run **Aeolis**, ✆ 22 321, ✉ 23 600 (*C; mod*), and the smaller **St George** on the beach, ✆ 23 162 (*E; mod*); **Barbouni**, ✆ 22 535, ✉ 23 137 (*C; mod*) is a nice family-run operation near the beach. *Open all year.* **Camping Naxos**, ✆ 23 501, is by the beach.

If you want to splash out for dinner, there are two fine places up in Bradóuna Square, just under the Kástro's walls: **Oneiro** has candlelit tables in a courtyard, and a roof garden with a dreamy view over town; try the *arni bouti yemistó*, lamb stuffed with garlic and bacon; a few steps away the **Kastro**, ✆ 22 005, has delicious rabbit *stifádo* and *exochikó*, filo pastry parcels. **Apolafsis**, by the waterfront serves fine Greek food with live Greek music; at the south end of the waterfront the **Meltemi** is one of the oldest and best, with fresh fish; other haunts are unpretentious **Psigaria**, with home-raised meat, and **Apostolis**, also good for fresh fish. **Kavouri** is an old favourite on Ag. Georgios beach, serving good fish soup and other dishes with Naxian wine for over 40 years. Out of season, try the **Panorma**, a very Greek taverna on the Gallini road. You can taste the local Kítron liqueur (regular, mint or banana flavour) in the **Probonas** shop on the waterfront; Náxos wine is good as well, but best drunk from a barrel in situ; it's famous for not travelling well.

Beaches: Ag. Prokópios, Ag. Ánna, Pláka, Mikri Vigla & Kastráki

At Ag. Prokópios the **Kavouras Village**, ✆ 25 580, ✉ 23 705 (*B; exp*) offers flower-bedecked studios and villas and a pool; here too is **Camping Apollon**, ✆ 24 117, with minibus service. At Ag. Ánna the new **Iria Beach Apartments**, ✆ 24 178, ✉ 23 419 (*C; mod*) is right on the beach with a range of facilities including car hire; **Ag. Anna**, ✆ 23 870, ✉ 24 204 (*C; mod–inexp*) is also good, as is immaculate, German-run **Camping Maragas**, ✆ 24 552. For dinner, try **Faros** for fresh fish or **Paradise Taverna** for tasty Greek dishes, a terrace shaded by a vast pine tree, and an infectious atmosphere. At Pláka, 6km from Náxos Town, **Villa Medusa** (book in Athens, ✆ (01) 894 6469, ✉ 412 0422, *A; exp*) is a favourite of sophisticated wind surfers; rooms are furnished with antiques from around the world, mini bars and satellite TV. There's also a new campsite that rents out tents and sleeping bags: **Plaka Camping**, ✆ 42 701, ✉ 42 700, with its own bus service to town running late into the night, bar and taverna, and a guide Panos, who leads walking excursions into the valleys. At Mikrí Vígla, the new **Mikri Vigla**, ✆ 75 241, ✉ 75 240 (*B; mod-exp*) is a low-rise mini-resort in Cycladic style, on the beach with a pool, surfing centre and restaurant; at Kastráki, **Summerland Studios**, ✆ 75 461, ✉ 75 399 are pleasant flats, with a jacuzzi, pool, tennis and barbecue.

Apóllonas

Flora's Apartments, ✆ 67070 *(mod)* are pleasant, built around a garden. **Adonis**, ✆ 81 360 *(D; mod)* is comfortable, but if you want to get away from it all head for Abram and the **Pension Efthimios**, ✆ 63 222 *(inexp)*.

<hr>

Entertainment and Nightlife

Náxos has a buzzing nightlife with masses of bars; two of the most popular are **The Loft** and smartish **Veggera**. In Kástro, **Notos** is the place to mellow out with jazz in the courtyard. You can dance the night away, watching the sun rise through the giant window at the **Ocean Club** right on the sea, or **Opera,** with terraces over the sea, or **Empire Club**, playing traditional, new wave and *rembetíka* in Grotta (live at weekends). There's a **bouzouki** club for Greek entertainment just outside town. In Ag. Ánna, **Enosis**, ✆ 24 644 is a popular club in a warehouse, playing Greek music.

Páros (ΠΑΡΟΣ)

Despite the tens of thousands who descend on Páros each summer, the Cycladic houses, narrow alleys, little bridges and balconies overflowing with potted plants seem to dilute their presence. The Parians have approached the boom in tourism with less fervour than their neighbours on Mýkonos, managing, against overwhelming odds, to maintain a Greek island atmosphere. The inhabitants have, for the most part, remained fun-loving and hospitable and, if you can find a place to stay, it's a fine spot to while away a few days on golden beaches and in charming villages whose main building material comes from Páros' gentle mountain, Profítis Ilías (771m)—some of the finest, most translucent marble in the world, prized by Classical sculptors and architects. Páros is one of the larger and more fertile Cyclades, with vineyards, wheat and barley fields, citrus and olive groves, and—an unusual sight in the archipelago—pastures of grazing cattle and sheep. Apart from its beaches, the island has several other attractions, including a famous Byzantine cathedral and a valley filled with butterflies.

History

With the trade in its famous marble, Páros prospered early on. Its thriving Early Cycladic town traded with Knossós, then later with the Mycenaeans in the Late Cycladic period (1100 BC). In the 8th century BC Ionians moved in and brought about a second wave of prosperity, which enabled the island to establish colonies, most notably on the northern island of Thássos. It was during this period that it produced the charming 7th-century BC soldier poet Archilochos, the first to write in iambic meter and whose ironic detachment inspired Horace. In one of his best

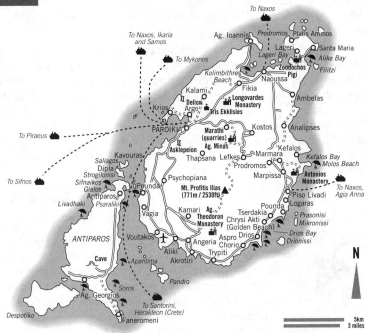

known poems he writes of leaving his shield and running for it in a battle. 'Some Thracian must be happy with it now,' he writes, and, 'to hell with it, I can always get another one, just as good'—a far cry from the implacable Spartan mothers, who handed their sons their shields with the advice: 'Come back with it or on it.'

The Athenians had an implacable streak as well. During the Persian Wars, Páros hated Athens enough to support the Persians at both Marathon and Salamis. The Athenian General Miltiades, the great hero of Marathon, whose bold charge against the Persian front line saved the day for the Greeks and Athens' new democratic government, came to punish Páros, but the islanders withstood his month-long siege and forced Miltiades to retire. Back in Athens the high court found their hero guilty of failure and sentenced him to be thrown off the walls of the Acropolis. The head judge eventually gave him a reprieve, although the unfortunate Miltiades died soon after anyway, perhaps as much from a broken heart as the gangrene from his broken leg.

During the Peloponnesian Wars Páros remained neutral until forced to join the second Delian league in 378 BC. The island produced the great sculptor Skopas in the Hellenistic period and did well until Roman times, exporting marble to make the Temple of Solomon, the *Venus de Milo*, the temples on Delos and, much later, part of Napoleon's tomb. When the Romans took over Páros, their main concern was to take over the marble business.

Later invasions and destructions left the island practically deserted, and after 1207 the Venetian Sanudos ruled Páros from Náxos. Barbarossa captured the island in 1536, and from then on the Turks ruled by way of their proxy, the Duke of Náxos, although his control was often shaky, especially in the 1670s, when Páros was the base of Hugues Chevaliers, the original of Byron's *Corsair*. In 1770, the Parians had to put up with more unlikely visitors when the Russian fleet wintered on the island. During the War of Independence Mantó Mavroyénous, whose parents were from Páros and Mýkonos, led guerrilla attacks against the Turks throughout Greece; after the war she returned to Páros and died there.

Páros ✆ (0284–) — Getting There

By air: minimum 3 flights daily from Athens. **Airport**: ✆ 91 256.

By sea: Páros is one of the great crossroads of the Aegean, with daily **ferry** and **hydrofoil** connections to Sýros, Rafína, Piraeus, Náxos, Tínos, Mýkonos, Íos, Santoríni, and Antíparos, and at least once a week with all the other Cyclades (except Kéa, Kýthnos, and Andrós), Kárystos (Évia), Sámos, Ikaría, Herákleon (Crete), the Dodecanese and Rhodes, Skiáthos, Skýros, Vólos, and Thessaloníki; frequent boats to Antíparos from Paroikiá and Poúnta. **Port authority**: ✆ 21 841.

By road: frequent **buses** go from the port to the airport and all the towns and villages, and in season between Náoussa and Dríos, ✆ 21 113. Beware if you want to hire a car or bike: some places are ripe rip-offs; **Cyclades**, on the waterfront towards Livádi, ✆ 21 057, is one of the most reliable.

Páros ✆ (0284–) — Tourist Information

Tourist police: Plateía Mandó Mavroyénous, Paroikiá, ✆ 21 673. **Information office**: by the bus station in Náoussa, ✆ 52 158, ✆ 51 190.

Festivals

23 April, Ag. Geórgios at Agkairia; **21 May**, Ag. Konstantínos at Paroikiá; **Good Friday–Easter**, at Marpissa, with re-enactments of the Crucifixion; **40 days after Orthodox Easter**, Análypsis at Píso Livádi; **15 August**, Ekatontapyliani at Paroikiá; **23 August** Náoussa sea battle; **29 August**, Ag. Ioánnis at Léfkas.

Paroikiá (ΠΑΡΟΙΚΙΑ), the island's chief town and main port, still greets arrivals with its old, now empty windmill. Behind it, however, the town has quintupled in size in the last couple of decades, so obscuring the original version that it's almost been forgotten; the locals have put up signs pointing the way to the 'Traditional Settlement'. Once you've found it, Paroikiá shows itself to be a Cycladic beauty, traversed by a long, winding main street that invites leisurely exploration, without trudging up a single stair. The centrepiece in the heart of town is the walls of the **Venetian Kástro**, built wholesale out of the white marble temples of Apollo and Demeter into an attractive collage of columns and pediments; a tiny white chapel tucked underneath adds to the effect. Three windmills close off the waterfront on the south end of town, where the *ouzeries* are a popular evening rendezvous.

Most of Paroikiá's sprawl, in the form of hotels, bars and restaurants, is in the direction of **Livádi** and its tamarisk-lined beach. Digging here in 1983 uncovered part of the **ancient cemetery**, in use from the 8th century BC to the 3rd AD; it lies below sea level and has to be constantly drained. If you get fed up with the crowds you can ride away: there's a stables nearby (ask at the Scouna restaurant, ✆ 57 981).

The Church of a Hundred Doors and the Archaeology Museum

Set back between Livádi and the 'Traditional Settlement' is Páros' chief monument, the cathedral **Ekatontapyliani** or 'Church of a Hundred Doors' hidden behind a modern wall (*open 8–1 and 4–9, no shorts*). In 326, St Helen, mother of the Emperor Constantine, was sailing from Rome to the Holy Land when her ship put into Páros during a storm. She prayed that, if her journey was a success and she found the True Cross she was seeking, she would build a church on Páros. She did, and told Constantine her promise, and he dutifully built a church on the site of the ancient gymnasium. What stands today is a 6th century building by the Byzantine Emperor Justinian. The story goes that he hired an architect named Ignatius, an apprentice of the master builder of Hagia Sophia in Constantinople and, when the master came to view his pupil's work, he was consumed by jealousy and pushed Ignatius off the roof—but not before Ignatius had seized his foot and dragged him down as well. They are represented by two bizarre, lardy figures with big belly buttons under the columns of the marble gate to the north of the church, one holding his head and the other covering his mouth; some say they are really satyrs taken from an old temple of Dionysos that originally stood here.

After two shattering earthquakes and subsequent restorations and repairs, the church was restored to approximately its 6th century appearance in 1966, with its dome on pendentives and a women's gallery running along the nave. Originally the interior was entirely covered with gleaming white marble. Another story says that only 99 entrances (anything a mouse could squeeze in apparently counts) have ever been found but once the 100th is discovered, Constantinople will return to the Greeks. In fact, the name itself is a 17th-century Greek fantasy; the original was probably *Katapoliani*, 'towards the ancient city.'

The marble iconostasis has an especially venerated icon of the black Virgin, which is silver-plated and worked all around with intricate little scenes (all made in Bucharest, in 1788), and here and there are other exceptional works, including the 16th-century Virgin called 'the Pure One' made by the Cretan school. Some frescoes survive, and behind the marble ciborium sheltering the altar there's a little marble amphitheatre, known as a *synthronon*—in the earliest churches, before the iconostasis totally blocked the view of the sacred area, the high priest and clergy used to stand and sit here.

In an alcove in the north wall is the silver-handed icon and tomb of the 9th century Ag. Osia Theóktisti. A nun captured by pirates on Lésbos, Theóktisti managed to flee into the forests of Páros, when the ship landed for water. For 35 years she lived a pious existence in the wilderness. A hunter finally found her and, when he brought her the communion bread she requested, she lay down and died. Unable to resist a free saintly relic, the hunter cut off her hand and made to sail away, but he was unable to depart until he had returned it to the saint's body.

Note the great 18th-century semi-circular icon on the wall near the tomb of the Holy Trinity, St Zion and the Consecration of St Jacob the Adelfotheos. The **Baptistry** to the right of the church has a 4th-century sunken cruciform font—the oldest one in Orthodoxy—adult-size, with steps leading down, and a column for the priest to stand on; baptism of children only began in the reign of Justinian.

Behind the church, next to the school, a row of sarcophagi with cartoon faces painted on marks the **Archaeology Museum** (*open Tues–Sun 8.30–2.30; adm*), containing a section of the renowned 'Parian Chronicles'—an art-orientated history of Greece, from Kekrops (*c.* 1500 BC) to Diognetos (264 BC) carved in marble tablets and discovered in the 17th century; the rest is in the Ashmolean in Oxford. There are finds from the temple of Apollo, a mosaic of the Labours of Hercules, found under the Ekatontapyliani, a 5th-century BC Winged Victory, a 7th-century BC amphora with the Judgement of Paris and swastikas (ancient solar symbols) going every which way, and a segment of a monument dedicated to Archilochos, who took part in the colonization of Thássos by Páros before he turned to lyric poetry.

Archilochos was buried along the road to Náoussa, and in the 4th century BC a *heröon*, or tomb-shrine of a hero or notable, was erected over his tomb, and in turn, in the 7th century, the basilica **Tris Ekklisíes** (or Ag. Charálambos) was built over the site. Northeast of Paroikiá a marble foundation and altar mark the **Temple of Delian Apollo**. Together with temples to Apollo on Délos and Náxos, it forms part of a perfect equilateral triangle. One of the triangle's altitudes extends to Mycenae and Rhodes town, site of the Colossus—the biggest of all the statues of Apollo. Another heads up to holy Mount Áthos.

Náoussa

Frequent buses connect Paroikiá with the island's second port, the lovely fishing village turned jet-set hang-out of **Náoussa** (ΝΑΟΥΣΑ). In 1997 it made history as the first place where the Greek government at last clamped down on shoddy indiscriminate building. Near the harbour stand the half-submerged ruins of the Venetian castle, with colourful caiques bobbing below and octopus hung out to dry for later scorching into chewy titbits to go with ouzo. On the night of 23 August 100 boats lit by torches re-enact the islanders' battle against the pirate Barbarossa, storming the harbour, and all ends in merriment, music and dance. Náoussa's church **Ag. Nikólaos Mostrátos** has an excellent collection of icons.

There are beaches within walking distance of Náoussa, or you can make sea excursions to others, notably **Kolimbíthres**, with its bizarre, wind-sculpted rocks; other sands nearby are at **Lágeri**; take the caique from Náoussa harbour, then walk to the right for about ten minutes. Lágeri is nudist, a relaxed mix of gay and straight. **Santa Maria** is even further around the coast, with a good wind surfing beach; the fishing village of **Ambelás** has sandy coves, an ancient tower, a taverna and a quiet hotel. Páros' main wine growing area is just south.

Into the Land of Marble

From Paroikiá, the main road east leads to Páros' ancient marble quarries at **Maráthi**, not far from the fortified but abandoned monastery of Ag. Mínas. The quarries, re-opened in modern times for the statues and decorations around Napoleon's tomb in the Invalides, are still in use—the longest tunnel stretches 90m underground. It produces the finest of all white marble, called 'Lychnites' by the ancients, or 'candlelit marble', for its translucent quality, admitting light 3.5cm into the stone (light penetrates the second most translucent Carrara marble only 2.5cm). The Venus de Milo, the Victory of Samothrace, the Hermes of Praxiteles, the Temple of Solomon, the Athenian Treasury at Delphi were all made of the stuff. Blocks and galleries, some with ancient inscriptions, lie off the road.

The road continues to Páros' attractive medieval capital **Léfkes**, with churches from the 15th century and one made of marble, Ag. Triáda; there's also a small museum dedicated to another local speciality, here and in nearby Kostos: ceramics. East of Léfkes, **Pródromos** is an old farming village; **Mármara**, another village, lives up to its name ('marble')—even some of the streets are paved with it. Prettiest of the three, though, is shiny white **Márpissa**, laid out in an amphitheatre. Above its windmills are the ruins of a 15th-century Venetian fortress and the 16th-century **monastery of Ag. Antónios,** constructed out of ancient marbles and containing lovely frescoes (note the 17th-century *The Second Coming,* which seems a bit out of place in *bon-vivant* Páros). The ancient city of Páros stood somewhere near by.

Down on the east coast **Píso Livádi** served as the port for these villages and the marble quarries, and now has excursion boats to Náxos, Mýkonos and Santoríni. It is the centre of Páros' beach colonies: **Mólos** just north,where luxurious villas line the bay where the Turkish fleet used to put in on its annual tax-collecting tour of the Aegean, and just south **Poúnda** (not to be confused with the ferry port for Antíparos), where beautiful people flock to a nightclub even bigger than the beach, the hip place for Athenians and foreigners to chill out and pick up. The winds on Páros blow fiercely in July and August, and the next beach, **Tserdakia** (or **Néa Chrysí Aktí**) in particular has become a Mecca for serious windsurfers; early every August since 1993 it has hosted the Professional Windsurfers' World Cup as well as the 'Odyssey ' a windsurfing relay race beginning on Mýkonos. Just to the south the island's best beach, **Chrysí Aktí,** 'Golden Beach', stretches 700m. Further south **Driós** is a pretty green place with a duck-pond, tavernas and sandy coves, and the remains of ancient shipyards.

Southwest of Paroikiá

Just south of Paroikiá, by a spring, are the ruins of a small Classical-era **Asklepeion** (dedicated to the god of healing); originally a temple to Pythian Apollo stood nearby. The road south continues 6km to **Psychopianá,** where swarms of tiger moths set up house in July and August and fly up in clouds as you walk by. Petaloúdes/Psychopianí has the ruins of a Venetian tower, while just outside the village stands the convent of Páros' second patron saint, **Ag. Arsénios,** the school-teacher, abbot and prophet who was canonized in 1967. The saint is buried in the convent, but this time men are not allowed in. At **Poúnda** there is a beach and the small boat that crosses to Antíparos. There's another beach at **Alikí** which has some facilities—and the airport, and now, perhaps inevitably, a roadside attraction, the **Historical Museum Scorpios** (*open 10–2 and 6–8; adm*), with 'animated handmade miniatures' depicting the old days on Páros.

Páros © *(0284–)*	***Where to Stay and Eating Out***

Páros is packed in the summer, and it may be hard to find a place if you just drop in, although the various well-organized reservations desks on the quay will do their darnedest to find you a place to flop. Beware—in season prices are high. At some point, try Paros' dry white, red or rosé bottled under the KAVARNIS label.

Paroikiá ✉ 84400

Fanciest here is the attractive **Yria**, 3km from the centre on Parasporos Beach, ✆ 24 154, 📧 21 167 (*A; exp*), a good family choice with air-conditioned bungalows, playground, tennis, pool and big American breakfasts. In the old town, **Dina**, ✆ 21 325 (*mod*) is the most charming, with simple pretty rooms and a little garden. **Argo**, on Livadia beach, ✆ 21 367, 📧 21 207 (*C; mod*) was renovated in 1995 and offers billiards and air-conditioning. **Argonaftis**, ✆ 21 440 (*C; exp–mod*) just back from the waterfront, is a pleasant family-run place. **Bayia**, ✆ 21 068 (*C; mod*) is a small family-run hotel, set back on the Naoussa road, surrounded by olive trees. **Kapetan Manolis**, ✆ 21 244 (*C; mod*) is also recommended, while **Kypreou**, ✆ 21 383 (*D; inexp*) is a simple budget option. **Xenia**, ✆ 21 394 (*B; exp*) has a lovely view over the village in its green amphitheatre, and there's a bar and good restaurant. Páros is especially popular among campers: **Camping Koula**, ✆ 22 082, and **Parasporos**, ✆ 21 100, for the laid back, are near Paroikiá, and **Krios Camping**, ✆ 21 705, is at Kríos Beach, opposite the port. Most have minibuses that meet ferries.

The best food on Páros is at **To Tamarisko** (*mod*), where you can dine delectably on international cuisine in the secluded garden. **Argonautis,** ✆ 23 303, in the big square by the National Bank, is well-known for its fresh food and grills; vegetarians can find sustenance, including good falafel, just behind at the **Green Cow**. The **Levanti** (*exp*), back from the harbour to the right of the Venetian castle walls, has good Greek, French and Lebanese dishes like *tabouleh* and *falafel*. For a simple taverna try **Nissiotissa** (*inexp*), behind the hospital; everything's good, especially the fresh fish. The **Paros**, signposted from Ekatoapylani, serves simple home-cooking and seafood under a trellis. **May-Tey**, in the backstreets of the old town, has a limited but high quality choice of southeast Asian dishes.

Náoussa and Around ✉ 84401

The island's most luxurious hotel is the **Astir of Paros**, ✆ 51 976, 📧 51 985 (*lux*), on Kolymbithres beach, with all your heart's desires. **Porto Paros**, at Ag. Ioánnis, ✆ 52 010, 📧 51 720 (*A; exp*) is pretty plush, too, a neo-Cycladic complex with an atrium, stone arches, painted pergolas and even a small church, plus 130 rooms, 70 apartments, all air-conditioned with mod cons, two pools, tennis, watersports and a disco. Little neo-monastic **Antrides**, ✆ 51711, 📧 52 079 (*B; exp)* is quiet, with gardens, verandas and balconies. **Calypso**, on the beach, ✆ 51 455, 📧 51 607 (*C; mod*) is simple and straightforward, while the new **Petres**, ✆ 52 467, 📧 52 759 (*C; mod*) is small, but has comfy air-conditioned rooms, and a pool. **Atlantis**, ✆ 51 340, 📧 52 087 (*C; mod*) has a pool, good facilities, and mountain bikes to hire. **Aliprantis**, ✆ 51 571 (*C; inexp*) has balconies overlooking the busy main square; **Galini**, ✆ 51 210 (*C; inexp*) is a friendly little place; **Glaros** (*inexp*) has rooms in the centre, ✆ 51 186. **Lilly Apartments**, ✆ 51 377, 🖷 51 716 (*A; exp*) are stylish and upmarket, right on the beach. Just east in Ambelas, **Miltiadis**, ✆/🖷 52 020 *(mod)* has rooms in a lush garden. Náoussa is one of the most picturesque places to eat with *ouzeries* by the water. **Diamante** up the hill serves good food at good prices; **Barbarossa** by the port serves super fresh fish. Ritzy **Christos** is Náoussa's finest for seafood and Greek cuisine.

Píso Livádi and East Coast Beaches ✉ 84400

Mostly simple accommodation here: **Andromachi**, ✆ 41 387, 🖷 42 153 (*C; mod*) is right on the sea; little **Marpissa**, ✆ 41 288 (*C; mod*) has an attractive view, although rooms are without bath. **Elina Residence**, UK contact ✆ (01274) 832771 (*mod*) is a lovely British-owned apartment overlooking the bay with views of Náxos. **Lodos**, ✆ 41 218, 🖷 41 135 (*C; mod–inexp*) is basic, but OK. **Stavros Taverna** is excellent for vegetable dishes and Greek favourites while next-door **Vrochas** does good grills. Just south in Logarás, **Albatross**, ✆ 41 157, 🖷 41 940 (*C; exp–mod*) has family oriented bungalows and a pool. **Fisilani's** is a good bet for food. Up in Márpissa, **Afendakis Apartments**, ✆ 41 141 (*C; mod*) are beautifully appointed and **Laini**, just off the main road, is a year- round favourite for grills, and often live Greek music.

Holiday Sun, in Poúnda, ✆ 91 284, 🖷 91 288 (*A; lux–exp*), has all mod cons. **Paros Philoxenia**, ✆ 41 778, 🖷 41 978 (*B; exp–mod*) is a hotel/bungalow complex at Tserdakia beach, with surf club, sea sports, and pool; **Driós** has Cycladic-style rooms, a good taverna on the beach; **Anezina**, ✆ 41 037, 🖷 41 872 (*C; mod*) has a lovely garden restaurant.

Entertainment and Nightlife

Páros has something for everyone, from the rowdy waterfront bars at Paroikiá to the sophisticated haunts of Náoussa. Paroikiá has an outdoor cinema, **Cine Paros**, set back from the waterfront, **Black Barts** and the **Salon d'Or** for cocktails on the strip, **Pirate's** for jazz, and a complex of four disco bars, the **Paros Rock,** including the **Dubliner**; there's dancing all night, often to live music, at the **Irish Bar** on the edge of town. Along Náoussa's covered-up torrent bed is one of the trendiest nightclub strips in Greece; the big news here is the recent opening of a **Varrelathiko**, summer headquarters of the hippest club in Athens. The **Golden Garden** at Chrysí Aktí is a popular, laid-back garden bar with a wide range of international sounds; in Píso Livádi **Remezzo** is a favoured watering hole.

Antíparos (ΑΝΤΙΠΑΡΟΣ)

Just a mile to the west, mountainous little Antíparos (the name means 'opposite Páros') was known as Oliaros when it was first mentioned as a base of Phoenician merchants of Sidon. A deep cave full of stalactites was discovered on Antíparos in antiquity (tradition has it that Antilochos himself was the first to carve his name on a stalactite in the 6th century BC) and ever since it has been a must-stop for every traveller in the region. Antíparos is the octopus capital of Greece, and it just may be that the tasty eight-legged, sucker-bedecked mollusc is an unsung aphrodisiac, considering the little island's current reputation. Even the local year-round population is rising, and that, in the Cyclades, is rare.

Antíparos ✆ (0284–)   **Getting There and Around**

Every two hours or so by **caique** from Paroikiá, Páros, and hourly **car ferry** from Poúnta, Páros. Buses link the port with the cave. **Port authority**, ✆ 21 240.

Antíparos ✆ (0284–)   **Tourist Police**

See regular police in town, ✆ 23 333.

Festivals

23 April, Ag. Geórgios; **8 May**, Ag. Ioánnis Theológos.

Kástro and the Cave

Lacking any defences, Antíparos was uninhabited after the fall of Rome until the Venetians, under Leonardo Lorentani, built a small castle, its thick walls doubling as the outer walls of the houses; **Kástro** is the alternative name of the main settlement. Everyone tos and fros down the Kampiara, the wide street linking the port to the charming square, lined with *ouzeries* and bars. Kástro has a good beach, **Psaralíki**, just south, and another one for skinny-dippers a five-minute walk north by the campsite. In the late afternoon everyone wanders over to **Sifnaíkos Gialós**, also known as Sunset Beach. The best beach, **Ag. Geórgios**, just south of the cave, is being developed as a resort.

The **Cave** (*open daily 10.45–3; adm*) remains Antíparos' star attraction, and buses now do the old donkey work of getting you there from the village. The old ropes visitors once used to descend have been replaced by 400 steps, descending 210ft into the fantastic, spooky chamber. The cave is really about twice as deep, but the rest is too dangerous for visits. Perhaps to make up for breaking off the stalactites, famous visitors of the past have smoked and carved their names on the walls, including Lord Byron and King Otho of Greece (1840). One stalagmite attests in Latin to a Christmas mass celebrated in the cavern by the French ambassador Count Novandel in 1673, attended by 500 (paid) locals. Many inscriptions were lost in 1774, when Russian officers chopped off stalactites as souvenirs. In the last war the Italians and Germans shot up the cave, destroying one of the oldest inscriptions, in which its several authors declared that they were hiding in the cave from Alexander the Great, who had accused them of plotting an assassination attempt. The church by the entrance of the cave, **Ag. Ioánnis**, was built in 1774. Of the islets off Antíparos, **Strogilónisi** and **Despotikó** are rabbit-hunting reserves. On **Sáliagos**, a fishing village from the 5th millennium BC has been excavated by John Evans and Colin Renfrew, the first Neolithic site discovered in the Cyclades.

Antíparos ✉ *84007*, ✆ *(0284–)*   **Where to Stay and Eating Out**

Antíparos has a desk at Paroikiá port on Páros, so you can book accommodation before you go, but beware, prices have now risen to match its big sister. **Artemis**, ✆ 61 460, ✆ 61 472 (*C; mod–inexp*) is new, 500 yards from the port, and all rooms have fridges and sea-view balconies. **Kouros Apartments**, on the Paralía, ✆ 51 688, has several types of flats available, ideal for families; there's a pool, pool bar, garden, restaurant and barbecue area as well. Little **Chryssi Akti**, ✆ 61 220 (*C; mod*) is an elegant hotel on the beach; recently renovated **Mantalena**, ✆ 61 206 (*D; mod*) on the waterfront offers tidy rooms, all with bath; just in from the beach; **Bergleri**, ✆ 61 080, ✆ 61 425 (*E; mod*) is similar, with a decent taverna and library of bestsellers. **Antiparos**, ✆ 61 358, ✆ 61 340 (*E: mod–inexp*) is simple, all rooms with shower, with a restaurant and bar. **Korali**, ✆ 61 236, is about the cheapest pension, with a restaurant. There's also a famously laid-back campsite, **Antiparos**, ✆ 61 221, clothes optional; freelancers are tolerated away from town. The **Garden** has good food, and the **Time Marine Beach Bar** is a popular hang out. Soros and Ag. Georgios beaches also have summer tavernas.

Santoríni/Thíra (ΣΑΝΤΟΡΙΝΗ/ΘΗΡΑ)

> *…We found ourselves naked on the pumice stone*
> *watching the rising islands*
> *watching the red islands sink*
> *into their sleep, into our sleep.*
> *Here we found ourselves naked, holding the scales that*
> *tipped towards injustice.*
>
> George Seféris, *Santoríni*
> (trans. by Edmund Keeley and Philip Sherrard)

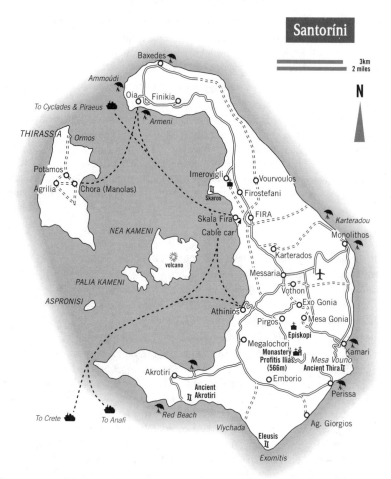

Santoríni

3km
2 miles

N

Baxedes
Ammoúdi
Oia · Finikia
To Cyclades & Piraeus
Armeni
THIRASSIA   Ormos
Potamos
Agrilia · Chora (Manolas)
Imerovigli · Vourvoulos
Skaros · Firostefani
NEA KAMENI
Skala Fira · FIRA
Cable car · Karteradou
Monolithos
Karterados
volcano
Messaria
PALIA KAMENI
Vothon
Exo Gonia
ASPRONISI
Athinios
Pirgos · Mesa Gonia
Episkopi
Megalochori · Kamari
Monastery
Profitis Ilias · Mesa Vouno
(566m) · Ancient Thira
Akrotiri
Ancient · Emborio
Akrotiri
Perissa
To Crete · To Anafi
Red Beach
Ag. Giorgios
Vlychada
Eleusis
Exomitis

As many people's favourite Greek island, the pressure is on Santoríni to come up with the goods. And it does. The awesome mixture of sinister multi-coloured volcanic precipices, dappled with the most brilliant-white, trendiest bars and restaurants in the country, gives the island a splendid kind of schizophrenia; forget *Under the Volcano*, here you're teetering on the edge. Usually bathed in glorious sunshine, but occasionally lashed by high winds and rain, everything seems more intense here, especially daily life. Some call it Devil's Island, and find a stay here both exhilarating and disturbing. And it's the honeymoon capital of Greece.

There are plenty of flights, but there's nothing like arriving by sea. As your fragile ship sails into the caldera, Santoríni looms like a chocolate layer cake with an enormous bite taken out of it, frosted with coconut cream towns slipping over the edge, while the charred islands opposite look suitably infernal. All of this little archipelago has, literally, had its ups and downs: throughout history parts have seismically appeared and disappeared under the waves.

Human endeavours have fared similarly: you can visit no fewer than three former 'capitals'—the Minoan centre of Akrotíri, a favourite candidate for Metropolis, the capital of Atlantis; the Classical capital Thíra at Mésa Vouná; and the medieval Skáros, as well as the picturesque modern town of Firá, perched on the rim. But this, too, was flattened by an earthquake in 1956. Although the island is now a must on the cruise ship itinerary, older inhabitants can remember still when Santoríni hosted more political prisoners than tourists, and nights were filled with the rumour of vampires rather than the chatter of café society sipping Bloody Marys, watching the sun go down in one of the world's most enchanting settings.

History

In the distant past Santoríni was a large round island called Strogyle, with a crater in the centre. Its regular eruptions created a rich, volcanic soil, which attracted inhabitants early on—from Karia originally, until they were chased away by the Minoans. One of the Cretan towns was at Akrotíri. Its rediscovery resulted from one of the most intriguing archaeological detective stories of the 20th century.

In 1939, while excavating Amnisós, the port of Knossós on the north coast of Crete, Greek archaeologist Spirýdon Marinátos realized that only a massive natural disaster could have caused the damage he found. At first Marinátos believed it was an earthquake, but over the years evidence of a different kind of catastrophe came in: southeast of Santoríni oceanographers discovered volcanic ash from Strogyle on the sea bed, covering an area of 900 by 300km; on nearby Anáfi and Eastern Crete itself a layer of volcanic tephra 3–20mm thick covers Minoan New Palace sites. Another clue came from the Athenian reformer Solon, who in 600 BC wrote of his journey to Egypt, where the scribes told him of the disappearance of Kreftia (Crete?) 9000 years before, a figure Solon might have mistaken for a more correct 900.

The Egyptians, who had had important trade links with Minoan Crete and Santoríni, told Solon about the lost land of Atlantis, made of red, white and black volcanic rock (like Santoríni today) and spoke of a city vanishing in 24 hours. In his *Critias*, Plato described Atlantis as being composed of one round island and one long island, a sweet country of art and flowers connected by one culture and rule (Santoríni and Crete, under Minos?). Lastly, Marinátos studied the eruption of Krakatoa in 1883, which blew its lid with such force that it could be heard 3000 miles away in Western Australia. Krakatoa's volcano formed a caldera of 8.3sq km, and as the sea rushed in to fill the caldera it created a *tsunami* or tidal wave over

200m high that destroyed everything in a 150km path. The caldera left by Strogyle (the present bay of Santoríni) is 22sq km—almost three times as big.

In the 19th century French archaeologists had discovered Minoan vases at Akrotíri, and it was there that Marinátos began to dig in 1967, seeking to prove the chronology of his theory: that Minoan civilization owed its sudden decline to the eruption, earthquakes, and tidal waves caused by the explosion of Santoríni in c. 1450 BC. Marinátos hoped to unearth a few vases. Instead he found something beyond his wildest dreams: an entire Minoan colony buried in tephra, complete with dazzling frescoes.

The rest of the island's history has been fairly calm by comparison. In the 8th century BC the Dorians settled the island, naming it Thíra, building their capital at Mésa Vouná, and colonizing the city of Cyrene in Libya. The Byzantines covered the island with castles, but the Venetians under the Crispi got it anyway. Skáros near Imerovígli was their capital and Irene their patron saint, hence the island's second name, Santoríni, which has stuck, as hard as officialdom tries to change it back to the Classical era Thíra.

Santoríni ℂ (0286–)   **Getting There**

By air: 3 flights from Athens; 5 a week from Mýkonos, 2 a week in season from Herákleon (Crete); 3 a week from Rhodes, Thessaloníki, and Kárpathos. Airport ℂ 31 523.

By sea: daily **ferry** connections with Piraeus, Íos, Páros, Náxos, and Mýkonos. Frequently ferries and hydrofoils with other Cyclades and Rafína, 2–3 times a week with Herákleon (Crete) Kássos, Kárpathos, Chálki, and Rhodes, Skiáthos and Thessaloníki. Ferries call at Athiniós. **Port authority**, ℂ 22 239.

By road: Santoríni has a decent if often crowded bus service to all major villages; buses depart from Fíra for Athiniós an hour before each ferry. **Taxis**: ℂ 22 555.

Tourist Information

English-speaking tourist information (*mornings only*) in Fíra: ℂ 22 220.

Festivals

19 and **20 July**, at Profítis Ilías; **15 August**, Panagía at Mésa Goniá and Fíra; **September**, Santoríni Music Festival, in Fíra, with Greek and international music. **20 October**, Ag. Artemiou in Fíra; **26 October**, Ag. Dimítríou in Karteráthos.

Most ferry passengers disembark at the chaotic port of **Athiniós** and take the bus to the capital **Firá**, where their first taste of the city is a zoo-like modern square where tourists are processed and fattened on fast food before being sacrificed to the volcano god. Cruise ships rather more pleasantly anchor beneath the towering cliffs at Firá, where motor launches ferry passengers to the tiny port of **Skála Firá**, where donkeys wait to bear them up the winding path to the town 885ft above. An Austrian-built **cable car** (*every 15 minutes from 6.45am to 8.15pm*), donated to the island by ship-owner Evángelos Nomikós does the donkey-work in two minutes. Profits go to a community fund—and to the donkey drivers.

Those who remember Firá before 1956 say that the present town can't compare to its original, although it's pleasant enough—perfectly Cycladically white, spilling over the volcano's rim on several terraces, adorned with pretty blue-domed churches, all boasting one of the world's most magnificent views. Understandably, the families who sold their damaged caldera-front properties for peanuts after the big quake have been kicking themselves ever since; the little lanes are now chock-a-block with shops, bars, hotels and restaurants. Firá now blends into quieter **Firostefáni**, a kilometre to the north; here some magnificent old *skaftá*, barrel-roofed cave houses, Santoríni's speciality, are now equipped with all mod cons.

The **Archaeological Museum** (© 22 217, *open Tues–Sun, 8.30–3; adm*) is near the cable car on the north side of town and houses finds from Minoan Akrotíri, Dorian-Hellenic Ancient Thíra at Mésa Vouná (which produced the fine 'Santoríni vases') and Early Cycladic figurines found in the local pumice mines. The famous frescoes from Akrotíri are in the National Museum in Athens, although there are rumours that a new museum may some day be built in Firá to bring them home. The handicraft workshop founded by Queen Frederíka, where women weave large carpets on looms, is also worth a visit. The **Mégaron Gýzi Museum**, (© 22 244, *open daily 10.30–1.30 and 5–8 pm; adm*) located in a beautiful 17th-century mansion, houses exhibits on the island's history—manuscripts from the 16th–19th centuries, costumes, old maps of the Cyclades, and photographs of Santoríni before the 1956 quake. Another, privately run, **Folklore Museum** (© 22 792, *open 6–8; adm*) occupies a cave house of 1861, with all of the owner's uncle's belongings on display and a gathering of machinery and old tools.

Firá ☑ 84700, © (0286–) **Where to Stay**

Firá isn't the only village with hotels spilling over the caldera rim, but it's the most expensive. Out of season, even in early July, you can wheel and deal with the room-owners who mug you as the bus pulls into town.

Top of the list for luxury is the **Santoríni Palace**, ✆ 22 771, ✉ 23 705 (*A; lux*) followed by **Atlantis**, ✆ 22 232, ✉ 22 821 (*A; lux*), overlooking the volcano. For mod cons (including a counter-swim unit in the pool) in a traditional, antique-furnished cliff side *skaftá*, there's **Egialos**, ✆ 25 191, ✉ 22 856 (*A; lux*). **Kavalari**, ✆ 22 455, ✉ 22 603 (*C; exp*) has rooms dug out of the cliff, as has **Lucas**, ✆ 22 480, ✉ 24 882 (*D; exp*). **Porto Karra**, ✆ 22 979 (*C; exp*), on the central square, faces the volcano. The air-conditioned **Pelican**, ✆ 23 113, ✉ 23 514 (*C; exp*) has a tank of odd fish in the lounge. *Open all year.* Just north along the cliff edge at Firostefáni **Galini**, ✆ 22 095, ✉ 23 097 (*C; exp–mod*) offers nice, simple rooms with caldera views, and port transfers; **Dana Villas** (not mine, unfortunately!) ✆ 22 566, ✉ 22 985 (*C; exp*) are self-contained apartments for two to six people, in traditional island style, with swimming pool and fabulous sunsets; **Efterpi Villas**, also in Firostefáni, ✆ 22 541, ✉ 22 542, are similar but more reasonable.

Cheaper, view-less places in Fíra include friendly **Argonaftis**, ✆ 22 055 (*inexp*), with breakfast served in the garden; and bohemian **Tataki**, in the centre, ✆ 22 389 (*D; mod–inexp*). *Open year-round.* There are two youth hostels in Firá: **Kamares Hostel**, ✆ 23 142, near the cable car and the better **Kontonari**, ✆ 22 722, with snack bar and English videos. *Open April–Oct.* **Camping Santorini**, ✆ 22 944, is a superb site.

Firá ✆ (0286–)   **Eating Out**

Besides wine, Santoríni is famous for its fava bean soup (puréed, with onions and lemon) and *pseftokeftédes*, 'false meatballs', made of deep-fried tomatoes, onion and mint; the island's tiny tomatoes are said to be the tastiest in Greece. The owner and chef of one of Athens' most innovative restaurants, Vitrina, spend the summer serving up similar refined fare at **Tomates** (*exp*). *Open mid April–10 Oct.* Up on top of the Fabrica Shopping Centre, **Meridiana**, ✆ 23 247 claims to be the only restaurant on the island with views on both sides of the island, as well as gourmet or Thai cusine and live jazz most evenings. *Open from lunch until 3am.*

Kastro with big views near the cable car will set you back a bit for one of its lavish international spreads. On the main street, try and squeeze in at **The Roosters**, a fun little restaurant with tasty Greek dishes and an inquisitive owner. **Alexandria** on the caldera is very expensive but even serves up ancient Greek specialities. Italians flock to **Bella Thira** for freshly made pasta and pizzas. The locals go to **Kokoroulia** for excellent cooking, grilled lamb and reasonable prices; the 24-hour diner, **Poseidon**, under the bus stop, has reasonably priced filling food. On the caldera south of town, you'll find the ultimate in tongue-in-cheek Greek silliness: a Mexican restaurant called **McZorbas**.

Entertainment and Nightlife

Café and bar life takes up as much time as eating in Santoríni. **Bebis** is the watering hole for a pleasantly loony young crowd. **Two Brothers** draws the backpackers and is a hot spot for rock; **Kira Thira Jazzbar** appeals to all ages for jazz, blues and *sangria*, while **Alexandria** is more sedate and attracts an older set. **Franco's**, playing gentle classical music, is still *the* place to go for sunset, even if the price of a coffee is sky-high. Cocktails are works of art, but a bottle of wine and *mezédes* are the best deal. **Enigma** and the adjacent **Koo Club** are big, central and packed; the lively **Marmounia Club** plays Greek hits, or rock away at **Tithora Club**, the disco in a cave on the steps to Skála Firá.

Way Down South: Minoan Akrotíri

Akrotíri (ΑΚΡΩΘΗΡΙ), a pleasant wine village on the south tip of the island, was a Venetian stronghold, and although damaged in the earthquake the fort still stands at the top of the town. There are beaches nearby on either coast, and a pretty walking path along the caldera rim. The first clues indicating that something else may have once been here came in the 1860s during the excavation of pumice for the rebuilding of Port Said during the Suez Canal project: cut stone blocks belonging to ancient walls kept getting in the way. A French geologist named Fouqué, who came to study Thíra's eruption of 1866, began digging, and with later French archaeologists he unearthed carbonized food, vases, frescoes and a pure copper saw. In 1967 Spirýdon Marinátos, following his hunch about the destruction of Minoan Crete through a volcanic eruption, led a team back to the site. The trenches were disappointing until they reached the level of volcanic ash 15ft below the surface, when suddenly they broke through into rooms full of huge storage vases, or *pithoi*. Excavations are still under way.

The **Minoan city**, buried in *c*. 1550 BC (*buses from Firá end up here; open Tues–Sun 8.30–3; adm*), laboriously revealed beneath its thick sepulchral shell of volcanic tephra—a material so hard that it's used to make cement for tombstones—is wonderful and strange, made even more uncanny by its huge modern protective roof. A carpet of volcanic dust silences all footsteps on paved lanes uncovered after 3500 years, amid houses up to three storeys high, many still containing their *pithoi* and linked up to a sophisticated drainage system. A series of earthquakes and eruptions must have warned residents that their island was about to blow: no jewellery or other valuables were found, and the only skeleton found so far belonged to a pig. As they escaped, the inhabitants must have shed more than a few tears, for life at Akrotíri was sweet judging by the ash imprints of their elaborate wooden furniture, their beautiful ceramics and the famous frescoes full of colour and life—every house had a least one frescoed room; one, unique in peace-loving Minoan art, showed a sea battle, or a naval regatta. The size of the storage areas and cooking pots suggests a strong communal life and collective economy. In one of the houses is the grave of Marinátos, who died after a fall on the site and requested to be buried by his life's work. For more details, pick up *Art and Religion in Thira: Reconstructing a Bronze Age Society*, by his son, Dr Nannó Marinátos.

Below the site, the road continues to Mávro Rachidi, where cliffs as black as charcoal offer a stark contrast to the white chapel of Ag. Nikólaos; a path over the headland leads to **Kókkino Paralía** or Red Beach, with sun beds under startling blood-red cliffs.

The Southeast: Embório, Périssa and Ancient Thira

West of Akrotíri, farming villages encircle the Mt Profítis Ilías. **Megalochóri**, 'big village', actually has a tiny, resolutely old Greek core, with a tiny outdoor taverna. **Embório** (EMΠOPEIO) still has its Venetian Goulas or fort; with its lone palm, like something out of the Sahara. A modern church replaces the Byzantine St Irene, the island's namesake and patroness of the Greek police. Another 3km east of Embório, in a pretty setting under the seaside mountain Mésa Vouna, the black sands of **Périssa** (ΠΕΡΙΣΣΑ) have attracted a good deal of development, and can be pleasant at either end of the season because the sand warms quickly in the sun. Eucalyptus groves provide shade, bars and clubs provide plenty of nightlife; a Byzantine church is being excavated on the edge of town. The coastal road south of Périssa leads around to **Cape Exomítis**, guarded by one of the best-preserved Byzantine fortresses of the Cyclades; submerged nearby are the ruins of the ancient **Eleusis**. The road ends by the wild cliffs and often big waves at **Vlycháda**, with a pretty beach, a snack bar and end of the world air, in spite of nearby smokestacks.

Pírgos (ΠΥΡΓΟΣ) shares with Embório the title of the oldest surviving village on the island, with interesting old barrel-roofed houses, Byzantine walls, and a Venetian fort. Much of the surrounding country is covered in vineyards, which swirl up the white flanks of **Mount Profítis Ilías**, Santoríni's highest point (566m). On a clear day you can see Crete from here, and on an exceptionally clear day, it is said, even Rhodes hovers faintly on the horizon. The locals say the monastery, built in 1712, is the only place that will protrude above sea level when the rest of Santoríni sinks into the sea to join its other half. Don't miss the scenes at the entrance, of the narrow road to heaven and the considerably wider one to hell, where the devil whiles away time playing the *laouto*. If you have bare knees, the monks won't let you any further; unfortunately the monastery's little museum is closed. At the foot of Profítis Ilías, by the village of Mésa Goniá, the 11th-century **Panagía Episkopí** has fine Byzantine icons, although 26 that managed miraculously to survive earthquakes and fires were stolen in 1982. On 15 August the church holds the biggest *panegýri* on the island (note how all the churches on Santoríni proudly fly the Greek flag).

North, another black beach and a million sun beds and umbrellas announce **Kamári** (ΚΑΜΑΡΙ) (tourist information, © 31 390) with 300 hotels and pensions, and just as many tavernas, bars, and tourist shops, while a mile away women thresh fava beans in the field. Above, on the rocky headland of Mésa Vouna, **Ancient Thíra** (ΠΑΛΑΙΑ ΘΗΡΑ) is spread over its great terraces. Founded in the 8th century BC by the Dorians (who also settled Mílos, but left all the other Cyclades for the Ionians), it remained a thriving town for 900 years. Discovered and excavated by the German archaeologist Hiller von Gortringen in 1895, most of what you see today dates from the Ptolemies, who used the city as a base for their enterprises further north and built temples to the Egyptian gods, as well as to Dionysos, Apollo Karneios, to the town's mythical founding father Thira, and to the Ptolemies' semi-divine selves, with a *temenos* (sacred area), dedicated by their admiral Artemidoros. There are the impressive remains of the *agora* and theatre, with a dizzying view down to the sea, several cemeteries and a gymnasium. Numerous houses still have mosaics; Dorian graffiti dating from 700 BC may be seen on the Terrace of Celebrations, recording the names of competitors and naked dancers of the *gymno paidiai*. Note the enormous Cyclopean walls. The church by the entrance, **Ag. Stefanos**, is the island's oldest, from the 5th century.

The coastal road north leads to **Monolíthos**, a soft grey sandy beach, with a big isolated lump of rock draped with a few ruins, tamarisks along the shore, windsurfers to hire and a few places to stay and eat. **Messariá**, an important wine and market village, has the **Archontiko Argyrou Museum**, in a 19th-century neoclassical mansion owned by a wealthy vintner, with murals and traditional furnishings (© 31 669, *guided tours April–Oct at 11, 12, 1, 5, 6, and 7; adm*).

Santoríni in a Glass

Santoríni is one of Greece's premier white wine producers, although only 3750 acres are still under cultivation as tourism and the easier money it brings in competes with winemaking. The exclusively volcanic soil makes for unusual, interesting wines, and also spared the vines from the deadly plant lice *phylloxera*, that devastated so many vineyards in Europe and required the importation of phylloxera-resistant American rootstock. On Santoríni the original rootstock remains intact; the average age of an *assyrtiko* vine, the main variety of white grape, is 80 years; the oldest vines, near Akrotíri, are estimated at over

150 years. *Assyrtiko* yields everything from a bone dry light wine to a sweet aged Vinsanto made from sun-dried grapes. Black *Mandilaria* is Santoríni's second variety (20%), and the third is white *Aidani*, known for its jasmine bouquet; there are another 12 varieties of grapes grown, mostly as a hobby and to keep alive species unique to the island. The vineyards themselves have a rather unexpected appearance. Because of the wind, the vines are pruned low and protected by woven cane—some fields look as if they were planted with baskets. Moribund for many years, churning out high-alcohol, low-quality wine, the Santoríni wine industry has recently had a shot in the arm from the national winemaker Boutari, who in 1988 built a new high tech domed winery, restaurant, and accessory shop at Megalochóri, towards Akrotíri (℗ (0286) 81 011). A second winery, Koutsoyanópoulos, on the road to Kamári, also offers tastings. One traditional wine to look out for is *nychteri*, which was pressed all night long—hence its name, 'night wine.'

Santoríni ℗ (0286–)　　　　　**Where to Stay and Eating Out**

Akrotíri/Megalochóri ✉ 84700

Plush **Villa Mathios**, ℗ 81 152, ✆ 81 704 (*exp*) has a swimming pool on a veranda overlooking the island; and air-conditioning and colour TVs in the rooms. **Atlante Star**, ℗ 81 647, ✆ 88 227 (*mod*) is isolated on the cliffs, near the road down to a caldera rim. Small and family-run **Villa Kalimera**, ℗ 81 855, ✆ 81 915 (*mod*) is near the caldera rim; there's a pool and courtyard, and all rooms have balconies.

For sunset views over all Santoríni, dine at the cliffside **Panorama**; **Glaros** down towards the Red Beach has good fish. In Megalochóri, a former winery has been converted into **Vedema**, ℗ 81 796, ✆ 81 798, one of the 'Small Luxury Hotels of the World' (*A; lux*), offering every amenity: art gallery, marble baths, in-house movies, a private beach 3km away with minibus service. Nearby in Pírgos, the **Pyrgos** taverna occupies a huge panoramic terrace just below town, a favourite for Greek parties and weddings. *Open year-round.*

Périssa ✉ 84700

Right on the black sands, **Sallada Beach**, ℗ 81 859, ✆ 81 492 (*exp*) offers handsome traditional flats; **Veggera**, ℗ 82 060, ✆ 82 608 (*exp*) has comfortable, fully equipped rooms with a neoclassical touch, pool and laundry; **Boubis**, ℗ 81 203 (*E; mod–inexp*) is a simple place near the beach.

Messariá ✉ 84700

Archontiko Argyrou, ☎ 31669, 🖷 33064 (*A; exp*) occupies a lovely mansion (partially used as a museum) from the 1860s, with rooms on the ground floor.

Kamári ✉ 84700

Kamari Beach, ☎ 31 243, 🖷 32 120 (*C; exp–mod*) is smack on the black sands, with a large pool; all rooms have big verandas. The **Matina** ☎ 31 491, 🖷 31 860 (*C; mod*) is comfortable, as is the **Sunshine**, ☎ 31 491 (*C; mod*) next to the sea. Modest **Andreas** ☎ 31 692, 🖷 31 314 (*D; mod*) has a lush garden. **Alkyon**, ☎ 31 956 (*C; mod*) is a friendly family-run place a short walk from the beach. Quiet **Sigalas**, ☎ 31 260 (*D; mod*) is at the end of the beach, with a shady garden and taverna. **Kamari Camping**, ☎ 31 453, is up the main road from the beach at Kamári.

Camille Stefani on the beach is one of the island's best restaurants, with a French-influenced Greek menu and their own wine label; **Kamari** is a good, inexpensive family-run taverna, serving *fáva* soup. Next to the sea, **Almira** has a good selection of starters and lemon chicken. The locals drive out to Monolithos and the seaside **Taverna Galini** for good cheap home-cooking and *pseftokeftédes*. Kamári throbs with bars. The **Sail Inn** has loud music, fun evenings and glamorous bar girls, and **Valentino's** always has a large crowd. Drop in at the **Yellow Donkey** and dance till dawn—there's very little point in trying to get an early night anyway.

North of Firá to Oía

Imerovígli has just about but not quite merged into Firostefáni and can be a good base if you prefer your caldera minus the crowds and daytripper paraphernalia. A traditionally Catholic village, it has views as magnificent as Fíra or Oía, this time over a startling great big lump of volcanic crud with a knob on top in the foreground. This, incredibly, was the site of **Skáros**, the medieval capital of Santoríni, once defended from below by an impregnable **castle** of 1207 built by Marco Sanudo; another, the Rocca, once sat on the top of the rock until a volcanic eruption in 1650 destroyed the town. A path (do it first thing in the morning, before it gets too hot, and don't do it if you're subject to vertigo) leads in about half an hour to the site of the Rocca, now occupied by a little white chapel. The views are sublime, awe-inspiring, terrifying. Other ruins belong to a Catholic convent, built after a young girl's vision in 1596. The nuns stuck it out in extreme hardship until 1818 when they moved to the new **Ag. Nikólaos**. In the 19th century it was one of the biggest convents in Greece, and has a fine collection of bishops' portraits.

The road north continues to that trendy mouthful of vowels called **Oía**, or Ía (OIA), the third port of Santoríni, although these days only yachts and caiques to Thirassía call here. In 1900, 9000 people lived here, mostly seamen; today most are in Piraeus, although the 500 who remain are fiercely independent of Fíra. Half-ruined by the earthquake, its houses, painted in rich, Fauvist colours, are nearly all restored now (beautifully enough to have won major international restoration prizes) and piled on top of one another over the jumble of broken red and white cliffs; the roofs of the lower houses are courtyards for the neighbours above. There's a half-ruined Venetian lookout fort, and working windmills; if you want the sea, it's 286 steps down to **Arméni** beach with a little clutch of houses, or 214 steps down to **Ammoúdi** beach with tavernas, where you can fill your pockets with pumice-stone souvenirs, or 3km by bus to **Baxédes**, with coarse blackish sand and shade. An old mansion houses the **Nautical Museum** (*open 10–1 and 5–8, closed Tues*), created by an old sea captain; it has ships' models, rare instruments and ships' figureheads. Oía is reputedly haunted, but most of the spirits these days seem to come out of bottles, especially when everyone gathers down on the tip by the Kástro to watch the sun call it a day.

Islets Around the Caldera

Santoríni's caldera, the biggest underwater volcanic crater in the world, is 10km wide and 380m deep. After the big bang that created it at the expense of Minoan civilization in *c.* 1450 BC, the restless volcano occasionally rearranged the topography. Boats from Oía frequently make the 20 minute journey to the **Thirassía**, the islet curving around the caldera's northwestern rim. This was part of Santoríni until another eruption-earthquake in 236 BC blasted them apart. In one of the quarries a Middle Cycladic settlement was discovered, pre-dating Akrotíri, though there are no traces of it now. The main business on Thirassía, pop. 245, is growing tomatoes and beans on the fertile plateau, 150 steps up above; the largest village, **Manolás**, has tavernas and rooms to rent by the sea. The old, nearly abandoned settlement of **Agrilia** has some lovely houses excavated out of the living rock.

Excursion boats from Oía also make trips out to the 'burnt isles'. **Palía Kaméni** emerged in 157 BC and an altar to Poseidon was built there as soon as it cooled off. **Néa Kaméni** was born in 46 BC, and both grew several times over the centuries as the big volcano rumbled and spat. Both are still active to a degree, especially the Metaxá crater on Néa Kaméni, which last erupted in 1950 and still spews steam. The worst recorded eruption happened in 1650, which went down in the history books as 'the evil times' when people and animals on Santoríni were killed by the noxious fumes, and a tidal wave (a mini one compared to the monster of 1450 BC) wrecked most of the ships and ports on its neighbouring islands and Crete. However, even though a local brochure advertising the excursion refers to it as 'the strange volcano which cause you greatness', most people who visit the Burnt Isles come away disappointed. The tourist trail up the mountain is rubbish-strewn, stinks of sulphur, and there's plenty of black ash to look at. There are also tourist excursion boats taking people to swim in the 'healthy' sulphurous mud nearby and hot volcanic waters around Palía Kaméni, which, if nothing else, makes an unusual chat-up line ('Gosh, you stink!') in the bars.

| *Santoríni ☎ (0286–)* | ***Where to Stay and Eating Out*** |

Imerovigli ✉ 87400

Heliotopos, ☎ 23 670, 🖷 23 672, (*A; exp*), an intimate, elegant Cycladic hideway, has a restaurant and grand views. **Villa Spiliotica**, ☎ 22 637, 🖷 23 590, has similar views and lower prices for its apartments and studios. **Katerina's Castle**, ☎ 22 708 (*E; mod*) offers simple rooms on the caldera. **Blue Note** is a good bet for dinner with grand views, or for something Greek, simple, and cheaper, **Marilos**, near the car park, has no views but is run by a kindly old gent. **Skaros Fish Taverna** is also excellent.

Oía ✉ 84702

The swishest places to stay are the luxury *skaftá* of **Fanari Villas**, ☎ 71 321, 🖷 71 235 (*exp*), below the windmill, with small bar, and steps down to Ammoúdi Bay. **Katikies**, ☎ 71 401, 🖷 71 129 (*exp*) are beautifully decorated rooms and apartments with great views, a spectacular pool and homemade breakfasts on the terraces. **Perivolas**, ☎ 71 308 (*A; exp*) has 14 lovely traditional houses, with a unique pool. **Zoe-Aegeas Traditional Houses**, ☎/🖷 71 466 (*exp*) are four caldera-rim double studios and four flats sleeping up to six. **Anemones**, ☎ 71 220 (*E; mod–inexp*) is OK. The **youth hostel**, ☎ 71 290 has cheap dorm beds. For a romantic dinner by candlelight, **1800**, in a shipowner's house on the main street, ☎ 71 485, serves imaginative international cuisine; the **Blue Sky Taverna**, a bit further down, is reasonable and deservedly popular; **Neptune** and **Thalami** are best for fish. If you want to have aperitifs and dinner by the famous Oía sunset, arrive early to get a table at **Kastro**.

Sérifos (ΣΕΡΙΦΟΣ)

Where its neighbour Sífnos welcomes the visitor with green terraces and dovecotes, Sérifos, 'the barren one', tends to intimidate with its stark rocks. The island owed its prosperity in antiquity to its iron and copper mines, among the richest in Greece, and minted its own coins, depicting a frog. A violent miners' strike in 1916 followed by a decline in the mines' profitability led to their abandonment, and since

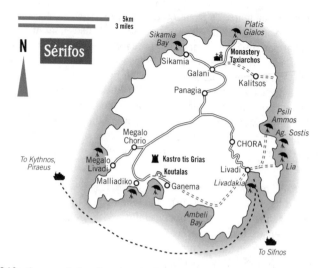

the 1960s the population has drastically decreased to around 1500. Otherwise, Sérifos' history follows that of the other Cyclades; Chóra, high above the sea, seemingly inaccessible as it tumbles impressively down the steep slopes, was once fortified with a Byzantine-Venetian castle and walls, ruled in the late 14th century by the exceedingly nasty tyrant, Niccolò Adoldo, who fortunately spent most of his time in his palazzo in Venice, until he thought his subjects weren't paying him enough taxes. Off he sailed to Sérifos, hiring a band of Cretan brigands to kidnap all the important men of the island and lock them in his castle, to torture them into revealing where they hid their money, and when they still couldn't come up with the goods Adoldo had them all thrown over the walls. The Signory in Venice, which usually didn't give a hoot about the behaviour of its freebooting lordlings in Greece as long as they remained loyal and kept the sea lanes open, was offended enough to imprison Adoldo for two years and take Sérifos away from him.

The appealing port Livádi provides an informal foreground to its dramatic setting, and has learned to cope with the arrival of yachties and a strong German and French contingent. Beware of water shortages in August.

Mythology

When it was prophesied to Akrisius, King of Argos, that he would be slain by the son of his daughter Danaë, Akrisius locked his daughter in a tower, but even there her beauty did not fail to attract the attentions of Zeus, who came to her in a shower of golden rain and fathered Perseus. Enraged but unable to put his daughter or grandson to death, Akrisius decided to leave the issue to fate and set them adrift in a box. Zeus guided them to Serifos, where a fisherman discovered them and brought them to Polydectes, the king of the island. Struck by her beauty, Polydectes wanted to marry Danaë but she refused him, and as Perseus grew older he defended his mother's decision. Polydectes pretended to lose interest in Danaë, while he plotted to remove Perseus from the scene by asking him to do him a favour: fetch the head of the Gorgon Medusa, the only mortal of the three horrible Gorgon sisters, who had hair made of living snakes, whose eyes bulged and whose teeth were fangs. The sisters were so ugly that a mere glance at one of them turned a human to stone.

Despite Danaë's horror at this treachery of Polydectes, Perseus accepted and accomplished the task, assisted by Athena, who helped him procure a mirror shield, winged shoes, and a cloak of invisibility. With Medusa's awful head in his pouch Perseus returned to Sérifos (saving Andromeda from a sea monster on the way), to find his mother hiding from Polydectes in the hut of the fisherman who had saved them so long ago. Angrily Perseus went up to the palace, where he found a very surprised Polydectes at a banquet. Perseus told him that he had succeeded in his quest and held up Medusa's head as proof, instantly turning everyone in the room and the whole island into stone. The kind fisherman was declared King of Sérifos in his place by Perseus, and the hero and his mother went home to Argos. Still fearing the old prophecy, Danaë's father fled before them. But fate finally caught up with him in another town, where Perseus was competing in a game and accidentally killed his grandfather with a javelin in the foot.

Sérifos ☎ (0281–)

Getting There

By sea: daily with Piraeus, Kýthnos, Mílos and Sífnos; 4 times a week with Kímolos, 3 times a week with Santoríni, Folégandros, Síkinos and Íos; twice a week with Mýkonos and Páros, once a week to Sýros and Tínos. **Port authority**: ☎ 51 470. Six **buses** go up to Chóra from Livádi; other villages are served once a day in the summer.

Tourist Information

Police: Livádi, ☎ (0281) 51 300.

Festivals

5 May, Ag. Iríni at Koutalás; **27 July**, Ag. Panteleímonos at Mount Óros; **6 August**, Sotíros at Kaló Ábeli; **15–17 August**, Panagía near the

Monastery and at a different village each day; **7 September**, Ag. Sosoudos at Livádi; **23 September**, Ag. Theklas

Livádi and Chóra

Most people stay in **Livádi** (ΛIBAΔI), the port and island green spot, a simple, pleasant spot where many of the streets are still unpaved. There's a long pebbly-sandy beach lined with tamarisks, and many rooms to rent. There are two other beaches within easy walking distance from Livádi, crowded **Livadákia** and, a 30 minute walk south over the headland, sandy **Karávi Beach**, more secluded, and popular with nudists and freelance campers; **Lía** to the east is another sandy alternative, and **Ag. Sóstis**.

Chóra, the capital, is 6km up, linked by bus or ancient stair. Set high over Sérifos's forbidding slopes, terraced to resemble corrugated iron as if Medusa's head had really done the business, Chóra is a whitewashed oasis, a fascinating jumble of narrow lanes and steps, where geranium trees tucked in corners grow 12ft high. Many houses are built of stone salvaged from the fortress; others date back to the Middle Ages, and a few are being bought as holiday homes by trendy Athenians and a handful of Brits and Germans. At the very top of Chóra there is a very pretty neoclassical square, with a **town hall** built in the moneyed days of 1908. The old windmills still turn in the wind, and in the spring you may see a rare carnation that grows only on Sérifos. From Chóra a 20-minute walk (or there's a road) leads down to **Psíli Ámmos**, an excellent beach with a pair of tavernas on the east coast.

Around Sérifos

The road continues beyond Chóra to **Megálo Chorió**, believed to occupy the site of the ancient capital of Sérifos; below, **Megálo Livádi**, now visited for its beach and tavernas, was once the loading dock for the iron and copper mined near Megálo Chorió. From Megálo Chorió the road continues to **Koutalás,** guarded by the 6th-century white marble **Kástro tis Grías.** During mining operations, a cave, instantly dubbed the **Cave of the Cyclops,** was discovered: inside are two stalactite chambers, a small lake, and a floor of petrified seashells (bring a light). There are two beaches nearby, **Malliádiko** and **Gánema**, and a track back to Livádi.

A second road, now paved, passes **Panagía**, named after the oldest church on Sérifos, from the 10th century. At **Galaní** you can visit **Taxiárchos Monastery**, built in 1500 and containing a precious altar, 18th-century frescoes by Skordílis, and Byzantine manuscripts in the library, then continue into the petrified island's land of milk and honey, **Kalítsos**, where almonds and olives and the island's stubborn vine, *rhodites*, prosper. There's a beach, Platís Giálos, just beyond the monastery, or, on the other side of Galaní, **Sikamiá Bay**, a good place to get away from it all, with a beach, taverna, rare bit of shade and fresh water.

Sérifos is well-known enough for its hotels and rooms to fill up in the summer. In Livádi, the further along the beach you go, the cheaper the accommodation. Handy for the ferries, **Areti**, ✆ 51 479, 📠 51 298 (*C; mod*) has a quiet garden and comfortable rooms with terraces overlooking the sea. New **Asteria**, ✆ 51 191, 📠 51 209 (*B; mod*) has a balcony with sea view for every room, TVs and a restaurant. **Albatross**, ✆ 51 148 (*D; mod*), smothered in oleander, is further around the bay but the owner meets the ferry with a minibus.

Naias, ✆ 51 749, 📠 51 587 (*C; mod*) has balconies, breakfast, and stays open all year. **Serifos Beach**, ✆ 51 209, (*C; mod*) is the island's biggest, with a nice taverna downstairs; the **Maistrali**, ✆ 51 220, 📠 51 298 (*C; exp–mod*) has lovely airy rooms and balconies. **Kyklades**, ✆ 51 553 (*E; mod*) has rooms by the sea, and delicious shrimp casserole with feta cheese and tomatoes in the restaurant. **Captain George Rooms** ✆ 51 274 (*inexp*), near the square are good value; other budget **rooms**, ✆ 51 160 with balconies are above the Cavo d'Oro supermarket. **Korali Camping**, Livadákia Beach, ✆ 51 500 has good facilities.

The sea is clean and subsequently the fish is especially good. Like the accommodation, the tavernas get cheaper further along the beach. Popular with locals and tourists alike, **Takis**, on Livádi's waterfront under an enormous tamarisk, offers excellent and inexpensive food and friendly service.

For a pleasantly zany atmosphere, with good, wholesome food (spaghetti, chicken curries) apart from the usual Greek fare, try **Mokka** at the end of the port where the locals, yachties, tourists, various children and an assortment of cats and dogs mingle happily together. **Ouzerie Meltemi** will give you a *karafáki* (enough for three or four good drinks) and vast choice of tasty nibbles, including local cheeses and the mysterious 'single yellow pea' or 'married yellow pea'. Round the bay, sit right on the water at **Stamati**, and enjoy his excellent food, vegetarian dishes, or grilled meats. **Serfanto** has pizza and bargain Italian-based set menus.

Up in Chóra, on the top square by the town hall, **Manoulis** serves *mezédes* with a difference; try the sun-dried tomatoes sautéed in butter, or wild fennel fritters, and Serifot specialities such as *keftédes*, *spetsofái* and chick peas from the wood oven, and the family's own wine. Neighbour

Zorba serves snacks with view; ditto the affable **Stavro**, by the bus stop, whose dad starred in a famous EOT tourist poster in the 60s.

Entertainment and Nightlife

There's a mix of nightlife in Livádi with several music bars and seasonally changing discos from heavy metal and pop at **Metallein**, to **Kastro** and **Veggera**, and a new little cluster of clubs **Praxis**, **Aiolos** and **Alter Ego**.

Sífnos (ΣΙΦΝΟΣ)

Sífnos in recent years has become the most popular island in the western Cyclades, with good reason—it is an island of peaceful serendipity, with gentle green hills, vineyards, watermelon patches and olives, charming villages and long sandy beaches, beloved by its 2000 inhabitants who keep it spick and span. It is exceptionally pleasant for walks, and is famous for its pottery and its cooks, ever since Sifniot Nikolas Tselemntes wrote the first modern Greek cookery book (to this day any cookbook in Greece is a *tselemntes*). Sífnos produces the best olive oil in the Cyclades, and the people speak with a sweet singsong lilt. The landscape is strewn with Venetian dovecotes, windmills, 300 little chapels, and 52 ancient towers (more than the rest of the Cyclades combined) left over from a sophisticated signalling system devised in the 5th century BC—a bit after the fact in Sífnos' case.

History: the Island that Laid Golden Eggs

Pliny, who often got it wrong, wrote that the Phoenicians called the island Meropia and were the first to mine its gold; according to recent archaeological research, this time Pliny was right: the oldest gold, silver and lead galleries on Sífnos date back to the 3rd millennium BC—the oldest mines yet discovered in Europe. And when these first miners exhausted their galleries, the archaeologists note, they religiously filled them in to heal the wounds of the earth.

The Phoenicians were replaced by the Minoans, who founded Minoa near Apollonía, and who were in turn replaced by Ionians who lived near Ag. Andreas and elsewhere. Meropia, meanwhile, had become famous for its gold; at one time, it is said, there was so much that the islanders simply divided it among themselves each year, and had enough extra in the 6th century to afford to pave their market with the finest Parian marble. Apollo at Delphi heard rumours of this wealth and demanded that the island contribute an annual tithe of gold in the form of a solid egg. In 530 BC Meropia constructed a magnificent treasury at Delphi to house its golden eggs and adorned it with a fine frieze and pediment which can still be seen; for many years it was the richest of all the oracle's treasures. But one year the islanders, who began to have a reputation for greed and cunning, sent the god an egg of gilded lead. Apollo soon discovered he had been duped and cursed the island.

This gave Polycrates, Tyrant of Sámos, a good excuse to extract a fine from Meropia; his 40 triremes plundered the island's gold, and Apollo's curse caused the mines to sink and give out. Thus the island became empty or, in Greek, *sífnos*. Nowadays most of the ancient mines at Ag. Mína, Kapsálos and Ag. Sostis are underwater, or just barely above the sea.

With egg on its face, Sífnos went into decline and the inhabitants moved up to Kástro. In 1307 the Da Coronia family ruled the island for Venice; in 1456 Kozadinós, the Lord of Kýthnos, married into the family and his descendants ruled Sífnos until the Turks took the island in 1617. Towards the end of the 17th century the Ottomans attempted to reopen the ancient mines, or at least sent out experts from Istanbul to examine them. Supposedly, when they got wind of these plans, the islanders hired a band of French pirates to sink the Sultan's ship. The experts, in turn, heard of the deal with the pirates, and simply went home. Later the French themselves exploited the local deposits of iron ore and lead; mining ended in 1925.

Sífnos has also made an important contribution to Greek letters. At the end of the 17th century the 'School of the Holy Tomb' was founded to keep ancient Greek and the classics alive during the Turkish occupation, drawing students from all over Greece. Nikólaos Chrysoyélos, the most famous headmaster, led a contingent of Sifniots in the War of Independence, and became modern Greece's first Minister of Education. Another islander, the 19th-century poet-satirist Cleánthis Triandáfilos, who wrote under the name Rabágas, was a thorn in the side of the monarchy until he was imprisoned and committed suicide. Ioánnis Gypáris (*d.* 1942) was another Sifniot of note; along with Caváfy, he was the first poet to espouse the use of the demotic language (as opposed to the formal *katharévousa*) in literature.

Sífnos ℂ (0284–)   **Getting There and Around**

By sea: daily with Piraeus, Kýthnos, Sérifos and Mílos; 4 times a week with Kímolos, 2–3 times a week with Íos, Santoríni, Folégandros and Síkinos, once a week with Páros, Tínos, Karystos (Évia) and Rafína. Excursion **boats** from Kamáres to Váthi and Cherónissos; 3 times a week around the island tours. **Port authority**: ℂ 31 617.

By road: frequent reliable **buses** between Kamáres, Appolonía, Aretmónas, and from there to Platýs Gialós; not quite as often to Fáros, Kato Petali, Kastro and Vathí. Pick up the detailed schedule at the tourist office. **Taxis**: ℂ 31 656/793/626.

Sífnos ℂ (0284–)   **Tourist Information**

Municipal tourist office, womanned by the helpful Sofia, near the quay in Kamáres, ℂ 31 977. In Apollonía **Aegean Thesaurus**, ℂ 33 151, ℮ 32 190, is helpful and offers guided walking tours around the island.

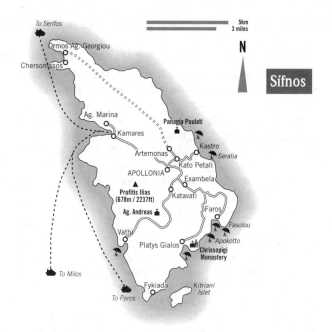

Sífnos

2 February *Lolopangyrio* 'crazy festival' of pagan origins, at Panagaía Ournofora, Apollonía; **25 March** and **21 November**, Panagía tou Vounoú; **40 days after Greek Easter** (Analypsis) at Chrissopigí; **20 July**, Profítis Ilías near Kamáres; **15 August**, Panagía ta Gournia; **29 August**, Ag. Ioánnes near Váthi; **31 August**, Ag. Simeon near Kamáres; **14 September**, Stavrós, at Fáros.

From Kamáres to Apollonía and Artemónas

The island's port, shady **Kamáres** (ΚΑΜΑΡΕΣ), has become a typical waterside jumble of tourist facilities. Situated between two steep, barren cliffs that belie the fertility inland, Kamáres has a sandy beach safe for little kids, with some shady places to camp, and a range of cafés and tavernas. Only two of the many pottery workshops that once lined the north side of the harbour still survive, and specialize in decorative glazed chimney pots. The exceptionally fine clay on Sífnos has been used for ceramics since pre-Cycladic times, and over the thousands of years, the islanders have become expert potters. In the early 19th century, there were so many that they began to emigrate to other corners of Greece, to the extent that someone has discovered that every Greek potter has a Sifniot in their family tree. Just after the war, there were still some 90 workshops, employing 600 potters, and after nearly dying a death the old tradition is undergoing something of a revival.

The bus makes the dramatic climb up to the capital **Apollonía** (ΑΠΟΛΛΟΝΙΑ), a Cycladic idyll of two-storey houses and bougainvillea, spread out across the hills, a circle of white from the distance; note how most of the houses have terraces on the side, designed for talking; the Sifniots are known for being a sociable lot. The town's name comes from a 7th-century BC temple of Apollo, superseded in the 18th century by the church **Panagía Ouranofóra** in the highest part of town. Fragments of the temple can still be seen, and there's a marble relief of St George over the door. Another church, **Ag. Athanásios** (next to the pretty square dedicated to Cleánthis Triandáfilos) has frescoes and a carved wooden iconostasis. In the bus stop square the **Museum of Popular Arts and Folklore** houses a fine ethnographic collection of Sifniot pottery, embroideries and costumes (*opening hours depend on who has a key*).

Artemis is Apollo's twin sister; similarly **Artemónas** (ΑΡΤΕΜΩΝΑΣ) is Apollonía's twin village and the second largest on Sífnos, a pretty mile's walk away. Beneath its windmills, cobblestoned lanes wind past the island's most ambitious neoclassical residences and churches. The church of **Kochí**, with its cluster of domes, occupies the site of a temple of Artemis; little 17th-century **Ag. Geórgios tou Aféndi** contains several fine icons from the period, and **Panagía ta Gourniá**, near the bridge, has a beautiful interior (keys next door). **Panagía Pouláti**, down on the coast, is in a superb setting overlooking sea and cliffs, with a beach down below.

Kástro and Panagía Chrissopigí

Kástro (ΚΑΣΤΡΟ), on the east coast, is 3km from Artemónas by road or the old scenic coastal path. The ancient and medieval capital of Sífnos, Kástro is a charming village overlooking the sea, if a bit forlorn with only 30 families in residence, still defended by Byzantine-style walls made from the backs of the tall narrow houses, many with wooden balconies and their Venetian coats-of-arms. Ruins of the Classical acropolis and walls remain, and there are many churches with attractive floors, among them the **Panagía Eleoússa** (1653), **Ag. Ekateríni** (1665) and **Panagía Koímmissi** (1593), where the altar is decorated with Dionysian bulls' heads. An old Venetian church of St Anthony of Padua houses the **Archaeological Museum** (*open Tues–Sun, 9–2; out of season, ask the lady opposite*). The site of the School of the Holy Tomb, closed in 1834, is now Kástro's cemetery. At Kástro there's plenty of deep blue sea to dive into, or if you prefer sand, a path from Kástro leads down to **Serália**, with remnants of the medieval port, and a lovely beach.

Just south of Artemónas the bus passes through **Exámbela**, a quiet flower-filled village famous for its songs. In the middle of one of the island's most fertile areas, the still-active **Vrísi Monastery** is surrounded by springs (1612) and contains many old manuscripts and objects of religious art. On the road to Platýs Gialós the monastery of **Ag. Andréas**, sitting on a hill, has some ruins of the double walls that once encircled the ancient citadel, and a little further north, a path from Katavatí continues up in two hours to Sífnos' highest peak (681m) named for its monastery of **Profítis Ilías**, built in the 8th century, with thick stone walls and a small network of catacombs and cells and a 12th-century marble iconostasis in the church (*check opening hours before setting out*); the views, over the white villages below, are delightful.

Further south, the old seaside village of **Fáros** with its sandy beaches is a friendly, low-key resort with cheap accommodation and good tavernas. There's a footpath to the island's most famous monastery, **Panagía Chrissopigí**, built in 1650 on a rocky cape. The story goes that two girls accidentally disturbed some pirates napping in the church. With the pirates in hot pursuit, the girls desperately prayed to the Virgin, who saved them by splitting the cape in the pirates' path—spanned in these pirate-free days by a bridge. The long beach here, **Apókofto**, has golden sands while **Fasoloú** is popular with nudists; both have tavernas.

Platýs Gialós, and other Beaches

Platýs Gialós (ΠΛΑΤΥΣ ΓΙΑΛΟΣ) with its broad sandy beach—said to be the longest in the Cyclades—is the island's busiest resort, though you can escape its worldly concerns by lodging in the serene convent of **Panagía tou Vounoú** up on the cliff, with a gorgeous view over the bay below. The nuns left nearly a century ago, but the church with its ancient Doric columns is still used for island *panegýria*. Platýs Gialós' pottery of Franzesko Lemonis was founded in 1936. There are boat excursions from Kamáres and now buses to the lovely pottery and fishing hamlet of **Vathí**, probably the prettiest place to stay on the island, with few rooms to rent, a lovely clean beach and shallow water. **Cherónissos** on the island's windy northern tip is another pottery centre, also best reached by boat, although there's a rough road (most car hire firms make you promise not to use it, however). Here master potter Kóstas Depastás upholds the island's old ceramics tradition, with local clay, his kiln fired by driftwood. There's a taverna if you feel peckish.

Sífnos ✉ *84003,* ☏ *(0284–)*   ***Where to Stay and Eating Out***

The tourist office has a complete list of all the rooms on the island. Sífnos is famous for *revíthia*, baked chick pea stew, served only on Sundays; *revithokeftedes,* chick pea patties*; xynomyzíthra*, a hard sheep's-milk cheese, steeped in wine and kept in barrels until it stinks but tastes great; *stamnás*, meat, cheese and potatoes in a clay pot; and *ambelofasola*, made from green beans. Dill is the favourite herb.

Kamáres

Boulis, ✆ 32 122, ✉ 32 150 (*C; exp–mod*), is by the beach and has a green lawn. **Stavros**, ✆ 31 641 (*C; inexp*) has basic rooms, some with shared bath. **Kamari Pension**, ✆ 31 710, ✉ 31 709 (*B pension; mod–inexp*) is a better bet on the waterfront; **Dimitris and Margarita Belli**, ✆ 31 276 (*inexp*) also have good little rooms with seaview balconies. There's a campsite just behind the beach, **Mikis**, ✆ 32 366. **Boulis Restaurant** on the road has good-value rooms (don't confuse it with the hotel) and serves traditional, excellent and cheap Greek fare. **Kapetan Andreas** has a good selection of fish; **Parapanda**, up on a lovely terrace, has a lot of choice and traditional grill favourites like *kokoretsi*; **Artyris**, right on the sea, has good grills too.

Apollonía/Artemónas/Kástro

In Apollonía, **Sofia**, ✆ 31 238 (*C; mod–inexp*) is set on a quiet little square. **Angelo's Rooms**, ✆ 31 533, are cheap with garden views. **Sífnos**, ✆ 31 624, ✉ 33 067 (*C; mod*) is another good choice; the charming **Apollónia**, ✆ 31 490 (*C; inexp*) is a budget gem. By the bus stop, **Orea Sifnos**, ✆ 33 069, serves tasty traditional food and barrelled wine. In Artemónas the little **Artemonas** guest house, ✆ 31 303, ✉ 32 385 (*C; mod*) is one of the most charming places on Sífnos with a cool courtyard, while the bigger **Artemon**, ✆ 31 303 (*mod*), under the same management, has a garden restaurant; for furnished apartments, the recently renovated **Apostolidis**, ✆ 32 143, includes minibars and views over Platis Gialos. **Liotrivi** ('Olive Press'), ✆ 31 246, on the main square in Artemónas, is the island's best-known and one of the best eating places in the Cyclades. Among the specialities are *kápari*, local capers, and *revíthia* and other Sifniot specialities; it's also high on atmosphere and wine. Up in Kástro, there are rooms to rent, food to eat at **Leonidas** or **Sifakis**, and drinks at the **Castello**.

Fáros/Apókofto

There are ten furnished apartments in **Blue Horizon**, ✆ 71 441 (*B; exp*), and the old standby **Sifneiko Archontiko**, ✆ 71 454, ✉ 71 454 (*D; mod–inexp*), plus some of the cheapest rooms on the island. Amid the clutch of jolly tavernas, try **Faros**, ✆ 31 826, with charcoal grilled lobster, octopus and fish. At Apókofto, the small, family-run **Flora**, ✆ 71 388 (*B; mod–inexp*), has great views; try taverna **Lembesis'** traditional food.

Platýs Gialós

The **Platys Yialos Beach**, ✆ 71 324, ✉ 71 325 (*B; exp*) is built in traditional Cycladic style with well-equipped air-conditioned bungalows, all facilities and sports. The **Alexandros Sífnos Beach**, ✆ 32 333, ✉ 71 303

(*B; exp*) is also smart with bungalows on the hillside above the beach. **Angeliki**, ☎ 31 688 (*mod*) near the bus stop is nice; there are several rooms to rent and **Camping Platys Yialos**, ☎ 71 286, in an olive grove set back from the beach. There are several beach tavernas and rooms—some available in the 16th-century monastery of **Taxiárchis**, ☎ 31 060. There is a good choice of fish restaurants: try the **Kyklades Beach** or **Sofia** for Sifniot dishes; for Italian food **Mama Mia** is popular.

Entertainment and Nightlife

Nightlife centres on Kamáres with numerous beachside cocktail bars and discos: **Café Folie** is lovely for a sundowner, then dance away at the **Mobilize Dancing Club**. In Apollonía **Aloni**, ☎ 31 543, often has live Greek music. For a spot of culture the **Sifniot Cultural Society** presents summer concerts at Artemónas.

Síkinos (ΣΙΚΙΝΟΣ)

If you want to escape the outside world, its newspapers and noise, or just practise your Greek, you can always visit Síkinos, Folégandros' little sister, with a sleepy port and the stunning white twin villages of Chóra and Kástro perched high above. Recently declared an 'Ecosystem of European Importance', its shores host wild pigeons, black-headed hawks, and sea birds; monk seals live in its sea caves, rare cat vipers and sand snakes slither about on land. Unaffected as yet by organized tourism, the island still has farming and fishing as its mainstay. Light years away from next-door Íos—although there are day trips from the fleshpots—there are a few beaches but little else to see or do. Most people call in for a few days to catch their breath, then move on. In August it gets busy with returning Greeks. Named after the child of banished Limnian Thoas who was set adrift in a tea chest, washed up on the island and saved by a nymph, Síkinos is the place to savour the simple pleasures of old-fashioned island life. There are many paths over the mountains, and the hillsides are neatly tended with little wheat fields and vines in the terraces and valleys. In ancient times Síkinos was one of several islands called Oenoe, or 'wine island', and the local stuff still packs a punch.

Síkinos ☎ *(0286–)*   ### Getting There and Around

By sea: daily summer **tourist boats** to Folégandros and Íos, and **ferries** most days as well; also 5 times a week to Piraeus, Santoríni, Kýthnos, Kímolos, Mílos, 3 times a week to Páros, Náxos, Sífnos, and Sérifos; once a week to Mýkonos and Sýros. **Excursion boat** to the beaches in summer. **Port authority**: ☎ 51 222.

By road: hourly island **bus** to Chóra and Kástro meets most ferries.

Villages and Walks Around Síkinos

Síkinos' port, **Aloprónia** (ΑΛΟΠΡΟΝΙΑ) or **Skála**, has been enlarged so ferries can now dock. It's still very shallow with a sandy beach, ideal for children; fishing boats bob by the quay, there are a few tavernas and a shop-cum-café, a scattering of holiday homes behind the port, and a new hotel complex sums up the rest. **Chóra** (XOPA), the capital, one of the most authentic villages in the Cyclades, is a good hour's walk up from the jetty, if the bus hasn't put in an appearance. Looming over the village is the ruined 18th-century **Monastery of Zoodóchos Pigí**, fortified against the pirates. The 300 inhabitants are most proud, however, of their 'cathedral' with its icons by the 18th-century master Skordílis. The main square is formed by 18th-century stone **mansions**, their walls used as bastions of defence. Some have bright wooden balconies like those in Folégandros. One ruined marble portico has intricately carved grapes and Byzantine symbols. The church of the **Pantánassa** is the focal point with bees buzzing in the trees. A few minutes' walk up the next hill, **Kástro** (ΚΑΣΤΡΟ), with its labyrinthine lanes, ruined windmills, tiny rooms and *kafeneíons*, is a last relic of what Cycladic villages looked like before tourism hit. Some nationalist goofball has brightly illustrated his opinions on his walls and a little **folk museum** has been set up by ex-pat American John Margétis in memory of his mother, Kalióped (*open July–August pm*).

From **Chóra** a new paved road leads past ruined **Cyclopean** walls south west to Episkopí, originally thought to have been a Roman shrine to Pythian Apollo but now believed to be a 3rd-century mausoleum, converted in the 7th century to the Byzantine church of Koimísis Theotókou. The church in turn was remodelled in the 17th century, after an earthquake, to become **Moní Episkópi**. A rough path to the northeast leads in about an hour and a half to the rather scant remains of a Classical fortress at **Paliókastro**, near the sandy beach, **Málta**. Tracks from this path lead south to the sandy beaches of **Ag. Geórgios** (with a taverna) and **Ag. Nikólaos**, but there is also a caique in summer. From the harbour beach you can walk up over the mountain to the next cove at **Gialiskári**; while the pebble beach at **Ag. Panteleímonas**, about 40 minutes away, is the site of a *panegýri* on 27 July.

Síkinos ✉ *84010,* ✆ *(0286–)*　　**Where to Stay and Eating Out**

Aloprónia

The smart hotel **Porto Síkinos**, ✆ 51 247, 🖂 51 220 (*B; exp–mod*) is right on the beach, prettily laid out in traditional design, with bar, restaurant and tourist office; up the hill **Flora** ✆ 51 239/214 (*C; mod*), a lovely Cycladic-style development of eight self-contained rooms built round a courtyard, has wonderful views. **Kamares**, ✆/🖂 51 281 (*mod*) has charming traditional rooms, all with bath and phones. There are also basic harbourside rooms to let: try **Loukas**, © 51 076, @ 51 075, above the fish restaurant, or **Sigalas** or **Panayiotis Kouvdouris**, © 51 232. There are several seasonal tavernas, but if you go after late September everything is closed except **Flora's Shop**, which doubles as a makeshift taverna. Otherwise you can eat at **Braxos Pizzaria**, aka **The Rock Café**, or have a coffee or ouzo or simple lunch at the **Meltemi** where the fishermen gather.

Chóra

There are a few rooms: **Haroula** and **Dimitris Divolis** on the way to the post office and **Nikos** over one of the *kafeneía* are all worth a try. The main taverna is **To Kastro** with a roof garden and excellent home-cooking; **Klimateria** is a pretty vine-covered *kafeneíon* which also does snacks and omelettes. **Zacherias** is another possibility for basic Greek fare. The main nightspot is **To Liotrivi**, a trendy music/dancing bar converted from an olive press. Or dance at **Themonies**, the new disco halfway to Aloprónia.

Sýros (ΣΥΡΟΣ/ΣΥΡΑ)

Inhabitants of Sýros, or Sýra as they call it, affectionately call their island home 'Our rock', and it's as dry and barren a piece of real estate as you can find. But at the beginning of the Greek War of Independence in 1821 it was blessed with three important qualities: a large natural harbour, the protection of the King of France, and a hardworking population. The result is Sýros' capital, Ermoúpolis, once the premier port in Greece, and today the largest city and capital of the Cyclades. Don't come here looking for Cycladic sugar cubism: Ermoúpolis is the best-preserved 19th-century neoclassical town in the whole of Greece.

A sophisticated island, with many Athenians working there in law or local government, Sýros can afford to snap its fingers at tourism, but it's booming nonetheless. However, it remains very Greek and tourists are treated more like guests than customers—except when it comes to *loukoúmia*, better known as Turkish Delight (both Greeks and Turks claim to have invented it; no one really knows). These sweet, gummy squares, flavoured with roses, quinces or pistachios, smothered in icing sugar, are an island speciality, and vendors stream aboard the ferries to peddle it. The other Sýros sweetmeats are *halvadópittes*, rather like nougat.

History

Homer's swineherd Eumaeus, who helped Odysseus when he finally returned to Ithaca, was actually a prince of Sýros who had been captured by Phoenician pirates, and he described his native island as a rich, fertile place where famine and disease were strangers, and inhabitants died only when they were struck by the gentle arrows of Apollo or Artemis after living long, happy lives. The first inhabitants, who may have been the same Phoenicians who made off with Eumaeus, settled at Dellagrácia and at Fínikas. Poseidon was the chief god of Sýros, and in connection with his cult one of the first observatories in Europe, a heliotrope (a kind of sundial), was constructed in the 6th century BC by Sýros' own philosopher Ferekides. Ferekides was a keen student of ancient Chaldaean and Egyptian mysteries, and spent two years in Egypt being initiated into secret cults; on his return to Greece, he became Pythagoras' teacher, imparting a mix of astrology and philosophy, and beliefs in reincarnation and the immortality of the soul; he was also the first Greek to write in prose.

In Roman times the population emigrated to the site of present-day Ermoúpolis, at that time known as 'the Happy' with its splendid natural harbour and two prominent hills. After the collapse of the *pax Romana*, Sýros was abandoned, until the 13th century when Venetians founded the hilltop town of Áno Sýros. Like all the lordlings on the islands, these regarded life as something of a game, and on one memorable occasion sent their tiny fleet and army against their counterparts on Tînos in a war over a donkey.

Because Áno Sýros was Catholic, the island enjoyed the protection of the French, and remained neutral at the outbreak of the War of Independence in 1821. War refugees from Chíos, Psará and Smyrna brought their Orthodox faith with them and founded settlements on the other hill, Vrondádo, and down at Sýros' harbour. This new port town boomed from the start, as the premier 'warehouse' of the new Greek state where cotton from Egypt and spices from the East were stored, and as the central coaling station for the entire eastern Mediterranean. When the time came to name the new town, Ermoúpolis—'the city of Hermes' (the god of commerce)—was the natural choice.

For 50 years Sýros ran much of the Greek economy, and great fortunes were made and spent not only on elegant mansions, but also on schools, public buildings and streets. Ermoúpolis built the first theatre in modern Greece and the first high school, financed by the citizens and government; and when the Syriani died they were so pleased with themselves that the most extravagant monuments to be seen in any Greek cemetery were erected in their memory. By the 1890s, however, oil replaced coal and Piraeus, with the building of the Corinth Canal, replaced Ermoúpolis as Greece's major port; Sýros declined, but always remained the largest city and capital of the Cyclades, supporting itself with shipyards and various industries, prospering just enough to keep its grand old buildings occupied, but not enough to tear them down to build new concrete blocks. Today Ermoúpolis is a National Historical Landmark.

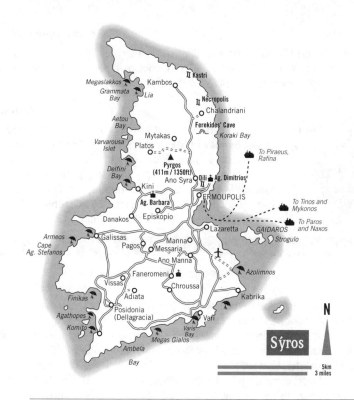

Map labels:
II Kastri
Megaslakkos
Grammata Bay
Lia
Kambos
II Necropolis
Chalandriani
Ferekides' Cave
Aetou Bay
Mytakas
Koraki Bay
Varvarousa Islet
Platos
To Piraeus, Rafina
Pyrgos (411m / 1350ft)
Delfini Bay
Ano Syra
Dili II Ag. Dimitrios
Kini
ERMOUPOLIS
Ag. Barbara
To Tinos and Mykonos
Danakos
Episkopio
Lazaretta
GAIDAROS
To Paros and Naxos
Armeos Cape
Ag. Stefanos
Galissas
Pagos
Manna
Messaria
Strogulo
Ano Manna
Vissas
Faneromeni
Chroussa
Azolimnos
Adiata
Kabrika
Finikas
Posidonia (Dellagracia)
Agathopes
Vari
Komito
Varis Bay
Megas Gialos
Ambela Bay

N

Sýros

5km
3 miles

Sýros ℂ (0281–)   ***Getting There and Around***

By air: at least two daily flights from Athens; airport ℂ 22 255.

By sea: daily with Mýkonos, (including day excursions to Délos) Tínos, Piraeus, Páros, Náxos and Amorgós; 4–5 times a week with Ándros, Santoríni, Íos and Rafína; 3 a week with Síkinos and Folégandros, 1–2 a week to Astypálaia, Koufoníssia, Schinoússa and Heráklia; once to Ikaría, Sámos, Sérifos, Sífnos, Kýthnos, Kímolos, Mílos, and Anáfi; **catamaran** daily to Piraeus and other Cyclades. Doudouris, ℂ 83 400 has caiques to hire. **Port authority**: ℂ 82 633.

By road: good **bus** service around the island, ℂ 82 575, departing from by the ferry port; 3 times a day a bus circles the island, by way of Azólimno. **Taxi rank**: ℂ 86 222.

Tourist Information

Friendly **NTOG** information office on Dodekanesou St, by the port and bus station, ✆ 86 725, ✉ 82 375. **Tourist police** ✆ 82 610. The **Teamwork** travel office in the port, ✆ 83 400 has rooms and tours of Ermoúpolis.

Festivals

Carnival, with dancing to the ancient *tasmbouna* and *toubi*, in Áno Sýra. The **last Sunday in May**, celebrating the finding of the icon at Ag. Dimitríou. In **June**, a folklore festival is held at Azólimnos with three days of dancing, wine and song. **June/August**, the Ermoupoleia Arts Festival. **24 September**, an Orthodox and Catholic celebration at Faneroméni. **26 October**, also at Ag. Dimitríou; **6 December**, Ag. Nikólaos in Ermoúpolis.

Ermoúpolis

Greece was reborn in Ermoúpolis.

Elefthérios Venizélos

As you sail into the **commercial port**, Ermoúpolis (ΕΡΜΟΥΠΟΛΗ), pop. 12,000, presents an imposing, unexpected sight much commented on by early travellers: a sweeping crescent meringue rising in twin peaks, one for each religion; older Catholic **Áno Sýros** to your left (or north), and **Vrondádo**, on the right, the Orthodox quarter, founded during the War of Independence. The whole wears a stately elegance, especially now that the buildings have been restored to their original soft colours; in the evening, horse-drawn carriages clopping down the marble lanes, softly illuminated with old street lamps, with the silhouettes of palms outlined against the moon, create a rare urban idyll—'Who could ever imagine finding such a city on a rocky island of the Aegean sea!' as Gautier marvelled, when he visited it, back when it was new. Yet at the same time there's no doubt that the city works for a living; prominent on the harbour are the Neórion shipyards, now back in business under new management.

Ermoúpolis' central square, **Plateía Miaoúlis**, is the most elegant in Greece, with its marble bandstand and palms, its worn, lustrous marble pavement, its cafés and statue of Admiral Miaoulis, revolutionary hero and old sea-dog, looking down to the port, the whole embraced by fine neoclassical buildings and wrought-iron balconies. In *Aegean Greece*, Robert Liddell wrote that he could think of no square 'except St Mark's that more gives the effect of a huge ballroom, open by accident to the sky.' Grandest of all is the neoclassical **town hall**, designed in 1876 by the German architect Ziller; pop inside for a coffee and look at the old fire engine in the courtyard. The **Archaeology Museum** (✆ 28 487, *open 8.30–3, closed Mon*) up the steps to the left contains proto-Cycladic to Roman era finds from Sýros and other islands: note the Hellenistic era 'Votive relief to a hero rider from Amorgos' with a snake crawling on the altar as a sheep is led to sacrifice, and more snakes on a marble plaque referring to Homer, from Íos. The **Historical Archives**, on the same side of the town hall, host the Ermoúpolis Seminars in summer, when the archives are on show (*same hours*). To the right, behind the square, the **Apóllon Theatre**, a copy of La Scala, Milan, was the first ever opera house in Greece; until 1914 it supported a regular Italian opera season, and has now been restored after a botched repair in 1970 that wrecked more than it fixed. Up the street a little way from here, the **Velissarópoulos Mansion**, now housing the **Labour Union**, is one of the few places you can get in to see the elaborate ceiling and wall murals characteristic of old Ermoúpolis. In the lanes above the square, the **Metamórphosis** is the Orthodox cathedral, with a pretty *choklakía* courtyard and ornate Baroque interior—rare in Orthodoxy. Chíos Street, descending towards the port, has the town's bustling **market**. Down towards the port, just up from the bus terminal, the church of the Annunciation, built by refugees from Psára, contains the rare icon of the *Assumption* painted and signed by Doménicos Theotokópoulos (*aka* El Greco) after he left for Venice. Nearby the old Europa hotel with a lovely *choklakia* courtyard is now part of Sýros' new **Casino**.

Here begins the elegant **Vapória** quarter of fantastic old shipowners' mansions with marble façades, lavishly decorated inside with frescoes and painted ceilings. The main square here has one of the town's best churches, blue and golden-domed **Ag. Nikólaos**, dedicated to the patron saint of the city and boasting a carved marble iconostasis by the 19th-century sculptor Vitális of Tínos. In front of the church, a memorial topped by a stone lion, also by Vitális, is the world's first **Monument of the Unknown Soldier**. Vapória's grand houses hug the coastline above the town beaches of **Ag Nikólaos**, **Tálliro** and **Evangelídis** which have marble steps down from the street.

Crowning **Vrondádo Hill** (take the main street up from behind Plateía Miaoúlis), the Byzantine church **Anástasis** has a few old icons and superb views stretching to Tínos and Mýkonos. Vrondádo has some excellent local tavernas spread out in its steps at night—follow your nose. More remote—870 cobbled steps, or a hop on the bus—is its twin, the medieval quarter of **Áno Sýros** (Apáno Chóra), a Cycladic enclave on top of Ermoúpolis: a pretty pedestrian-only labyrinth of whitewashed lanes and archways, a close-knit community where public and private spaces meld. Herman Melville, who visited in 1856, wrote that 'the houses seemed clinging around its top as if desperate for security, like shipwrecked men about a rock beaten by billows.' Since the Crusades, most of the families in Áno Sýros have been Catholic, and some have lived in the same mansions for generations and attended the **Catholic Cathedral of St George**, known as **Ai-Giórgi**, on top of the rock.

The main entrance, the **Kámara**, is an ancient arched passageway which leads past tavernas and little shops to the main street or **Piátsa**. There's a town hall, the **Women's Association of Handicraft Workers**, with a folklore collection and workshop, the **Cultural Centre** and **local radio station**. The large, handsome **Capuchin Convent of St Jean** was founded there in 1635 by France's Louis XIII as a poorhouse and contains archives dating from the 1400s; the Jesuits, just above at 16th-century **Panagía Karmilou**, have a cloister from 1744 with an important library. Áno Sýros was also the birthplace of the famous *rembetiko* composer Márkos Vamvakáris whose bust graces the square named after him. On your way up or down the hill, don't miss the **Orthodox cemetery of Ag. Geórgios**, with its elaborate marble mausoleums and dolorous decorous damsels pining over wealthy shipowners and merchants.

A 45-minute walk from Ermoúpolis leads to the pretty seaside church of **Ag. Dimítrios**, founded after the discovery of an icon there in 1936. All ships coming into port hoot as they pass and a bell is rung in reply—cup your hand and you'll hear it. In **Díli**, just above, are the remains of a **Temple of Isis** built in 200 BC. Across the harbour at **Lazarétta** stood a 5th-century BC temple of Poseidon, although the only traces of it are a few artefacts in the museum; it may have been the Poseidonia mentioned in the *Odyssey*.

Around Sýros

'Our Rock' is a pretty wild place on the whole but it isn't quite as barren as it sounds; olives, pistachios and citrus grow here, and the bees make an excellent thyme honey. Other ancient sites are in the quiet, seldom visited north side of the island. At lagoon-like **Grámmata Bay** (reached only by boat), sailors from Classical to Byzantine times who found shelter from storms engraved epigrams of gratitude, still legible on the rocks. If you want a beach away from it all this is the place; sea-lilies grow here and on the beaches of **Lía** and **Mégas Lakkos**. Towards the east coast, the wealth of grave-goods discovered in 1898 in the 500 tombs at the Bronze Age necropolis at **Chalandrianí** (2600–2300 BC) contributed much to the understanding of Early Cycladic civilization. **Kástri** an hour's walk north was their citadel: its walls, six towers, and foundations of houses remain in the undergrowth. The **cave** where philosopher Ferekides lived in the summer may be seen just south of Chalandrianí.

Buses from Ermoúpolis travel to the main seaside resorts: **Kíni** (KINI), a small west coast fishing village with two sandy beaches, is a popular rendezvous for sunset-watching, and home to a famous singing family who play authentic bouzouki music at their beachside taverna. North over the headland is **Delfíni Beach**, for that all-over tan. In the middle of the island, **Episkópio** claims the oldest Byzantine church on Sýros, **Profítis Ilías**, prettily set in the pine-covered hills. The

Orthodox convent **Ag. Barbára**, inland from Kíni, has a school of arts and crafts with needlework on sale. The walls of the church are decorated with frescoes depicting Barbára's martyrdom—her father locked her in a tower and put her to death, but immediately afterwards was struck down by a thunderbolt, making her the patron saint of bombardiers.

The foreign tourists who come to Sýros concentrate in lively **Galissás** (ΓΑΛΗΣΣΑΣ), which has the best sheltered beach on the island, a sweeping crescent of sand fringed by tamarisks, with the island's two campsites. You can hire sail boats; on shore, however, it's all mini-markets and heavy metal, backpackers and bikers in high season. Nearby **Arméos** is for nudists. Further south **Fínikas** (ΦΟΙΝΙΚΑΣ), 'Phoenix', originally settled by the Phoenicians and mentioned in Homer, is another popular resort with a gritty roadside beach.

The grandees of Ermoúpolis built their ornate summer houses at **Dellagrácia** or **Posidonía** (ΠΟΣΕΙΔΩΝΙΑ), a genteel resort with a serene film set atmosphere of ornate Italianate mansions and pseudo castles, and a blue church. Further south, quieter **Agathopés** has a sandy beach and islet opposite and you can take the track from here to **Kómito**, a stony stretch in front of an olive grove. **Mégas Gialós** (ΜΕΓΑΣ ΓΙΑΛΟΣ) is a pretty family resort, with shaded sands. **Vári** (ΒΑΡΗ) to the east, first settled in the Neolithic era, is now a major resort, but still has its fishing fleet. **Azólimnos** is particularly popular with the Syriani for its *ouzeries* and cafés, but there are no hotels or rooms. Inland, **Chroússa** is a pleasant, pine-shaded village, home to more shipowners' villas, while nearby **Faneroméni** ('can be seen from everywhere') itself has panoramic views of the island.

Sýros ✉ *84100,* ✆ *(0281–)*   ***Where to Stay and Eating Out***

Sýros has some stylish new hotels in restored neoclassical buildings. The **Rooms and Apartments Association,** ✆ 82 252, publishes an excellent booklet with a map. Culinary specialities include smoky San Michaeli cheese, *loúza*, salt pork, various delicious sausages, and the excellent Vátis wines.

Ermoúpolis

The swish **Omiros**, 43 Omirou, ✆ 84 910, ✉ 86 266 (*A; lux–exp*) is a 150-year-old neoclassical mansion, the elegantly restored family home of sculptor Vitális. There's more history at the **Diogenis**, Plateia Papagou, ✆ 86 301, ✉ 83 334 (*B; lux–exp*) on the seafront, once a coal store then a cabaret club, now lavishly converted. The stylish **Palladian**, Stamatoú Proioú, ✆ 86 400, ✉ 86 436 (*C; exp–mod*), including breakfast, is another gem. For modern comforts, **Syrou Melathron**, 5 Babagiotou St, ✆ 86 495, ✉ 87 806 (*A; exp*) is brand new, and offers a roof-garden restaurant as well as rooms with all the amenities. *Open all year.* By the beach just north or town, **Sea Colours Apartments**, Athinas, ✆ 81 181 (*A; exp–mod*) are luxurious and modern with marble terraces and wonderful views. In the same area the **Ypatia**, ✆ 83 575 (*B; mod*) is a super neoclassical mansion with brass bedsteads. **Villa Nostos**, ✆ 84 226 (*B; mod*) is another fine old house, as is **Hermes**, ✆ 28 011, ✆ 27 412 (*C; exp–mod*), on the harbour, tastefully extended and revamped. **Venetiko**, up stepped E. Roídi Street, ✆ 81 686 (*mod–inexp*) is a very friendly pension in an old house near the square with a pretty walled garden and bar; owner Pétros is a mine of information. **Dioskouri**, Kl & Kyp Stefanou 9, ✆ 22 580 (*inexp*) has a colonnaded terrace, and quiet rooms. **Silvia**, 42 Omirou, ✆ 81 081 (*mod*) are elegantly furnished rooms in another old mansion.

For tighter budgets **Tony's**, no phone (*B; inexp*) on Vokotopoúlou is a favourite backpackers' haunt; **Ariadne**, 9 Filini, ✆ 80 245 (*inexp*) has rooms with bath 50m from the port, convenient if you arrive at an ungodly hour. For a more reclusive holiday you can always stay at the **Capuchin Monastery Guest House** in Áno Sýros, ✆ 22 576, rates on request.

The **Folia Taverna** up in Vrondádo is the most well-known in Sýros and one of the best in the Cyclades for classic dishes like pigeon, rabbit and cauliflower patties at reasonable prices; in Áno Sýro, **Lilli's** is famous for its wonderful views, excellent food (try the *louza*, the local sausage) and *rembétika* music at weekends. Opposite the ferry port, barrel-lined **Bouba's**, a fine old island *ouzerie*, has exquisite barbecued octopus and local, smelly *kopanistí* cheese on *paximádia* bread rusks.

The waterfront is heaving with eateries and bars. **Muses** is good, just up from the port, although tables near the water's edge can get a bit whiffy. **Taverna 1935** is smart with international as well as Greek food. For the best roasts and barbecues, as well as take-aways, there's **Ta Yiannena Psistaria** further along the quay with *kokorétsi*, chicken and some imaginative vegetable dishes too. **Archontika**, in the alley behind the post office, is very popular for good Greek basics. By the sea north of town, towards Ag. Dimítrios, **Haravgi** serves excellent fare.

Kíni/Galissás

In Kíni, the little **Sunset**, ✆ 71 211 (*C; mod*) is right on the sea and has fine views of you know what; you can also enjoy it over delicious stuffed aubergines at **Delfini's**. In Galissás, **Akti Delfiniou**, ✆ 42 924, ✆ 42 843 (*A; exp*) is a complex of apartments with everything from volleyball to disco. The newish **Benois**, ✆ 42833 (*C; mod*) is open all year; family-run **Semiramis**, ✆ 42 067 (*C; mod*) and **Petros**, ✆ 42 067 (*E; inexp*) are both near the beach. **Two Hearts Camping**, ✆ 42 052/321, has minigolf, motorbike hire and a minibus to meet ferries. The other site is **Yianna**, ✆ 42 418.

Posidonía and Around

Eleana, ✆ 42 601, ✉ 42 644, (*C; mod*) is a very pleasant hotel with lovely grounds right on the beach. **Chroussa**, up in the little village of the same name, has the best food on Sýros; the menu changes weekly.

Entertainment and Nightlife

There's no shortage of both on Sýros, from culture at the **Apollon Theatre**, movies at the **Pallas outdoor cinema** near the market, and a huge range of bars from sophisticated to rowdy. The new **Aegean Casino** by the ferry port occupies two buildings, the old Europa Hotel and a port-side warehouse, and both the game tables and restaurant are the rage. The evening *vólta* up and down Miaoúlis Square is still important; at one time the square was even specially paved so that the unmarried knew on which side to stroll to show they were available!

The waterfront buzzes with bars. Laid-back **Dizzy Bar**, in an alley, plays soft music; **Tramps** is for ex-pats, **Highway** for loud music, **Corto** is chic, or you can dance at the **Cotton Club**. Trendy Ermoúpolis flocks to the **Rodo Club**, 3 Arcimidous, in a half ruined, half beautifully restored building behind the Neorian shipyards. For *rembétika* music head to **Lilli's** and **Rahamos** in Áno Sýros or **Dakrotsides** in Kíni. The **Neraida Bouzouki Club** opens nightly in summer at **Manna**.

Tínos (ΤΗΝΟΣ)

If Délos was the sacred island of the ancient Greeks, Tínos, the Lourdes of Greece, occupies the same place in the hearts of their modern descendants. Chances are that in ancient times Délos had much the same atmosphere as Tínos—a harbour with a permanent carnival atmosphere, inns and mediocre restaurants, shaded stoas (here awnings over the street) merchants selling holy pictures, *támata* (votives) and backscratchers to throngs of pilgrims who come to seek the healing powers of the island's miraculous icon. Tínos is also famous for its 800 Venetian dovecotes, little white embroidered towers scattered across the sloping terraces, inhabited by clouds of white doves. You almost believe the locals when they say there's a hole in the ozone layer giving them a direct line to the Almighty—if chapels are God's phone booths, Tínos has one for every ten inhabitants. Sinners disturbing the peace will be politely but firmly placed on the first ferry—to Tínos' glitzy neighbour, Sodom and Gomorrah.

History

Originally infested with vipers (its name apparently comes from the Phoenician *Tunnoth*, 'snake'), Tínos was settled by the Ionians in Archaic times. The Persians grabbed it in 490 BC, but it was set free after the Battle of Marathon. In the 4th century a sanctuary of the sea god Poseidon was founded here after he sent a flock of storks to gobble all its snakes; pilgrims would come to be cured and participate in the December festivals of the Poseidonia. Tínos had two ancient cities, both called Tínos, one at the site of the present town and the other high up at Exómbourgo. In his war with the Romans, Mithridates of Pontus destroyed both in 88 BC.

Not much happened until the Fourth Crusade brought the island, along with Mykonos, under the Ghisi brothers, members of one of the noblest families in Venice. They re-used the stone of the ancient acropolis and city to build the citadel of Santa Elena on the commanding 1700ft-high crag at Exómbourgo. When the last Ghisi died out in 1390, he bequeathed Tinos to the Serene Republic, which really didn't want it and auctioned off its lease. They had a change of heart a couple of decades later, when the islanders sent a petition begging the Signory of Venice to govern them directly, because 'no ruler under heaven is as just and good as Venice'. In general the Greeks despised the Venetians as the wicked schismatics who led the sack of Constantinople, but Tinos was different; it was not only proud to be loyal to lagoon land but so many islanders converted to Catholicism that the Greeks called it 'the Pope's island'. One Venetian chronicler called it 'the rose among the thorns'.

Their Santa Elena was the strongest fortress of the Cyclades, and both Venetians and Tiniots were proud that it stood impregnable to eleven assaults by the Turks, including one by Barbarossa himself. It stood as the rest of the Cyclades and Aegean spent 200 years falling to the Turks. In 1715, long after the rest of Greece, except for the Ionian islands, had submitted to Ottoman rule, an army of 25,000 Turks sailed into Tínos, and the islanders, expecting that the 12th attack would go the same as the others hurried up to their well-stocked citadel with their weapons, ready to hold out for however long. They met the first terrible onslaught with a spirited defence. Meanwhile the Venetians decided that this time Santa Elena would not hold out and, to the surprise and dismay of the Greeks who were ready to fight to the finish, the island's governor Bernardo Balbi and his officers struck a deal with the Turks. The Turks allowed the Venetians to leave in safety, with all the honours of war, while all the islanders had to stay. Nearly all were sold into slavery in Africa. Back in Venice, the surrender caused a scandal. Balbi and his captains were put on trial for treason, accused of taking bribes from the Turks. Balbi was imprisoned for life, and his captains were supposedly given a coating of molten silver as a lesson.

Tínos was the Ottoman Empire's last addition, but the Turks had only been there a century when a nun, Sister Pelagía, had a vision of the Virgin directing her to a rock where she duly discovered an icon. It was 1822, the second year of the Greek

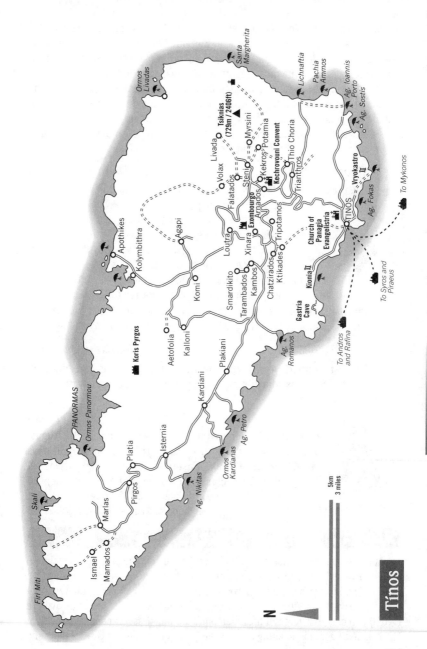

War of Independence. The holy discovery gave the Greek fight the morale-boosting aura of a *jihad* and, what's more, the icon was found to have extraordinary healing powers. A church, Panagía Evangelístra, was built over the spot where it was found and it quickly became the most important pilgrimage site in Greece, and a great national shrine. On 15 August 1940, during the huge annual pilgrimage to the church, an Italian submarine sneaked into the harbour and sank the Greek cruise boat *Elli*—a prelude to Mussolini's invasion of Greece. Under the Colonels' regime the island was declared holy (as part of its 'moral cleansing') and women of Tínos had to wear skirts and behave at all times as if they were in church.

Tínos ✆ *(0283–)* | **Getting There and Around**

By sea: daily **ferries, hydrofoils** and/or **catamarans** from Piraeus, Mýkonos, Sýros, Ándros and Rafína; 6 times a week with Páros, 5 times a week with Amorgós, 3 times a week with Santoríni, Íos, Sérifos, Sífnos, Koufoníssia, Schinoússa, Heráklia, Kárystos (Évia), Thessaloníki, Skíathos and Skýros. N.B. Ships from Tínos to Piraeus are often brim-full on weekends. Two landing areas operate, often simultaneously; when departing be sure to check you find the right one. **Port authority**: ✆ 22 220.

By road: there's an excellent **bus** service all over the island from the big square near the ferry dock, ✆ 22 440, and plenty of **taxis**: ✆ 22 470.

Tínos ✆ *(0283)* | **Tourist Information**

Tourist council: ✆ 23 780. **Tourist police**: 5 Plateía L. Sóchou, ✆ 22 255. **Tínos Mariner** travel agency, ✆ 23 193 on the waterfront is also very helpful.

Festivals

19 January, Megalómatas at Ktikádes; **25 March** and **15 August** at the Panagía Evangelístra, the two largest in Greece; **50 days after Greek Easter** (mid-June), Ag. Triáda at Kardianí; **29 August**, Ag. Ioánnes at Kómi (Catholic); **20 October**, Ag. Artemíou at Falatádos; **26 October**, Ag. Dimítri in Tínos town; **21 December**, Presentation of Mary at Tripotámos.

Tínos Town: Panagía Evangelístra

As your ship pulls into Tínos, the port and capital, the outline of the yellow church Panagía Evangelístra and its neon-lit cross floats above the town. The modern Sacred Way, Evangelístra Street, becomes a solid mass of pilgrims on the two principal feast days of the Virgin, 25 March and especially 15 August, when an average 17,000 descend on Tínos and the ceremonies are broadcast on national television. The icon itself goes for an airing in a jewelled pavilion, carried by Greek sailors and accompanied by a military band and national dignitaries. Pilgrims stroke the passing pavilion. Many of the devout, elderly women in particular, cover the distance from the ferry to the church on all fours, with padded knees and arms, crawling in penance for the health of a loved one—a raw, moving and often disturbing sight.

Outside of the high holidays, do as the Greeks do: buy an ice cream and wander up Evangelístra, perusing the stalls full of candles, tin *támata*, holy water bottles and one of the finest displays of kitsch this side of Italy: sprawling ceramic nymphs with huge salt and pepper breasts and seashell frogs shooting pool mingle merrily among the icons and Panagía thermometers. When you reach the church, a red carpet covers the grand marble stair where the only thing to do is join the queue to light a candle, kiss the icon and pray; the church employs men who do nothing all day but remove candles from the stands—the largest are the size of elephants' tusks. Through the smoke and incense, the church glimmers like Aladdin's cave with hundreds of precious offerings, and ex votos: an orange tree made of silver and gold, and lamps dangling ships (including one with a giant fish stuck in its side), heads, a foot, a truck, a bucket—blind pilgrims pledge to give the icon an effigy in precious metal of whatever they first see if their sight is restored. The icon itself, the *Megalóchari*, or Great Grace, is so smothered in gold, diamonds and pearls that you can barely see the dark slip of the Virgin's face.

Around the courtyards, hostels have been built for pilgrims waiting for dreams of the Virgin or to be healed by the icon, but there is still not enough room to house them, and the overflow camp out patiently. The crypt, where Ag. Pelagía discovered the icon, is now the **Chapel of Evróseos** ('discovery'). Silver lines the spot in the rocks where the icon lay; the spring here, believed to be holy, is said to have curative properties. Parents from all over Greece bring their children here in August to be baptized in the font. Next to the chapel the victims of the *Elli* are interred in a mausoleum, next to a fragment of the fatal Fascist torpedo.

Enough art has been donated for the Panagía to fill several **museums** (℗ 22 256; *all open 8–3.30, free*): an **art gallery**, with works from the Ionian school, a reputed Rubens, a dubious Rembrandt partially hidden by the radiator, and many 19th-century works; a museum devoted to the works of the Tiniot sculptor **Lázarou Sóchou**, and above it the **Sculpture Museum** housing pieces by Greek sculptors such as Ioánnis Boúlgaros and Vitális; old icons in the **Byzantine Museum**; and another museum containing items used in the church service.

Around Tínos Town

There are other museums as well: parallel with Evangelístra Street, opposite a pine grove, the **Archaeological Museum** (℗ 22 670; *open 8–3, closed Mon; free*) contains artefacts from the Sanctuary of Poseidon and Amphitrite, including a sundial (a copy of Ferekides' Heliotrope on Sýros?), a sea monster in various pieces and decorated storage vessels from the Archaic period. There's also a **Folklore Museum** on Loutrá Street (*open 9–12 and 4–7; adm free*).

The rest of the town is pretty much single-mindedly devoted to feeding and lodging pilgrims. From the port buses go the 4km west to **Kiónia** ('the columns'), with beaches and the famous **sanctuary of Poseidon and Amphitrite** (*© 22 670, open Tues–Sun 8–2, free*), excavated by the Belgian archaeologist Demoulin in 1902: bits remain of two temples, treasuries, baths, fountains and inns for pilgrims; votive offerings show that, like Panagía Evangelístra, Poseidon also was a great one for rescuing sailors, and his wife Amphitrite was known for granting fertility. Pilgrims to Delos often stopped here first to take a purifying bath. Further west, there's a little beach under **Gastriá Cave** with its stalactites. East of town, the closest and busiest beach is shingly nondescript **Ag. Fokás**; a few minutes further east, at **Vryókastro**, are the walls of an ancient settlement, and a Hellenistic tower. Further east at **Ag. Sóstis** the beach tends to be less crowded, but sandy **Ag. Ioánnis Pórto** is now a busy resort.

Around the Island

Buses wend their way north to the 12th-century **Kechrovoúni Convent**, one of the largest in Greece, with five churches and lanes lined with cells—it looks more like a village. It is here that Sister Pelagía, canonized in 1971, had her two visions, in which the Virgin told her where to find the icon. You can visit her old cell, with her little bed and a box containing her embalmed head. The nearby villages **Arnados** and **Dío Choriá** are real charmers.

Tínos may be the centre of Orthodox pilgrimage, but of all the Cyclades it has the highest percentage of Catholics; many villages have campaniles for landmarks. Between the mountains and ravines, Tínos is all sloping terraces, lush and green until May (it is one of the few Cyclades naturally self-sufficient in water) and golden brown in the summer, brightened by the dovecotes and the white doves. Having a dovecote, once a privilege of the nobility (the doves gobbled the peasants' grain for free, and master got nice plump birds for dinner and fertile guano to sell back to the peasants) was granted to all the islanders by the Venetians during their last decades on the island, and everyone wanted one, and built them with the typical Venetian love of fanciful ornament. Nests filled each nook and cranny created by the intricate weave of stone slabs into geometrical patterns, stars, and suns; these days the doves, still prized for their fertilizer, are more often pets than lunch.

Dovecotes decorate all the villages encircling **Exómbourgo** (1700ft), the great rocky throne of the famous Venetian fortress of Santa Elena, affording a superb view over neighbouring islands, and east to Chíos and Ikaría, and Tínos' 50 villages. The main feature recalling the fortress are the steep steps, a fortified gate, ruined houses—there were once 500—a fountain and three churches. In 1700, not long before the last battle, a French visitor found it defended by only 'fourteen ragged soldiers, seven of whom are French deserters'. After its ignominious surrender, the Turks blew up Santa Elena in case the Venetians should change their minds and come back.

The road goes up from **Kámbos,** seat of the Catholic archdiocese, which keeps its discreet distance inland, away from the Orthodox pilgrimage. From here, too, you can walk to the site of one of the two 8th-century BC towns called Tínos, where a large building and Geometric period temple were discovered, and head up the valley to the charming villages of **Smardákito** and **Tarambádos**, with the island's most beautiful dovecotes. North of Exómbourgo, pretty **Loutrá** has a 17th-century Jesuit monastery where a school is run by the Ursulines; for wild scenery, continue around to little **Vólax** ('rocky') where basket-makers work in a landscape of granite outcrops and weird formations. **Mt Tsikniás**, looming above, is no mere mountain, but the tomb of Calais and Zetes, the sons of Boreas the north wind, who puffed so hard that Jason and the Argonauts could not land to rescue Hercules at Mysia; the furious Hercules killed Calais and Zetes and buried them here, setting up the sombre crags as a marker along with two columns, one of which was famous for moving when the north wind blew. To this day the north wind blows here, cooling Tínos even in August. From **Kómi**, another pretty village, a long valley runs down to the sea at **Kolymbíthres**, a horseshoe bay with sandy beaches.

A paved road follows the mountainous ridge overlooking the southwest coast. At Kardianí a driveable track winds down to a remote beach; otherwise, from Istérnia, a pleasant village with plane trees, you can drive down to popular Ormós or Ag. Nikíta beach, the latter with rooms and tavernas. Often gusty northern Tínos is famous for its green marble, and has a long tradition in working the stone. There's a new **sculpture museum** in Istérnia (*open daily till 3, closed Mon*). Several well-known Greek artists came from or have worked in **Pírgos**, a large traditional village, with a small museum and the residence of sculptor Giannolís Halépas (*open April–Oct daily 10–2 and 5–7.30; adm*). The old grammar school, built in the first flush of Greek independence, is now a School of Fine Arts. A shop near the main square exhibits and sells students' works—two-headed Byzantine eagles are still popular motifs. Below Pírgos buses continue down to the beach at Pánormos bay, with a good fish taverna and rooms. Marlás, further north, is in the centre of the old marble quarries. From the wild, barren northwest tip of Tínos it's only one nautical mile to the island of Ándros; watch the red sunsets from here and be bowled over, by the drama—and the wind.

Tínos ✉ *84200,* © *(0283–)*   **Where to Stay**

Avoid August 14–15 if you haven't a room, although sleeping rough isn't a terrible price to pay to witness the greatest pilgrimage in all Greece. Otherwise a chorus of rooms-people greet ferries.

Aeolos Bay, ✆ 23 339, 🖷 23 086 (*B; exp*) is a smart but friendly hotel with a pool overlooking Ag. Fokás beach. **Meltemi**, ✆ 22 881, 🖷 23 000 (*C; mod*) is quite luxurious despite its grade. **Alonia**, ✆ 23 541, 🖷 23 544 (*B; exp*) is in a verdant spot with springs east of town. The Grande Dame of older hostelries, the **Tinion**, ✆ 22 261, 🖷 24 754 (*B; mod*) is on the left of the harbour as you sail in, and has brass beds in hospital-like rooms; **Vyzantion**, 26 Alavanoú, ✆ 22 454, (*C; mod*) is a pleasant alternative. **Argo**, ✆/🖷 22 588 (*C; mod*) is another good bet a little out of town, by the sea at Agiali. **Leandros**, 4 L. Lamera, ✆ 23 545, 🖷 24 390 *(C; mod)* is a favourite, with friendly owners; **Aphrodite** ✆ 22 456 (*C; mod*) is handy for ferries, as is **Delfinia**, on the waterfront, ✆ 22 288, 🖷 22 989 (*C; mod*). Inland, **Favie-Souzane**, ✆ 22 693, 🖷 22 176 (*C; mod*) is pleasant; or there's modest portside **Eleana**, ✆ 22 561 (*D; inexp*). On the beaches either side of town: at Ag. Fókas, **Golden Beach**, ✆ 22 579, 🖷 23 385, offers well-furnished studios and a shuttle bus into town. **Tinos Beach** at Kiónia, ✆ 22 626/8, 🖷 23 153 (*A; lux–exp*) has fancy furnished apartments; **Cavos**, at Ag. Sóstis, ✆ 24 224, 🖷 22 580 (*B; exp*) has airy bungalows with kitchens near the sea. **Porto Tango** at Ag. Ioánnis Pórto, ✆ 24 411, 🖷 24 416 (*A; lux–exp*) has all the comforts of a major complex, tennis, pool, and sauna. **Camping Tinos** ✆ 22 344 or ✆ 23 548, is a good site south of town.

Tínos ✆ *(0283–)*   ***Eating Out***

You can find inexpensive food throughout the town, especially the local speciality, *froutália* omelettes, though the waterfront restaurants tend to be hurried and mediocre. Try to order something cooked with the island's famous stinky garlic, which Aristophanes recommended for improving eyesight. In town, try **Nine Muses**, a nice *ouzerie*-cum-taverna, or head back from the harbour to **Michaelis** for rabbit *stifádo*, or **Pentelis**, another authentic taverna. Smart **Xinari** at the foot of Evangelistrias has Cycladic specialities and pizza and tables on the verandas. **Palea Palada** near the fish market is good. The beautiful village of Kardianí has the exotic **To Perivoli**, a popular haunt with Athenians.

Entertainment and Nightlife

Although no one comes to Tínos for a wild time, there are some music bars; **Allothis** offers 'imperishable night mystagogy' at 27 Taxiárchon; or look for live Greek music at **Aithrio** in Kiónia.

Greek holds a special place as the oldest spoken language in Europe, going back at least 4000 years. From the ancient language, Modern Greek, or Romaíka, developed into two forms: the purist or *katharévousa*, literally 'clean language', and the popular, or Demotic *demotikí*, the language of the people. But while the purist is consciously Classical, the popular is as close to its ancient origins as say, Chaucerian English is to modern English. These days few purist words are spoken but you will see the old *katharévousa* on shop signs and official forms. Even though the bakery is called the *foúrnos* the sign over the door will read ΑΡΤΟΠΟΛΕΙΟΝ, bread-seller, while the general store will be the ΠΑΝΤΟΠΟΛΕΙΟΝ, seller of all. You'll still see the pure form on wine labels as well.

At the end of the 18th century, in the wakening swell of national pride, writers felt the common language wasn't good enough; archaic forms were brought back and foreign ones replaced. Upon independence, this artificial construction called *katharévousa* became the official language of books and even newspapers. The more vigorous Demotic soon began to creep back; in 1901 Athens was shaken by riots and the government fell when the New Testament appeared in *demotikí*; in 1903 several students were killed in a fight with the police during a *demotikí* performance of Aeschylus. When the fury subsided, it looked as if the Demotic would win out by popular demand till the Papadópoulos government (1967–74) made it part of its 'moral cleansing' of Greece to revive the purist. *Katharévousa* was the only language allowed in schools and everything had to be written in the pure form. The great debate was settled in 1978 when Demotic was made the official tongue.

Language

Greeks travel so far and wide that even in the most remote places there's usually someone who speaks English, more likely than not with an American, Australian or even South African drawl. On the other hand, learning a bit of Greek can make your travels more enjoyable. Usually spoken with great velocity, Greek isn't a particularly easy language to pick up by ear. But even if you have no desire to learn Greek, it is helpful to know at least the alphabet—so that you can find your way around—and a few basic words and phrases.

Greekspeak

Sign language is an essential part of Greek life and it helps to know what it all means. Greekspeak for 'no' is usually a click of the tongue, accompanied by raised eyebrows and a tilt of the head backwards. It could be all three or a permutation. 'Yes' is usually indicated by a forward nod, head tilted to the side. If someone doesn't hear you or understand you properly they will often shake their heads from side to side quizzically and say '*Oríste?*' Hands whirl like windmills in conversations and beware the emphatic open hand brought sharply down in anger. A circular movement of the right hand usually implies something very good or in great quantities. Women walking alone might hear hissing like a demented snake emanating from pavement cafés. This will be the local Romeos or *kamákis* trying to attract your attention.

Greeks also use exclamations which sound odd but mean a lot, like *po, po, po!* an expression of disapproval or derision; *brávo* comes in handy for praise while *ópa!* is useful for whoops! look out! or watch it!; *sigá sigá* means slowly, slowly; *éla!*, come or get on with you, *kíta!* look. Other phrases you'll hear all the time but won't find in your dictionary include:

paréa	gang, close friends	*listía*	rip-off
pedhiá	guys, the lads	*alítis*	bum, no-good person
ré, bré	mate, chum, slang for friends	*palikári*	good guy, brave, honourable
endáxi	OK	*pedhí mou/*	my boy/my girl
malákka	rude, lit. masturbator, used	*korítsi mou*	
	between men as term of endearment	*yasoo koúkla/os*	Hi doll, hello gorgeous
kéfi	high spirits, well-being	*etsi íne ee zoí*	that's life!
kaïmós	the opposite, suffering, sad	*ti na kánoume*	what can we do!
lipón	well, now then	*kaló taxídhi*	good trip, Bon Voyage!
hérete	formal greeting	*kalí órexi*	Bon appetit!
sto kaló	go with God, formal parting		

The Greek Alphabet (*see* also **Introduction** p.x)

Pronunciation			English Equivalent	Pronunciation			English Equivalent
A	α	*álfa*	short 'a' as in 'father'	N	ν	*ni*	n
B	β	*víta*	v	Ξ	ξ	*ksi*	'x' as in 'ox'
Γ	γ	*gámma*	guttural *g* or *y* sound	O	ο	*ómicron*	'o' as in 'cot'
Δ	δ	*délta*	hard *th* as in 'though'	Π	π	*pi*	p
E	ε	*épsilon*	short 'e' as in 'bet'	P	ρ	*ro*	r
Z	ζ	*zíta*	z	Σ	σ	*sígma*	s
H	η	*íta*	long 'e' as in 'bee'	T	τ	*taf*	t
Θ	θ	*thíta*	soft *th* as in 'thin'	Υ	υ	*ípsilon*	long 'e' as in 'bee'
I	ι	*yóta*	long 'e' as in 'bee';	Φ	φ	*fi*	f
			sometimes like 'y' in 'yet'	X	χ	*chi*	German *ch* as in 'doch'
K	κ	*káppa*	k	Ψ	ψ	*psi*	*ps* as in 'stops'
Λ	λ	*lámtha*	l	Ω	ω	*oméga*	'o' as in 'cot'
M	μ	*mi*	m				

Dipthongs and Consonant Combinations

ΑΙ	αι	short 'e' as in 'bet'
ΕΙ	ει, ΟΙ οι	'i' as in 'machine'
ΟΥ	ου	*oo* as in 'too'
ΑΥ	αυ	*av* or *af*
ΕΥ	ευ	*ev* or *ef*
ΗΥ	ηυ	*iv* or *if*
ΓΓ	γγ	*ng* as in 'angry'
ΓΚ	γκ	hard 'g'; *ng* within word
ΝΤ	ντ	'd'; *nd* within word
ΜΠ	μπ	'b'; *mp* within word

Useful Phrases

Yes	*né/málista* (formal)	Ναί /Μάλιστα
No	*óchi*	Οχι
I don't know	*then xéro*	Δέν ξέρω
I don't understand... (Greek)	*then katalavéno... (elliniká)*	Δέν καταλαβαίνω...(Ελληνικά)
Does someone speak English?	*milái kanis angliká?*	Μιλάει κανείς αγγλικά?
Go away	*fíyete*	Φύγετε
Help!	*voíthia!*	Βοήθεια!
My friend	*o fílos moo (m)*	Ο φίλος μου
	ee fíli moo (f)	Η φίλη μου
Please	*parakaló*	Παρακαλώ
Thank you (very much)	*evcharistó (pára polí)*	Ευχαριστώ (πάρα πολύ)
You're welcome	*parakaló*	Παρακαλώ
It doesn't matter	*thén pirázi*	Δέν πειράζει
OK, alright	*endaxi*	Εντάξι
Of course	*vevéos*	Βεβαίος
Excuse me, sorry	*signómi*	Συγγνώμη
Pardon? Or, from waiters, what do you want?	*oríste?*	Ορίστε?
Be careful!	*proséchete!*	Προσέχεται!
Nothing	*típota*	Τίποτα
What is your name?	*pos sas léne? (formal)*	Πώς σάς λένε?
	pos se léne?	Πώς σέ λένε?
How are you?	*ti kánete? (formal/pl)*	Τί κάνεται?
	ti kanis?	Τί κάνεις?
Hello	*yásas, hérete (formal/pl)*	Γειάσας, Χέρεται
	yásou	Γειάσου
Goodbye	*yásas, hérete (formal/pl)*	Γειάσας, Χέρεται
	yásou, adío	Γειάσου, Αντίο
Good morning	*kaliméra*	Καλημέρα
Good evening/good night	*kalispéra/kaliníchta*	Καλησπέρα /Καληνύχτα
What is that?	*ti íne aftó?*	Τί είναι αυτό?

What?	ti?	Τί?
Who?	piós? (m), piá? (f)	Ποιός? Ποιά?
Where?	poo?	Ποιός?
When?	póte?	Πότε?
Why?	yiatí?	Γιατί?
How?	pos?	Πώς?
I am/ You are/He, she, it is	íme/íse/íne	Είμαι /Είσε /Είναι
We are/ You are/They are	ímaste/ísaste/íne	Είμαστε /Είσαστε /Είναι
I am lost	échasa to thrómo	Εχασα το δρόμο
I am hungry/I am thirsty	pinó/thipsó	Πεινώ/Διψώ
I am tired/ill	íme kourasménos/arostos	Είμαι κουρασμένος /άρρωστος
I am poor	íme ftochós	Είμαι φτωχός
I love you	s'agapó	Σ'αγαπώ
good/bad/so-so	kaló/kakó/étsi kétsi	καλό /κακό /έτσι κ'έτσι
slowly/fast/big/small	sigá sigá/grígora/megálo/ mikró	σιγά σιγά / γρήγορα / μεγάλο / μικρό
hot/cold	zestó/crío	ζεστό /κρίο

Shops, Services, Sightseeing

I would like...	tha íthela...	Θά ήθελα...
where is...?	poo íne...?	Πού είναι...?
how much is it?	póso káni?	Πόσο κάνει?
bakery	foúrnos/artopoleion	φούρνος /Αρτοπολείον
bank	trápeza	τράπεζα
beach	paralía	παραλία
church	eklisía	εκκλησία
cinema	kinimatográfos	κινηματογράφος
hospital	nosokomío	νοσοκομείο
hotel	xenodochío	ξενοδοχείο
hot water	zestó neró	ζεστό νερό
kiosk	períptero	περίπτερο
money	leftá	λεφτά
museum	moosío	μουσείο
newspaper (foreign)	efimerítha (xéní)	εφημερίδα (ξένη)
pharmacy	farmakío	φαρμακείο
police station	astinomía	αστυνομία
policeman	astifílakas	αστιφύλακας
post office	tachithromío	ταχυδρομείο
plug, electrical	príza	πρίζα
plug, bath	tápa	τάπα
restaurant	estiatório	εστιατόριο
sea	thálassa	θάλασσα
shower	doush	ντούς
student	fititís	φοιτητής
telephone office	Oté	ΟΤΕ
theatre	théatro	θέατρο
toilet	tooaléta	τουαλέττα

Time

What time is it?	*ti óra íne?*	Τί ώρα είναι
month/week/day	*mína/evthomáda/méra*	μήνα /εβδομάδα /μέρα
morning/afternoon/evening	*proí/apóyevma/vráthi*	πρωί /απόγευμα /βράδυ
yesterday/today/tomorrow	*chthés/símera/ávrio*	χθές /σήμερα /αύριο
now/later	*tóra/metá*	τώρα /μετά
it is early/late	*íne norís/ argá*	είναι νωρίς/αργά

Travel Directions

I want to go to ...	*thélo na páo sto (m), sti (f)...*	Θέλω νά πάω στό, στη...
How can I get to...?	*pós boró na páo sto (m), sti (f)...?*	Πώς μπορώ νά πάω στό, στη...?
Where is...?	*poo íne ...?*	Πού είναι...?
How far is it?	*póso makriá íne?*	Πόσο μακριά είναι
When will the... come?	*póte tha érthi to (n), ee (f), o (m)...?*	Πότε θά έρθη τό, ή, ό...?
When will the... leave?	*póte tha fíyí to (n), ee (f), o (m)...?*	Πότε θά φύγη τό, ή, ό...?
From where do I catch...?	*apó poo pérno...?*	Από πού πέρνω...?
How long does the trip take?	*póso keró pérni to taxíthi?*	Πόσο καιρό πέρνει τό ταξίδι?
Please show me	*parakaló thíkste moo*	Παρακαλώ δείξτε μου
the (nearest) town	*to horió (to pió kondíno)*	Το χωριό (το πιό κοντινό)
here/there/near/far	*ethó/ekí/kondá/makriá*	εδώ /εκεί /κοντά /μακριά
left/right	*aristerá/thexiá*	αριστερά /δεξιά
north/south	*vória/nótia/anatoliká/thitiká*	βόρεια /νότια /ανατολικά /δυτικά

Driving

where can I rent ...?	*poo boró na nikiáso ...?*	Πού μποπώ νά νοικιάσω ...?
a car	*éna aftokínito*	ένα αυτοκινητο
a motorbike	*éna michanáki*	ένα μηχανάκι
a bicycle	*éna pothílato*	ένα ποδήλατο
where can I buy petrol?	*poo boró nagorásso venzíni?*	Πού μπορώ ν'αγοράσω βενζίνη?
where is a garage?	*poo íne éna garáz?*	Πού είναι ένα γκαράζ?
a mechanic	*énan mihanikó*	έναν μηχανικό
a map	*énan chárti*	έναν χάρτη
where is the road to...?	*poo íne o thrómos yiá...?*	Πού είναι ο δρόμος γιά...?
where does this road lead?	*poo pái aftós o thrómos?*	Πού πάει αυτός ο δρόμος?
is the road good?	*íne kalós o thrómos?*	Είναι καλός ο δρόμος?
EXIT	*éxothos*	ΕΞΟΔΟΣ
ENTRANCE	*ísothos*	ΕΙΣΟΔΟΣ
DANGER	*kínthinos*	ΚΙΝΔΥΝΟΣ
SLOW	*argá*	ΑΡΓΑ
NO PARKING	*apagorévete ee státhmevsis*	ΑΠΑΓΟΡΕΥΕΤΑΙ Η ΣΤΑΘΜΕΥΣΙΣ
KEEP OUT	*apagorévete ee ísothos*	ΑΠΑΓΟΡΕΥΕΤΑΙ Η ΕΙΣΟΔΟΣ

Numbers

one	*énas* (*m*), *mía* (*f*), *éna* (*n*)	ένας, μία, ένα
two	*thío*	δύο
three	*tris* (*m, f*), *tría* (*n*)	τρείς, τρία
four	*téseris* (*m, f*), *téssera* (*n*)	τέσσερεις, τέσσερα
five	*pénde*	πέντε
six	*éxi*	έξι
seven/eight/nine/ten	*eptá/ októ/ ennéa/ théka*	επτά/οκτώ/εννέα/δέκα
eleven/twelve/thirteen	*éntheka/ thótheka/ thekatría*	έντεκα/δώδεκα/δεκατρία
twenty	*íkosi*	είκοσι
twenty-one	*íkosi éna* (*m, n*) *mía* (*f*)	είκοσι ένα, μία
thirty/forty/fifty/sixty	*triánda/ saránda/ peninda/ exínda*	τριάντα/σαράντα/ πενήντα/εξήντα
seventy/eighty/ninety	*evthomínda/ ogthónda/ enenínda*	ευδομήντα/ ογδόντα/ ενενήντα
one hundred	*ekató*	εκατό
one thousand	*chília*	χίλια

Months/Days

January	*Ianooários*	Ιανουάριος
February	*Fevrooários*	Φεβρουάριος
March	*Mártios*	Μάρτιος
April	*Aprílios*	Απρίλιος
May	*Máios*	Μάιος
June	*Ioónios*	Ιούνιος
July	*Ioólios*	Ιούλιος
August	*Avgoostos*	Αύγουστος
September	*Septémvrios*	Σεπτέμβριος
October	*Októvrios*	Οκτώβριος
November	*Noémvrios*	Νοέμβριος
December	*Thekémvrios*	Δεκέμβριος
Sunday	*Kiriakí/*	Κυριακή
Monday	*Theftéra*	Δευτέρα
Tuesday	*Tríti*	Τρίτη
Wednesday	*Tetárti*	Τετάρτη
Thursday	*Pémpti*	Πέμπτη
Friday	*Paraskeví*	Παρασκευή
Saturday	*Sávato*	Σάββατο

Transport

the airport/aeroplane	*to arothrómio/aropláno*	τό αεροδρόμιο /αεροπλάνο
the bus station/bus	*ee stási leoforíou/leoforío*	ή στάση λεωφορείου /λεωφορείο
the railway station/the train	*o stathmós too trénou/to tréno*	ό σταθμός τού τραίνου/τό τραίνο
the port/port authority	*to limáni/ limenarchío*	τό λιμάνι/λιμεναρχείο
the ship	*to plío, to karávi*	τό πλοίο, τό καράβι
the steamship	*to vapóri*	τό βαπόρι
the car	*to aftokínito*	τό αυτοκίνητο
a ticket	*éna isitírio*	ένα εισιτήριο

The Menu (ΚΑΤΑΛΟΓΟΣ)

Finding your way round a Greek menu, *katálogos*, takes some doing, but there's a basic lay-out with prices before and after local tax. You begin with Orektiká, ΟΡΕΚΤΙΚΑ; dishes cooked in olive oil are known as Laderá, ΛΑΔΕΡΑ; main courses are Entrádes, ΕΝΤΡΑΔΕΣ; Fish are Psária, ΨΑΡΙΑ; dishes with minced meat, Kimádhes, ΚΥΜΑΔΕΣ and things grilled or barbecued to order are either Psitá, ΨΗΤΑ or Tis Oras, ΤΗΣ ΩΡΑΣ.

Ορεκτικά (Μεζέδες)	Orektiká (Mezéthes)	Appetisers
εληές	eliés	olives
κοπανιστι (τυροσαλατα)	kopanistí (tirosaláta)	cheese purée, often spicy
ντολμάδες	dolmáthes	stuffed vine leaves
μελιτζανοσαλατα	melitzanosaláta	eggplant (aubergine) dip
ποικιλια	píkilía	mixed hors-d'œuvre
μπουρεκι	bouréki	cheese and vegetable pie
τυροπιττα	tirópitta	cheese pie
αξινι	eahíni	sea urchin roe (quite salty)
Σούπες	**Soópes**	**Soups**
αυγολέμονο	avgolémono	egg and lemon soup
χορτόσουπα	chortósoupa	vegetable soup
ψαρόσουπα	psarósoupa	fish soup
φασολαδα	fasolada	bean soup
πατσας	patsás	tripe and pig's foot soup (for late nights and hangovers)
Λαδερά	**Latherá**	**Cooked in Oil**
μπαμιες	bámies	okra, ladies' fingers
γιγαντες	yígantes	butter beans in tomato sauce
μπριαμ	briám	aubergines and mixed veg
φασόλακια	fasólakia	fresh green beans
φακή	fakí	lentils
Ζυμαρικά	**Zimariká**	**Pasta and Rice**
πιλάφι, ρυζι	piláfi/rizi	pilaf/rice
σπαγκέτι	spagéti	spaghetti
μακαρόνια	macarónia	macaroni
Ψάρια	**Psária**	**Fish**
αστακός	astakós	lobster
καλαμαρια	kalamaria	squid
χταπόδι	chtapóthi	octopus
γαρίδες	garíthes	prawns (shrimps)
ξιφιας	ksifias	swordfish
μαρίδες	maríthes	whitebait
συναγρίδα	sinagrítha	sea bream
φαγρι	fangri	bream
σαρδέλλα	sardélla	sardines
σκουμβρι	skoumbri	mackerel
στρείδια	stríthia	oysters
λιθρίνια	lithrínia	bass
μιδια	mídia	mussels

Αυγά	**Avgá**	**Eggs**
ομελέττα μέ ζαμπόν	omeléta me zambón	ham omelette
ομελέττα μέ τυρί	omeléta me tirí	cheese omelette
αυγά τηγανιτά (μπρουγέ)	avgá tiganitá (brouyé)	fried (scrambled) eggs
άυγά και μπεικον	avgá kai bakón	egg and bacon
Εντραδεσ	**Entrádes**	**Main Courses**
κουνέλι	kounéli	rabbit
συκώτι	seekóti	liver
μοσχάρι	moschári	veal
αρνι	arní	lamb
λουκάνικο	lukániko	sausage
κατσυκι	katsíki	kid
κοτόπουλο	kotópoulo	(roast) chicken
χοιρινό	chirinó	pork
Κυμάδες	**Kymadhes**	**Minced Meat**
παστίτσιο	pastítsio	mince and macaroni pie
μακαρόνια με κυμά	makarónia me kymá	spaghetti Bolognese
μπιφτεκι	biftéki	hamburger, usually bunless
σουτζουκάκια	soutzoukákia	meat balls in sauce
μελιτζάνες γεμιστές	melitzánes yemistés	stuffed aubergines/eggplants
πιπεριές γεμιστές	piperíes yemistés	stuffed peppers
Της Ωρας	**Tis Oras**	**Grills to Order**
μπρισολα	brisóla	beefsteak with bone
μπριζόλες χοιρινές	brizólas chirinés	pork chops
σουβλάκι	souvláki	meat or fish kebabs on a skewer
παιδακια	paidakia	lamb chops
κεφτέδες	keftéthes	meat balls
Σαλάτες	**Salátes**	**Salads and Vegetables**
ντομάτες	domátes	tomatoes
αγγούρι	angoúri	cucumber
ρώσσικη σαλάτα	róssiki saláta	Russian salad
σπανακι	spanáki	spinach
χοριάτικη	choriátiki	salad with *Feta* cheese and olives
κολοκυθάκια	kolokithákia	courgettes/zucchini
πιπεριες	piperiés	peppers
κρεμιδι	kremídi	onions
πατάτες	patátes	potatoes
μαρούλι	maroúli	lettuce
αγκιναρες	angináres	artichokes
Τυρια	**Tiriá**	**Cheeses**
φέτα	féta	goat's cheese
κασέρι	kasséri	hard buttery cheese
γραβιέρα	graviéra	Greek 'Gruyère'
μυζήθρα	mizíthra	soft white cheese
προβιο	próvio	sheeps' cheese
Γλυκά	**Glyká**	**Sweets**
παγωτό	pagotó	ice cream
μπακλαβά	baklavá	nuts and honey in fillo pastry
γιαούρτι (με μελι)	yiaoúrti (me méli)	yoghurt (with honey)

ρυζόγαλο	*rizógalo*	rice pudding
μπουγάτσα	*bougátsa*	custard tart
Φρούτα	***Froóta***	**Fruit**
πορτοκάλι	*portokáli*	orange
ροδι	*ródi*	pomegranate
μήλο	*mílo*	apple
κερασι	*kerási*	cherry
ροδάκινο	*rothákino*	peach
πεπόνι	*pepóni*	melon
καρπούζι	*karpoúzi*	watermelon
ακτινιδι	*aktinídi*	kiwi
σύκα	*síka*	figs
σταφύλια	*stafília*	grapes
μπανάνα	*banána*	banana
βερύκοκο	*veríkoko*	apricot
φραουλεs	*fráoules*	strawberries

Miscellaneous

ψωμί	*psomí*	bread
βούτυρο	*voútiro*	butter
μέλι	*méli*	honey
μαρμελάδα	*marmelátha*	jam
αλάτι	*aláti*	salt
πιπέρι	*pipéri*	pepper
ζάχαρη	*záchari*	sugar
λάδι	*láthi*	oil
λεμόνι	*lemóni*	lemon
πιάτο	*piáto*	plate
μαχαίρι	*mahéri*	knife
πηρούνι	*piroóni*	fork
κουτάλι	*koutáli*	spoon
λογαριασμό	*logariasmó*	the bill/check

Drinks

άσπρο κρασί	*áspro krasí*	wine, white
ασπρο/κοκκινο/κοκκινελι	*áspro/kókkino/kokkinéli*	white/red/rosé
ρετσίνα	*retsína*	wine resinated
νερό (βραστο/μεταλικο)	*neró (vrastó/metalikó)*	water (boiled/mineral)
μπύρα	*bíra*	beer
χυμόs πορτοκάλι	*chimós portokáli*	orange juice
γάλα	*gála*	milk
τσάι	*tsái*	tea
σοκολάτα	*sokoláta*	chocolate
καφε	*kafé*	coffee
φραππε	*frappé*	iced coffee
παγοs	*págos*	ice
ποτίρι	*potíri*	glass
μπουκαλι	*boukáli*	bottle
καραφα	*karáfa*	carafe
στήν γειά σαs!	*stín yásas (formal, pl)*	to your health! Cheers!
στήν γειά σου!	*stín yásou (sing)*	

Glossary of Terms

acropolis	fortified height, usually the site of a city's chief temples	**kore**	Archaic statue of a maiden
agíos, agía, agíi	saint or saints, or holy abbreviated **Ag.**	**kouros**	Archaic statue of a naked youth
ágora	market and public area in a city centre	**larnax**	a Minoan clay sarcophagus resembling a bathtub
amphora	tall jar for wine or oil, designed to be shipped (the conical end would be embedded in sand	*límani*	port
		limenarchíon	port authority
		loutrá	hot spring, spa
		megaron	Mycenaean palace
áno/apáno	upper	**metope**	sculpted panel on a frieze
caique	a small wooden boat, pronounced '*kaEEki*' now mostly used for tourist excursions	*meltémi*	north wind off the Russian steppe that plagues the Aegean in the summer
		moní	monastery or convent
cella	innermost holy room of a temple	*monopáti*	footpath
choklakía	black and white pebble mosaic	**narthex**	entrance porch of a church
		néa	new
(or *hokalaía*)		*nísos/nísi*	island/islands
chóra	simply, 'place'; often what islanders call their 'capital' town, although it usually also has the same name as the island itself	*nomós*	Greek province
		OTE	Greek national telephone company
		paleó	old
		panagía	Virgin Mary
		panegýri	Saint's feast day
chorió	village	*pantocrátor*	the 'Almighty'—a figure of the triumphant Christ in Byzantine domes
dimarchíon	town hall		
EOT	Greek National Tourist Office		
epachía	Orthodox diocese; also a political county	*paralía*	waterfront or beach
		períptero	street kiosk selling just about everything
exonarthex	outer porch of a church	*pírgos*	tower, or residential mansion
heroön	a shrine to a hero or demigod, often built over the tomb		
		pithos (pithoi)	large ceramic storage jar
		plateía	square
iconostasis	in an Orthodox church, the decorated screen between the nave and altar	*skála*	port
		spilio	cave or grotto
		stoa	covered walkway, often lined with shops, in an *ágora*
kalderími	stone-paved pathways		
kástro	castle or fort		
katholikón	monastery chapel	**temenos**	sacred precinct of a temple
káto	lower	**tholos**	conical Mycenaean temple

254

Index